THE COMPACT TIMELINE
OF
MILITARY HISTORY

The Charge of the Light Brigade at the
Battle of Balaclava, 25 October 1854.

THE COMPACT TIMELINE
OF
MILITARY
HISTORY

A. A. EVANS AND DAVID GIBBONS

METRO BOOKS
NEW YORK

Designed and produced by
DAG Publications Ltd., London.

Metro Books
122 Fifth Avenue
New York, NY 10011

ISBN: 978-1-4351-1137-0

Printed and bound in China.

10 9 8 7 6 5 4 3 2 1

Publisher's Note Every effort has been made to ensure
the accuracy of the information presented in this book.
The publisher will not assume liability for damages caused
by inaccuracies in the data and makes no warranty
whatsoever expressed or implied. The publisher
welcomes comments and corrections from readers,
emailed to info@worthpress.co.uk, which will be
considered for incorporation in future editions. Every
effort has been made to trace copyright holders and seek
permission to use illustrative and other material. The
publisher wishes to apologize for any inadvertent errors
or omissions and would be glad to rectify these in future.

Illustrations Bukvoed, via Wikipedia, 186, 203. Radomil,
via Wikipedia, 190. *Signal* magazine, 187, 189. Stephen
Turnbull, Pages 112–13; United States Department of
Defense, 154, 158, 161, 163, 172–3, 182–3, 188, 193,
195, 196–7, 198–9, 200–1, 202–3, 204–5, 206–7, 208–9,
210–11, 212–13, 212–13, 216-17, back endpaper. Other
illustrations PageantPix and compilers' collections. While
every effort has been made to trace copyright holders and
seek permission to use illustrative material, the Publishers
wish to apologize for any inadvertent errors or omissions
and would be glad to rectify these in future editions.

Front endpaper: *Eighteenth-century French ships
of the line deploying on the starboard tack.
Maneuvering in lines enabled an admiral to bring
broadsides to bear on his opponents. Note that the
flag flown is the white flag of the Bourbon (pre-
Revolutionary) monarchy.*

Back endpaper: *US Marines from the 15th Marine
Expeditionary Unit, aided by an armored vehicle,
move toward an objective in Iraq during March 2003.*

Below: *The corner of a British square under attack
at the Battle of Waterloo, June 18, 1815. The
square formation, with ranks of infantry facing
outward, proved generally successful in repelling
cavalry attacks, but infantry needed to redeploy
back to line to bring maximum firepower to bear on
advancing enemy infantry.*

CONTENTS

Preface, 7

Introduction: Warfare and Weapons, 8

THE TIMELINE OF MILITARY HISTORY, 21

The Great Battles of History: An A–Z, 218

Further Reading, 254

Military Biographies

CONTENTS

PREFACE

The timeline in this book provides a guide to the thousands of wars and campaigns fought by humankind since records began, to the kings and generals who fought them, and to the weapons that their armies wielded.

The events presented are organized on an overall chronological basis, but, in order to maintain the essential flow within the context of the preceding and succeeding narrative, the timeline has been organized into sections, essentially geographical but also historical. Thus the timeline is not simply set out as a year-by-year list of battles and campaigns but presents a succession of chronologies within the overall timeline, each listing events in a particular area of the globe or a particular war in turn, which affords continuity without interruption.

The timeline is set principally on the right of each double-page spread, and facing this are illustrated sections expanding upon, and providing background to, the facts in the chronology, with brief summaries of certain wars and biographies of the great commanders of history, plus maps and illustrations.

Beginning the book is a summary of warfare in the context of weapons development, tracing the evolution of armor and edged weapons, fortification and siege warfare, artillery, small-arms, armored fighting vehicles, warships, and aircraft. Following the timeline is a comprehensive A–Z reference guide to some two thousand of the great battles of history, with their dates, victors, and vanquished.

So vast is the scope of this book that the timeline sometimes cannot enter into great detail about each specific event, so a guide to further reading lists some of the many good books in which the reader can explore particular periods or wars in more depth.

The timeline ends with the last (thus far) of the 'conventional' military campaigns, in which the United States led a coalition force into Iraq, armored formations advancing through the desert to Baghdad while aircraft pounded enemy positions. That campaign has been succeeded by a drawn-out occupation of the country by Western forces, attempting to impose law and order upon a country torn apart by internecine conflict. The same applies to Afghanistan, where the resurgent power of local warlords limits the effectiveness of central authority. Meanwhile the ongoing 'War on Terror', declared by US President George W. Bush after the '9/11' attack on the World Trade Center in New York, continues. Around the world, the military 'frontline' is increasingly invisible, as the threat from militants and terrorists to pursue their aims by attacking civilians with bombs forces governments to devote resources to security measures and forestalling such outrages.

Civil wars continue, particularly in the Middle East and north-east Africa, where ethnic, tribal, genocidal, and religious conflicts result in thousands of innocent deaths every year. An end to such conflicts seems difficult to imagine while attempts at diplomacy and negotiation by international organizations so often appear doomed to fail. This, increasingly, is the face of war today.

INTRODUCTION: WARFARE AND WEAPONS

This book chronicles the wars and battles of five thousand years of human history – since records began. For four and a half of those millennia, human muscle supplied the power to win wars – with spear, sword, arrow, and club. Only in the last half-millennium has muscle power been supplanted by mechanism, and in the last few decades by microchip.

From the ancient Egyptians to the close of the Middle Ages, there are many similarities apparent in the armies and fleets that went to war. Indeed, military styles appeared to have come full circle in the late sixteenth and seventeenth centuries, when bodies of armored men advanced into combat armed with long pikes not very different from those wielded by the hoplites of ancient Greece. The galleys that fought at Lepanto were powered by oars in much the same way as the triremes that defeated the Persians at Salamis two thousand years before.

Yet from the middle of the fifth millennium in our chronicle to the present, warfare has altered dramatically – to global communications networks, battles, and campaigns directed from across the world using computers, satellite surveillance, and aircraft capable of delivering missiles from halfway across the earth.

ARMOR AND CAVALRY

The transition from tribal warfare to organized city-state conflict is not recorded, but the earliest weapons were probably fire-hardened sticks, stone axs, spears, flint daggers, together with slings and primitive bows. By the middle of the third millennium BC, Sumerian smiths were casting socketed ax heads, the ax having developed from the mace, and bronze heads were also being made for spears and javelins (the latter used for throwing, as against shock combat). Bas reliefs of Assyrian and Egyptian warfare show regimented warriors, relatively sophisticated in dress and armament, with spears, bows, and shields of bronze and wood. Bronze helmets were relatively expensive items. The sword began with the ax, developing into the sickle sword by the middle of the second millennium BC; because of the structural limitations of bronze, only with the coming of iron (about 1200 BC) were long, straight swords possible.

By the time of the Greek–Persian Wars, the Greek phalanx manned by hoplite warriors represented the peak of military organization. Dressed with bronze helmet and body armor, each man carried a sword, spear, and shield. When standing in sixteen-deep phalanx formation, the nine-foot long spears presented a formidable battle front. Philip of Macedon, father of Alexander the Great, equipped his phalanxes with spears more than twice that length, called sarissas. Perceiving that the phalanx was a relatively difficult mass to maneuver, Philip and Alexander made the formations smaller and thus more flexible to deploy.

Alexander's great battles were won – in part at least – by the shock effect of cavalry. The first highly mobile shock weapon was the chariot, which was in use by about 1700 BC, the first chariot battle to be recorded being at Meggido in 1457. Around the middle of the second millennium the ridden horse began to usurp the role of the chariot, Scythian cavalrymen from the north-east irrupting into the civilized world, as would many other such people in succeeding centuries.

Infantry, however, remained the principal component of armies, the legions of Rome, disciplined, well organized, and equipped, becoming supreme on the battlefield for some six hundred years from the middle of the third century BC to the mid-fourth century AD. Organized in smaller sub-units, or cohorts, the legionaries were armed with short stabbing swords and throwing javelins. The Roman army was a formidable fighting machine, able to march long distances at speed, make camp for the night, then hurry onwards, the spade being as important as the sword.

During the third century AD, pressure from barbarian tribes upon the borders of the Roman Empire intensified, and warfare was increasingly dominated by cavalry. Mobility was vital to counter the irruptions of tribes along the Rhine–Danube frontier, and during the great crisis of the mid-second century cavalry corps were established at key locations, ready to move against incoming tribal raids. The Battle of Adrianople in 378, at which the Emperor Valens perished, has traditionally been seen as the beginning of the Age of Cavalry. The Roman infantry had long

Left: *The siege of a fortified city during the 15th-century phase of the Hundred Years War in France. The walls have been breached by cannon – a new weapon at this time – and the besiegers are storming the walls. The attackers are covered by the fire of handgun men, crossbowmen and archers.*

been in decline, a very different instrument of war from Republican days, when it was essentially a citizen army; increasingly the troops were of barbarian origin taken into service by the empire.

The Huns, who terrorized Europe and the Middle East during the middle years of the fifth century, were essentially fast-moving horse archers. Such tribes emerged periodically throughout history, the most dramatic being the Mongols, whose hordes of mounted archers spread terror across the Far East, Asia, and the Middle East, and even briefly into Europe during the thirteenth century. Their tactics were not based upon shock. Essentially, they were light cavalry, swarming around an opponent and able to escape before being brought to combat by heavier armed troops. Essentially too they were nomads; they appeared quickly, and as quickly disappeared.

The shock effect of cavalry has been ascribed to the introduction of the stirrup during the seventh century, but the breeding and training of suitable horses were more important factors, possibly a result of Arab breeds, spread by Islamic conquerors during that century. By the eighth century improved breeds produced heavier war horses that could carry greater weight, making possible the development of the armored knight. The improved war horses and increasingly sophisticated armor were expensive, so that armies of this period tended to be smaller than those of earlier centuries, consisting of relatively small numbers of 'élite' mounted warriors supported by footmen. The break-up of the Roman Empire ushered in a period of smaller-scale conflicts between the new kingdoms that replaced it, with the rise of feudal states in which tenancy of land was awarded in return for military service. This system, which lasted to the fourteenth century, originated with the Franks in the eighth century and spread to North Italy, Spain and Germany, the Normans taking it to England and southern Italy.

Armor took a variety of forms, evolving over the centuries. Roman armor could be chain mail, scale (overlapping small pieces of metal sewn on to a supporting fabric), lamellar (laced pieces of metal) or laminated (segments of metal bound together) as illustrated on Trajan's Column. Scale and mail were very ancient methods of armoring, dating back to the Assyrians, and lamellar armor was known to the Etruscans. All were relatively expensive to manufacture. During the eleventh century the armor of the Norman knight was typically as depicted in the Bayeux Tapestry: a conical helmet, long hauberk of chain mail, and a kite-shaped shield. Weapons consisted of spear and sword.

Soon after 1200, plate armor began to be manufactured. Helmets with hinged visors appeared about 1300, and the first suits of full armor date from the early years of the fifteenth century. Such suits were heavy and cumbersome, requiring very strong horses to support them; vision was limited and communication made difficult. Arrows and crossbow bolts could be stopped by heavy armor, making the later-period knights the equivalent of modern tanks, powerful shock weapons but requiring support for sustained combat. Ultimately the coming of firearms rendered armor obsolete: plate thick enough to keep out musket balls was impracticable.

FORTIFICATION

During four and a half of the millennia of warfare chronicled here, fortification and siege warfare remained recognizably the

Above: *Château Galliard, Richard the Lionheart's great fortress on the Seine, north of Paris. Built at the end of the 12th century, it was one of the finest of medieval castles; nevertheless, his enemy, King Philip Augustus of France, captured it after a prolonged siege in 1204.*

same. Many of the earliest wars recorded are between walled cities, and the bas reliefs of the Ancient Egyptians and Assyrians bear witness to the methods employed to break into fortifications.

Heavy artillery, catapults, and battering-rams were used to dislodge part of the city walls, enabling a breach to be made through which an assault might be launched. Such operations took time, and besiegers often looked for the more vulnerable parts of the defenses to attack. In particular the city gates would receive attention, and battering rams, often of great size and weight, would be pulled into place under a constant rain of missiles and arrows from the ramparts above. The rams needed to be protected, and these can be seen quite clearly on early bas reliefs. Siege towers, tall mobile structures protected with wood and hides, would also be constructed and hauled into place against the walls, enabling the attackers to reach the

ramparts by means of drawbridges and get to grips with the defenders. Such constructions could be huge, requiring the building of long ramps – again under constant enemy harassment – for the approach to the walls, the towers having been fabricated well out of missile range. A further hazard for the besiegers, were the garrison strong enough, was an unexpected sally from the city or fortress to destroy the towers and siege engines under construction.

The relief of besieged places by field armies often made necessary the construction of a double set of siege lines by the attackers – facing outwards (lines of circumvallation) instead of inwards (lines of contravallation). Sieges were thus lengthy and manpower-consuming – and often awe-inspiring. Caesar's siege of Vercingetorix in Alesia in 52 BC involved the construction of double siege lines some dozen miles in circumference, with towers at intervals and a free, open space between the inward and outward defense lines to enable the speedy reinforcement of threatened zones. In front of the defensive walls, cunning traps – the equivalent of modern minefields – were set for the Gauls: sharpened stakes in concealed pits, blocks of wood with iron hooks, and trenches, all covered by brushwood.

If the walls of a city continued to defy the besiegers, hunger and starvation would eventually succeed in reducing the garrison's ability to resist. The victims 'in the middle' of the combatants were often the civilians living within the walls. The fighting men would take priority for food and water; and there are many recorded instances of civilian populations being ruthlessly expelled from besieged towns, to waste away in the no-man's land between besieged and besiegers. In the nineteenth and twentieth centuries this seems less shocking, 'total war' having become a recognized form of warfare, with cities bombarded from the air as well as from the land. During World War II, Leningrad withstood a terrible siege over 29 months, during which the privations of the inhabitants, made worse by the Russian winter, earned them heroic status.

The gunpowder revolution made its impact on siege warfare before having much effect on the battlefield. Large bombards were in use by the last phases of the Hundred Years War and at the Ottoman capture of Constantinople in 1453, and as artillery and small-arms improved, the design of fortifications changed. Previously, it had been enough to build defenses thick and high, on hills or crags if possible, giving the defenders the advantage of height as well as the solidity of stone walls. Bastions – towers placed at intervals along

the walls, provided extra strength and were a place of refuge for the defenders if the walls were damaged or breached. Gunpowder changed all that. During the Renaissance period a distinct break with previous fortification is apparent, defenses becoming lower, rounder, and even more massive. But this was not enough. Fortification became a science, the plan of a fortified place being carefully designed to take into account the fields of fire available to both attacker and defender. The bastion became arrow-shaped with a long sloping earthen rampart so that guns could dominate the areas in front of the linking curtain walls. In front of the main defenses, ditches, and walls were built to impede the approach of infantry – but constructed in such a way as to avoid interfering with defensive fire. Fortifications during the late seventeenth century became ever more complex and effective, featuring outworks such as ravelins and demilunes, the science of fortification being taken to a new level by the works of Vauban, whose fortifications survive in many parts of northern France.

In addition to artillery fire, the besieged city or fortress would also be threatened – perhaps more insidiously – by the stealthy approach of trenches and tunnels dug by the besiegers. If the underlying geology permitted, one way to bring down a defensive wall was to tunnel beneath it, digging as large a space beneath the wall as possible and shoring up the roof with timbers. When set ablaze, the 'mine' would collapse, bringing down a section of the wall. It was a technique used throughout the history of siege warfare against stone fortifications and even made its contribution to the Vicksburg and later eastern-theater campaigns of the American Civil War.

With the stalemate parallel lines of trenches on the Western Front in World War I, stretching across Belgium and northern France and often no farther apart than a few hundred yards, tunnelers were employed to dig out below no-man's land to beneath the enemy trenches with precisely the same purpose, now using explosives of far greater power. Beneath the trench lines, a dark, horrifying war was waged between the opposing miners, each side listening in the dark for the sounds of enemy digging.

Perhaps the ultimate in fortification, built between World Wars I and II, was the French Maginot Line, a vastly expensive complex with thicker concrete and heavier guns than ever before. Running along France's border with Germany, it was 87 miles in length, permanently manned, with air-conditioned barracks and underground connecting rail lines. Its effectiveness, however, was entirely negative, breeding complacency in the French command that led to disaster in 1940, when the Germans simply outflanked it through Belgium.

The fortification of towns and cities has now been rendered obsolete by modern weaponry and the speed of communications. A city can be attacked from the air – as was the case during World War II, when London was 'blitzed', and an aerial campaign was waged against Germany's cities. No defense on earth could have prevented the atomic destruction of Hiroshima and Nagasaki.

ARTILLERY

A notable characteristic of warfare has been the increase in the distance at which armies can wage war. In ancient times, the killing range of an army was the length of a sword arm, the distance a spear could be thrown or an arrow shot. Artillery provides a means of extending that distance and increasing the weight of the projectile – and its killing power. Ancient artillery was based upon throwing or slinging projectiles by means of torsion or tension. Ballistae were based upon the latter. Tightly twisted bundles of rope or other fibre generated the energy that, when released, threw the projectile. Tension – as in the bow – was used to power catapults and large horizontal bows. In general these were clumsy and heavy pieces of apparatus, more useful in conducting siege warfare than on the field of battle. Smaller pieces of artillery, however, were useful in defense of fortified lines, typical of Roman warfare.

For siege warfare, the heavier the artillery the better the chance of knocking holes in the defenders' walls. Josephus describes Roman catapults at the siege of Jerusalem in AD 70 as throwing stones of 55 pounds more than 400 yards. With the demise of the Roman Empire, the science of artillery seems to have declined. The trebuchet, however, which appeared about the twelfth century, provided a simple means of propelling large objects considerable distances. They worked by counterpoise, a heavy weight, when released, pulling the launch-arm sharply upwards. Modern experiments indicate the power of such machines: with a ten-ton weight, and an arm about 50 feet long, a 300-pound stone could be lobbed some 300 yards.

Such artillery was only of use in siege warfare, however. Only with the coming of gunpowder did artillery take its place as the arbiter of battles. Early guns were wrought iron tubes, bonded with hoops and loaded at the muzzle end with a spherical stone ball. By the last quarter of the fourteenth century, wrought-iron bombards were capable of projecting 450-pound stone cannonballs. Cast guns were infinitely superior, initially manufactured from brass or bronze, later from iron and steel, and had the advantage of being able to shoot metal cannonballs instead of stone. (Stone anyway was proving too expensive, being too labor-intensive by the fifteenth century.) Gradually the classic artillery piece emerged: a cast metal tube, muzzle-loaded, fired from the breech via a touch-hole, and mounted on a carriage with a pair of wheels and 'cheeks' projecting backwards for training the gun, moving it and absorbing recoil.

By the seventeenth century artillery was becoming lighter and more maneuverable, Gustavus Adolphus of Sweden being a particular innovator in designing light battalion guns to support infantry in the field. During the eighteenth century lighter car-riages and standardized calibres made manufacture and deployment more practicable. Napoleon (who began his military career as an artilleryman) was able to field 'grand batteries' to blast his opponents' infantry before sending in cavalry and infantry to the attack – at Waterloo his army deployed nearly 250 pieces of artillery.

During the nineteenth century great advances in metallurgy and ballistics improved artillery dramatically, as it did small-arms, and rifling increased accuracy. The gun began to take its modern form, high-velocity, breech loading, and rapid firing. By World War I, artillery dominated the battlefield, and during the three and a half years of virtual stalemate on the Western Front, artillery effectively pinned troops to the ground, making infantry assaults almost suicidal. Vast bombard-ments by huge howitzers failed to cut the

Above: Artillery today. Soldiers from the United States 151st Field Artillery Regiment prepare to fire a M198 155mm howitzer during annual training in July 2007. The 155 was used extensively during the wars in Iraq – Operations 'Desert Storm' and 'Iraqi Freedom'.

barbed wire defending enemy lines and served only to churn up the ground so that it became an almost impassable morass.

Maneuver returned at the end of World War I, but the artillery now had new targets: tanks and aircraft. A seesaw development race developed between the tank and the anti-tank gun, tanks becoming bigger and more heavily protected to keep out higher velocity artillery shells designed to penetrate armor. War in the air was contested by fighter aircraft, but anti-aircraft weapons were made more effective by the development of proximity fuzes, which detonated without needing to strike the aircraft. By the end of the war in the Pacific, the US Navy's warships were covered by anti-aircraft guns, in the latter stages to knock down Japan's kamikaze suicide aircraft. Meanwhile the battleships' big guns were now capable of shooting over distances in excess of twenty miles.

Today's artillery has the advantage of satellites and computers to target and range; propellants are many times more powerful than gunpowder; and rockets, tentatively tried by the British inventor Congreve during the Napoleonic Wars, have now come of age, providing power and accuracy that is supplanting conventional artillery.

SMALL-ARMS

The so-called 'gunpowder revolution' (of *c.*1300–1650) brought forth modern artillery, small-arms, and bombs. Early small-arms were crude and often as dangerous to the user as to the target. In the middle of the fifteenth century the development of slow match and the serpentine made possible the matchlock musket, the first practical firearm. Heavy and cumbersome, it was slow to fire and needed a forked rest to support the muzzle end. Proper gunstocks and butts enabled more accurate and less painful shooting, and during the Dutch War of Independence and the Thirty Years War large formations of musketeers took the field, their slowness of fire requiring them to be protected by bodies of pikemen. With the disappearance of armor towards the end of the sixteenth century, muskets could be lighter and smaller. Also during the sixteenth century, the flintlock was invented, a cheaper, easier to use mechanism for igniting the charge. This came into military use a century later, flintlocks gradually supplanting matchlocks by 1700. In the eighteenth century standardization of parts and the ability of nation states to manufacture weapons en masse made possible large armies of infantry uniformly equipped.

The short range of these weapons, however – much shorter than for the longbow – meant that battles retained the old linear formations and maneuvers, small-arms being accurate only up to about seventy-five yards and liable to kill at well under 200 yards. Volley fire increased effectiveness at these short ranges, and battles were often stand-up exchanges of fire between lines of infantry until one side had had enough, the battlefields disappearing into a dense fog of smoke.

The flintlock was the standard infantry weapon of the eighteenth and early nineteenth centuries, but while the method of ignition was relatively reliable, these muzzle-loaders took a long time to load and fire – volley fire probably averaged no more than two or three shots per minute – and the accuracy of the spherical lead balls used, even with rifling, was poor. In 1843 the Prussian army adopted the Dreyse needle-gun, a breech-loader with percussion ignition, and this increased the rate of fire. The French Minié of 1846/8 extended the range to 1,000 yards by means of an improved bullet that expanded on firing, gripping the rifling. By the latter part of the nineteenth century, small-arms had been revolutionized – metallic cartridges and smokeless propellants instead of the old black powder making accurate fire possible to 5–600 yards while the firer was virtually undetectable – so that close-order battle formations were suicidal. The major powers were slow to grasp this, as casualties in the Boer War demonstrated.

World War I saw these improved firearms used on a large scale, but it was the machine-gun – notably the recoil-operated Maxim design – that eliminated tactical maneuver and set in train the events leading to the 'siege'-line trenches of the Western Front. With a battlefield rate of fire of 5–600 rounds per minute and a range of up to 2,000 yards, they brought unprecedented destructive power to the battlefield.

Modern small-arms include more automatic and semi-automatic weapons of the sort that we see on TV every night. Their firepower is massive, and infantry tactics

Left: General Wolfe steadies his red-coated grenadiers on the Heights of Abraham during the storming of Quebec in 1759. The infantry have their bayonets fixed on their Brown Bess flintlock muskets ready for the close-combat that ensued.

Right: A German Tiger Tank – Panzerkampfwagen VI – in North Africa during the middle part of World War II. The Tiger was a fearsome weapons system, so heavily armored that Allied tanks had great difficulty in knocking them out, and with a massive punch from its 88mm gun.

today emphasize small groups in concealment, working in close cooperation with tanks, artillery, and air power.

ARMORED FIGHTING VEHICLES

With the overwhelming superiority of the defense at the close of the nineteenth century and the beginning of the twentieth, high-velocity firearms and artillery dominating the battlefield at long range, maneuver became almost impossible. The opening moves of World War I saw vast armies transported to their staging areas by railway, then advancing to meet one-another. After a brief period of maneuver, in which the Germans' modified Schlieffen Plan failed at the Battle of the Marne, a virtual stalemate settled across Belgium and north-eastern France, broken by infantry offensives that were unacceptably costly in human lives. Sophisticated and complex trench systems evolved, defended by barbed wire and machine-guns, with considerable underground workings and shelters from artillery fire. The Western Front became a giant killing ground, the mud

often churned to liquid by the density of continued bombardment.

It was in this situation that the tank was conceived and built, its purpose to cross the trenches and penetrate enemy lines. With caterpillar tracks, tanks could indeed cross formidable obstacles, while their armor would keep out small-arms fire, and cannon or machine-guns mounted in the hulls fired back. In time, it had an impact on the course of events on the Western Front, but it was only in World War II that it came of age. Between the wars, such theorists as Fuller, Liddell Hart, Guderian, and de Gaulle argued that the tank should be the cutting edge for an attacking army, rather than deployed as infantry support. In this role it brought maneuver, shock, and speed back into warfare, the German blitzkrieg campaigns in Poland, Belgium, France, and Russia demonstrating that properly used tanks were decisive weapons. Since then the tank has been an essential element of land warfare. During World War II the threat of anti-tank artillery was met by heavier armor, and by the time of the epic Battle of

Kursk in 1943 each side was fielding thousands of armored fighting vehicles.

In the last half of the twentieth century the tank became increasingly sophisticated, with computerized armament able to lock on to targets despite the vehicle's maneuvers across rough terrain; and modern communications systems made possible improved coordination of attack. However, the threat from the skies – from jets with 'smart' weapons, attack helicopters that can rise from behind cover to unleash missiles and such aircraft as the heavily armored A-10 'tankbuster' – has led many to predict that the tank is obsolete.

WAR AT SEA

For almost four and a half of the millennia covered in this book, warships depended on oars for propulsion. During the Ancient period, the Greeks developed a warship that has been considered a classic in ship design: the trireme. Three banks of oars enabled these long, narrow ships to attain bursts of high speed, and the principal method of attack was to ram an opponent. The bows of the ship were sharp and heavily reinforced so as to pierce the side of the victim. This was characteristic of sea battles from Salamis to Actium and beyond, the ships themselves becoming larger and more powerful over the centuries. However, these were not ocean-going ships, and no complete ancient warship has ever been discovered by archaeologists. Much of the design remains a mystery, but during the 1980s an Anglo-Greek team reconstructed a trireme, using evidence from pottery, bas reliefs, archaeological evidence and the writings of the ancient historians; the result was a convincing warship, but much detail remains conjectural.

The trireme was essentially the warship of the Greek democracies. The galleys of Rome were propelled by slave rowers, and, with the invention of boarding ramps, offensive action depended less upon ramming, the Romans effectively turning sea battles into extensions of war on land.

Slave-propelled galleys remained typical of many navies until the sixteenth century, when the advent of gunpowder revolutionized war at sea just as it did land warfare. Lepanto in 1571 was the last of the great sea battles fought with galleys; seventeen years later the Spanish Armada was in large measure a very different type of naval action, fought between fully ocean-going ships propelled by sails and armed with rows of cannon. About the twelfth century, the compass had been discovered, enabling ships to venture more confidently across the seas. By the sixteenth century the earth was being circumnavigated, and war could now be projected across the oceans.

For three and a half centuries, sailing warships ruled the seas, battles and individual combats being characterized by much maneuver until the enemies came within cannon range – a few hundred yards – and proceeded to blast broadsides into each others' hulls. Battles between navies were characterized by great fleets in line ahead, carefully maneuvering to gain advantage and bring the greatest possible number of guns to bear on the enemy.

Trans-oceanic war enabled the conquest of great empires across the globe, wars in Europe now continuing in North America, the Caribbean, India, and across the trade routes. By the middle of the nineteenth century, sail power gave way to steam, and the iron-hulled, steam-powered warship, equipped with breech-loading, high velocity weapons, ushered in the age of the battleship. Britain's launch of *Dreadnought* in 1906 set in train a new arms race, and battleships became ever bigger and more powerfully armed. The 18,000-ton *Dreadnought* mounted ten 12-inch guns; during World War II the Japanese had two 70,000-ton giants with nine 18-inch guns.

The age of the battleship did not last long. At sea, as on land, new factors were at hand. Mines and torpedoes were cheap to make and very effective against expensive battleships. Torpedoes fired from submarines posed a new threat to surface fleets as they did to merchantmen. In both World Wars, a vast battle was waged across the North Atlantic as Germany's U-boats sought to cut off supplies to Britain of food, fuel, munitions and men from America.

Most dramatically, it was from the air that came the greatest threat. Aircraft carriers developed between the two wars and during World War II usurped the battleship's place as the capital ship of the world's fleets. The turning-point Battle of Midway in 1942 was fought between fleets that never came within visual distance – they exchanged aerial attacks over a distance of more than 100 miles. Air power now dominates sea warfare as it does war on land. The United States, the remaining world superpower, can project its military might across the world by means of vastly powerful carrier battle groups, developed from the great fleets of World War II in the Pacific. It was from such fleets that the US launched part of the aerial bombardments of Iraq in 1991 and Kosovo in 1999.

MILITARY AVIATION

The impact of aviation has altered warfare almost out of recognition over the last three-quarters of a century. Flight was in its infancy as World War I began, and aircraft were initially deployed for reconnaissance purposes. The elimination of the enemy's reconnaissance aircraft immediately became a prime concern, and the fighter aircraft was the result. The first aerial combats took place between slow aircraft whose pilots sported pistols and rifles. Machine-guns mounted behind the pilot and operated by a second aviator followed, but fixed forward-firing machine-guns were the true key to fighter effectiveness. The problem of the propeller obstructing forward fire was solved by Fokker, giving the ability to fire through the propeller arc by means of mechanical synchronization. This made true aerial combat possible, and a series of fighters with improving performance and armament led to the classic 'dog-fights' over the trenches. Aerial 'aces' became skilled at maneuver, the highest exponent of this new art being Manfred von Richthofen, who scored 80 kills before being brought down, possibly by ground fire, in 1918.

One vital role for the early fighters was shooting down observation balloons and airships. Propelled lighter-than-air craft were deployed as bombers, Zeppelin raids on England – the first planned use of aircraft against civilians – being seen as barbaric. But it was merely a foretaste of what was to come. Between the wars the bomber was seen as the ultimate weapon, with the idea that 'the bomber will always get through' conjuring up to a terrified populace the vision of cities razed to the ground by fleets of aircraft. It was not as simple as that, but ground-attack would come to dominate World War II. During the blitzkrieg campaigns of 1939–41, the Germans used Stuka dive-bombers as close-support 'aerial artillery' for ground

Above: *An American P-38 Lockheed Lightning long-range fighter of World War II, here painted with recognition 'Invasion Stripes' for the Normandy landings in June 1944. It was aircraft of this type that shot down the aircraft carrying the Japanese Navy C-in-C Admiral Yamamoto off Bougainville in April 1943.*

troops. In the Far East, the Japanese used air power from their carriers to strike at Pearl Harbor and pre-emptively cripple the US fleet. As Singapore was about to fall, two British capital ships were sunk by Japanese aircraft, proving beyond doubt that at sea as well as on land, air power was now the dominant arm.

Over Europe, bombers struck military and civilian installations indiscriminately, attacked and protected by swarms of fighters, and by the end of the war the Mustang provided the Allies with a long-range fighter that could accompany the bombers on the longest of bombing penetrations. The last, dramatic act of the war came from the air when atomic bombs dropped on two cities finally induced the Japanese to desist in their fanatical resistance to the overwhelming military might of the USA.

The Cold War between the Eastern bloc and the Western powers saw the construction of nuclear bombs sufficient to destroy humanity several times over. The addition of technology developed initially by the Germans as a last-ditch attempt to stave off defeat – the V-2 missile – gave the world the inter-continental ballistic missile, each side targeting the other's cities in a deterrent stand-off. Missiles were, and still are, deployed in land-based silos and at sea in nuclear submarines, each with awesome destructive potential. During the last decades of the twentieth century, however, the Cold War ended; agreements were reached to limit nuclear weapons and the testing of warheads. But many of these terrible weapons remain in being, and nuclear weapons are no longer restricted to the superpowers.

Air power remains dominant, however. The USA's great aircraft carriers can deploy rapidly to any part of the world, bringing to bear weaponry that is generally far in advance of the potential enemy's. Air power, with new 'smart' weapons and cruise missiles, demonstrated its worth in the Gulf War of 1991 and again in Iraq in 2003.

THE TIMELINE OF MILITARY HISTORY

Middle East

By beginning of 3rd Millennium a dozen city states including Kish, Erech, Ur, Lagash compete for domination

By 2900 Narmer or Aha becomes King of all Egypt

2800 Kish unites city states of Sumer

2600 Uruk overthrows Kish

2300–2200 Akkad. Sargon I, the first great conqueror of history, conquers Mesopotamia, Syria, part of Asia Minor

About 2000 Expansion of Ur

Mid-20th century Ur overthrown by Elamites and Amorites. Two centuries of city-state anarchy follow

2270–2230 Naram-Sin renews Akkadian vigor. Late third millennium Hurrians infiltrate northern Mesopotamia and Syria from the north

2200 Pharaoh Pepynakht campaigns against Nubia

About 2150 death of Pepy II, last of 6th Dynasty, ends Old Kingdom of Egypt

2150–2050 Guti from Iran destroy the Akkadian Empire, then are expelled by Erech and Uruk

1st Intermediate period, after which Monjunotep II reunites Egypt. Beginning of the Egyptian Middle Kingdom. Fragmentation of Egypt

Gradual disintegration into Kingdoms of Avaris, Thebes, Kush

2064–1990 Thebes conquers Wawat and upper Egypt

2050–1950 Ur reconstructs the Sumer-Akkad empire

1993 fortification of 1st and 2nd cataracts of the Nile

1937–1908 Amenemhat I builds the 'Walls of the River' about Suez

1919–1903 Senuset I gains control of Wawat (north Nubia)

19th century Rise of Babylon to become the main political and cultural center in Southern Mesopotamia

1830 Senusret III campaigns to the north of Jerusalem

1829–1818 Senuset III campaigns beyond 2nd cataract of the Nile and builds a second series of forts

18th–early 17th centuries Assyrian wars of conquest

1800 Assyrians conquer northern Babylonians Foundation of 'Old Assyrian Empire'

1760 Kassites enter Mesopotamia introducing horse and chariot

1728–1686 Amorite Hammurabi of Babylon conquers southern Mesopotamia, uniting the six main states

Late 18th to mid-17th centuries gradual disintegration of Egypt into Kingdoms of Avaris, Thebes and Kush

18th century Hyksos enter north Egypt and take control during the mid-17th century. Capital: Avaris. They bring technology of the horse in war, with chariots, the compound bow, battleaxes and skill in fortification

Late 16th century Thutmosis I defeats Hittites on the Euphrates

Egyptian 2nd Intermediate Period. Egypt divided into three states: Thebes, Kush and the North, controlled by the Hyksos

1650 Kassite kings

17th–16th centuries Babylon fights continuously with Kassites and Hurrians

1573–1550 Pharaoh Ahmose expells Hyksos and pursues them into Palestine. Foundation of the Egyptian Empire

1521 Avaris falls to Egyptians

1500 Hurrians unite as Mitanni

Late 17th century Mursilis, 3rd king of united Hittite state, destroys Aleppo, raids Babylon, defeats Hurrians on the Euphrates. First Hittite Empire

Sargon of Akkad (reg. 2334–2279 BC)

The first great empire-builder, he rose from being a servant of the king of Kish to found his own state around the city of Agade. He may have conquered all southern Mesopotamia and south-west Persia as well as parts of Lebanon. His successors were continually at war defending the empire, which finally succumbed to the Guti by about 2050.

Shamshi-Adad I (reg. 1813–1781 BC)

Founder of the first Assyrian Empire. Conquered all northern Mesopotamia.

Thutmosis I (reg. 1525–1512 BC)

Pharaoh of 18th Dynasty Egypt, he campaigned deep into Nubia, beyond the 4th cataract, securing Nubia's rich gold mines. He pursued the Hyksos to the Euphrates, which he claimed as the boundary of the Egyptian Empire.

Thutmosis III (reg. 1504–1450 BC)

One of the greatest pharaohs of Egypt. Faced with a major revolt in Syria, he won the Battle of Meggido (1457), the first military engagement of recorded history. Seventeen subsequent campaigns subjugated Syria and Palestine, while campaigns up the Nile extended Egyptian control as far as the 4th cataract.

Above: Egyptian Pharoah Thutmosis 1.
Below: Assyrian King Tiglath-Pileser in his war chariot.

Europe

Crete: Minoan civilization may have begun as early as 3000. 2200–1400 Crete is leading power in the Aegean

2000 arrival of Greek-speaking peoples in mainland Greece: Mycenaean warriors consolidate power in Greece and raid overseas

2000–1600 Minoan 'Old Palace' period

1600–1400s Minoan 'New Palace' period until a wave of destruction about 1425 leaves only Knossos intact

1450–1400 Probable Mycenean conquest of Crete; 1370 destruction of Knossos. 14th and 13th centuries are the great age of Mycenae

13th century: more massive fortifications are built and the Isthmus of Corinth fortified against invaders from the north

Mid-14th to mid-12th centuries: period during which the siege and fall of Troy is thought to have taken place, according to the account of Homer's *Iliad*, which did not exist in written form until the 8th or 7th centuries

13th century: General breakdown of settled conditions and overall decline; by 1150 Mycenaean civilization collapses; from 1100 to 800 a dark age descends on the Aegean and the coast of Asia Minor, as invaders from the north (Ionians, Aeolians, Dorians, etc.) enter the area in the 11th and 10th centuries. These invaders have traditionally been referred to as the 'Sea Peoples'; but there remains much uncertainty about this period

India

About the beginning of the 3rd Millennium to c.2300 Harappan Civilization begins in Indus Valley. After 2000 and by 1750 Harappan culture breaks down, with collapse of city civilization, causes yet unknown

1500 Vedic Age begins. Indo-European (Aryan) tribes enter Punjab, semi-nomad pastoralists and tribal societies led by rajas (warrior chiefs). Inter-tribal conflicts ensue

1500–1200 Ganges Valley Civilization

China

By about 3000 Civilization in the Huang Ho (Yellow River) valley appears; after 2500 walled settlements appear

2200–1760 Yü (Hsia or Xia) Dynasty

1760–1100 Shang (Yin) Dynasty. They conquer the area between the Yellow River and the Yangtse

1100 Revolt against last of the Yin Dynasty, Zhouxin, and foundation of Western Chou (Zou) Empire. Wars of expansion c.1000–900

By 771 Chou central authority overall is lost. Fragmentation into more than 100 individual states

770–475 'Spring and Autumn' Period (or The Age of Hegemons)

Middle East

By 1600 Fragmentation of Mesopotamia into areas dominated by Hurrians, Kassites and 'Sealand' in the south

1457 Battle of Megiddo. Pharaoh Thutmosis III defeats Canaanites and their allies and advances north to Galilee

By 1450 Assyrians become vassals of Mittani

15th century: Thutmosis III fights 17 campaigns into Palestine

1427–1400 Pharaoh Amenhotep II campaigns to north of Byblos and Damascus

Late 16th century to early 12th century Wars of Imperial Egypt

Thutmosis III extends Egyptian control south to 4th cataract of the Nile

Hittite wars of conquest. Foundation of second Hittite Empire, the 'Hittite New Kingdom'

1400–1390 campaigns of Pharaoh Thutmosis IV ends with treaty with Mitanni

1390–1364 Eriba-Adad wins Assyrian independence from Mitanni

Suppiluliamas (reg. 1380–1340 BC)
Founder of the Hittite Empire; conquered Mitanni c.1360 and invaded Syria; captured Carchemish c.1354.

Ramses II the Great (1304–1237 BC)
One of the greatest of Egypt's rulers, who fought a series of campaigns against the Hittites in Syria and Palestine. The Battle of Qadesh (Kadesh) against the Hittites is the first great battle in history to be recorded in detail. Other campaigns were generally punitive expeditions in outlying provinces, in addition to the defense of Egypt against invaders from Libya. His reign marks the last peak of Egypt as a military power.

Ashurnasirpal II (reg. 883–859 BC)
Assyrian king of particular cruelty. Extended Assyrian power to the shores of the Mediterranean. He founded Nimrud, to become the military capital of the empire. He reorganized the army, the first great power to use iron weapons en masse, and his annual campaigns spread terror far and wide.

Tiglath-Pileser (reg. 745–727 BC)
Founder of the Neo-Assyrian Empire after a period of relative weakness. Campaigned against Urartu, Aramaeans, in Palestine, Syria, Iran and Babylonia, extending Assyrian domination to the Egyptian frontier and the Persian Gulf. 729 annexed Babylon. 732 took Damascus. Replaced militia system with a standing army and began cruel policy of mass deportations (today euphemized as 'ethnic cleansing'), such as that of the 'lost ten tribes' of Israel in 722.

Above: *Ramses II the Great in his war chariot.*

Top: *Assyrians besiege a city; and below, the capture of the city of Astartu.*
Left: *Assyrian slingers.*

1380–1340 Hittite King Suppiluliamas. He conquers the Mitanni (c.1360), which becomes a buffer state betwen the Hittites and the Assyrians

1294–1279 Pharaoh Seti I campaigns in Palestine

c.1275 Battle of Qadesh. First battle in history to be recorded in detail. Ramses II and Muwatalli fight an inconclusive battle. A treaty c.1263–1258 divides Palestine and Syria between Egypt and Hatti

By 13th–12th centuries, Nubian gold (reason for Egyptian imperialism to the south) is exhausted

1272–1243 Shalmaneser I begins Assyrian expansion and conquers Mitanni

1242–1206 Tukulti-Ninurta I, Assyrian dominion expands south and temporarily (c.1210) takes Babylon

1200–900 General decline in face of invasions

Europe

End of 2nd millennium: hill forts are being constructed in Western Europe

815 Foundation of Carthage (traditional date)

By 800 Sparta has emerged as a military state in the Peloponnese

8th century Phoenicians, already trading widely in the Mediterranean, establish outposts on the Iberian coast

8th century Rise of aristocracies in Greece. Evolution of city-states, with hoplite armies, the phalanx battle formation and pentekonter warships

753 Foundation of Rome (traditional date)

750 Sparta conquers Amylae

8th century Greeks colonize Sicily and southern Italy

735 Syracuse founded by Corinthians

730–710 Spartan conquest of Messenia

About 700 Greeks penetrate the Black Sea

Early 7th century Predominance of Argos in the Peloponnese

669 Battle of Hysiae. Argos defeats Sparta

By 650 Sparta defeats Messenian revolt

Mid-7th to mid-6th centuries Age of Tyrants in Greece

580 Carthaginian-Phoenician clashes with Greeks begin on Sicily

600 Phocaeans found Massilia (modern Marseilles)

600 Athens takes Salamis from Megara

600–550 Sparta extends dominion over most of the Peloponnese

570 War between Athens and Megara

560–550 War between Sparta and Tegea

550 Sparta takes Thyreatis from Argos

546–5 Persia conquers the Greek city-states on the Aegean coast of Asia Minor

540–523 Polycrates, Tyrant of Samos, is the first great naval imperialist

535 Battle of Alalia. Phocaeans expelled from Corsica by Etruscans and Phoenicians

525–524 Unsuccessful Spartan-Corinthian expedition against Samos

509–508 Sparta invades Attica and frees Athens from tyranny

By 500 Sparta is established as the greatest military power in mainland Greece. 494 Cleomenes, King of Sparta (520–490), crushes the revival of Argos

Middle East

Mid-13th century Conquest of Palestine by Hebrews. Wars of Joshua (including fall of Jericho)

1190–1150 Hittite Kingdom overthrown by Phrygians, Luvians etc.

1184–1153 Pharaoh Ramses III repulses invaders from the Sahara: depicted on bas-reliefs is a naval battle

1180 Phrygians invade Asia Minor

Great invasion including possibly those of peoples formerly identified by historians as the 'Sea Peoples' cause widespread disruption and fragmentation

1180–1177 Pharaoh Merenptah repulses invasions from Libya and 'Sea Peoples' in raiding along the coast and into the Nile delta

By the reign of Ramses VI (1143–1136)

Sargon II (reg. 721–705 BC)

Assyrian king who spent much of his reign crushing rebellions and reconquering lost territories, Egypt, Elam and Urartu all fostering resistance to Assyrian rule. 714 invaded and crushed Urartu. Reconquered Babylon 710 (which had been taken by the Chaldeans in 720).

Sennacherib (reg. 705–681 BC)

Quelled revolt in Palestine and Phoenicia; ended Babylonian revolts by recapturing and sacking the city in 689. Attacked Elam. Enlarged and rebuilt Nineveh.

Left: Assyrian troops. Top to bottom: cavalry, assorted infantry, archers in action behind a battering ram, and chariot-borne archers.

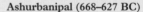

Esarhaddon (680–669 BC)

Assyrian king who repulsed Scythian and Cimmerian invaders from the north and north-east. 671 crushed revolt in Sidon, took Tyre and invaded Egypt, taking Memphis in 671. His campaigns brought the Assyrian Empire to its greatest territorial extent.

Ashurbanipal (668–627 BC)

The last great king of Assyria. Quelled two revolts in Egypt, but was unable to hold the province after 655. In 648 conquered Babylonia from his brother. In 642 invaded Elam and destroyed Susa.

Nebuchadnezzar II (605–562 BC)

Son of the founder of the Chaldean Empire, he was a brilliant tactician and strategist who pursued a policy aiming at having 'no opponent from horizon to sky'. He smashed the Egyptian army at Carchemish and Hamath, thereby gaining control of Syria. Subsequent campaigns in Palestine culminated in the capture of Jerusalem in 597 and 586. His attempted invasion of Egypt in 568/7 was not successful.

Egypt has lost her Palestine dominions

Late 13th to 12th centuries Rise of Elam

1124–1103 Nebuchadnezzar I defeats Elam

1114–1076 Tiglath-Pileser expands Assyrian control to Mediterranean coast

Late 12th to early 10th century Philistines dominate Palestine

1087 King Panehsy of Nubia invades and temporarily occupies Thebes. In 1080 his regime separates from Egypt

By 1060 Egypt has withdrawn to her original valley boundaries. End of Egyptian Empire

1025–1006 Wars of Israelite King Saul

1006–968 Wars of Israelite King David. He captures Jerusalem

975 David defeats Philistines

11th and 10th centuries Babylonia fought over by Assyrians, Aramaeans, Chaldeans etc.

925 Division of Kingdom of Israel into Israel (north) and Judah (south)

Egyptian 3rd Intermediate Period. Egypt fragmented. Sporadic wars between component states

911–891 Adadnivan II begins Assyrian revival and expansion. Foundation of 'Neo-Assyrian Empire'

9th to 7th centuries: Constant warfare waged by Assyrians, based on terror to dominate Mesopotamia and beyond

877 Assyria reaches the Mediterranean

853 Battle of Quaquar. Assyrians halted by Phoenicians, Syrians and Ahab of Israel

8th century Assyria conquers all Babylonia and much of Palestine

By 800 Egypt is three kingdoms: Herakleopolis, Thebes and Kush

Mid 8th century Rise of Kush

750 Nubia advances north to the confluence of the two Niles

745–725 Conquest of Palestine by Tiglath-Pileser III of Assyria

Late 8th century Egyptian incursions in Palestine and Syria provoke Assyrians

727 Piy (or Piankhi) of Kush conquers the Nile Delta and is acknowledged King of all Egypt

722 Assyria takes Samaria

720 Al-Mina overrun by Assyria

717 Assyria takes Carchemish

705 Cimmerians conquer Phrygia

701 Judaean revolt

Battle of Elteka. Assyrians defeated by Judaeans and Egyptians

700 Assyria takes Byblos

688–663 Sennacherib drives Egypt from Palestine

677 Sidon destroyed

674 Assyrian invasion of Egypt repulsed

671 Assyrians sack Memphis and take Tyre

664–656 Assyria takes control of Egypt

664–610 Psamtek I ejects Assyrians from Egypt

652 Gyges, King of Lydia, killed by Cimmerians

630 Psamtek occupies Ashdod

c.627 Last Assyrian King of Babylonia dies: Civil War ensues. Nabopolassar

626–625 Babylon independent of Assyria

625 Rise of Media Empire

625–539 Chaldean dynasty reinstates Babylon as the dominant power in Mesopotamia, the 'Neo-Babylonian Empire'

Cyaxares defeats Scythians

616 Psamtek campaigns against Babylonians in Syria

612 Collapse of Assyrian Empire and destruction of Nineveh

Late 7th to mid 6th centuries War of the Medes v. Urartu, Lydia, etc.; the Median Empire extends to Syria and East Anatolia and East to the Indus

610 Battle of Megiddo. Egyptian Neko II defeats Josiah of Judah

By 610 Saite dynasty rules Egypt

605–562 Nebuchadnezzar II conquers Syria and Palestine

605 Battle of Carchemish. Neko defeated by Nebuchadnezzar who takes southern Mesopotamia

601 Babylonian invasion of Egypt repulsed

c.600 Lydia introduces world's first coinage

597 Nebuchadnezzar captures Jerusalem

Cyrus the Great (reg. 559–530 BC)

Founder of the Achaemenid, or Persian, Empire. After defeating his Median overlord by 550, he conquered Media, Assyria and part of Asia Minor before taking Lydia and the Ionian cities. In 539 he captured Babylon. His empire, 4,000km in width and 1,500km from north to south, was vast, with a population of some 35 millions. His son, Cambyses, conquered Egypt and Cyprus.

Darius I (The Great) (549–486 BC)

Aided by his predecessor Cambyses' bodyguard (the Ten Thousand Immortals), he ousted the usurper Bardiya and then set about expanding the already huge Persian Empire. By 513 he had conquered east as far as the Indus. In 510 he launched a major expedition in the Balkans against the Scythians and encroached upon the city states of mainland Greece. The revolt of the Ionian Greeks was met with the destruction of Miletus and deportations, but this sparked full-scale war with the Greeks. Defeated at Marathon, and with a rebellion in Egypt, Darius died before he could counterattack.

Above: Cyrus the Great.

Above: Darius I, the Great.

28

594–589 Psamtek II sends expedition to Nubia. His force includes Greek mercenaries

590–589 Sacred War against Crisa

590–585 Media-Lydian War

586 Siege and destruction of Jerusalem by Nebuchadnezzar

581 Babylonian invasion of Egypt repulsed

574–570 Campaigns of Apries

570 Battle of Kyrene

561–547 Croesus King of Lydia

560 Ahmose II asserts Egyptian domination of Syria and Palestine and occupies Cyprus

555–539 Nabonides last king of Babylon

550 Cyrus the Great (559–530) ousts Median dynasty and founds Persian Empire

547–545 Cyrus conquers Lydia and takes Sardis and the coastal cities of South Asia Minor

539 Cyrus takes Babylon from Nabonides

530 Cyrus killed campaigning on Jaxertes

525 Battle of Pelusium. Babylonian king Cambyses conquers Egypt, which becomes a province of the Persian Empire

Above: Persian infantry.

Above: Greek infantry.

522–521 Civil War in Persia

513 Darius of Persia's great Danube expedition

India

c.800 Beginning of Kali era (traditionally set earlier, 3102). Conflict between Kauravas and Pandavas of the Kurv tribe

600 Rise of the Republics (Mahajanapandas). Conflict for hegemony in Ganges Valley. 16 'great states' coalesce into 3 kingdoms – Kashi, Koshala, Magadha, and the Vrjjian Republic

543 King Bimbasara of Magadha conquers Kashi and Koshala and breaks the Vrjjian confederation

537 Darius of Persia conquers Indus Valley

491 King Ajatasatru (491–459) builds fort at Patua; annexes Kasi and Kosala

Wars of Ajatasatru. Over 16 years he subdues Vrjji

By about 400 Nandas field large armies

495–448 Greek-Persian Wars

497 Greek uprisings against Persians in Miletus, Cyprus etc

494 Battle of Lade: Persians defeat Ionian fleet

492 1st Campaign. Thracians repel Persians

490 2nd Campaign. Battle of Marathon. Greeks defeat Persians

480 3rd Campaign. Battle of Thermopylae

480 Battle of Cape Artemisium. Sack of Athens by Persians

480 Battle of Salamis

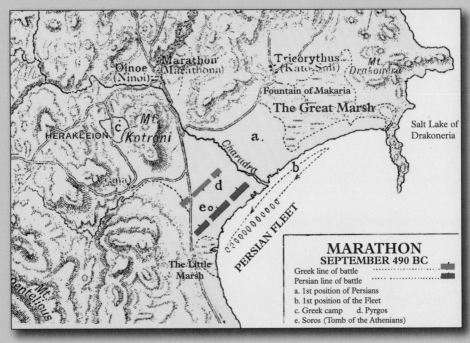

MARATHON
SEPTEMBER 490 BC
Greek line of battle
Persian line of battle
a. 1st position of Persians
b. 1st position of the Fleet
c. Greek camp   d. Pyrgos
e. Soros (Tomb of the Athenians)

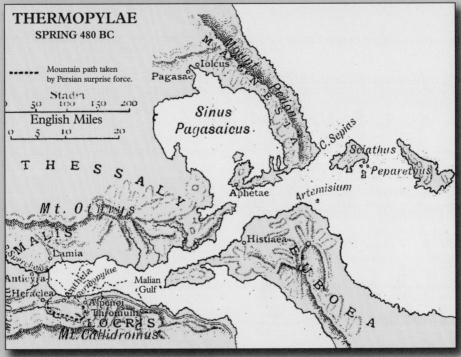

THERMOPYLAE
SPRING 480 BC

Mountain path taken
by Persian surprise force.

Stadia
50 100 150 200

English Miles
0   5   10   20

Battle of Marathon

Context Greek-Persian Wars

Date September 490 BC

Location 26 miles north-east of Athens, Greece

Commanders/Forces Datis commanding 15,000 to 20,000 Persians. Miltiades and Callimachus commanding 10,000 Athenians and 1,000 Plataean hoplites

Objectives Greeks aimed to eject Persian expeditionary force from the Greek mainland

Casualties Said to be 192 Greeks, unknown number of Plataeans; 6,400 Persians

Victor Greeks

Consequences Seen as one of the decisive battles of history, demonstrating the superiority of the Greek infantry and encouraging resistance to the Persians among the Greek city-states. It broke the spell of Persian invincibility. The battle saved the Greeks from the Persian invasion and was long celebrated

Battle of Thermopylae

Context Greek-Persian Wars

Date Spring 480 BC

Location Narrow mountain pass south of Lamia on northern shore of Lamian Gulf, east-central Greece

Commanders/Forces Leonidas, King of Sparta, commanding 300 Spartans and 5–7,000 Greek allies. Mardonius commanding (for King Xerxes) Persians said to number 100,000 but probably a fraction of that

Objectives Greeks sought to delay the advance of the invading Persians and give time for the withdrawal and concentration of their Greek allies

Casualties Greeks overall unknown, but the Spartan element fought to the death after a traitor showed the Persians a route bypassing their defensive position. Persians unknown

Victor Persians

Consequences An epic of heroic resistance to overwhelming force, and an inspiration to the Greeks who were thereby given time to withdraw to the Corinth Isthmus defense line

Below: In contrast to later times, no ancient warship has yet been found complete – only fragments, including the massive pointed beaks used for ramming enemy ships. Details of ancient warship design can be gleaned from illustrated pottery, painting, and murals, but the arrangements of oars and rowers in biremes, triremes, etc., remain conjectural. A reconstruction of a Greek trireme was designed and built in 1987 and propelled successfully by teams of rowers from British universities and rowing clubs.

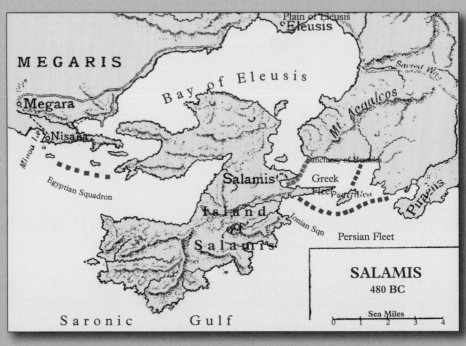

MEGARIS

Megara

Nisaea

Minou I.

Egyptian Squadron

Plain of Eleusis

Eleusis

Bay of Eleusis

Sacred W

Mt. Aegaleos

Salamis

Sanctuary of Heracles

Greek Fleet

Psyttaleia

Ionian Sqn

Piraeus

Island of Salamis

Persian Fleet

SALAMIS
480 BC

Sea Miles
0   1   2   3   4

Saronic   Gulf

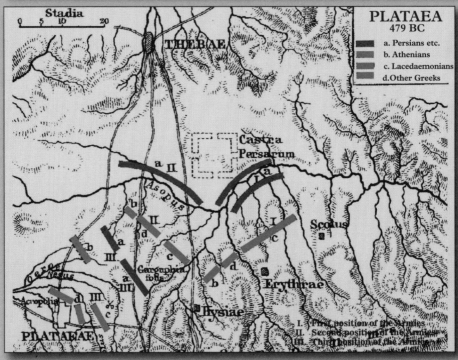

Stadia
0   5   10   20

THEBAE

PLATAEA
479 BC
a. Persians etc.
b. Athenians
c. Lacedaemonians
d. Other Greeks

Castra
Persarum

a II

Asopus

a

b

II

b   a   d

III

c

Scolus

I

c

Gargaphia
fons

d

b

a   III

Oeroe

Nesus

Erythrae

d   III

c

Acropolis

PLATAEAE

Hysiae

I.   First position of the armies
II.   Second position of the armies
III.   Third position of the armies

Battle of Salamis

Context Greek-Persian Wars

Date September 480 BC

Location Saronic Gulf off Piraeus, the port of Athens

Commanders/Forces Themistocles and Eurybiades commanding 366 Greek triremes from Athens and Aegina. Persians 600 galleys

Objectives Persians aimed to capture Athens and conquer Greece. Greeks aimed to defeat and eject the Persian invaders

Casualties 2–300 Persian ships. 40 Greek triremes

Victor Greeks

Consequences The first decisive naval battle of history. Persian fleet driven out of Greek waters, delaying the attack of the Persian army. The battle secured the Peloponnese, but central Greece remained in the hands of the Persians until the Battle of Plataea.

Battle of Plataea

Context Greek-Persian Wars

Date 479 BC

Location Southern Boeotia 12 km south of Thebes

Commanders/Forces Pausianius commanding the forces of the Peloponnesian League; 26,500 hoplites and 11,500 Athenians, Aeginetans, Plataeans and Megarians. Mardonius commanding an unknown, but large, number of Persians

Objectives Persians aimed to conquer Greece. Greeks sought a decisive battle to eject them

Casualties 1,360 Greeks and over 50,000 Persians according to Plutarch; evidently much exaggerated

Victor Greeks

Consequences Decisive end to the Persian attempt to conquer Greece and another demonstration of the superiority of Greek formations and discipline

479 Persians re-occupy Athens. Battle of Plataea
479 Battle of Mycale and Greek liberation of Asia Minor city states
478 Greeks capture Byzantium and Cyprus under Pausanias. Athens organizes Delian League against Persia
467 Battle of Eurymedon. Athens defeats Persians
458 Battle of Aegina
459 Greek fleet supports Egyptian uprising. Expeditions to Memphis
454 Greek fleet annihilated by Persians
449 Battle of Salamis/Cyprus
448 Treaty of Callias ends war

Greek-Etruscan Wars (Western Mediterranean)
540 Battle of Alalia
535 Greeks expelled from Corsica
474 Battle of Cyme/Cumae

481–480 Carthage in Sicily
480 Battle of Himena (Syracuse, Carthage)

509 Revolution v. Tarquinius Superbus in Rome

China
475–221 Era of the Warring States.
By about 300 China has coalesced into seven principal states; vast conscript armies now take the field, a massive increase in scale over previous eras of war
c.255 End of Zhou Dynasty and final disintegration of any sort of imperial structure

431–404 Peloponnesian Wars
457–1 1st War, Athens defeated
457 Athens conquers Aegina. Battle of Tangra
451 Truce
447 Boeotia frees itself from Athens
446 Euboea and Magara. Revolt against Athens. '30 Years Peace'. Athens returns war gains

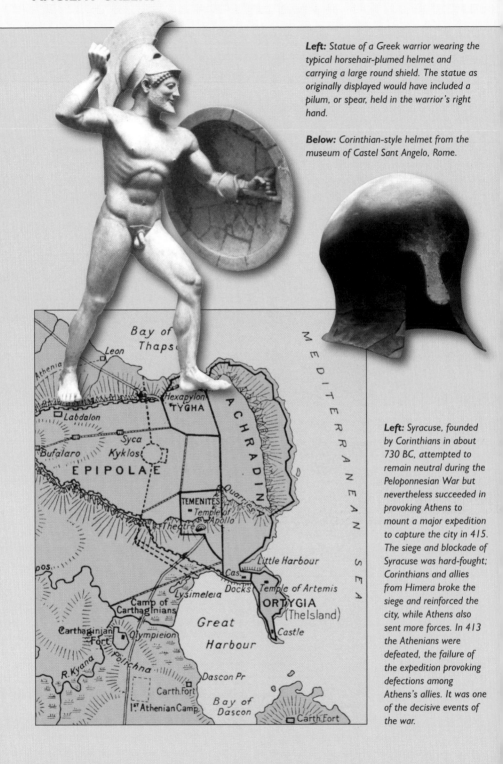

Left: Statue of a Greek warrior wearing the typical horsehair-plumed helmet and carrying a large round shield. The statue as originally displayed would have included a pilum, or spear, held in the warrior's right hand.

Below: Corinthian-style helmet from the museum of Castel Sant Angelo, Rome.

Left: Syracuse, founded by Corinthians in about 730 BC, attempted to remain neutral during the Peloponnesian War but nevertheless succeeded in provoking Athens to mount a major expedition to capture the city in 415. The siege and blockade of Syracuse was hard-fought; Corinthians and allies from Himera broke the siege and reinforced the city, while Athens also sent more forces. In 413 the Athenians were defeated, the failure of the expedition provoking defections among Athens's allies. It was one of the decisive events of the war.

431–21 2nd War, indecisive
431–421 Archidamian War
Sparta devastates Attica; plague in Athens
425 Battle of Pylos. Athens victory.
  Sphacteria capitulates
424 Thracian campaign. Battle of Amphipolis
421 Battle of Niceas
Sparta dominates the land; Athens the sea
430–427 Plague weakens Athens
428–7 Revolt of Mytilene
425 Battle of Pylos. Athens victorious
424 Battle of Delium. Athens defeated
421 Treaty of Nicias, resulting from war-
  weariness
418 Battle of Mantinea. Sparta defeats Argos
415–413 Athens' disastrous expedition to
  Sicily. Fleet annihilated
413–404 Decelian War
410 Battle of Cyzicus. Athens regains naval
  supremacy
407 Sparta gains Persian cooperation
406 Battle of Arginusae. Athens victorious.
  But internal dissention
405 Battle of Aegospotania. Athens' fleet
  destroyed
404 Siege and surrender of Athens

409 Carthage advances towards Syracuse

Continuing expansion of Rome in Italy
431 Battle of Algidus
498–493 Latin Wars
403–400 Dionysus of Syracuse conquers
  most of Sicily

401–400 March of the 10,000. During
  Persian Civil War (Artaxerxes II v. Cyrus
  the Younger), Greek mercenaries win
  Battle of Cunaxa, but then make epic
  retreat across mountains in winter (as
  recorded by Xenophon)

Sparta
399–394 SPARTA-PERSIAN WAR
396–394 SPARTAN EXPEDITION TO ASIA MINOR
395–387 CORINTHIAN WAR
395 Battle of Haliartus

394 Siege of Corinth (to 390)
394 Battle of Coronea
394 Battle of Cnidus. Spartan fleet defeated
  by Persia
382 Sparta occupies Thebes citadel
379–371 THEBAN WAR OF INDEPENDENCE
379 Thebes expels Spartan garrison
376 Battle of Naxos. Athens defeats Sparta
  at sea
371 Battle of Leuctra. Thebes defeats Sparta

370–362 Theban Wars
370 Theban invasion of Peleponnese and
  Laconia
364 Theban naval expedition to Byzantium
364 Battle of Cynoscephalae
363 Thebans defeat Thessalians
362 Thebes invades Peloponnese again
362 Battle of Mantinea

Dionysian Wars with Carthage
398–397 1st War. Carthage pushed back
  from Syracuse
392 2nd War. Carthage almost ejected from
  Sicily
390–379 Dionysius conquers part of S. Italy
389 Battle of Elleponus. Dionysius defeats
  Italians
385–376 3rd War
368–367 4th War
366–344 Turmoil in Syracuse after 367
  death of Dionysius

Roman conquest of Italy
405–396 Etruscan Veii besiege Rome
391 Gauls besiege Clusium
391 Gauls defeat Rome at Battle of Allia
  and sack Rome
367 2nd Gallic invasion repulsed
362–345 Rome contains Latin uprisings
343–341 1ST SAMNITE WAR
343 Battles of Astura, Suessula, Salicula
342 Battle of Mt Gaurus
341 Battles of Veseris, Tifernum; Roman
  conquest of Campania
340–338 LATIN WARS
338 Battles of Sinnessa, Pedum

Alexander the Great (Alexander III of Macedon) (356–323 BC)

Perhaps the greatest warrior-hero of all time, a military genius, whose legend persists to this day in folklore throughout the vast empire he conquered in the Middle East. He was the son of Philip II (380–336 BC), who created an élite military force and won control of the Greek city states. Alexander participated in his father's victory at Chaeronea in 338 and succeeded to the throne of Macedon upon Philip's assassination two years later. He invaded Asia in 334, aiming at nothing less than the conquest of the Persian Empire. This he accomplished in four years of

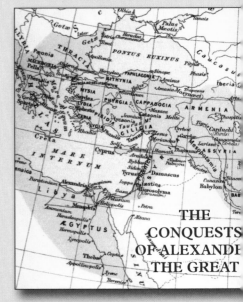

THE
CONQUESTS
OF ALEXANDER
THE GREAT

Left: Alexander (left) and Darius (right) in battle as depicted on the Roman mosaic discovered at Pompeii.

campaigning, proclaiming himself Great King in 331. His principal battles were the Granicus (334 BC), Issus (333), Gaugamela (331) and the Hydaspes (327). As much explorer as soldier, he led his army east and north, into modern Afghanistan and to the frontier of India until his troops refused to march farther. He died at Babylon before his plans for conquests in the west could be undertaken.

360–1, 350–349 Gauls raid to the Tiber valley

Carthage and Syracuse
344–339 Carthaginian war against Timoleon of Syracuse. Siege of Syracuse
340 Battle of Crimissus

Wars of Philip of Macedon
358 Philip unifies Macedon
357–355 War of the Allies
357, 356 Philip expands to Chaldice
355–346 Philip seizes much of Thessaly
355–346 2nd Holy War. Philip is drawn into central Greek conflict

352 Battle of Crocus Field
348 Philip conquers Chaldice, Thrace
345–339 Philip consolidates hold on north of Greece
342 Persia meanwhile regains control of Egypt
341–338 Macedonian war against Hellenic League
338 Battle of Chaeronaea. Philip defeats Hellenic League
337 Philip's general Parmenion leads vanguard for projected invasion of Persia
336 Philip assassinated

335–323 Wars of Alexander the Great
335 Campaign v. Danube tribes: suppresses revolts in Thessaly, Athens, Thebes
334–331 *CONQUEST OF PERSIA*
334 Battle of Granicus
333 Battle of Issus
332–331 Conquest of Syria
332 Siege of Tyre, siege of Gaza and conquest of Egypt
331 Spartan uprising. Battle of Megalopolis. Antipater defeats Agis
331 Battle of Gaugamela/Arbela
330 Occupation of Mesopotamia
331–323 CONQUESTS OF EASTERN PERSIA TO HYDASPES
326 Battle of the Hydaspes
323 Death of Alexander

Western Mediterranean
327/6–304 2nd Samnite War against Rome
323 Carthage begins reconquest of Sicily
321 Battle of Caudine Forks/Passes. Humiliating Roman defeat by Sabines

India
c.325/321 Chandragupta Maurya overthrows Nanda power in Magadha and campaigns in northern and central India
Wars of Chandragupta: he conquers northern India and founds Mauryan Empire
305 Chandragupta fights Seleucus I Nicator. Ends with friendly relationship. Seleucus

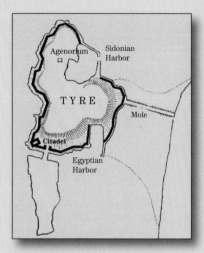

Above: *Alexander's great battlefield victories are well known. But he had also to carry out lengthy sieges, as at Tyre, from January to July 332. This involved the construction of two half-mile-long moles with catapults and siege engines, fighting off naval attacks that included a fireship. In contrast to his fiery impetuosity on the battlefield, Alexander displayed formidable patience and determination.*

BATTLE OF GAUGAMELA (Arbela)
October 331 BC

Alexander's second, decisive victory over the Persians, fought on the eastern bank of the River Tigris not far from Nineveh. Alexander advanced in an oblique formation to offset the Persians' great advantage in numbers. Darius's army included 15 elephants and some 200 scythe-chariots, the deployment of which he aided by preparing his battlefield carefully, flattening out the ground between the armies.

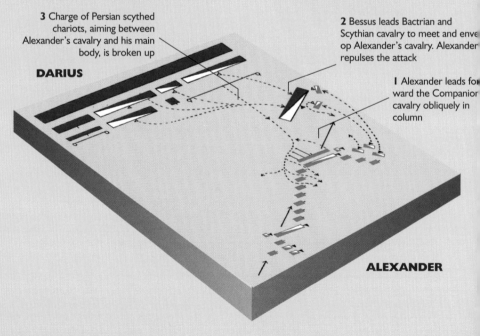

3 Charge of Persian scythed chariots, aiming between Alexander's cavalry and his main body, is broken up

DARIUS

2 Bessus leads Bactrian and Scythian cavalry to meet and envelop Alexander's cavalry. Alexander repulses the attack

1 Alexander leads forward the Companion cavalry obliquely in column

ALEXANDER

From age 13 to 16 Alexander was taught by the philosopher Aristotle. He inherited the leadership of Greece, which his father Philip had achieved after twenty years of political opportunism and hard campaigning. At the Battle of Chaeronea Philip had defeated Athens and Thebes, thereafter uniting the Greek city-states in a federation to strike back at the mighty Persian Empire, avenging the wrongs of earlier wars and liberating the Greek cities of Asia Minor.

On the death of Philip, the Greeks rapidly came to understand that his 20-year-old son was in every way equal to his father – lightning descents on Thessaly and Thebes forestalled any attempts at independence.

In contrast to the seasonal, limited warfare of the Greek cities, the Macedonians waged a new type of warfare, with a professional standing army able take the field at all times of the year and to follow up victory on the battlefield, exploiting success to make lasting gains. Alexander fully understood the importance of a relentless pursuit, so that the set-piece battle was but the first step to total victory. Only thus could he contemplate the conquest of a great empire. His exploits were achieved in just a dozen years.

At Issus, Darius fled. After an interlude in Egypt, Alexander set off in pursuit of the Persian king in 331, defeating him again at Gaugamela. Again Alexander pursued Darius, but was to find him dying, betrayed by his officers led by Bessus, Satrap of Bactria. By 330 the Persian Empire was Alexander's.

Four years of guerrilla fighting and mountain warfare ensued in the north-east of the empire, subduing the tribes at the very edges of the great empire. In 327 a new enterprise drew the Greeks towards the Indus, and on the banks of the Hydaspes Alexander defeated an Indian army. Further conquests beckoned, but the army had had enough. Having followed him for more than 2,000 miles from Greece, now they would go no farther; their king had turned explorer. The Greeks returned to Babylon, by land and by sea, Alexander's new fleet braving the Indian Ocean, the army marching across the Gedrosian desert.

Alexander came as a liberator from the Persians, but not all the cities saw him as such. The siege of Tyre was a massive undertaking, lasting fully seven months and involving the construction of two moles and lengthy naval operations. Some 8,000 Tyrians died in the fighting.

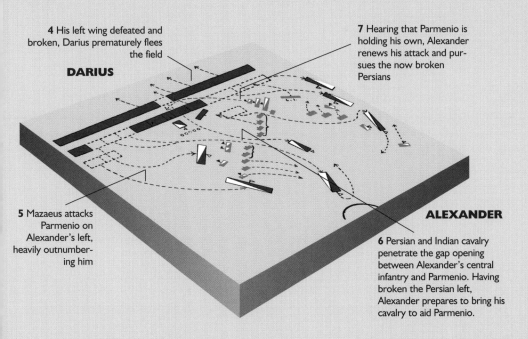

4 His left wing defeated and broken, Darius prematurely flees the field

DARIUS

7 Hearing that Parmenio is holding his own, Alexander renews his attack and pursues the now broken Persians

5 Mazaeus attacks Parmenio on Alexander's left, heavily outnumbering him

ALEXANDER

6 Persian and Indian cavalry penetrate the gap opening between Alexander's central infantry and Parmenio. Having broken the Persian left, Alexander prepares to bring his cavalry to aid Parmenio.

Demetrius I Poliorcetes (336–283 BC)

Son of Antigonus Monopthalmus, one of Alexander's successors competing for control of the Macedonian Empire, whose appellation Poliorcetes means 'the Besieger'. Principal battles were Gaza (312 BC), Salamis/Cyprus (306 BC), Ipsus (301 BC). More ambitious and energetic than successful, his resilience and ability to rebound vigorously from one defeat to another are impressive. He campaigned widely, gaining control of Greece (293–289 BC) but lost Macedon in 288 BC, ending his career trapped with a small force of mercenaries by Seleucus in Cilicia. Rather than execute him, his captor encouraged him to drink himself to death.

Ptolemy I Soter (c.367–282/3 BC)

Friend, general and biographer of Alexander the Great, and founder of the Macedonian dynasty that ruled Egypt from 305/4 BC to the death of Cleopatra in 30 BC. During the wars of Alexander's successors he established himself as king of Egypt and extended his dominion to Palestine, Cyprus and parts of the Aegean.

Seleucus I Nicator (c.358–280 BC)

The most successful of Alexander the Great's generals competing to reunite and rule his huge empire after his death. By 312 BC Seleucus controlled Babylon and much of Mesopotamia.

Above: Seleucus I Nicator.

Victory at Ipsus (301 BC) brought control of Syria and (in 296 BC) Cilicia. He founded Antioch in 300 BC and Seleuceia on the Tigris in 312 BC. The Battle of Corupedium (281 BC) won Asia Minor, so that at his death he had reunited most of Alexander's empire in Asia. Recognising the limits of his empire in the east, about 304 BC he ceded his Indian provinces to Chandragupta, founder of the Mauryan Empire. He was assassinated while embarking on a campaign to win Macedonia; his dynasty lasted for two centuries.

DIADOCHI

The successors of Alexander the Great were a number of his top generals, who partitioned the empire shortly after Alexander's death. Some of the more important were:

Antigonus I
(Monopthalmus, the One-Eyed) took possession of Anatolia and Syria and attempted to reunite the empire. He died at the Battle of Ipsus in 301.

Antigonus II
Grandson of Antigonus, secured Macedon for his dynasty, which remained in control of the country until its conquest by the Romans.

Antipater
Regent of Macedon, he imposed Macedonian control over

Greece following a revolt shortly after Alexander's death.

Cassander
Antipater's son; in c.317 he captured Macedon but died in 297.

Lysimachus
Took control of Thrace and expanded his dominion until his death at the Battle of Corupedium in 280; his kingdom was absorbed by the Seleucids.

Ptolemy I Soter
Seized Egypt and for a while

successfully expanded his empire to include Palestine, Syria and the coastline of what is now southern Turkey. Ptolemaic Egypt remained independent until the defeat of Cleopatra VII at Actium in 31, and its annexation by Rome.

Seleucus I Nicator
Took possession of the eastern portion of Alexander's empire and founded a kingdom that would stretch from the Aegean to the border of India. The victor of Corupedium, he was assassinated soon after.

cedes his trans-Indus provinces in return for 500 elephants

c.297–272 or 268 Bindusara: 'Amitrochates' ('Destroyer of Foes') establishes 'Second' Mauryan Empire, which he extends south, stopping only at Mysore

272/268–c.231 Asoka

Pliny records the Mauryan army as consisting of 9,000 elephants, 30,000 cavalry and 600,000 infantry

260 Asoka campaigns against Kalinga

Bactrian King Demetrius (c.190–167) enters Punjab and gains control of north-west India: Indo-Greek rule

185 Last of Mauryas, Brhadratha, assassinated by Pusyamitra, who founds Sunga Dynasty, with its nucleus at Magadha

After 88 Scythians (Sakas) sweep through Parthia into Indus valley

Kanva Dynasty and Aandhras (Deccan)

323–280 Diadochian Wars: Wars of Alexander's Successors

323–322 LAMIAN WAR

322 Battle of Abydos. Cleitus defeats Athenian fleet

322 Battle of Amorgos. Cleitus defeats and blockades Athens

322 Battle of Crannon. Antipater invades Thessaly and defeats the Greeks

322 Perdiccas invades Cappadona and gives it to Craterus. Perdiccas is now regent of almost the whole empire

322–319 WARS AGAINST PERDICCAS

321 Battle of Lysimachia. Eumenes, for Perdiccas, defeats Craterus

321 Perdiccas invades Egypt. Army mutinies and kills him. Antipater is elected regent by the army in Syria; he gives Babylon to Seleucus

320 Antigonus invades Cappadocia and defeats Eumenes at the Battle of Oraynian Fields. Siege of Nova

319 Antipater dies. Macedonian army elects Polyperchon regent. Antigonus, Cassander and Ptolemy ally against him

WAR WITH POLYPERCHON

Antigonus conquers Asia Minor, Ptolemy takes Syria

318 Cassander invades Greece

318 Battle of the Bosporus. Cleitus defeats Antigonus' fleet. Eumenes takes Babylon

317 Antigonus fights Eumenes in Mesopotamia until Eumenes is betrayed. Antigonus now controls Asia and the East

317 Cassander conquers Athens and Macedon

317–16 Siege of Pydna. Death of Olympias, mother of Alexander

315–312 1ST ANTIGONID WAR

All ally against Antigonus and his son Demetrius. Much maneuvering ensues

312 Battle of Gaza

Ptolemy defeats Demetrius, but Antigonus restores his position by 311 when peace is made. Antigonus has lost the East

311–308 Confused, futile campaigns on all sides

307–301 2ND ANTIGONID WAR

Antigonus mounts second attempt to reunite Alexander's empire: all ally against him and Demetrius

307 Demetius seizes Athens

306 Battle of Salamis. Demetrius defeats Ptolemy's fleet. Antigonus and Demetrius assume titles of Joint Kings of the Empire; Ptolemy declares himself king of Egypt

304 Battle of Thermopylae. Demetrius defeats Cassander and wins most of Greece and Thessaly

302–1 The allies invade Asia Minor and Syria, overwhelming Antigonus

301 Battle of Ipsus. Seleucus and Lysimachus defeat Antigonus, who is killed. They divide his kingdom and Cassander is recognized as king of Macedon. The war against Demetrius, with various re-alignments of alliance continues

294 Demetrius takes Athens and Macedonia

293 Demetrius expands into Thessaly etc.

292 Demetrius invades Thrace

288 Lysimachus and Pyrrhus of Epirus invade Macedonia

Antiochus III the Great (241–187 BC)

Seleucid king whose expansionist ambitions led, after much success, to the eventual downfall of the Seleucid kingdom at the hand of Rome. After restoring lost parts of his empire in the east (Armenia, Parthia, Bactria), he conspired with Philip V of Macedon against Egypt. In 202–198 BC he conquered Ptolemaic Syria and Palestine, then came up against Roman interests in Greece (192 BC). At Thermopylae (191 BC) and Magnesia (189 BC) he was defeated by Rome, ending the Seleucid kingdom as a major power in the Mediterranean.

Pyrrhus (319–272 BC)

King of Epirus who aspired to be 'the Alexander of the west'. His Italian campaigns (281–275 BC) were initially to aid Tarentum against Rome. Principal battles were Heraclea (280 BC), Ausculum (279 BC) and Beneventum (275 BC). He also fought the Carthaginians in Sicily, inconclusively. His 'Pyrrhic victories' (as at Heraclea, which were won at an unsupportable cost) gained no lasting success, however.

Top: *Antiochus III the Great.*

Left: *Statue of Pyrrhus in the town of Arta, Epirus.*

Below: *Coin of Pyrrhus.*

283 Death of Demetrius
281 Battle of Corupedium. Seleucus defeats Lysimachus
280 Death of Seleucus
279 Gauls raid Macedonia
277 Battle of Lysimachia. Antiochus, son of Seleucus defeats the Gauls
The rivals are now into a new generation, with established kingdoms: Antigonus II Gonatas (son of Demetrius) rules Macedon; Antiochus, son of Seleucus rules Asia Minor and Mesopotamia (Seleucid Empire), Ptolemy II rules Egypt
275 Battle of the Elephants. Antiochus defeats the Galatians
274–272 Pyrrhus' wars of conquest in Greece/Macedon
274 Pyrrhus conquers Macedon
273 Antigonus Gonatas retakes Macedon

267–261 War of of Chremonides between Egypt and Macedon
265–261 Siege of Athens by Antigonus Eioriatas

263–261 War of Eumenes (Pergamine breakaway)
263 Battle near Sardis. Antiochus I defeated

258–255 '2nd Syrian War': Macedonians and Seleucids against Egypt
258 Battle of Cos. Macedon defeats Egyptian fleet. Seleucids take Syria

245–241 '3rd Syrian War'
245 Battle of Andros. Macedon and Rhodes defeat Egypt. Egypt fails to regain Syria

WAR OF THE BROTHERS (Seleucus II against Antiochus Hierax)
240 or 239 Battle of Ancyra. Hierax defeats Seleucus
239–229 Wars of Demetrius II of Macedon
233 Battle of Phylacia. Demetrius defeats Achaean League
229–222 War of Cleomenes
227 Battle of Megalopolis. Cleomenes of

Sparta defeats Achaean League
222 Battle of Sellasia. Macedon and Achaeans defeat Cleomenes
219 '4th Syrian War'. Seleucid Antiochus III attacks Egypt in Syria
217 Battle of Raphia. Egyptians defeat Seleucus
220–217 Battle of the Allies (Macedon v. Aetolia/ Sparta) and Philip V of Macedon begins encroachments on Roman theater
207 Battle of Mantinea. Achaean League defeats Sparta

230–228 Roman campaign in Illyria

238–179 Wars of Philip V of Macedon
217–205 1st Rome-Macedonian War
203–200 Macedonian/Seleucid War against Egypt
201 Battle of Lade. Macedon defeats Rhodes' fleet
201 Battle of Chios. Macedon defeated by Pergamum
200–196 2nd Rome-Macedonian War
199–198 Flamininus defeats Philip
197 Battle of Cynoscephalae. Philip defeated
184, 183, 181 Philip's Balkan campaigns

Sicily
312 Agathocles begins conflict with Carthage
311 Carthage wins Battle of Himera and besieges Syracuse
310 Agathocles besieges Carthage to 307
302 Agathocles invades southern Italy

Rome
2nd Samnite Wars continued
316 Battle of Lantulae
315 Battle of Ciuna
309 Battle of Lake Vadimo
306 Battle of Mevania
305 Rome takes Bovanium
304 Peace. Rome annexes Campania
298–290 3RD SAMNITE WAR
298 Battle of Camerinum
295 Battle of Sentinum

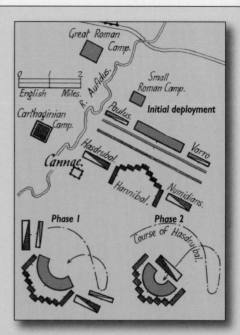

Above: *The Battle of Cannae is considered one of the great masterpieces of generalship and was cited as late as 1991 by General Schwartzkopf as an inspiration for his strategy in his offensive against Saddam Hussein's forces in Kuwait and Iraq.*

Below: *Hannibal's elephants cross the River Rhône en route to the Alpine passes.*

Hannibal (247–183 BC)

One of the Great Captains of History, famous for crossing the Alps into Italy with an army that included elephants. He took command of the Carthaginian army in Spain in 221 BC and captured Saguntum two years later, precipitating the 2nd Punic War with Rome. He devised the bold strategy of invading Italy (from Spain, via the Alps) to raise revolt among Rome's allies in the peninsula. Principal battles were Ticinus (218 BC), the Trebbia (218 BC), Lake Trasimeno (217 BC), Cannae (216 BC) and Zama (202 BC). The victory at Cannae stands as one of the classic battles of history, exemplar of double envelopment. However, despite divided command, the strategy of Fabius (avoiding set-piece battles to wear down the Carthaginian army) and the reluctance of Rome's allies to join the Carthaginian cause, led to the gradual erosion of his army. After 16 years of campaigning without a decisive result, Hannibal returned to defend Carthage in 203 BC. The following year he was defeated by Scipio at Zama.

Publius Cornelius Scipio Africanus Major (c.236–184 BC)

One of Rome's greatest generals, who led the Republic to victory in the 2nd Punic War. Elected to an unprecedented proconsular imperium at the age of 25, he revised legionary tactics and proceeded to defeat Hannibal's brother Hasdrubal at Baecula. His victory at Ilipa effectively decided the course of the war in Spain. He was consul in 205 BC, then led the invasion of the Carthaginian homeland, capturing Utica and Tunis before defeating Hannibal at Zama. His triumphant campaign won him the appelation 'Africanus'.

Left: A bust of
Scipio Africanus.

293 Battle of Aquilonia

285–282 ROMAN CONQUEST OF CELTIC ITALY

285 Battle of Arretium

283 Battle of Lake Vadimo

282 Battle of Populonia ends Etruscan
resistance

281–272 Pyrrhic Wars

280 Battle of Heraclea

279 Battle of Auschlum

275 Battle of Beneventum

272 Blockade and fall of Tarentum. Rome
now dominates southern Italy too

269 Last Samnite uprising against Rome
crushed

264–241 1st Punic War

262 Rome takes Agrigentum

260 Battle of Lipari Islands

260 Battle of Mylae

259 Roman invasion of Corsica, Malta,
Sardinia

256 Battle of Cape Ecnomus

256 Battle of Adys

255 Battle of Tunis

251 Battle of Panormus I

250 Battle of Panormus II

250/49 Battle of Drepanum

242 Rome takes Lilybaeum and Drepanum

241 Battle of Aegates Islands

241 Peace. Carthage gives up Sicily

241–237 Mutiny of the Carthaginian army

238 Rome seizes Corsica and Sardinia

238–229 Carthage conquest of south-
eastern Spain to Ebro frontier

219 Carthage captures Saguntum provoking
full-scale war with Rome

218–202 2nd Punic war

219–203 HANNIBAL'S CAMPAIGN IN ITALY

218 Hannibal crosses Alps. Battles of
Ticinus, Trebbia

217 Battle of Lake Trasimene

217 Battle of Gerunium

216 Battle of Cannae

215 Neapolis/Bruttium campaign

214 Battle of Beneventum

Below: A Roman trireme puts to sea, marines parading on deck.
Above is an impression, put together from evidence at Herculaneum,
of a trireme under sail rather than oar power.

213 Hannibal takes Tarentum
212–11 Siege of Capua
212 Battle of Herdonea I
210 Battle of Herdonea II
207 Battle of the Metaurus
205 Mago takes Genoa
203 Hannibal returns to Africa

SPANISH THEATER

218 Battle of Celsa
217 Battle of Ebro (naval)
215 Battle of Ibera (Dertosa)
213 Rome takes Saguntum

211 Battle of Lorqui
209 Rome takes Nova Carthago
208 Battle of Baecula
206 Battle of Ilipa

SICILY AND OTHER THEATERS

218 Carthage attacks Lilybaeum but is
repulsed
215 Sardinia revolts against Rome. Battle of
Cavales
215–212 Sicily campaign. Romans storm
Syracuse
210–9 Carthage incursion to Agrigentum

AFRICA

204 Scipio invades and besieges Utica
203 Battle near Utica
203 Battle of Great Plains
203 Hannibal returns to Africa
202 Battle of Zama. Final defeat of Hannibal
by Scipio

200–191, 186, 181 Insubre, Boii uprisings in
Cisalpine Gaul (sporadic)

China

Qin or Ch'in Dynasty
c.221 'The First Emperor' Qin Shi Huang-Ti
unites 'civilized' China, improves the
Great Wall and institutes great centralising
reforms (uniform coinage, writing, canals,
roads, etc). Armies of terracotta warrior
effigies guarding his vast tomb are being
unearthed today
206 Massive rebellions rock China after
death of First Emperor
c.206 or 202 Liy-Bang again re-unites China
and founds the Han Dynasty, which
colonizes southern and south-western
China, Korea, Vietnam and Central Asia,
opening the Silk Road to the West and sea
routes to Burma and India
Wars of expansion of Han rulers, 206–113:
campaigns eliminate Yuen Kingdoms of
the south-east coast
Mid-2nd century offensive against the
Hsiung-Nu
Mid-2nd century northern Vietnam
occupied

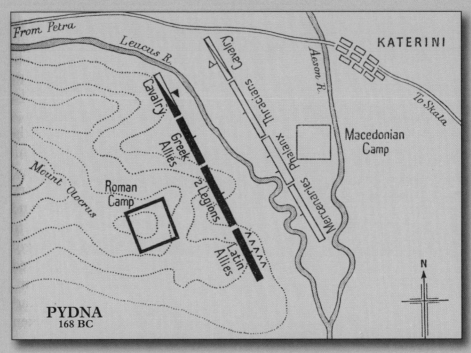

From Petra

Leucus R.

Cavalry

Greek Allies

Roman Camp

2 Legions

Latin Allies

Mount Olocrus

Cavalry

Thracians

Macedonian Phalanx

Mercenaries

Aeson R.

KATERINI

To Skata

Macedonian Camp

N

PYDNA
168 BC

Above: *The Battle of Pydna marked the end of the Kingdom of Macedonia, the greatest power in the eastern Mediterranean for nearly two centuries. It also saw the end of the famed Macedonian phalanx: here it proved initially successful but was disorganized by rough ground and fell victim to the more flexible formations of the Romans.*

Caius Marius (157–86 BC)

First of the great Roman warlords whose ambitions and rivalries brought about the fall of the Roman Republic. He rose to prominence during the Jugurthine War, revolutionising the composition of the Roman army by taking volunteers irrespective of the established property qualifications, creating a semi-professional army more apt to be loyal to its general than to the state. He defended Italy from the invasion of the Cimbri and Teutones, defeating them at Aquae Sextiae (102 BC) and Vercellae (101 BC). He was consul for an unprecedented six times and subsequently became involved in the political struggle between the *Optimates* and *Equites* in alliance with Saturninus and, later, Cinna, and in opposition to Sulla. He died before Sulla triumphed. He was, by marriage, the uncle of Julius Caesar.

117–115 Chiang tribes conquered

117–100 Western expansion

108 Invasions of China and Indochina

2nd half of 1st century sees beginning of Han decline

c.33 Peasant Revolts

Rome's Macedonian Wars

215–205 1ST MACEDONIAN-ROMAN WAR

214 Philip V seizes Oricum

213 Philip invades Illyria

212–11 Operations in central Greece

207 Battle of Mantinea (Sparta defeated by Achaean Leauge)

205 Peace

202 Philip campaigns in the Bosporus

201 Battle of Lade

200–106 2ND MACEDONIAN-ROMAN WAR

Rome invades Epirus

199 Battle of Ottalobus

197 Battle of Cynoscephalae ('Jena of Macedon')

195 Flamininus campaigns in Greece

216–196 Wars of Antiochus the Great

(Seleucid King of Syria)

216–213 Antiochus' Sardis campaign

210 Antiochus regains Armenia

202 Antiochus invades Syria

200 Battle of Panion and siege of Sidon (to 199)

199 Antiochus secures all Palestine

197 Antiochus conquers south-west coast of Asia Minor and Thrace

192–188 ROME'S WAR WITH ANTIOCHUS THE GREAT

192 Antiochus invades Greece

191 Battle of Thermopylae loses Greece for Antiochus.

191 Battle of Cape Corycus

190 Rome invades Asia Minor across the Hellespont

190 Battle of Myonnesus

189 Battle of Magnesia. L. Scipio defeats Antiochus. End of strong Seleucid kingdom

140 Battle of Side

Rome in Spain

195–133 1st Celtiberian War.

153–151 Renewed war

134–133 Numantine War. Final siege and fall of Numantia

154–137 Lusitanian War

Cisalpine Gaul

197–6 Roman campaigns v. Insubre, Boii, etc

193 Roman campaigns v. Insubre, Boii, etc

183–177 Roman campaigns in Istria

181–177 Sardinian revolt and pacification

169 Egyptians invade Palestine v. Antioch IV (Seleucid). Antiochus counter-invades Egypt

167 Antiochus temporarily controls Egypt and Cyprus

171–168 3rd Macedonian War

171 Battle of Callicinus

168 Battle of Pydna

186 Bithynia-Pergamum War

167–160 Revolt of the Maccabees (Palestine)

165 Battle of Emmaus

164 Battle of Beth-Sur

162 Battle of Beth-Zachariah

160 Battle of Adsa

160 Battle of Elasa

151 Carthage-Numidian War

149–146 3rd Punic War.

Carthage city razed to the ground by Rome

154 Roman campaign v. Ligurians

152–145 Egyptian-Seleucid War in Palestine/Syria

145 Battle of Oenoparas

149–148 4th Macedonian War (pretender)

146 End of Achaean League

146 Battle of Scarpheia. Rome takes control of all Greece

133 King Attalus bequeaths Pergamum to Rome

Left: *Lucius Cornelius Sulla.*
Above: *Mithridates the Great of Pontus*

Lucius Cornelius Sulla (138–78 BC)
Second of Rome's great warlords during the 1st century BC and dictator of Rome 81–79 BC. Rivalry with Marius over command in the 1st Mithridatic War led to his march on Rome and seizure of power. He defeated Mithridates and returned to civil war in Rome. The issue was settled in 82 BC at the Battle of the Colline Gate and he took control of Rome. His régime restored the power of the *Optimates*, but after his retirement Rome was set for a further half-century of civil strife that would be ended by the rule of one man.

Quintus Sertorius (c.122–72 BC)
Roman general who allied with Marius and Cinna against Sulla; he fled to Spain after the Battle of the Colline Gate. Brave and resourceful, he proved brilliant in irregular warfare. With Lusitanians and an army of exiles from Sullan Rome, he defied the best efforts even of Pompey until being assassinated in 72 BC.

Mithridates VI the Great (120–63 BC)
King of Pontus and implacable enemy of Rome. In 88 BC he seized Cappadocia, Bithynia and the Roman province of Asia, but was defeated and expelled by Sulla by 84 BC. He defeated the activities of Sulla's lieutenant Murena (83–82 BC) and invaded Bithynia again (bequeathed to Rome in 74 BC). The Roman general Lucullus's successful campaigns against Pontus were frustrated by politics, and Mithridates was finally driven from his kingdom by Pompey.

Left: *Reconstruction of a Roman artillery piece.*

132–130 Pergamine revolt quelled by Rome

135–132 1st Servile War against Rome

129–118 Egyptian Civil War
129–76 Rome conquers Dalmatia
125–120 Rome conquest of southern Gaul
(to Cevennes)

117–105 Jugurthine War
111 Roman intervention
110 Battle of Calama
109 Battle of 'Muthul'

113–101 Invasion of Gaul and Italy by Cimbri and Teutones
113 Battle of Noreia
109 Battle in Rhône valley
105 Battle of Arausio
102 Battle of Aquae Sextiae
101 Battle of Vercellae: Marius and Catulus
decisively defeat the invaders

104–101 2nd Servile War

103–76 Wars of Alexander Jannaeus
His aggressive policy results in the
expansion of Judaea but conflict with
Egypt and other local powers and a
Jewish revolt 82–85

102 Roman campaign against Cilician
pirates

Spain
99, 98–93 Lusitanian revolts

91–98 The Social War against Rome (War of Rome's allied tribes)
90 Battle of Tolenos River
89 Battle of Fucine Lake
89 Battle of Asculu
89 Battle near Pompeii

88 Turmoil in Rome. Sulla marches on Rome
87 Counter-coup of Marius and Cinna in
Rome

89–88 Egyptian Civil War

88–85 1st Mithridatic War (Pontus against Rome)
88 Mithridates invades Cappadocia
Battle of Amnias River
Athens rises against Rome
87 Sulla in command of operations in the
East
87–85 Sulla campaigns in Greece
86 Battle of Mileopolis. Fimbria defeats
Pontic army
86 Athens retaken by Sulla
86 Battle of Chaeronea. Sulla defeats Pontic
army
86 Battle of Cyzicus. Lucullus victorious
85 Battle of Orchomenus. Sulla defeats
Pontic army
85 Battle of Rhyndacus
85 Battle of Lectum, Battle of Tenedos
85 Sulla crosses to Asia Minor

83–82 Sullan War
83 Sulla's return from the East. Battle of Mt
Tifata. Sulla victorious
82 Battles of Sacriportus, Faventia, Clusium,
Colline Gate. Sulla victorious over
Marians
82–80 Pompey campaigns against rebels in
Africa/Sicily
81–79 Sulla Dictator

83 Parthian conquest of Syria

83–72 Sertorian War (Spain)
77 Pompey joins Metellus in Spain
76 Sertorius wins Battles of Lauro and Italica
75 Pompey is victorius at Turia, but defeated
at Sucro and Turia. Subsequently
Sertorius' support in Iberia wanes and in
72 or 73 he is assassinated

83–82 2nd Mithridatic War (Mithridates repulses Murena)
77 Revolt of Lepidus
Battle of Cosa (then Pompey transfers to
Spain)

Above: Pompey the Great.

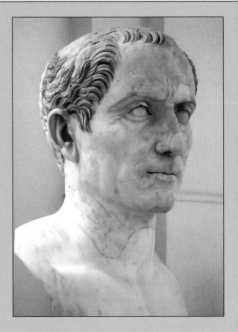

Above: Julius Caesar.

Pompey the Great (Gnaeus Pompeius Magnus)(106–48 BC)

Dominant Roman general between the régimes of Sulla and Caesar. Rose to prominence with his father, Strabo, during the Social War. Aided Sulla (83–82 BC) and helped put down revolt of Lepidus in 77 BC. Campaigned in Spain against Sertorius, then returned to Italy at the end of the rebellion of Spartacus. With Crassus, overawed Rome to become consul for 70 BC. Undertook vast campaign against pirates in the Mediterranean (67 BC) then took command of the war against Mithridates, thereafter settling Roman affairs in the east. Returned to Rome to form 1st Triumvirate with Crassus and Caesar. Fought Caesar (49–48 BC) in the Roman Civil War (War of the 1st Triumvirate), meeting defeat at Pharsalus (48 BC) and assassination in Egypt.

C. Julius Caesar (100–44 BC)

One of the greatest generals in history, Caesar conquered Gaul for Rome, invaded Britain twice, and defeated his enemies, led by Pompey the Great, in the Roman Civil War of 49–45 BC. Assuming the dictatorship of Rome, he effectively brought the Roman Republic to an end, ushering in an imperial regime, the founder of which was his adopted nephew Octavius (later known as Augustus). With Pompey and Crassus, he had formed an alliance (the 1st Triumvirate) and after his consulship assumed the governorship of Gaul, then a small part of the area that is modern France. Between 58 and 52 he systematically conquered the rest of Gaul, pausing in 55 and 54 to invade, but not conquer, Britain. A full-scale revolt in Gaul was suppressed after hard fighting in 52–1. Tension with the Senate and his erstwhile ally Pompey led to Civil War in 49. Caesar invaded Italy, defeated a Pompeian army in Spain, then faced Pompey at Dyrrhachium before defeating him at Pharsalus in Greece (48 BC). His pursuit of Pompey to Egypt led to a campaign in Alexandria and on the Nile, after which he returned to Rome, defeating Pontic forces at Zama in modern Turkey (47) en route. His enemies had meanwhile rallied in Africa, where Caesar defeated them at Thapsus (47–46) before tracking down Pompey's last supporters at Munda in Spain (45). Caesar was assassinated while planning a new campaign against the Parthians.

Above: Napoleon III's statue to Vercingetorix.

78–76 Roman campaign *v.* Cilician pirates
74 Marcus Antonius' campaign against the pirates fails

72–71 3rd Servile War (Revolt of Spartacus)

72 Battle of Mt Garganus
72 Battle in Picenum, Battle of Mutina
71 Crassus and Pompey march on Rome

74–62 3rd Mithridatic War

74 River battle of Rhyndacus. Mithridates invades Bithynia
73 Battle of Lemnos
69 Battle of Tigranocerta. Lucullus defeats Pontic army
68 Battle of Arsanias River
67 Battle of Zela. Mithridates defeats Romans
66 Pompey assumes command against Mithridates
64–62 Pompey campaigns in upper

Mesopotamia and Syria and settles Roman affairs in the East

67 Pompey's campaign against piracy in the Mediterranean
65 R intervenes in Judaea. Battle of Papyron

63–2 REVOLT OF CATILINA

62 Battle of Pistoria
60 1st Triumvirate rules Rome (Pompey, Crassus, Caesar)

58–50 Caesar's Conquest of Gaul

58 Campaigns against Helvetii and Suebi
58 Battle of Toulon-sur-Arroux
58 Battle near Cernay
57 Campaign against Belgae
57 Battle of Neuf-Mesnil
56 Campaign against maritime tribes of the west
56 Battle of Quiberon Bay
55 Campaigns on northern border of Gaul
55 1st invasion of Britain
54 2nd invasion of Britain
54 Rebellion of Ambiorix
53 Revolt of Ambiorix. Battle of Aduatuca. Ambiorix defeats Sabinus. Campaigns against the Nervii, etc.
52 Rebellion of Vercingetorix
52 Battle of Gergovia
52 Battle of Lutetia
52 Siege and battle of Alesia
51 Siege of Uxellodunum

55 Gabinius intervenes in Egyptian succession crisis
55 Parthian succession crisis

54–53 Parthian campaign of Crassus

53 Battle of Carrhae. Romans defeated, Crassus killed

Roman Civil War

49 Near bloodless conquest of Italy by Caesar

49 1ST SPANISH CAMPAIGN

49 Maneuvers of Ilerda
49 Siege of Massilia

JULIUS CAESAR

Caesar was not essentially an innovator but a supreme exponent of Roman warfare. The Roman cohort was a much finer instrument of war than the old phalanx, enabling him to move and maneuver with speed. He took risks, and sometimes these failed, condemning him to a long, hard campaign where the spade was as important as the sword. Always, however, his indomitable will-power – and the endurance of his veterans – brought victory.

Top: *Life-size reconstruction of Roman defense lines as constructed during Caesar's siege of Alesia. In front of the wall, which is strengthened with towers, are trenches and pits covered with brushwood hiding sharpened stakes – the ancient equivalent of today's minefield.*

Above: *Model in the Museum of Roman Civilization, Rome, showing a siege tower in action, with bridge dropped over the defending wall to allow the attacking troops to storm the defenses. Behind the tower are covered ways to protect the engineers and the assaulting troops from arrows and other missiles. Roman legions possessed formidable skills with wood, being able to construct camps, siege engines, catapults, bridges (such as Caesar's across the Rhine) and even warships on campaign.*

BATTLE OF NEUF-MESNIL (or The Sambre) July 57 BC.
Caesar's army ambushed by Belgic tribes during the conquest of Gaul.

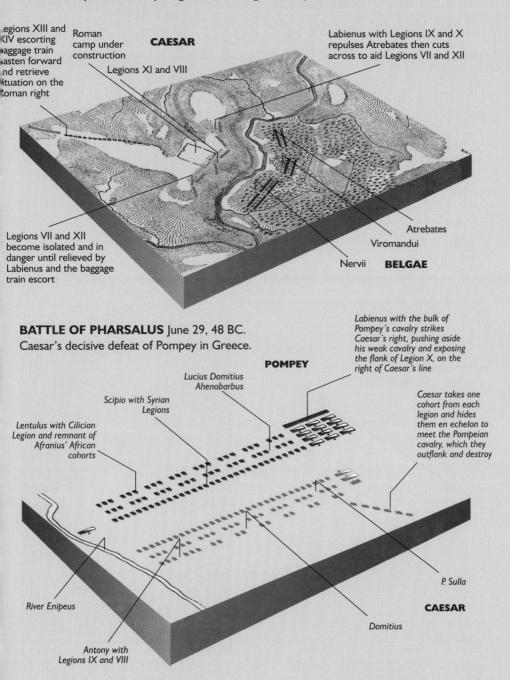

Legions XIII and
XIV escorting
baggage train
hasten forward
and retrieve
situation on the
Roman right

Roman
camp under
construction

CAESAR

Legions XI and VIII

Labienus with Legions IX and X
repulses Atrebates then cuts
across to aid Legions VII and XII

Legions VII and XII
become isolated and in
danger until relieved by
Labienus and the baggage
train escort

Atrebates

Viromandui

Nervii   **BELGAE**

BATTLE OF PHARSALUS June 29, 48 BC.
Caesar's decisive defeat of Pompey in Greece.

Labienus with the bulk of
Pompey's cavalry strikes
Caesar's right, pushing aside
his weak cavalry and exposing
the flank of Legion X, on the
right of Caesar's line

POMPEY

Lucius Domitius
Ahenobarbus

Scipio with Syrian
Legions

Caesar takes one
cohort from each
legion and hides
them en echelon to
meet the Pompeian
cavalry, which they
outflank and destroy

Lentulus with Cilician
Legion and remnant of
Afranius' African
cohorts

P. Sulla

River Enipeus

CAESAR

Domitius

Antony with
Legions IX and VIII

Mark Antony.

Mark Antony (Marcus Antonius) (c.82–30 BC)

Penultimate in the line of warlords whose rivalries led to the fall of the Roman Republic. Served with Caesar in Gaul and during the Civil War (War of the 1st Triumvirate). Allied with Octavian and Lepidus after the failure of the Mutina War to form 2nd Triumvirate (43 BC). Defeated Caesar's assassins at Philippi (42 BC). Divided the Roman world with Octavian and attempted unsuccessfully to conquer Parthia. Fell out with Octavian and, in alliance with Cleopatra of Egypt, was defeated at Actium (31 BC), subsequently committing suicide.

Marcus Vipsanius Agrippa (c.63–12 BC)

Associate and general of Augustus, 44–30 BC, victor at Actium (31 BC) over Antony and Cleopatra.

Augustus (C. Octavius/Octavian) (63 BC–AD14)

Heir to Julius Caesar and founder of the Roman Empire. A statesman rather than a general (see Agrippa). With Antony and Lepidus formed 2nd Triumvirate; defeated Pompey's son Sextus by 36 BC and Antony at Actium in 31 BC. Subsequently campaigned in Illyricum and in north-west Spain. Secured Rome's northern frontiers and stabilized the administration of Rome and her overseas relationships, ushering in a long period of relative peace and Roman domination of Western Europe and the Mediterranean.

Above: Augustus. Below: Marcus Vipsanius Agrippa

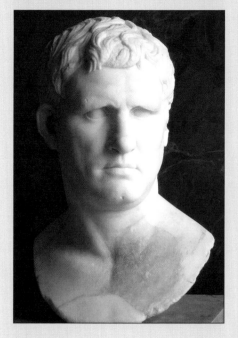

49 Curio defeated in Africa at Battle of the Bagradas

49 Mutiny of Caesar's army at Placentia

48 DYRRHACHIUM CAMPAIGN

48 Siege of Dyrrhachium

48 Campaign and battle of Pharsalus. Caesar defeats Pompey

48–47 CAESAR'S EGYPTIAN (ALEXANDRIAN) CAMPAIGN. Battle of Nile Delta. Battle of Canopus. Caesar secures Cleopatra on the throne of Egypt

47 Battle of Nicopolis. Pharnaces, son of Mithridates the Great, defeats Caesar's lieutenant Domitius

47 Caesar's Asian campaign. Battle of Zela. Caesar routs Pharnaces

47 Mutiny of troops in Rome

47–46 CAESAR'S AFRICAN CAMPAIGN

46 Battles of Ruspina and Thapsus. Caesar defeats Pompey's associates

46–45 CAESAR'S 2ND SPANISH CAMPAIGN

45 Battle of Munda

44 Assassination of Julius Caesar

Wars of the 2nd Triumvirate

43 Mutina war. Battle of Mutina

43 2nd Triumvirate rules Rome (Antony, Octavian, Lepidus)

42 Philippi Campaign

42 Battles of Philippi. Antony and Octavian defeat Brutus, Cassius and the other assassins of Caesar

40 Parthian conquest of Syria, southern Asia Minor

41–40 War of Perusia. Siege of Perusia

43–35 SEXTUS POMPEY'S WAR

36 Battle of Mylae

36 Battle of Naulochus

39–33 ANTONY'S PARTHIAN WAR

38 Battle of Gindarus

36 Antony's Parthian invasion fails

34 Antony's Armenian campaign

35–33 Octavian's Illyrian Campaign

32–31 WAR BETWEEN ANTONY (WITH CLEOPATRA) AND OCTAVIAN

31 Battle of Actium. Antony and Egyptians defeated. Antony and Cleopatra commit suicide. Octavian (Augustus from 27) is now sole ruler of the Roman Empire

25–24 Gallus's Arabian Expedition

26–24 Augustus' conquest of north-west Iberia

26 Battle of Vellica

30–28 Roman frontier operations in the Balkans

25–24 Gallus's Arabian expedition

17–14 Roman operations in Rhine-Danube area

14 Agrippa intervenes in Bosporan kingdom

12 German campaigns begin

12–9 Campaigns of Drusus

8BC Tiberius takes command in Germany

BC

AD

China

AD 9–23 Wang Mang usurps throne; 23 restoration of the Han

Meanwhile the external menace of the Hsiung-nu begins to become major threat

Late 1st century Emperor Wu-ti launches a drive against the Hsiung-nu west into central Asia

25 Eastern Han

Court factionalism weakens central authority by c.160; regional commanders become autonomous

184 Mass uprising – the 'Yellow Turbans'

220 Hsien-ti, the last Han emperor, abdicates and China splits into three kingdoms: Wei (North), which becomes Western Ch'in; Shu (West); Wu (South)

263 Wei conquer Shu

265 Ssuma coup in Wei

Middle East

4 Armenian succession crisis

5–6 Gaetrilian Revolt in Mauretania

Europe: Wars of Imperial Rome

6–9 Pannonian revolt put down by Tiberius

Above: *Tiberius was the second emperor of Rome (AD 14–37), stepson of Augustus. Before he succeded to the throne, he fought with distinction on the borders of Germany and Pannonia.*

Above: *Bust of the Trajan.*

Above: *Vespasian became Rome's emperor in 69, concluding the 'Year of the Four Emperors' (Galba, Otho and Vitellius being his predecessors). His legions in Syria and Palestine, putting down the Jewish revolt, proclaimed him emperor, and he defeated Vitellius at Cremona. The making of emperors by armies in the field was to become common during the 3rd century.*

Marcus Ulpius Traianus, Trajan (reg. 98–117) Of Iberian origin, Trajan was the epitome of Rome's great soldier-emperors, famous above all for his conquest of Dacia, which is commemorated on Trajan's Column in Rome. Provoked by the activities of the Dacian King Decebalus, Trajan conquered the area in two campaigns, establishing a dramatic salient resting on the Carpathian Mountains. This acted as a strategic shield for the Danube and its region until the crisis of the 3rd century, when Aurelian abandoned the province. Dacia also had the advantage of containing gold and silver deposits. Less lasting was Trajan's conquest of Armenia and Mesopotamia, provoked by one of many succession crises in Armenia and the interference of the Parthians. The Romans took the Parthian capital, Ctesiphon, and reached the mouth of the Tigris, but the area proved too difficult to hold and Trajan's successor, Hadrian, withdrew the frontier.

7 Battle of Volcaean Marsh. Tiberius, ambushed, defeats the rebels

9 Revolt in the newly won area of Germany by Arminius.

9 Battle of the Teutoburger Wald (or Clades Variana). A great disaster for Rome: P. Quintillius Varus is defeated with the loss of some 20,000 men. Effectively, this means the end of Roman plans to expand to the Elbe. Subsequent campaigns are raids rather than attempts at conquest

14–16 Revolt of German legions. Germanicus quells then campaigns into Germany

16 Battle of Idistaviso. Germanicus worsts Arminius. Germanicus is then deployed to the East, but dies, possibly poisoned, at Antioch

17–24 Revolt of Numidian chief Tacfarinus

22 Battle of Thala

21 Gallic Revolt of Julius Florus and Julius Sacrovir

25 Thracian Revolt

28–41 Frisian Revolt

35–52 Armenian succession operations

40–49 Conquest of Britain begun. After an aborted invasion in 40, Aulus Plautius leads a full-scale expedition in 43. By 49 the Romans have reached the Severn and the Wash. After the defeat of Caractacus, operations remain low-key until 61

35–52 Armenian succession operations

61 Revolt of the Iceni in Britain. Boudicca of the Iceni takes Camulodunum and Lincoln before Suetonius Paulinus defeats her near Lichfield

66–68 Judaean revolt

70–73 Siege of Massada

68 Revolt of Julius Vindex (suppressed), precursor to the major revolt against Emperor Nero, who kills himself when the Praetorian Guard support the usurper Galba

69–70 ROMAN WAR OF SUCCESSION

69 Year of the Four Emperors. A succession of coups raise Otho, then Vitellius to the throne

69 Battle of Locus Castorum. Otho's ally Caecina fails to defeat the Vitellians

69 First Battle of Bedriacum (Cremona). Vitellius vanquishes Otho

69 Second Battle of Bedriacum. Vespasian's legions defeat Vitellius

71–74 Brigantine War in Britain results in the advance of the Roman frontier farther north

72 Upper Euphrates campaign stabilizes frontier for half a century

73–74 'Basel re-entrant' annexed in Germany

78–84 Cn Julius Agricola campaigns in Scotland, but the Romans are now over-extended

84 Battle of Mons Graupius. Agricola defeats Picts

89 Revolt of Saturninus in Germany

97–98 Suebian War

WARS OF TRAJAN

101–102 First Dacian War. Trajan invades and wins at Tapae (101), but severe losses and difficult terrain slow the Roman advance

102 First Battle of Sarmizegethusa (Dacian capital); Trajan defeats Dacian King Decebalus

105–106 Second Dacian War. Trajan's major offensive conquers Dacia completely

106 Second Battle of Sarmizegethusa. The Roman province of Dacia is established

113–116 Trajan's conquest of Parthia and Armenia

115–117 Revolts in Cyrenaica, Egypt and Palestine

116–117 Mesopotamian revolt

122/3–c.128 Hadrian's Wall built in Britain; it will become Rome's northern frontier

132–135 Bar Kochba revolt in Palestine

134 Recapture of Jerusalem

Brigantine Revolt in Britain is crushed by 139–142 but further outbreaks occur in 155 and 158. Lollius Urbicus builds the

Lucius Septimius Severus.

Lucius Septimius Severus (reg. 193–211)

Founder of the Severan dynasty, and African by birth, Septimius had to fight for the throne, overcoming Didius Julianus in 193, Pescennius Niger in 194 and Clodius Albinus in 196. He understood the importance of the army and provoked the hostility of the senate by stationing troops near to the capital. He conquered Mesopotamia (195–202), taking Ctesiphon and annexing the area. In 208 he visited Britain and mounted an expedition against the Caledonians, after which, understanding that the Antonine Wall was a defense line too far north, ordered the upgrading of Hadrian's Wall. He died at Eboracum (York, England) leaving the empire to his unbalanced megalomaniac son Caracalla, who proceeded to undo much of the good work for the Roman Empire that Septimius had done.

Left: *Scenes of battle depicted on Trajan's Column in Rome. At upper right can be seen the 'testudo' formation, legionaries using their square shields to form a tortoise-like carapace against arrows and other missiles.*

Right: *Soldiers of the Praetorian Guard, the Roman Emperor's personal bodyguard. They became an important factor in palace politics, deserting Caligula and Nero, and assassinating Galba and Pertinax.*

Antonine Wall between the Clyde and the Forth

145–152 Mauretanian disturbances

152–153 Egyptian rising

161 Parthian War

157–158 Dacian operations

167, 172–5 and after Danube security operations. Pressure from Germanic tribes including Chatti, Marcomanni, Quadi, Iazyges, Roxolani, etc., provoke Roman trans-Danube punitive raids. The scale of imperial commitment to the northern frontiers increases dramatically. After two centuries of relative stability and peace, the Roman Empire is approaching a period of crisis within and without

175–176 Revolt of Aridius Cassius in Syria

184 Antonine Wall overrun

184–186 Mutiny of legions in Britain

190 African revolt

192–197 Emperor Commodus assassinated. Rivals for the throne are eliminated by L. Septimius Severus

193 Battle of Cyzicus

194–195, 197–199 Septimius Severus's Parthian campaigns

194 Battle of Issus

195–197 Revolt of Albinus

197 Battle of Lugdunum (Lyons); city destroyed, as Albinus is defeated by Severans

209 Major expedition to Moray Firth in Scotland led by Septimius Severus. Hadrian's Wall renovated to become new frontier in Britain

213–214 Alemanni campaign of Caracalla. Defensive *limes* completed in Rhine-Danube re-entrant

214 Theocritus's Armenian campaign

215 Caracalla's Alexandrian Massacres

216–217 Caracalla's Eastern Campaign

216 Battle of Nisibis

218 Battle of Antioch

Middle East

227 Ardashir Artaxerxes establishes Sassanid Empire

India

Yueh-chi Chief Kujula Kadphises conquers northern India

After 100, Zenith of Kushana under Kanishka

2nd century, Satarahanas (Deccan)

Early 3rd century Pandya King Nedunjeliyan wins major victory over Ceras

By about 250 Kushans reduced to Gandhara and Kashmir and become vassals of Sassanid Persia

China

280 China reunified by Western Ch'in

'Wars of the Eight Princes' – internal dynastic conflicts wreck the authority of

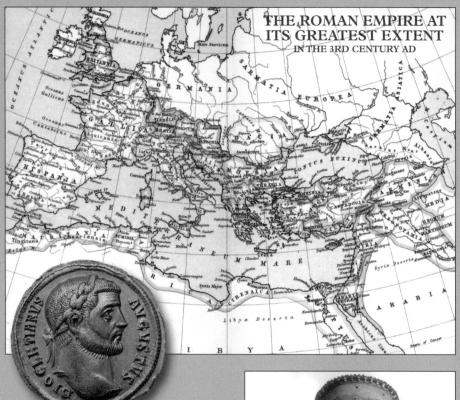

THE ROMAN EMPIRE AT
ITS GREATEST EXTENT
IN THE 3RD CENTURY AD

**Gaius Aurelius Valerius Diocletianus,
Diocletian (reg. 284–305)**
After two decades of short-lived emperors,
Dalmatian-born Diocletian stabilized and
reformed the Roman system of government to
take account of the demands on the ruler
imposed by the continuing wars against barbarian invasions and the threat of usurpers being
raised up by the various armies deployed about
the empire. Two senior and two junior emperors, with adoptive succession, were to rule the
empire. It did not work completely, but it did
provide a more sound, structured government
that would in essence survive to the middle of
the next century. Effectively (and with the subsequent contribution of Constantine) he re-
founded the empire. Discipline was restored to
the army, which included a larger standing force
as well as local defense units within smaller
provinces to guard the frontiers.

Above left: *Diocletian.*
Above: *The walls of Rome.*

the central administration

'The Sixteen Kingdoms' or 'The Five Barbarians' disruption of China'. Some five barbarian groups conquer China

Near-permanent warfare exists between the states of northern China and many refugees flee south from the northern barbarian invaders

383 Chien Ch'in invades south but is repulsed

South China Dynasties Eastern Ch'in; Song; Qi; Liang; Chen

End of the 6th century Yang Chien conquers the south and reunites China, founding the Sui dynasty

Crisis of the Roman Empire

After the assassination of Caracalla (217), a succession of emperors are raised to the throne by their legions, only to be assassinated, overthrown by a rival or even by their own troops. Records of this period are poor but point to almost constant warfare within the empire and with the tribes north of the Rhine and Danube, together with continuing conflict in the East. Many battles are fought during this period, but they are rarely named, and details are few. Alemanni and Goths are the principal enemies in Europe. The strain on manpower and the economic resources of the empire is immense. And plague hits Rome in 262.

231–233 Severus Alexander's Eastern campaign

234–235 Alemanni War

236–237 Sarmatian/Dacian campaigns

238 War with the Sassanids

240 Carthage rebellion

244 Balkan trans-Danube tribal invasions

251 Battle of Abritus. Emperor Decius perishes fighting the Goths

251 Battle of Forum Trebroni

253–260 Rome-Persian War

259 Battle of Edessa

260 Emperor Valentinian made prisoner by Persians

256 Saxons raid British coasts

258/9 Alemanni break into northern Italy where they are repulsed by Gallienus

269 Battle of Naissus. Claudius defeats the Goths

260–274/5 'Postumus's Gallic Empire'. C. Latinius Postumus proclaims himself emperor at Cologne. Gaul is recovered in 275 after Battle of Campi Catalaunii by Emperor Aurelian ('Restitutor Orbis', reuniting the Empire); but he is assassinated in 275. During his reign, construction begins on the walls of Rome, which has not been necessary since Republican times

262–267 Odaenathus of Palmyra's campaigns against Persia

273 Palmyra destroyed

282–283 Carus invades Mesopotamia

Persians occupy much of the East during Roman strife

285 Battle of Margus (against rival Carinus) establishes Diocletian as emperor who will 're-found' the empire

286–293 Carausius declares independence in Britain and northern Gaul but is assassinated by Allectus

293 THE TETRARCHY – The Collegiate Emperors.

Diocletian splits the running of the empire between two emperors with deputies/designated successors. The aim is continuity and increased efficiency in fighting off the incursions of barbarians from across the Rhine and Danube. The frontier is too long for one man to command it. And the capital, Rome, is no longer a strategic base for such operations

295–298 Crisis faces Rome: Narses of Persia is at war; Achilleus in Egypt; the Quinquegentanei in Africa; Carausius in Britain; plus there is warfare on Rhine and Danube fronts

296 Battle of Clausentum. Tetrarch Constantius recovers Britain for Rome

297 Battle of Carrhae – Persians defeat Galerius

Above: *Constantine the Great, depicted in a bust in Rome (left) and in a Byzantine mosaic reflecting his importance to the Christian church.*

Left: *From the third century onwards, the use of cavalry became increasingly important, and the once-mighty infantry of the legions were eclipsed on the battlefield. These are cataphracts, fully armored cavalry, as depicted on Trajan's Column.*

Flavius Valerius Constantinus, Constantine the Great (reg. 306-337)

First Christian emperor of Rome, who fought rivals for six years (306–312), then in 323 eliminated his colleague Licinius (Augustus of the East) to become sole ruler of the Roman Empire. Recognising that Rome was no longer the strategic capital of the empire, he established a new capital at Byzantium, renaming it Constantinople. According to legend, a vision before the decisive Battle of the Milvian Bridge led to his adoption of Christianity, and his military standard incorporated the *Labarum*, a monogram combining the first two letters of the word 'Christ' in Greek. It was Constantine that set Christianity on course to be the official religion of the Roman Empire.

297/8 Battle of Langres – great Roman victory over Alemanni

306–323/4 Wars of the Tetrarchs

312 Constantine takes Italy from Maxentius

312 Battles of Turin, Verona, Saxa Rubra. Constantine defeats the troops of Maxentius_

312 Battle of Milvian Bridge. Maxentius is killed. Constantine is converted to Christianity during the campaign and in future wears the sign of the labarum on his army's shields

313 Licinius defeats Maximin Daia

313 Constantine campaigns on Rhine

314 First War between Constantine and Licinius

315 Battle of Cibalis. Constantine defeats Licinius

315 Battle of Mardis is indecisive

323/324 War between Constantine and Licinius

323 Battle of Philippopolis-Adrianople. Constantine outmaneuvers Licinius

323 Battle of Chrysopolis. Licinius is defeated, surrenders and is later executed

328 Constantine consecrates his new capital Constantinople (formerly Byzantium); the city has been under reconstruction as the imperial capital for four years. Strategically it will be better placed than Rome to meet the threats to the empire from the north and from the east. Gradually the Roman Empire will become more permanently divided into West and East, but while the West will succumb in a century and a half to the barbarians from across the Rhine and Danube, Constantinople, as capital of the 'Byzantine' Empire, will remain the bastion of the empire, now officially a Christian state, for more than 1100 years. Traditionally historians have seen this development as ushering in the Middle Ages

332 Constantine's son, Constantine, fights Goths on the Danube and inflicts a significant defeat on them

340 Constantine II invades Italy after disputes with his brothers

340 Battle of Aquileia. Constantine II defeated and killed by Constans

341, 342 Constans defeats Gauls

350–353 War against Magnetius. 351 Battle of Mursa. Constantius defeats barbarian usurper Magnetius, the first major triumph of cataphract armored cavalry over infantry legions

354 Gallic crisis. Major incursions of barbarian tribes; from 364 constant operations on the Rhine-Danube frontier

356–361 Rhine-Danube operations

356–359 Julian (the Apostate)'s Rhineland campaigns

361 Julian's War with Constantius

358–361 Persian War

363 Julian's campaign in East. Jovian signs '30 Year Peace'

371–377 Valens' inconclusive Armenian operations in the East against Persians

370s Huns attack the Ostrogothic kingdom. Increasingly, the advance of the Huns from the steppe into eastern Europe is putting pressure on the tribes to their south and west; in turn, these tribes increase their attempts to cross the perimeter of the Roman Empire, seeking land on which to settle. And the frontier regions of the empire are becoming depopulated as a result of constant raids and depredations

376–382 Gothic War

378 Battle of Adrianople. One of the great decisive battles of history. The Huns defeat the Romans and the Emperor of the East, Valens, is killed. The Huns achieve their breakthrough into the empire. It is the beginning of the end of empire in the west. Fritigern leads the Goths into Thrace and Greece. That this disaster on the battlefield is not immediately fatal to the empire is due to Theodosius the Great (379–395), who

Theodosius the Great.

Theodosius the Great (reg. 379–395)

Last ruler of a united Roman Empire, Theodosius succeeded in avoiding total disaster for the empire after the massive defeat at Adrianople and the death of his predecessor in the East, Valens. He was forced to defeat two usurpers, Maximus and Eugenius, and temporarily ended the continuing conflict with Persia.

Flavius Stilicho (359–408)

Rome's chief general during the reign of the Emperor Honorius, and by strength of character an important stabilizer during a difficult period following the disaster of Adrianople and break-in of the Goths under Alaric. He maneuvered with them in Greece and foiled their invasion of Italy in 401–3, winning an incomplete victory at Pollentia. In 406 at Florence he destroyed a large number of invaders. Two years later, however, he was murdered by Honorius, leaving Italy leaderless and open to further invasion. The result in 410 was the first sack of Rome in 800 years.

Attila (434–453)

'The Scourge of God' succeeded his father as king of the Hun confederacy in 434 with his brother, whom he soon murdered. The Huns were nomadic peoples from central Asia, who had migrated gradually from the steppe to create a vast empire that encompassed much of Germany and east to the Caspian. From here Attila's horsemen terrorized their neighboring tribes and raided the frontier territories of the Roman Empire. Dramatic incursions were wholly destructive, each time the Huns returning home with vast booty and often considerable subsidies from Constantinople, the walls of which, however, defied them. Nevertheless great cities, such as Singidunum, Sirmium, Naissus, Serdica and Aquileia, were destroyed, and large areas of the Danube provinces laid waste. His defeat in 451 saved Gaul, but Attila was yet capable of a subsequent invasion of Italy which appeared unstoppable. His death ended the unity of the Hun confederacy and the great threat to Western civilization faded away.

Flavius Aetius (396–454)

Master of Horse (general in chief) for the Roman Emperor Valentinian III, Aetius fought a series of campaigns to reassert Roman authority in the West against Visigoths, Franks and Burgundians, the latter being destroyed during 435–7. His greatest battle was in 451 at the Catalaunian Fields, where, with Visigoth help, he defeated Attila's Huns. Aetius was murdered by his ungrateful emperor in 454.

Left: *Attila leads his Huns, in this reproduction of a romantic 19th century painting*

restores order in the empire. But the writing is on the wall

383–388 Revolt of Maximus

392–394 Revolt of Eugenius. 394 Battle of the Frigidus, near Aquileia. Theodosius defeats Eugenius, who is killed

395 Huns invade Cappadocia, Armenia, Thrace and Syria

395 The division between Eastern and Western Empires becomes permanent. After the death of Theodosius, the decline of the empire becomes steeper. His heirs are not up to the task of maintaining the empire and increasingly delegate the running of affairs to their chief ministers while isolating themselves from the realities of the world in Ravenna. In the West, a succession of Masters of Horse (commanders-in-chief of the armies) are left to decide policy.

395–398 Alaric the Goth's campaign in Greece. Stilicho, Western Emperor Honorius's Master of Horse, cannot prevent the Goths, under Alaric, going where they please: Greece, Illyricum and then into Italy.

399 Revolt of Tribigild

400 Revolt of Gildo

400 Goth uprising

401–403 Alaric the Goth's first invasion of Italy
402 Battle of Pollentia. Stilicho defeats the Goths, but not decisively

405 Barbarian crossing of the Alps repulsed

406–7 Great barbarian breakthrough into Gaul. At the end of December 406 barbarian hordes cross the frozen Rhine at Mainz. There is no Imperial army to halt them. This is the second great break-in. From here, the tribes pour into Gaul

407 Revolt of Constantinus in Britain. He invades Gaul, which is meanwhile being devastated by Vandal tribes progressing south

407–10 Alaric's second invasion of Italy.

410 sack of Rome

408 Huns are active on the lower Danube

409–11 Revolt of Maximus

412–418 The Visigoths leave Italy and enter Gaul and the Iberian Peninsula

413 Revolt of Heraclian

The Goths establish themselves in southern Gaul with sporadic footholds in northern Spain. There is almost constant warfare with other barbarian tribes and the Romans

422 Huns raid Thrace

424–425 On the death of the Western Emperor Honorius in 423, Theodosius II of the Eastern Empire sends an army to place Valentinian III (aged 4) on the Western throne. Aetius (390–454) is meanwhile Master of Horse, making use of barbarian mercenaries (including Huns) to maintain some sort of Imperial authority in the West

430s Led by Clodion, the Franks advance to the Somme

434/5 The Huns, raiding into Thrace, demand payment with menace from Constantinople

435–7 Aetius repulses Burgundian invasion of Upper Belgica

CAMPAIGNS OF ATTILA THE HUN

441–443, 447–448 Attila leads the great confederation of Huns against Constantinople, laying waste the land and taking away vast booty. In the field they are all but invincible, but they lack the ability to assault or lay siege to major cities

451 The Huns invade Gaul. Battle of Catalaunian Plains, or Châlons. Aetius, with a mixed Roman army that includes a significant Visigoth element under their king, Theodoric, defeats or holds the Huns, who retreat.

452 Attila invades Italy. With help, the Huns reduce and destroy the great city of Aquileia, but venture little farther south, ostensibly due to the intervention of the Pope, Leo, more plausibly because fodder for the Hun horses is in short supply and plague has broken out in Italy. This is the

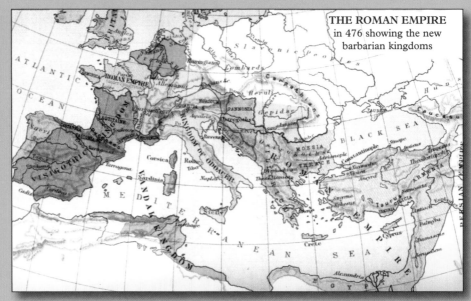

THE ROMAN EMPIRE
in 476 showing the new
barbarian kingdoms

Above: *The raids and invasions of the so-called barbarians into the area of the Roman Empire resulted in much anarchy and destruction, the Christian churches losing many items of gold and silver. The modern word 'vandal' derives from the Vandals, who, having established themselves in North Africa, mounted an expedition to sack Rome, which they carried out with a ruthless efficiency far beyond the sacking of 410.*

Right: *Euric, founder of the Visigothic kingdom. Originally established in France, the Visigoths expanded into the Iberian Peninsula, where Euric's successors were to rule a prosperous kingdom until the early 8th century.*

Gaiseric (428–477)

King of the Vandals who led his people from Spain to establish a kingdom in North Africa. Advancing from the Strait of Gibraltar, he took the Roman province of Africa (essentially Tunisia) by 439 when Carthage fell. Alone of the barbarian chiefs who set up kingdoms in the wreckage of the Western Roman Empire, he constructed a considerable fleet, which raided widely in the central Mediterranean. In 455 an expedition arrived at the mouth of the Tiber and proceeded to sack Rome. The activities of the Vandal pirates provoked the Empire into two major attempts to destroy the Vandals. These, in 460 and 468, were foiled, and the Vandals extended their control to the Balearic Islands, Sardinia, Corsica and Sicily (which was subsequently passed to the Ostrogothic Kingdom of Italy). Gaiseric's Vandal kingdom lasted until 533 when Belisarius reconquered North Africa for the Byzantine Emperor Justinian.

Euric (reg. 466–484)

Founder of the Visigothic kingdom in Spain, Euric altered Visigoth policy by setting out to make his Kingdom of Toulouse independent of Rome rather than a federate. Threatened by the Franks to his north, the Burgundians to the east and Roman attempts to reimpose control on Gaul, Euric went on the offensive. At Deols on the Indre he won a shattering victory over a coalition of Romans, the independent Syagrius, Bretons, Franks and Burgundians. In 472–3 his armies conquered much of the Iberian Peninsula.

last great incursion by the Huns

453 Attila dies; his empire does not long survive him

429 Vandals enter Africa

Vandals raid Mediterranean coasts

439 Persian invasion of Armenia

440–1 Great expedition against Vandals fails

455 Vandal expedition sacks Rome

456 Vandal invasion of Sicily repulsed by Ricimer

454 Visigoths attack the Bagaudae in north-west Gaul on behalf of Rome

455 Battle of Nedao (location unknown). Breakup of the Hun empire

455–456 Usurpation of Avitus

456 Visigoths enter the Iberian Peninsula in force

456 Battle of River Urbicus shatters the power of the Suebi tribes who have settled there

458–461 Emperor Majorian leads an expedition to Spain

By 464 The Visigoths (capital Toulouse) have advanced their domain north to Loire

466–484 Reign of Euric, founder of the Visigothic Kingdom in Spain

456–465 revolt of Aegidius in Gaul, which is a battleground between Franks moving south, Burgundians in the east, Visigoths in the south and Bretons in the north-west

Britain, meanwhile, cut off from Rome by these barbarian powers, is now deemed lost to the empire

468 and 472–3 The Visigoths conquer much of Spain

472–476 Anarchy in Italy, following the death of Ricimer (Master of Horse), who has made and unmade a series of unworthy emperors

475 Odovacar (Odoacer) leads army revolt.

476 End of Western Empire with enforced abdication of the young Emperor Romulus Augustulus.

476–493 Odovacar rules Italy, nominally for the empire

475–477 Eastern Emperor Zeno deposed and returns to power

Left: *The baptism of Frankish King Clovis by Saint Remigius (Apostle to the Franks) in 496 at Rheims.*

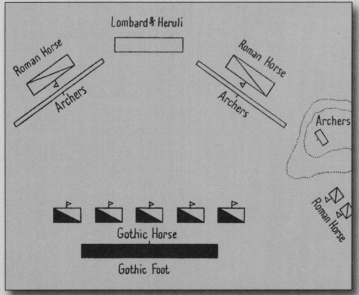

Lombard & Heruli

Roman Horse

Roman Horse

Archers

Archers

Archers

Roman Horse

Gothic Horse

Gothic Foot

Left: *The Byzantine Narses' victory over Totila at the Battle of Taginae in 552 was decisive in bringing the Ostrogothic Kingdom of Italy to an end. His deployments have been compared to those of Henry V at Agincourt.*

Clovis I (reg. 481–511)

Merovingian founder of the Frankish kingdom. Under his leadership the Franks advanced ever deeper into Gaul, defeating Syagrius, the last Roman ruler in Gaul, at Soissions in 486. He fought campaigns against the Burgundians and German tribes in Thuringia, and at Vouillé, near Poitiers, he defeated the Visigoths, subsequently taking temporary possession of their capital, Toulouse. He adopted Catholicism (in contrast to the Arian Christianity of his southern foes, the Visigoths) and established his capital at Paris. One of the great, central figures of French history, he established an enduring dynasty and the beginnings of a power-base for the future Carolingian Empire.

Belisarius (c.505–565)

Byzantine Emperor Justinian's greatest general, and a legendary figure thanks to the writings of Procopius and, in the twentieth century, Robert Graves. After fighting in the wars against Persia, he quelled the Nika Insurrection in Constantinople, which was dangerous to the imperial régime. He led the expeditionary force that destroyed the Vandal kingdom in 533. Two years later he was sent to retake Italy from the Ostrogoths and was initially successful, but inadequately supported by Constantinople. After being besieged in Rome during 537–8, he advanced north and accepted the Ostrogoth surrender, at the same time refusing their offer of the Italian throne. This made Justinian suspicious; Belisarius was recalled, and thereafter his military career was sporadic and at the mercy of court intrigue, made worse by the scandalous activities of his wife.

Narses (c.480–573/4)

A rare example of a Byzantine eunuch rising to high office, Narses was the general who completed Justinian's reconquest of Italy for the Roman Empire. He played a crucial role in suppressing the Nika riot of 554, thus gaining the Emperor's confidence. During his first campaign in Italy, he quarreled with Belisarius, which hampered the Byzantine war efort. During the second campaign, after Belisarius's recall, he returned with a well-equipped army. At Taginae he decisively defeated the Ostrogoths and went on to reconquer Italy.

476 Euric's Italian expedition repulsed
481–511 WARS OF CLOVIS expand the kingdom of the Franks
486 Battle of Soissons. Clovis defeats Syagrius
491 Frank campaign against the Thuringians
500 Campaign against the Burgundians
507 Battle of Vouillé. Clovis defeats Alaric and conquers all southern Gaul except Provence
523 Campaign against the Burgundians
542 Expeditions to Saragossa
Ongoing campaigns for Septimania (Provence) between Franks, Burgundians and Ostrogoths
488 Ostrogoths. Led by Theodoric the Great, invade Italy 'on behalf of' the Eastern Empire to reclaim it from Odovacar. After much campaigning, the two leaders meet and Theodoric treacherously slays Odovacar. Theodoric (493–526) will be a major player in international diplomacy and rule nominally within the ambit of the Byzantine Empire
RECONQUESTS OF JUSTINIAN
527–565 Justinian rules the Byzantine Empire and sets out to recover the West. His generals – especially Belisarius – are initially successful, but the enterprise places great strain on the empire's resources and cannot be sustained in the longer term
533–4 Belisarius conquers the Vandal kingdom of North Africa, defeating the Vandals at Ad Decimum and Ticameron
535–54 Gothic War in Italy
535 Belisarius takes Sicily followed by Naples and Rome in 536; By 540 he has taken Milan and Ravenna from the Ostrogoths
541–2 Belisarius wages an inconclusive campaign against Chosroes I of Persia
541 Ostrogoths elect Totila as their king and he retakes much of Byzantine Italy
544–8 Belisarius campaigns against Totila but with limited success owing to lack of supplies and support from the East; in 548 he is replaced by Narses

552 Narses defeats Totila at Taginae; Totila is killed and by 554 Narses reconquers Italy

520s–560s Sporadic conflicts between Slavs, Bulgars and Huns and Byzantium

India

Mid 4th century Samudragupta and son Chandragupta II campaign and found Gupta Empire

End of 5th century Hun incursions into northern India; after 500 the White Huns establish power in northern India until they are gradually expelled during the 6th century

510 Battle of Airikina. Hun victory

511 Huns sack Prayaya

3 major dynasties emerge. Pushyabhutis of Kanauj, Chalukyas of Badami and Pallavas of Kanci

600–630 Establishment of Pallava power by Mahendravarman I

608–42 Establishment of Chalukya power by Pulakeshin II

620 Pulakeshin II defeats Harsha

After 647 breakup of Kanavj Empire into small Rajput states

China, Korea and Tibet

c.600 Unification and expansion of Tibet

618 Establishment of T'ang dynasty followed by some ten years of internecine conflict for the throne

626–640 Chinese expansion into Central Asia and (temporarily) Korea

660 destruction of Paekche state in Korea

Autonomous military districts established to protect China's frontiers

By 660s Chinese armies have penetrated

Left: Sassanid King Chosroes II submitting to Byzantine Emperor Heraclius.

Heraclius I (reg. 610–641)

Byzantine emperor who restored the fortunes of the empire after a period of civil war and military defeat. In 610 he took power in Constantinople following a major mutiny of the army and virtual anarchy in the capital. Initial failures in Syria and Palestine were met by major campaigns into Armenia and Mesopotamia, leading to the downfall of the Persian king, Chosroes. He reformed the Byzantine army, creating a regional system of local farmer-soldiers to replace the previous reliance on irregular recruiting and mercenaries. This gave the defenses of the empire a new lease of life. However, Heraclius' declining years saw the whirlwind of Muslim conquest begin to blow through the empire.

India, the Tarim Basin, etc.

668 destruction of Korean state of Koguryo and occupation of northern Korea until 676 withdrawal leaving Silla state in control

751 Battle of Talas River. Muslims defeat Chinese

755 Mutiny of An Lu-shan leads to weakening of the T'ang state and eventual descent into turmoil with large-scale peasant uprisings

763–783 Tibet takes Tarim Basin after withdrawal of Chinese garrisons

c.790 Tufan Kingdom conquers China's Western provinces

By about 900, final collapse of central authority. China splits into ten states with five short-lived dynasties

'Five Dynasties and Ten Kingdoms' Period Coup d'etat ends the last (later Chou) dynasty

960 Northern Sung Dynasty

963–979 Sung re-unite much of China

979–1004 China-Liao border War

982–1126 China and Hsi-Hsia border wars

c.1125–1127 Northern tribes conquer northern China and establish Ch'in Empire

By 1127 Sung control reduced to southern half of China: Southern Sung Empire

Britain

Mid-5th century Angles, Saxons and Jutes invade Britain. Semi-legendary leaders Hengist and Horsa fight for the British king Vortigern against the Picts between 446 and 454; Hengis then establishes Jutish kingdom in Kent

c.480–500 Battle of Mount Badon (Mons Badiconus) victory over the invaders by legendary Arthur

491 Sack of Pevensey by Aelle (first bretwalda, or hegemon)

Resistance to invaders led by 'Aureius Ambrosius'

552 Battle of Old Sarum. Cynric of the Gewissae defeats Britons

577 Battle of Deorham. Ceawlin of the Gewissae defeats three British kings and

extends nascent Wessex to the Severn

Kingdoms of Deira and Bernicia form Northumbria, which gains supremacy. Edwin of Northumbria is 5th bretwalda and adopts Christianity

633 Battle of Heathfield. Penda of Mercia and Cadwallon of Gwynedd defeat and kill Edwin

634 Battle of Heavenfield. Bretwalda Oswald of Northumbria defeats Cadwallon

642 Battle of Oswestry/ Maserfield. Oswald defeated by Penda

655 Battle of Winwaedsfield. Christian Oswy of Northumbria defeats and kills heathen Penda and becomes bretwalda.

661 Mercia defeats West Saxons

675–704 Aethelred of Mercia defeats Northumbria decisively near the Trent. Northumbria declines

Mercia reaches zenith under Aethenbald (716–57) and Offa (757–96), latter styling himself King of all England. He builds defensive 'Offa's Dyke' from Dee to Wye, probably to prevent cattle raids. Mercia declines after Offa. Rise of Wessex

Byzantine Empire

602 Byzantine mutiny, anarchy and Civil War. Ongoing campaigns against Avar incursions

603 Revolt of Narsus. Persians involved in Edessa-Dara operations

605–628 Byzantine-Sassanid War

608–610 Revolt of Heraclius; becomes emperor 610–641

613 Battle of Antioch

626 Constantinople besieged by Avars, Bulgars, Slavs, Gepids and Persians

627/8 Battle of Ctesiphon

Wars of the Franks

c.575 Inter-family strife among the Merovingians because of a procession of minors (rois traînéants). These internecine conflicts in the Frankish

Charles Martel (c.688–741)

Mayor of Austrasia, Charles was the victor at the Battle of Tours (or possibly Poitiers, the location being uncertain) in 732, famously defeating the last significant Muslim expedition from Spain to penetrate deep into France. (Modern historians, however, dispute the size and significance of the battle.) As a result of this he received the nickname 'Martel' (the Hammer). After a civil war following the death of his father, Pepin, in 714, he had established control of the Frankish realms and subsequently campaigned tirelessly against Bavaria, Burgundy, Aquitaine and the Saxons. In 737 he took Avignon from the Muslims and in 739 drove them out of Provence. The fiction of Merovingian rule was maintained, but power rested firmly in his hands and was passed at his death to his two legitimate sons, following the Franks' lamentable custom of dividing the inheritance. However, he laid the foundations upon which his illustrious grandson Charlemagne would build a great empire.

Above: Charles Martel's victory at the Battle of Tours.

Below: Muslim horsemen as depicted in a European manuscript of the 16th century.

kingdoms lead to the rise of the Mayors who come to hold effective power

*c.*670 Ebroin, Mayor of Neustria conquers Burgundians

687 Battle of Tertry. Pepin II, Mayor of Austrasia, defeats Berthar, Mayor of Neustria, who is assassinated in 681. Effective fall of the Merovingians and beginning of the Carolingian rulers of the Franks. Pepin becomes undisputed master of all Gaul except Aquitaine. The Merovingians remain puppets

719–41 Charles Martel. He defeats Austrasians in two battles:

716 Battle of Amblève.

719 Battle of Vinay.

719 Battle of Soissons. He masters Burgundy

720–39 Arab invasion of France

720 Arabs seize Septimania

732 Battle of Tours or Poitiers (location unknown). Abd ar-Rahman defeated and killed by Charles

737 Charles takes Avignon from the Muslims

738 Charles's Saxon expedition

739 Charles repulses Muslim attack on Provence

Charles also campaigns against Aquitaine and Alemans

Wars of the Lombards

663 Byzantine expedition of Emperor Constans to Italy fails to expel the Lombards

678–81 Treaty and peace between Lombards and Byzantium

700–12 Lombard succession conflicts

712–44 Liutprand, King of the Lombards, consolidates Lombard power in Italy

751 Lombards take Ravenna, Byzantine capital in Italy

Middle East

630s–650s MUSLIM WARS OF CONQUEST

Muslim armies erupt from Arabia

636 Battle of Yarmouk

637 Battle of Qadisiya

640 Conquest of Egypt and Syria

642 Battle of Nahavend

650 Muslims take Persepolis

651 Battle of Merv: Muslim conquest of Persia; end of Sassanid Empire

Muslim Civil War

657 Battle of Camel

Battle of Basra

Battle of Siffiu

Muslim sea-borne campaigns against Byzantium

661–750 Umayyad Caliphate

674–8 Constantinople besieged by Muslims

690s–700s Muslim conquests

698 take Carthage

702 Muslims conquer Berbers

717–18 Constantinople besieged by Muslims

747–50 Muslim Civil War

750 Battle of the Zab. Abbasid Caliphate replaces Umayyads

755–72 Berber revolt in North Africa

763 construction of Baghdad

Byzantines recover Thrace from Slavs

776 to 843 Byzantium internal conflict over iconoclasm

798 Muslims take Ibiza

811–819 Abbasid Civil War

825 or 823 Crete captured

827–832 Muslim Aghlabids begin conquest of Sicily (achieved by 902)

830–8 Abbasid-Byzantine War

India

704–715 Muslims take Transoxania, Khwarazim and Tashkent

712–713 Muslim invasion of Sind

Arab conquest of Indus area to 745

740 Chalkyas defeat Pallavas

750 Gopal founds Pala dynasty. From 750s to *c.*950 Rashtrakutas constitute the main power in India

757 or 752–6 Rebellion of Rashtrakutas who defeat Chalukyas

*c.*840 Rise of Pratinaras (King Bhoja)

*c.*840 Collapse of central authority in Tibet

Charlemagne (768–814)

One of the great, towering figures of the Middle Ages, Charlemagne (Charles the Great) reunited the Frankish realms by 771 and by many wars of conquest welded almost all Western Europe (save the Iberian Peninsula) into a Christian polity. He was crowned Holy Roman Emperor by the Pope in Rome on Christmas Day 800 and, initially at least, used military force as a means of spreading Christianity among the heathen tribes of Germany. His campaigns are too many to list here, often taking the form of annual expeditions. In 773 he invaded Italy and put an end to the Lombard kingdom after besieging Pavia. In 778 he crossed the Pyrenees without intending permanent conquest. The rearguard battle (actually little more than a skirmish) of Roncesvalles during the withdrawal from Spain has passed into heroic legend. Subsequent invasions of Spain were to create (by 795) a Spanish march, or buffer state. Longer-term campaigns took place in Germany, deposing Duke Tassilo of Bavaria (787–8), defeating the Avars (788–796) and a long series of bitter wars in Saxony.

Below: Charlemagne, after a drawing by Dürer.

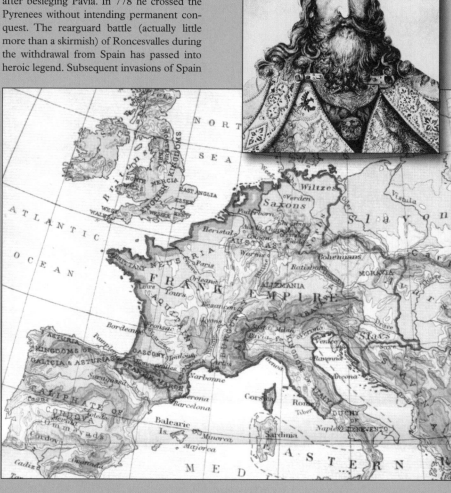

Wars of the Visigoths in Spain

610–12 King Witteric fights Vascons and Byzantines

629 last Byzantine possessions (Algarve) taken. Visigoths now rule almost all Iberian peninsula

631 Franks invade as far as Saragossa

653 rebellion of nobles quashed by King Receswinth (649–672)

672–80 King Wamba constantly at war against Vascons, rebels in Septimania and invasions from the Muslims

680 Wamba deposed. Erwig succeeds (to 678)

708 Muslim invasion of Iberian coast repulsed by King Witiza

709 Revolutions lead to reign of last Visigoth king: Roderick (Ruderico)

709, 710 Muslim invasions of Iberian peninsula

711 Tarik of Mauretania leads Muslim invasion of Iberian peninsula; takes Gibraltar, Algeciras

19 July 711 Battle of La Jauda. Muslims defeat Roderick and take Seville, Ecija, Cordoba, Toledo. Musa brings Muslim reinforcements

Sept 713 Battle of Segoyuela. Final defeat of King Roderick. End of the Visigothic Kingdom. At Toledo, Musa proclaims the Caliph sovereign.

Balkans

Khazaks expand to Crimea, Ukraine and Caucasus

679–80 Bulgars conquer areas of Danube

Franks

751–68 Pepin ('the Short') King of the Franks

By early 750s Muslims driven out of France

753 Saxon campaigns

754 Pepin invades Italy to aid the Pope against the Lombards, the Byzantines failing him and he having to take refuge with the Franks. Pope annoints Pepin King of the Franks and 'Patrician of the Romans'

At Pavia, Aistulf of the Lombards surrenders but subsequently reneges on agreements. By 755/6 he is at the gates of Rome again

756 Pepin invades Italy again; same result

759 Saxon campaign

759 Franks take Narbonne

760–8 Conquest of Acquitaine, not fully absorbed into Frankia

768–814 Charlemagne

771 Charlemagne unites the Frankish realms. Begins wars of conquest in Italy, Pyrenees, Bavaria against the Avars, and into north/north-east Germany against Saxons, Slavs and Danes

CHARLEMAGNE'S ITALIAN CAMPAIGNS

773–4 Charles invades Italy and besieges Pavia. 774 King Desiderius is made prisoner; thus Charlemagne destroys Lombard Kingdom. Subsequent operations in Italy and Istria (790)

805 Venetia and Dalmatia conquered

CHARLEMAGNE'S SPANISH CAMPAIGNS

778 Franks cross into Spain and take Pamplona, a raid rather than conquest

778 Roncesvalles reverse as the armies retire

785 Gerona voluntarily joins Frankish rule

793 Hisham I, Emir of Cordoba, invades, taking Gerona and penetrating to Narbonne and Carcassonne

Frank response leads to establishment of Spanish march (military border area) by 795

799 Balearic Islands place themselves under Frankish rule

801 Franks take Barcelona

806 Franks take Pamplona and Novara

811 Franks take Tortosa

CHARLEMAGNE'S EASTERN CAMPAIGNS

787–96 Franks conquer Bavaria and the Avars – destruction of Avar state 803 (main Avar ring taken 795). Practically annual campaigns. Depopulation results from the continual campaigning

772–85 Saxon campaigns. Annual campaigns, bitter and hard

Krum, Khan of the Bulgars (reg. 802/3–814)
The First Bulgarian Kingdom (681–1018) became a significant political power in the Balkans during the reign of Khan Tervel. Krum's reign was marked by dramatic conflict with Constantinople and an expansion of the Bulgarian realm. In 809 he captured Sofia from the Byzantine Empire, but in 811 the Emperor Nicephorus I attacked Bulgaria and destroyed Krum's capital, Pliska. However, Krum trapped the Byzantine army and in the ensuing battle the Emperor was killed. Krum again took the offensive and in 813 even laid siege to Constantinople. But lacking a fleet he was unsuccessful, and the following year he died while beginning a second siege.

Mahmud of Ghazna (reg. 999–1030)
Sultan of Ghazna, an Afghan Muslim ruler who was the first Muslim invader of India, mounting some seventeen expeditions into northern India (1001–1026) and winning a great battle against a confederacy of Hindu states in 1008. His last raid resulted in the sack of the Hindu temple at Somnath. He conquered most of Iran and ruled an empire that included Kashmir and the Punjab. The effects of his campaigns were to weaken the hold of the Hindu rulers in northern India and to prepare the way for subsequent Muslim invasions.

Above: Mahmud of Ghazna is to the right.

779 Battle of Süntel Hill smashes Saxon rising (4,500 Saxons beheaded in a day as punishment)
Subsequent risings, deportations, etc., over some thirty years
808–10 Confrontation with Danes
782 Sorbs attack Thuringia; 806 conquered by Charlemagne's son Charles
800 Christmas Day, Charlemagne crowned 'Emperor of the Romans' (or Holy Roman Emperor) in Rome
843 Empire divided. Temporarily reunited 885
887/8 Final disintegration of Carolingian Empire to become kingdoms of France, Italy and Germany

Balkans/Byzantium
803 Krum unites Bulgars
811 Krum defeats Nicephorus at Edirne (Adrianopolis)
805 Venetia, Dalmatia and Corsica conquered
893–927 Tsar Symeon: zenith of Bulgarian Empire

Japan
740 Battle of Itabitsu
764 Battle of Miohosaki
989 Conflict between Kyoto and Nara
1051–63 Early Nine Years War
1086–9 Later Three Years War
1146 Battle of Kyoto
1156 and 1160 Japanese succession wars
1180–5 Gempei Wars
1185 Battle of Dan No Ura
1331–3 Jojo regency overthrown
1333–92 Nanbokucho Wars between northern and southern courts

Scandinavia
808–810 Danish War
c.895 Battle of Hafsfjord. Harald Finehair unites southern Norway

Spain: Emirate of Cordoba
755/6 Umayyad dynasty of Spain founded
Aghlabid Campaigns

Muslim pirates raid central Mediterranean coastlines, especially from bases at Bari (841–71) and Taranto (840–80)

846 or 850 Muslim sack of Rome

847 Muslims seize Bari

The Christian states of northern Iberia combine, fragment and intermittently fight one another and the Muslims

Middle East

852 Byzantine naval expedition against Egypt

860 Rus attack Constantinople

867 Saffarids of Herat independent

867–886 Basil I emperor of Byzantium

868 Egypt independent under Tulunid emirs

874 Sarmarids of Bukhava independent

905 Abbasids recover Egypt from Tulunids

909 Rise of Fatimids of North Africa; they ravage the coasts of Italy, Corsica, Sardinia and Liguria

914 and 919 Fatimid expeditions against Egypt fail

960 Fatimids conquer Egypt

961 Byzantines recover Crete

965 Byzantines recover Cyprus

966–8 Byzantine invasion of Syria

969 Byzantines retake Antioch

974–5 Byzantine invasion of Syria

Meanwhile Abbasid Caliphate continues in little but name until 1258

983–1055 Buwayhid Civil War in Iraq/Iran

989–1025 Wars of Basil II

997 or 999–1030 Wars of Mahmud of Ghazna in Transoxonia, Iran and Iraq

998 Collapse of Samarids

1032 Byzantines take Edessa

1039 Zendecan Turkish invasion of Afghanistan

1050 Hilali and Sullaym tribes from Upper Egypt invade Cyrenaica and Turkey

1050s–1060s Almoravids conquer Morocco

SELJUK WARS OF CONQUEST

1055 Seljuks take Baghdad

1060s Seljuks conquer northern Syria and the Hejaz

1060–1073 Civil strife in Fatimid Egypt

1069 Seljuks take Fez

1071 Battle of Manzikert: Seljuks take most of Asia Minor from the Byzantines

1073–7 Baar al-Jamah establishes military regime in Egypt

Three Seljuk Sultanates now exist: Rum, Hamadan and Merv

1096 The People's Crusade is massacred by the Turks

Americas

c.980 First European landing in America

c.993, 995 battles between Vikings and native Americans

India

900 Samarids overthrow Saffavids

907 Parantaka I establishes Chola power in southern India

c.950 to c.1200 establishment of the Chola Empire

972 Paramara King Siyaka II sacks Rashtrakuta capital, Manyakheta

985–1014 Rajaraja I extends Chola power. Major campaigns of the Cholas: 999, 1017 to Sri Lanka

1000 naval expedition to Maldives

1022 to Ganges

1022 or 1023 Northern campaign of Rajendra Chola

1025 Chola naval expeditions to SE Asia

997 or 999–1030 Wars of Mahmud of Ghazni in India. Conquest of Punjab

1001 Battle of Peshwar. Second Muslim invasion of India

1024 or 1025 Battle of Somnanth. Shiva temple destroyed

1040 Dandanquan Seljuks defeat Ghaznavids

1040 Seljuks break away from Ghazni. Decline of Ghaznis

1018 Turkic armies sack Kanauj, ending Pratihara

Mediterranean

870 Muslins conquer Malta

871 Holy Roman Emperor Louis II retakes Bari, Muslim headquarters in Italy, for the Pope

Above: *Viking longships – these fast, clinker-built, ocean-going ships could also penetrate deep into estuaries and rivers, giving the Scandinavian traders turned brigands great strategic advantages. During the 9th to 11th centuries, the great period of Scandinavian expansion, the Vikings proved superb navigators in their oar- and sail-powered ships and are credited with the first visits of Europeans to North America.*

Left: *Alfred the Great.*

Alfred the Great (reg. 871–899)

King of Wessex, scholar and energetic defender against the seemingly invincible Danes. Despite suffering great setbacks, he ultimately succeeded in driving the Vikings back to a line between London and Chester. He established a semi-professional army and began the construction of the West Saxon fleet. He also refortified London, which had practically been abandoned for several centuries.

Britain

825 Battle of Ellendune. Egbert of Wessex decisively defeats Beornwulf, King of Mercia

838 Battle of Hingston Down. Egbert defeats large Viking invasion

851 Viking incursion into the Thames to London

865 'Great Army' of Vikings invades East Anglia

869 Battle of Hoxne. Vikings defeat East Anglians

871 Battle of Reading. Aethelred I defeated by Vikings

871 Battle of Wilton. Alfred. King of Wessex, defeated by Viking Guthrum

871 Battle of Chippenham. Guthrum defeats Alfred

871 Battle of Edington/Ethandun. Alfred decisively defeats Guthrum. Peace of Chippenham and Guthrum's conversion to Christianity

910 Battle of Tettenhall. Edward the Elder of Wessex defeats the Danes of York

937 Battle of Brunanburgh. Athelstan of Wessex defeats a coalition of Vikings, Scots and Britons and can claim to be King of all Britain

944 Edmund I of Wessex annexes York

954 Battle of Stainmore. Viking Eric Bloodaxe defeated and killed by Eadred of Wessex. Subsequent weakening of Wessex by succession of royal minors

991 Battle of Maldon. Olaf Triggvason defeats Earl of Essex

994 Expedition of Olaf Triggvason and Sweyn Forkbeard. Olaf returns to take kingdom of Norway, Sweyn to reclaim kingdom of Denmark

1002 Aethelred II the Unready massacres all Vikings in royal service including hostage sister of Sweyn

1013 Sweyn (now King of Denmark) lands at Humber and marches south, effectively conquering the country. Dies 1014

1015 Canute (Sweyn's son) masters most of the realm

9th century: Confederation of 12 tribes create the city state of Venice

Vikings

793 Vikings raid Lindisfarne. Norse raiding expeditions to British Isles and coasts of France, Spain – even into the Mediterranean – follow

834–45 Norse raids on Rhine, northern France and northern Germany

856–62 Norse raids reach their peak

862 Vikings seize Kiev

865–7 Viking 'Great Army' raids England

870 Norse capture Strathclyde

882–92 Viking 'Great Army' raids France

882 Oleg unites Novgorod and Kiev

885–6 Vikings besiege Paris

911 Establishment of County of Normandy by the Viking Rollo. His descendents create a strong principality

Otto the Great (reg. 936–973)

German king from 936 and creator of the German Holy Roman Empire. He defeated the Magyars on the Lech River in 955, ending their career of penetrating raids that had terrorized central and western Europe for more than half a century. In 962 he was crowned Emperor in Rome after having been drawn into Italian conflicts in 951 and assuming the title of King of the Lombards. He was obliged to make two more expeditions to Italy (962 and 966), and also subdued the tribes of the middle Elbe and middle Oder. His main achievement was the consolidation of the Reich, bringing peace and security to Germany and establishing it as Europe's greatest power for several hundred years.

Sveyn Haraldsson (Forkbeard) (c.960–1014)

After overthrowing his father, Harold Bluetooth, Sveyn succeeded in extending Danish rule in Scandinavia and conquered England, founding an Anglo-Danish empire that continued under his son and grandson. He was acknowledged as King of England in 1013 and died a year later, being succeeded by his son Canute.

Boleslav the Mighty (or the Brave) (992–1025)

First king of Poland. He subjugated the West Slav tribes and worked to unify Poland. In 996 he conquered Pomerania and then Cracow. From 1003 to 1018 he was in conflict with the German Empire, but succeeded in increasing the size of his realm at the expense of all his neighbors. He made Poland a major European state, but his conquests were not lasting.

Above: Norman warriors wearing armor typical of the time, with long chainmain hauberks, kite-shaped shields and characteristic conical helmets with long noseguards.

Left: Otto the Great.

Right: The naval battle of Svelder, Sweyn Haraldsson's (Forkbeard) victory over King Olaf Tryggvason of Norway.

1016 Battle of Pen Selwood. Canute defeated by pretender Edmund Ironside

1016 Battle of Ashingdon. Decisive victory of Canute over Edmund

1016–35 Canute rules England and Denmark

Succession to English throne subsequently disputed

1066 Harold II elected king; challenged by Duke William of Normandy

Poland

992–1025 Wars of Boleslav I 'The Mighty' King of Poland

Magyars

895–900 Magyars conquer Hungarian Plain

First half of 10th century Magyars raid west into central Europe, inflicting major defeats on the Franks 899–910

906 Moravia destroyed

907 Battle of Pressburg

926, 933 North Italy, Germany and Swabia raided

929 Battle of Unstrut defeats Magyars

954 and 955 Northern France and Italy raided

955 Battle of Lechfeld. Defeat of Magyars by Otto the Great

977–1038 Stephen becomes Christian King of Hungary

939 Saracens sack Rome

941 Rus attack Constantinople

Umayyad Caliphate

920 Battle of Val de Junqueras. Emir of Cordoba defeats Navarre and León

962 Sancho I of Leon launches Reconquista, Christian reconquest of Iberian peninsula

981 Battle of Rueda

985 Andalusians sack Barcelona

Decline of Umayyads – by 1031 era of 'taifas' (fragmentation)

1008–28 Muslim Civil War

Germany

Henry I (the Fowler) of Germany (919–36) extends eastwards against the Slavs and fortifies areas against Magyar invasions

938–72 WARS OF OTTO THE GREAT

Imperial control imposed on Germany and northern Italy

951 Otto invades Italy

962 Otto crowned in Rome as Holy Roman (German) Emperor

983 Great Slav revolt against German rule

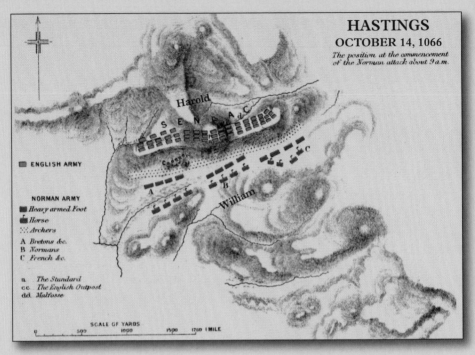

HASTINGS

OCTOBER 14, 1066

The position at the commencement of the Norman attack about 9 a.m.

Harold

SENLAC

William

ENGLISH ARMY

NORMAN ARMY
Heavy armed Foot
Horse
Archers

A *Bretons &c.*
B *Normans*
C *French &c.*

a *The Standard*
cc *The English Outpost*
dd *Malfosse*

SCALE OF YARDS
0   500   1000   1500   1760 1 MILE

Battle of Hastings

Context Norman invasion of England

Date October 14, 1066

Location Near town of Hastings, East Sussex, south coast of England

Commanders/Forces King Harold of England commanding c.7,500 men. Duke William of Normandy commanding c.7,000

Objectives William had invaded England in pursuit of his claim to the English crown

Casualties English c.2,000 including the King and two of his brothers. Normans c.2,000

Victor Normans

Consequences William went on to conquer England and be crowned King of England

Left: *Norman cavalry at the Battle of Hastings.* **Below:** *William the Conqueror. Both illustrations are from the Bayeux Tapestry.*

Basil II Bulgaroctonus (Slayer of the Bulgars) (963–1025)

One of the greatest soldier-emperors of Byzantium. He had to defeat internal opposition (by 989) before he could pursue his policy of extending and consolidating Byzantine authority. He expanded the empire in Syria, but his principal achievement, as his name suggests, lay in the conquest of Bulgaria (986–1018). After his victory at Ochrida (the Bulgarian capital), he is said to have blinded the whole of the surviving Bulgarian army, leaving but one man in a hundred with eyes to lead the rest home. (The Bulgarian king immediately expired in shock.) Basil never married or had children, so that on his death his achievements were rapidly frittered away.

Robert de Hauteville (Guiscard) (1015–1085)

Epitome of the heroic, larger-than-life characters that strode through these centuries, Guiscard was a man of action but shrewd too, an immediate predecessor of the leaders who would cut their way to Jerusalem at the end of the 11th century. In 1047 joining his Norman brothers (including William de Hautevile, elected count of Apulia after defeating the Byzantines), Robert carved out a major kingdom in the south of Italy and Sicily. In 1059 the Pope enfeofed him with the duchy of Apulia, Calabria and Sicily, the last-named being yet unwon. In 1061 he conquered Calabria; in 1071 Bari, the Byzantines' last city in Italy, fell to him; and in 1076 he took Salerno and made it his capital. With his brother Roger, and with Papal support, he conquered Sicily from 1081. Ambitious to the end, he died campaigning against the Byzantines on Cephalonia.

William I the Conqueror (1027–1087)

Initially facing serious threats to his dukedom, by 1066 he had annexed Maine and the Vexin and was laying claim to the throne of England. He defeated his rival, Harold Godwinson, at Hastings (Senlac) in 1066, and was crowned King of England on Christmas Day of that year. He spent the years from 1067 to 1071 consolidating his conquests before invading Scotland in 1072 and Wales in 1081, creating marches, or buffer areas. These activities in the British Isles led to the loss of Maine in 1077.

995 Germans conquer Pomerania
1002–37 German conquest of northern Italy

965–972 Wars of Prince Sriatoslav of Rus

Balkans
986–1018 Wars of Basil II against the Bulgars; end of Bulgar State by 1018
Byzantines conquer Serbs

1047–1107 Wars of the Normans
1047–71 Norman Conquest of southern Italy by Robert and Roger Guiscard
1052 Muslims ejected from Sardinia
1050s–1070s Norman-French ongoing conflict
1054 Battle of Mortemer. William of Normandy defeats Angevin-French coalition
1061–1091 Norman conquest of Sicily
1066–72 Norman conquest of England
1066 Battle of Stamford Bridge. Harold II of England defeats invader Harold Hardrada, King of Norway
1066 Battle of Hastings. William of Normandy defeats Harold II and takes the crown of England
1066–71 William consolidates his conquest of England
1069 Danes invade Yorkshire
Normans in the South
1071 Bari, last Byzantine city in southern Italy, falls to Normans
1072 Palermo taken by Normans
1079/80 Norman England at war with Scotland
1081 Norman invasion of Byzantium with Papal blessing. Robert and Bohemund take Corfu
1082 Durazzo captured by Normans
1083 Battle of Larissa. Bohemund's advance on Constantinople repulsed
1106 Battle of Tinchebray. Henry I defeats brother Robert Curthose and regains Normandy
1107 Bohemund's second invasion of Byzantium defeated by Alexis I

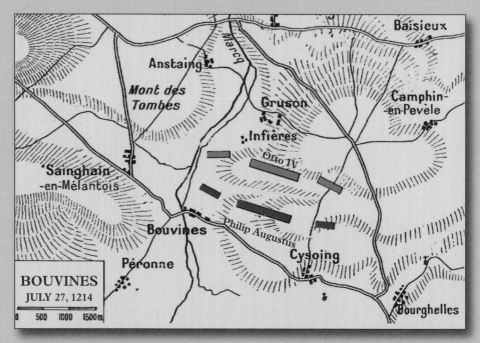

Battle of Bouvines

Context French-Angevin Wars of Philip II Augustus of France and King John of England

Date July 27, 1214

Location South-east of Lille, France

Commanders/Forces Otto IV, Holy Roman Emperor, commanding between 15,000 and 24,000 men. Philip Augustus commanding between 10,000 and 22,000 French

Objectives English attempt to regain lands in France already conquered by the French king. John was invading south-central France; John's allies, including Otto (with a force under the Earl of Salisbury), invading the north

Casualties Allies 170 knights and unknown number of infantry; Count of Flanders captured. French losses light

Victor French

Consequences Philip destroyed the coalition ranged against him and ended England's hope of recovering lands north of the Loire

Richard I the Lionheart (1157–1199)

The model Crusader and a great romantic hero, Richard led the Third Crusade to the Holy Land in the wake of the disasters that had befallen the Christians after the Battle of Hattin. The Battle of Arsuf (1191) was Richard's greatest victory against Saladin, but in the end he failed to retake Jerusalem. While returning to England, he was captured by his arch-enemy and held for ransom for two years (1192–4). Less glorious than his Middle Eastern adventure was his struggle against Philip Augustus of France, who took advantage of his absence to conquer much of his possessions in France.

Philip II Augustus (reg. 1180–1223)

King of France and principal founder of French monarchical power. As much Machiavellian statesman as soldier, he took considerable areas of the Angevin empire while his most formidable opponent, Richard I, was in the Holy Land on a crusade from which Philip had returned early. Richard's brother John was no match for him. The Battle of Bouvines (1214) against John's allies of Flanders and Germany sealed the fate of Angevin possessions in France, enabling France to become the greatest power in Western Europe.

The statue to Richard the Lionheart outside the Houses of Parliament in London.

The Seal of Philip II Augustus.

France

987–96 Hugh Capet King of France (Capetian dynasty to 1328)

1180–1223 Philip II Augustus ends the Angevin conflict, conquering English possessions north of the Loire

1214 Battle of Bouvines: Decisive victory of Philip Augustus over his coalition enemies

1209–29 Albigensian Crusade against heretics in the south of France

1223–6 Louis VIII

1224 Louis takes Poitou and Saintonge from England

1226 He takes Avignon and Languedoc

1226–70 Louis IX (St Louis) the Crusader (1248–54, 1270)

The Crusades

1095–9 FIRST CRUSADE

1097 Battle of Nicea. Christian victory

1098 Crusaders take Antioch

1099 Crusaders take Jerusalem and repulse counterattack from Egypt at Battle of Ascalon. Christians establish Kingdom of Jerusalem

1147–9 SECOND CRUSADE.

1148 Failed siege of Damascus

1187 Saladin defeats Crusaders at Hattin then captures Jerusalem and Acre

1189–92 THIRD CRUSADE

1191 Acre retaken by Crusaders

1191 Battle of Arsuf. Richard I of England defeats Saladin

1202–4 FOURTH CRUSADE

1204 Crusaders take and sack Constantinople. Foundation of Latin Empire (to 1261)

1218–21 FIFTH CRUSADE

1219 Damietta taken

1228–9 SIXTH CRUSADE

Frederick II of Germany succeeds by negotiation into becoming crowned King of Jerusalem

1248–54 SEVENTH CRUSADE

1250 Battle of Mansura indecisive

1250 Battle of Fariskur. Crusaders defeated and St Louis captured

Saladin (Salah al-Din) (1138–1193)

Zangid Sultan of Egypt, he ended the Fatimid regime there and fought during 1184–1187 in Mesopotamia to reconstruct the empire of Nur al-Din. His realm eventually surrounded the Crusader states, and for once the Christians were facing an enemy united and led by one man. From 1169 Saladin engaged in desultory operations against the Crusader states until in 1187 he won a truly decisive victory at Hattin. This broke the power of the Crusader states, and Jerusalem soon fell, as did Acre. In 1189 a new Crusade laid siege to Acre, and it was taken two years later by Richard the Lionheart. Saladin's attempts to expel the invaders was repulsed at Arsuf in 1191, but this was not decisive, and the campaign ended with Jerusalem still in Muslim hands. His Ayyubid dynasty lasted until 1250.

Louis IX of France (b.1215; r.1226–70), St Louis

The only canonized king of France, Louis was highly religious and spent much time in prayer, fasting and penance. Regarded as one of the greatest medieval kings of France, he fulfilled the ideals of medieval kingship, being both pious and just. But he was a poor general. He saw it as his duty to fight for Jerusalem, which had been taken back from the crusaders by the Muslims in 1187, and led two crusades. The seventh crusade, 1248–54, was to Egypt, and ended in disaster, Louis and much of his army being captured by the Mameluks. The Eighth and last crusade, 1270–2, involved an invasion of Tunisia, and Louis began to besiege Tunis. Already a sick man, however, he fell victim to the outbreak of an epidemic in the siege lines, and died. He was made a saint in 1297.

1270–2 EIGHTH CRUSADE (to Tunis). St Louis
dies in epidemic

Middle East
1129 CAMPAIGNS OF ZANGI AND NUR AL-DIN
1144 takes Edessa
1154 takes Damascus
1141 Seljuks of Merv defeated by Qarakhitai
Mongols
1140s Almohads replace Almoravids in
Morocco
1152–60 Almohads take Maghreband
Tripolitania
1146–1148 Second Crusade
1147 Normans attack Byzantium
1153 Seljuk Sultanate of Merv destroyed by
Ghuzz tribes
1157 Death of last Seljuk Sultan
1163, 1167 Zangi attacks Egypt and
conquers it in 1168–1169
1171 Saladin (1169–1193) establishes
Ayyubid Sultanate
1176 Battle of Myriokephalon: Rum Seljuks
defeat Byzantines
1184–1187 Saladin reconquers
Mesopotamian empire from Zangids
1185 Normans attack Byzantium

India
c.1149–1215 Wars of the Ghurids
1162–1206 Mohammed of Ghur
1175 Ghurids take Multan
1179 Ghurids take Peshawar
1186 Ghurids take Lahore
1187 Ghurids end Ghaznid State and rule to
1215
1192 Battle of Taraori: Mohammed of Ghur
defeats Rajputs
1206 Mohammed assassinated. Ex-slave
Qutbuddin Aibak revolts and establishes
new dynasty
Sultanate of Delhi; 1206–1290 Slave Dynasty
rules

German Empire
1024–1125 Salian Frankish Emperors of
Germany

Left: *St Louis.*

Above: *Nefs
carry his army
from Aigues-
Mortes on the
Rhône delta to
Tunisia on the
Eighth Crusade
in 1270*

Valdemar II the Victorious.

Valdemar II the Victorious / the Conqueror (reg. 1202–1241)

After involvement in the politics of the Holy Roman Empire, he was one of the Northern Crusaders, fighting to Christianize the eastern Baltic provinces. With the Knights of the Sword he fought in Estonia, winning control of the area at the Battle of Tallinn. The Danish Empire was now huge; but in 1281 he was surprised and imprisoned by his enemies, with the result that he lost much of the territory he had gained. In 1227 he took the field to restore his empire but met decisive defeat at the battle of Bornhöved in 1227. All prospects of a Danish north German empire were dashed, although he did retain part of Estonia. For a time, however, he had made Denmark the greatest power in the Baltic region

Left: *Statue to Rodrigo Diaz, known to history as 'El Cid', who led the armies of Alfonso VI of Castile to victories over the Muslims in Spain before being exiled by the king. He than fought for the Emir of Saragossa*

1033 Kingdom of Burgundy joined to the German Empire (Germany and Italy)

1026–7 Conrad II's 1st Italian campaign; he is crowned with the iron crown of Lombardy at Milan; 1027 Imperial coronation in Rome

1037–8 Conrad's 2nd Italian campaign, against Aribert of Milan

1041 Campaign to Prague; Bohemia becomes a German vassal

1044 Conrad's Hungarian campaign

Henry III: partition of Lorraine 1044, resulting in constant conflict between the Emperor and Duke Gottfried the Bearded

1056–1106 Henry IV

1075 Battle of Homburg on the Unstrut. Henry defeats Saxon uprising

1175 Beginning of Investiture conflict with the Papacy

1076–7 Henry IV excommunicated

1077–80 Civil War in the Empire.

1080 Battle of Hohenmölsen. Rival Rudolf of Swabia defeated and killed

1080 Henry is excommunicated again

1083 Henry conquers Rome in his 1st Italian campaign, defeating the Lombards

1084 Henry's Anti-Pope crowns him. Robert Guiscard relieves the Pope in Castel Sant'Angelo and Henry recoils. Normans sack Rome

1090–7 Henry IV's 2nd Italian campaign. But by 1106 he is forced to abdicate

1106–25 Henry V, last Salian emperor

1110–11 Henry V's 1st Italian campaign

1122 Concordat of Worms ends Investiture conflict

Iberian Peninsula

1085 Almoravids of Morocco invade Iberian peninsula and take Toledo

1086 Az-Sallaqg

1095 Take Badajoz

1087 Syracuse

By 1115 Almorovids conquer all Muslim Spain

1150–1172 Almohads conquer Iberia

1172 Almohads take Seville

PORTUGAL

1094 Portugal gains independence

1139 Portugal becomes a kingdom and expands to the south. Conflict with Castile ensues

1385 Battle of Aljubarrota. Portugal defeats Castile, establishing reign of John I in Portugal

CASTILE

1035–65 Ferdinand the Great

1037 He obtains Léon

1085 Castile conquers Toledo

1094 El Cid (Rodrigo Diaz) takes Valencia

1212 Battle of Navas de Tolosa. Alfonso VIII of Castile defeats Muslims, breaks Almohad power in Spain

ARAGON

1118 Aragon conquers Saragossa

1137 Aragon unites with Catalonia

1229–35 Aragon seizes Balearic Islands

1238 Aragon takes Valencia

1118 Aragon conquers Saragossa

1125 Almohad rebellion in Morocco begins

1134 Battle of Fraga

1139 Portugal becomes a Kingdom

1147 Alfonso Henriques of Portugal takes Lisbon

1148–9 Aragon conquers Lower Ebro

Northern Europe

1099 Revolt of Sigtrygg Silkbeard, King of Dublin

1121 Boleslav III of Poland subdues Pomerania

c.1130 to 1240 Civil Wars over Norwegian Succession

1157–82 Waldemar the Great begins the rise of Denmark

1157 Battle of Viborg

1184–1201 Denmark conquers Pomerania, Schleswig, Holstein, Lübeck and Hamburg

1202–41 Wars of Waldemar 'the Conqueror'. Denmark takes Norway, Estonia, Courland, etc., but loses all at Battle of Bornhöved 1227

1208–22 Dynastic struggles in Sweden

1226 Papal Golden Bull of Rimini tasks Teutonic Knights with conquest of heathen Prussia. By 1230 Livonia and Courland subjugated

c.1231–83 Teutonic Knights conquer Prussia

1236 Battle of Sante

1242 Battle of Lake Peipus

1261 Norwegians conquer Greenland and

1262–4 Iceland

Britain

1138 Battle of the Standard. Scottish raid on northern England repulsed

1139–53 Anarchy. Civil War between King Stephen and Matilda and son Henry (to become Henry II)

1141 Battle of Lincoln. Stephen temporarily imprisoned

1154–89 Henry II's Angevin Empire

1158 Henry II invades Brittany

1167–71 English invasion of Ireland

1173–4 Revolt of the sons of Henry II

1190 Richard the Lionheart takes Cyprus from Byzantines

1194–9 War between Richard the Lionheart and Philip Augustus

1198 Battles of Courcelles and Vernon

1203–5 Philip Augustus of France conquers Normandy and Poitou

1203–4 Siege and capture of Château Gaillard

1204 France conquers Normandy

1213 First Flemish campaign. John gathers a

Right: The tomb of the Angevin King Henry II (King of England 1154–89), whose empire took in a large portioin of western France including Aquitaine, which remained in the possession of his successors for 300 years.

Genghis Khan (1206–1277)

By violence he overcame rivals to become ruler of all the Mongolian steppe peoples. One of the great conquerors of history, whose armies of fast-moving horse archers everywhere outmatched their opponents, the vast campaigns of conquest he set in motion are awe-inspiring. In 1215 he captured Beijing and began the subjugation of China. During 1210 to 1223 he devastated Muslim Kwarzm. His successors continued the great conquests, which were universally destructive. They did not result in a truly unified empire, and Europe was saved from the full force of the Mongol terror by succession crises in distant Asia. Nevertheless the thirteenth century was dominated by the impact of the Mongols, whose empire at its peak extended from the Mediterranean to the Pacific and the Baltic.

Above: Frederick I Barbarossa (Holy Roman Emperor 1152–90), a great champion of chivalry and knighthood. He died while swimming in the River Saleph en route to the Third Crusade. Barbarossa became a subject of a 16th century legend whereby he was not dead but asleep in his castle at Kyffhaüser, waiting to return and restore the empire to its glory.

Left: Genghis Khan. *Below:* The seal of Edward I.

Edward I (reg. 1229–1307)

One of England's greatest soldier-kings, who emerged from the civil wars of thirteenth-century England by his victory at Evesham in 1265 to become virtual ruler of the country while still only heir to the throne. In two campaigns he conquered Wales (1277 and 1282), subsequently building massive and beautiful castles to overawe the Welsh. His wars in Scotland met with less success. In 1296 he invaded Scotland but immediately provoked uprisings, including that of Sir William Wallace. He died on campaign in Scotland.

formidable alliance against Philip Augustus (including Germany)

1213 Battle of Damme. William of Salisbury defeats Philip's fleet and frustrates his plan to invade England

1214 Campaign and Battle of Roch–au–Moine. Philip defeats John

July 27, 1214 Battle of Bouvines. Philip defeats the Allies

1263–65 Barons War in England

Simon de Montfort leads rebellion against Henry III

1264 Battle of Lewes. Simon captures Henry and his son Edward (the future Edward I)

1265 Battle of Evesham. Edward decisively defeats the barons

1277–84 Edward I conquers Wales

German Empire

1152–90 Frederick I Barbarossa

1154–5 Frederick's 1st Italian campaign. He promises the Pope he will attack the Normans but does not

1158–62 Frederick's 2nd Italian campaign

1163–4 Frederick's 3rd Italian campaign. Veronese League formed

1166–8 Frederick's 4th Italian campaign

1174–8 Frederick's 5th Italian campaign

1160–4 Campaign against the Wends

1168 Conquest of Rügen

Siege of Alessandria fails

1176 Battle of Legnano. Lombard League defeats Frederick Barbarossa

1180–1 War of Henry the Lion

1184–6 Frederick's 6th Italian campaign

Henry VI is crowned at Milan as King of Italy

1187 Frederick allies with Philip II Augustus of France against Guelphs and Anjous

1190–7 Henry VI

1191 Henry's 1st Italian campaign and coronation at Rome. Siege of Naples

1194–5 Henry's 2nd Italian campaign. 1194 Henry crowned King of Sicily at Palermo. He plans hereditary empire

1210–50 Frederick II

1214 Battle of Bouvines. Anglo-Guelphs defeated

1237 Battle of Cortenuova. Lombard League defeated

By the mid-13th century central authority of the German emperors has declined

Iberian Peninsula

1217–52 Ferdinand III conquers the south, taking Cordoba in 1236 to complete the Reconquista

c.1228–9 Almohads abandon Iberia

1229–35 Aragon seizes Balearic Islands

1236 Cordoba taken

1238 Aragon takes Valencia

1244 Treaty of Almiza agrees Portuguese reconquest on the Atlantic side of the peninsula; Aragonese on the Mediterranean side

1257 Only Granada left to Moors in Iberia

The Mongol Empire

1206–1227 Genghis Khan

1218 Battle of Karaku

1220 Battle of Samarkand

1221 Forces of Genghis Khan penetrate as far as the Indus

1221 Battle of Kandahar

1231 Mongols destroy Khwarazim

1237–42 Mongol invasion of Europe

1241 Battle of Leignitz

1241 Death of Ogedei Khan

1243 Battle of Kösedag: Mongols defeat Seljuks

1256 Assassins of Alamut destroyed by Mongols and Baybars

1259 Death of Monghe Khan

After 1260 the Mongol Empire has no unified political direction; it continues as Chagatai, Il-Khanate and the Golden Horde

1258–1365 Il-Khanate (breaks up after 1335)

MONGOLS IN CHINA

1205–1209 Mongols conquer Hsi-Hsia as base for conquest of China

1211–1234 Mongol conquest of Ch'in. Mongols rule as the Yüan Dynasty

Above: *The walls of Acre, the last bastion of the Christian crusaders in the Holy Land, which fell to the Muslims in 1291. But the battle between Christianity and Islam continued in the islands and shores of the Mediterranean.*

Left: *A Mongol horse-archer.*

Baybars I (reg. 1260–1277)

Founder of the Mameluke Sultanate of Egypt and Syria. After fighting in the campaign against Louis IX's crusade during 1249–50, and participating in the victory over the Mongols at Ayn Jalut in 1260, he usurped the throne and began a vigorous campaign to eliminate the remaining crusader states in Syria. In 1268 he took Antioch and in 1271 captured the impressive Christian castle of Krak des Chevaliers. A truce with the Christians was followed by campaigns against the Armenians in 1266, 1275 and 1277. Throughout his reign he was in almost constant conflict with the crusaders and the Mongols, against whom he fought nine battles. He united Syria and Egypt into one state and pursued an intelligent foreign policy, establishing good relations with the Byzantines. He died accidentally of poison intended for another victim.

1215 Mongol capture of Beijing

1227 Destruction of Hsi-Hsia

1260–79 Mongol conquest of Sung China

Mongol attacks on Burma and Java fail

Kublai Khan rules China as Shih-Tsu

1274 and 1281 Mongol invasions of Japan fail

1294 Death of Kublai Khan results in rivalry for the throne

1368–1398 Chu Yüan-Chang drives Mongols back to the Steppe (1368 Yüen (Mongols) expelled from Beijing) and establishes Ming Dynasty

1345 Great famine in China: 8 million people die. Uprising results

Middle East

1250 Mameluke slave-soldiers kill last Ayyubid Sultan

1258 Sack of Baghdad; end of Abbasid Caliphate

1261 Byzantines retake Constantinople from the Latin Empire

1263 Byzantines take Antioch

1280–1324 Osman, founder of Ottoman State

1260–1277 CAMPAIGNS OF BAYBARS

1260 Battle of Ain Jalut: Mamelukes defeat Mongols

1289 Mamelukes take Tripoli

1291 Acre falls to the Mamelukes, last Crusader toehold in Palestine

By about 1400 the Mameluke Empire extends to Syria, Palestine and Hejaz

Sicily

1266 Battle of Benevento. Charles of Anjou defeats regent Manfred

1266–8 Charles of Anjou conquers Sicily

1268 Battle of Tagliacozzo. Charles defeats Conradin, son of Emperor Conrad IV

1271 Charles captures Durazzo and campaigns into Albania and Greece and prepares to crusade against Constantinople

1282–1302 Sicilian Vespers revolt against Charles of Anjou

1302 Treaty splits Kingdom of Sicily in two

France

1285–1314 Philip IV the Fair

1297–1305 Philip IV's conquest of Flanders

1302 Battle of the Spurs (Courtrai). Flemish defeat French

1305 Flanders submits to France

1328–1498 House of Valois rules France

Germany

1273–91 Rudolf of Habsburg elected Holy Roman Emperor

1278 Battle of Marchfeld. Rudolf defeats and kills rival Ottokar II of Bohemia

1282 Rudolf of Habsburg gains control of Austria

1298 Battle of Göllheim. Emperor Adolf of Nassau defeated and killed by Albrecht of Habsburg, son of Rudolf. He becomes emperor 1298–1308

1314–47 Louis the Bavarian. He defeats the Habsburgs at 1322 Battle of Mühldorf

India

1290–1320 Sultanate of Delhi: Khalji Dynasty

1296–1316 Wars of Alauddin Khali; he breaks resistance of Rajputs and repulses Mongols in north-west India

1311 Alauddin Khali conquers India to its southern tip

1320–1414 Sultanate of Delhi: Tughluq Dynasty

1325–1351 Wars of Muhammed Ibn Tughluq. He conquers southern India but most is lost after his death

1336 Kingdom of Vijayanagara established

1347 Kingdom of Bahmani established

1358 Vijayanagara–Bahmani conflict begins (ongoing sporadic campaigns)

1370 Vijayanagara conquers Madurai

1382–1396 Khandesh, Malna, Jaunpur and Gujerat break away from Delhi

Middle East

OTTOMAN WARS

1326 Ottomans take Bursa

1361 Ottomans take Ankara

Timur (Tamerlane, Timur lenk) (1336–1405)

Last great Asiatic conqueror of the Mongol line, a military adventurer who erupted from his Transoxanian realm in the 1370s, dynamically filling the power vacuum in the area resulting from the decline of Il-Khanate. For over thirty years his armies of mounted archers spread terror and destruction far and wide – in Iran, against the Golden Horde (he held Moscow for a year in 1385) and against the Mamelukes, sacking Damascus in 1401 and taking Baghdad the same year. During 1398–9 he invaded India and sacked Delhi; and in 1402 defeated the Ottomans at Ankara, taking Bayazid I prisoner. The vast empire he created was ruled from his tent, constantly on the move, his administration an uneasy compromise between this Turko-Mongol style and settled Islam. He died while preparing to invade China.

1389–1403 Bayezid I Yildirim ('The Thunderbolt')
1394–1403 Blockade of Constantinople by Ottomans

China
c.1390–1449 Wars of conquest by Ming Dynasty
Ongoing sporadic operations v. Mongols
1392 Korea becomes a vassal State
1405–1433 Cheng-Ho is sent on seven great naval expeditions as far as the Indian Ocean and East coast of Africa
1407–1422 Chinese occupation of Annam
1448 Huge rebellions in China
1449 Attack on Mongols fails; Emperor taken prisoner
After period of aggressive expansion, Ming fall back to the defensive
1450s Pirates infest Chinese sea and coastline; famines, plagues and floods afflict China

Campaigns of Timur (Tamerlane)
1380–1405 Annual 'raids' of destruction
1381–8 Iran
1391–5 Against the Golden Horde and Crimea
1384–9 Timur penetrates India and sacks Delhi in 1398
1400–2 against Ottomans
1402 Battle of Ankara. Timur defeats Bayezid

By 1430s Ottoman position fully restored

After Timurid Shah Rukh Empire splits

Switzerland
1291 Swiss Eternal Union for protection against Habsburgs, etc.
1315 Battle of Morgarten. Swiss defeat Leopold I of Austria
1353 Swiss Confederation founded
Swiss War of the Cities
1386 Battle of Sempach. Swiss defeat Habsburgs.

1415 Swiss conquest of Habsburg Aargau
1422 Battle of Arbedo. Swiss defeated
1440–6 First 'Old War' of Zurich
1444 Battle of St Jacob
1474 'Perpetual Peace' signed

Germany and Northern Europe
1320 Battle of Rudau: Teutonic Knights defeat Lithuanians
1327 Poland loses Silesia and Bohemia
1327–8 Another German campaign in Italy
1330–55 Serbian Empire of Stefan Dushan
1340–75 Waldemar IV of Denmark Campaigns against Oland and Gotland
1346 Casimir II reunites Central Poland
1361 Casmir III conquers Galicia
1361–70 Danishconflict with the Hanseatic League
1373–1419 Wenceslaus, King of Bohemia, provokes uprising. 1394, 1402 he is taken prisoner after defeats
1381 Peasants' Revolt
1377–89 South German War of the Cities
1377 Battle of Ulm. Cities defeat Charles IV
1377 Battle of Reutlingen. Cities defeat Württemberg
1381 South German League of Cities formed; they ally with Swiss Confederation
1388 Battle of Döffingen. Allies defeated by the princes
1382 Teutonic Knights conquer Poland's Baltic provinces
1397 Union of Kalmar unites Norway, Sweden and Denmark
1390s–1402 Uprising of Wenceslus of Bohemia
1398 Teutonic Knights drive Vitalian Brethren from Gotland
1402 Teutonic Knights seize Neumark
1419–36 Hussite Wars
1415 Execution and martyrdom of John Hus of Bohemia
1419 Bohemian uprising and first defenestration of Prague. Hussite people's army repulses five Imperial/Crusader attacks

Left: *The statue to Robert the Bruce on the site of his great victory at Bannockburn.*

Robert I (the Bruce) (1274–1329)

Scotland's greatest warrior hero, who won independence from England. Of essentially Anglo-Norman lineage, he became leader of the anti-English party in 1306, after years of service to Edward I. His murder of John Comyn allowed him to proclaim himself King of Scotland, but long campaigning was necessary to make this a reality. In 1306 he was defeated at Methven and Dalry, becoming a fugitive (from which grew the famous legend of his taking new heart from the efforts of a spider repairing its web). Taking advantage of the weak reign of Edward II, he achieved a major victory at Bannockburn, but another fourteen years of fighting were necessary to bring English recognition of Scottish independence. The romance of his life continued after his death, his heart being taken in pilgrimage for burial in the Holy Land.

Edward III (1312–1377)

The first half of Edward's long reign were years of dazzling success. In 1333 at Halidon Hill he took revenge upon the Scots for Bannockburn. In 1337 disputes with the King of France over English possessions led to the outbreak of the Hundred Years War, the first phase of which Edward won in style. At Sluys in 1340 he achieved a major naval victory, practically annihilating the French fleet. In 1347 his celebrated victory at Crécy led to the capture of Calais. As the Black Death made its terrible impact upon Europe, only sporadic operations followed both in France and Scotland, until the victory at Poitiers in 1356 where the Black Prince captured the French king. A subsequent campaign was needed to bring peace on English terms, the zenith of Edward's reign, in 1360, by which

Edward gained all Aquitaine. The remainder of his reign was less successful, the King falling into an early senility. In his early years he had been a knight of outstanding vigor and energy, with a brilliant court. He instigated the Order of the Garter and in 1348 was offered the imperial crown of the Holy Roman Empire.

Above: *Edward III.*

Left: *Sluys, the opening major battle of the Hundred Years War, was fought on June 24, 1340 when Edward III's English fleet destroyed the French fleet. The result prevented any French invasion of England – the Hundred Years War would be fought almost entirely in France.*

1431 Battle of Taus. Indecisive

1434–6 Danish uprising of Englebrecht Engle–Brechtson

1471 Swedes defeat Danes

1466 Casimir IV of Poland/Lithuania takes much of Prussia from the Teutonic Knights

Mediterranean

1284 Battle of Meloria: Genoa defeats Pisa and takes Corsica

1298 Battle of Curzola: Genoese defeat Venetians

1309 Knights of St John establish base in Rhodes

1323–5 Pisa–Genoa war for Sardinia and Corsica

1340 Battle of Salano

1343 Aragon takes Majorca

1296–1346 Scottish War of Independence

1296 Edward I invades Scotland

1297 Battle of Stirling Bridge. Wallace defeats English force

1298 Battle of Falkirk. Wallace defeated by Edward

1303 Edward invades Scotland again

1305 Rebellion of Robert Bruce

1306 Battle of Methven

1307 Battle of Loudon Hill. Bruce defeats Pembroke

1314 Bruce takes Stirling Castle, stongest English fortress in Scotland

1314 Battle of Bannockburn. Bruce decisively defeats Edward II

1315–18 Bruce invades Ireland

1318 Bruce takes Berwick. Subsequent cross–border operations by both sides

1332 Battle of Dupplin. Edward Baliol usurps Scottish crown under suzerainty of Edward III of England

1333 Battle of Halidon Hill. Douglas defeated by Baliol

Iberian Peninsula

1311 Aragon takes Duchy of Athens

1323 Aragon takes Sardinia

1474–9 Castilian War of Succession against France and Portugal

1476 Battle of Toro. Defeat of Portugal

1479 Union of Aragon and Castile

1482 Aragon and Castile reduce Granada

1494 Spain takes Medilla

1509 Spain takes Oran

India

1414–1451 Sultanate of Delhi: Sayyid Dynasty

1451–1526 Sultanate of Delhi: Lodi Dynasty

1509–1530 Campaigns of Krishna Deva Raya bring Vijayanagara to zenith of power

1517–1526 Factions weaken Sultanate of Delhi

1338–1453 Hundred Years War

PHASE 1: PHILIP VI v. EDWARD III 1337–47

1337 The French fleet attacks Portsmouth, Southampton and Guernsey, making more raids the following year. Philip prepares for an invasion of England

1338 Edward III crosses to Flanders.

1340 Battle of Sluys. French fleet destroyed

1346 Battle of Crécy. Edward crushes French army of Philip VI

1346 Battle of Neville's Cross. David II of Scotland defeated while raiding England

1346–7 Calais taken by Edward III in one of the first actions involving artillery

Oct 1350 Battle of Winchelsea/Sandwich. Edward III's fleet defeats Spanish fleet

1350 Death of Philip VI of Valois. John II succeeds him.

Black Death ravages Europe. Estimated at least 25 million victims of the epidemic between 1347 and 1351

PHASE 2: JOHN II v. EDWARD III 1351–6

1355 Brief chevauchée of Edward III in Artois. Chevauchée of Black Prince in Languedoc.

1356 Battle of Poitiers. Black Prince defeats and captures King John of France

1358 Jacquerie peasant uprising in France

1360 Edward III seizes the suburbs of Paris. Peace of Brétigny

More properly a series of wars, the Hundred Years War was fought essentially between the kings of England and France, with the Duke of Burgundy as a third major player in the game. The first phase, 1337–60, was fought over the Duchy of Guyenne. Only in 1340 did Edward III make claim to the throne of France. 1360–1413 was a period of confused conflict with no decisive outcome. 1413–53 saw Henry V's revival of the claim to the French throne, but his early death threw all into the melting pot once again. Thereafter several events were decisive in favor of the French: the intervention of Joan of Arc, the return of Burgundy to alliance with the French and the weakness of the English monarchy during the reign of Henry VI.

Above: Edward III leads his army across the Somme.

Above: Prince Edward at Poitiers

Henry V (1387–1422)

Famed as Shakespeare's heroic victor of Agincourt, Henry's star blazed bright and died quickly. The victory at Agincourt was against the odds and justifiably takes its place as one of the great battles of the Middle Ages. Less well known are his subsequent operations in France, leading to the Treaty of Troyes and his recognition as next King of France. In three well-planned campaigns he conquered Normandy, but before his monarchical aim could be realized he died, just two months before his father in law, Charles VI of France. His courage and determination in the face of seemingly impossible odds remains a model of English cool-headed pluck.

Left: Henry V, after one of the very few portraits of this monarch.

1364 Battle of Cocherel. Du Guesclin beats Jean de Grailly's Anglo–Gascon–Navarrese army

1364 Auray captured by the English

PHASE 3: CHARLES V v. EDWARD III 1357–75

1367 Battle of Nájera. Black Prince and Pedro the Cruel of Castile defeat du Guesclin and the Count of Trasamara

1370 Battle of Pontvallain. Du Guesclin stops English chevauchée from Calais

1372 Du Guesclin and Clisson conquer Brittany.

1372 Battle of La Rochelle. English fleet destroyed by Castilian galleys (allies of the French).

Charles V reconquers Poitou and Saintonge.

1376 Death of the Black Prince.

1377 Death of Edward III.

PHASE 4: CHARLES V v. RICHARD II 1377–80

1378 Naval victory of Jean de Vienne at Cherbourg over Lancaster. English take Cherbourg and Brest

1380 English offensive from Calais.

Above: Men at arms of the period, showing a variety of helmets, armor and weapons. Men such as these made up the great 'companies' who often fought as mercenaries, inflicting much suffering over a wide swathe of France.

1380 Châteauneuf-de-Randon besieged and captured by du Guesclin, who dies in the process

Franco-Castilian fleet destroyed by the English off the coast of Ireland. Death of Charles V

PHASE 5: CHARLES VI v. RICHARD II 1382–96

1381 Truce between France and England. Peasants' revolt (Wat Tyler) in England

Nov 1382 Battle of Roosbeke. Charles VI of France defeats Flemish

1387 Battle of Margate. Engish fleet defeats Franco-Castilian fleet, ending the threat of a French invasion of England

1388 Battle of Otterburn. Scots raiding force defeats defending troops of Henry Percy

1394 Revolt in Ireland repressed by Richard II

1395–6 Anglo-French conference in Paris. Truce providing for 28 years

1399 Richard II dethroned in favor of Henry IV

PHASE 6: CHARLES VI v. HENRY V 1414–22

1405 French expeditionary force lands in Wales to help the Welsh uprising

1406 Welsh beaten by the English. French attempted offensives against Guyenne and Calais checked.

1407 Anglo-French truce. Beginning of Civil War in France.

1415 Henry V renounces the truce of 1396 and lands at Harfleur, which he besieges and takes

1415 Battle of Agincourt. Henry V defeats the French

1416 Battle of Harfleur. Franco-Genoese fleet defeated

1417 Henry V's second expedition to France.

1418 Conquest of Normandy by the English.

1418–19 Siege and capture of Rouen. Burgundians enter Paris

1419 Rouen taken by the English

1420 Treaty of Troyes: Henry V to be heir to the throne of France. Henry enters

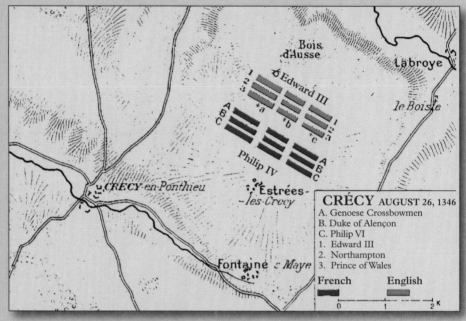

CRÉCY AUGUST 26, 1346
A. Genoese Crossbowmen
B. Duke of Alençon
C. Philip VI
1. Edward III
2. Northampton
3. Prince of Wales

French   English

0   1   2 K

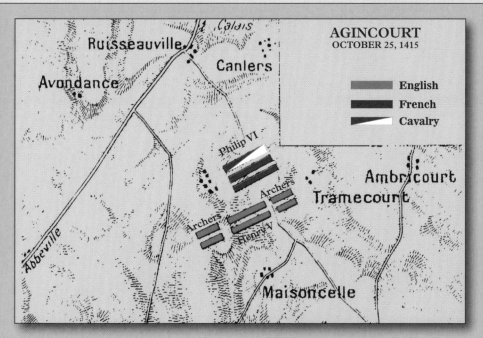

Battle of Crécy

Context Hundred Years War

Date August 26, 1346

Location 10 miles north of Abbeville, northern France

Commanders/Forces King Edward III of England commanding c.9,000 men. King Philip IV of France commanding c.30,000

Objectives Edward was brought to battle during a chevauchée across northern France; the French sought his destruction

Casualties English c.100. French more than 1,500 nobles and knights and c.10,000 infantry

Victor English

Consequences The French army was devastated, and Edward was free to march on to Calais, which he captured

Left: Artillery at Crécy. While this battle marked the introduction of the longbow as a decisive weapon of war and the corresponding decline of the amored knight, it was also one of the first battles where artillery was used.

Battle of Agincourt

Context Hundred Years War

Date October 25, 1415

Location Midway between Abbeville and Calais in northern France

Commanders/Forces King Henry V of England commanding c.5,700 English. King Philip VI of France commanding c.25,000 French

Objectives French attempt to intercept and destroy the invading English who were en route to Calais

Casualties English c.400 including the Duke of York. French c.8,000 including the Constable of France, 3 dukes, 90 nobles and more than 1,500 knights

Victor English

Consequences The cream of the French army was shattered. Henry continued to Calais rather than exploiting this spectacular success by a march on Paris

Left: *Joan of Arc at the siege of Orleans. 'The Maid of Orleans' (c.1412–31) was a country girl who claimed to have heard the voices of the saints instructing her to free France from the English. She inspired the raising of the siege and subsequently saw Charles V crowned at Rheims. But in 1430 she was captured by the Burgundians and sold to the English, who burnt her at the stake after a trial for heresy. She was canonized in 1920.*

Below left: *Bertrand du Guesclin (c.1379) served Charles V as his great champion in many victories over the English in the closing decades of the Hundred Years War.*

Below: *Men at arms, mid-15th century.*

Paris, which is under English control for the next 15 years

1421 Henry V's third expedition to France.

1421 Battle of Beaugé. Franco-Scottish force defeated by Clarence's English

1422 Truce. Death of Henry V and of Charles VI in Paris

PHASE 7: CHARLES VII v. HENRY VI 1423–53

1423 Battle of Cravant. Bedford defeats Franco-Scottish army

1424 Battle of Verneuil. Bedford defeats Franco–Scottish army

1427 Battle of Montargis. Dunois defeats Bedford and Warwick

1428 Salisbury besieges Orleans defended by Dunois.

1429 Rouvray ('The Herrings'). Falstolf repulses French attack on a convoy of supplies for the English besiegers of Orleans

1429 Siege of Orleans raised by Joan of Arc, leading to spirited counterattack by the French, which rapidly gathers momentum. Coronation of the Dauphin

Above: *Castillon, last battle of the Hundred Years War, which sealed the fate of Aquitaine.*

at Rheims as Charles VII

1429 English fortress of Jargeau taken by the French

1429 Battle of Patay. French surprise and defeat English army of Shrewsbury (Talbot)

1430 Joan of Arc checked before Paris and made prisoner

1431 Joan of Arc burnt at Rouen. Henry VI aged 10 is crowned king of France at Paris.

1436 English leave Paris. The French lay siege to Calais

1441 The French take Pontoise

1444–8 Successive truces of Tours

1448 Resumption of hostilities between France and England. French offensive in Normandy

1449 Rouen expels English garrison

1450 Battle of Formigny. Decisive French victory by Clermont over the English, leading to the fall of Caen and Cherbourg to the French

1450–1 French drive the English out of France, leaving only Calais in their hands

The people of Aquitaine revolt against the new French rulers and Shrewsbury takes an English expeditionary force to support them

1453 Battle of Castillon. Shrewsbury is defeated. Castillon, Bordeaux and all Aquitaine revert to French rule. End of the Hundred Years War. The English are left with only Calais, which they keep until 1558

Balkans

1360s–1390s Ottoman conquest of Thrace, Bosnia, Serbia, Greece and Bulgaria

1389 Kosovo Polje. Turks decisively defeat Serbs

1394–1403 Blockade of Constantinople by Ottomans

1396 Battle of Nicopolis: Christian Crusade defeated by Ottomans

1409–26 Venetian expansion in Dalmatia and Lombardy

Mehmet II the Conqueror.

Mehmet II the Conqueror (Mehmed Fatih) (1432–1481)
Ottoman sultan who ended the Byzantine Empire by taking Constantinople in 1453. Over the following two decades he campaigned in the Balkans, conquering the Morea, Serbia and Bosnia, Wallachia and, later, Moldavia. A war with Venice (1463–79) brought Negroponte and northern Albania, and in 1473 he repulsed an invasion of Turkomen at Otluk Beli. Otranto fell in 1480, but in the same year Ottoman forces failed to take Rhodes from the Knights of St. John. He took measures to repopulate Constantinople, now Istanbul, and reorganized the Ottoman army to incorporate increased use of cannon. Ushering in a golden age, he made the Ottoman Empire a major power in both Europe and the Middle East.

Above: *A contemporary illustration of a city under siege, with artillery bombarding the walls.*

Left: *A full suit of armor of the fifteenth century. By this date armor had reached the height of sophistication and design but, with the introduction of firearms was soon to become redundant.*

Right: *Contemporary illustration from the Chronicles of Froissart depicting the siege of a castle. It shows some of the most important weapons of the time: crossbows, longbows and early artillery. Crossbows were less accurate and of shorter range than longbows, but crossbowmen could be trained more quickly and the weapon could be kept cocked and ready to shoot at a moment's notice. Longbows in the hands of the English and Welsh proved battle-winning weapons at Crécy, Poitiers and Agincourt; however, they required years of training and practise to be fully effective.*

1451–81 Ottoman Sultan Mehmet 'The Conqueror' annexes Serbia, Bosnia, Greece, Crimea, etc.

1453 Siege and fall of Constantinople. End of Byzantine Empire. Constantinople is renamed Istanbul

Britain: Wars of the Roses

May 22, 1455 Battle of St Albans. York, Salisbury and Warwick defeat Royal army. Somerset and Northumberland are killed

Sept 23, 1459 Battle of Blore Heath. Salisbury wins for York at Ludlow

July 10, 1460 Battle of Northampton. Yorkists put Lancastrians to flight. Henry is captured

December 30, 1460 Battle of Wakefield. Margaret defeats York and Salisbury who are killed

February 2, 1461 Battle of Mortimer's Cross. Edward, new Duke of York, defeats Lancastrians and is proclaimed king

February 17, 1461 Battle of St Albans. Margaret and Somerset defeat Warwick

March 29, 1461 Battle of Towton. Lancastrians defeated with heavy loss of life. Edward controls England

1464 Battles of Hedgley Moor (April 25) and Hexham (15 May). Montagu (Warwick's brother) defeats Lancastrians

1465 Henry is captured

1468 Harlech, last Lancastrian stronghold, falls to the Yorkists.

Warwick and Edward's brother Clarence change sides

July 26, 1469 Battle of Edgecote Moor. Warwick defeats Pembroke

March 12, 1470 Battle of 'Lose-Coat Field' (Stamford). Rebels ambush Edward, but he defeats them

Sept 1470 Henry VI is restored to the throne

April 14, 1471 Battle of Barnet. Warwick is defeated and killed

May 4, 1471 Battle of Tewkesbury. Edward defeats Lancastrians and rules as Edward IV

1483 Edward IV dies. Richard of Gloucester usurps the throne as Richard III

Charles V (1500–1558)

Habsburg monarch whose reign dominated the first half of the sixteenth century. His vast inheritance – Spain in 1516, Austria and the Holy Roman Empire in 1519 – constituted a 'monarchia' of unprecedented proportions, taking in Spain, parts of Italy, the Netherlands, Germany and the Habsburg lands in the New World. His reign was colored by three main themes: the Reformation and his attempts to defeat Protestantism in Germany; the aggressive expansionism of the Ottoman Turks in Hungary and the Mediterranean; and a continuing feud with Francis I of France, the French seeing themselves as encircled and threatened by the huge empire of the Habsburgs. Charles was forced to travel constantly in Europe to deal with a succession of crises. His army defeated the French at Pavia in 1525, ensuring Spanish supremacy in Italy. In 1547 at Mühlberg he defeated the German Protestants. But his incessant wars outran his credit, the silver mines of South America were yet to come into production and provide the massive quantity of bullion that would

Above: Charles V, 'the world emperor', whose dominions spanned vast tracts of Europe and South/Central America.

enrich Spain during his son's reign. The responsibilities of state weighed heavily upon him, for ruling an empire this colossal in the sixteenth century was beyond the capability of one man. He abdicated in 1556, splitting the empire into its Spanish and Austrian components.

Left: The Battle of Marignano.

Below: The Battle of Pavia.

August 7, 1485 Lancastrian Henry Tudor lands in Wales

August 22, 1485 Battle of Bosworth. Richard is killed. Henry VII is king

June 16, 1487 Battle of Stoke. Impostor 'Edward VI' (Lambert Simnel) defeated

July 21, 1403 Battle of Shrewsbury. Henry VII defeats rebellion of Henry Percy (Hotspur)

Burgundy and Switzerland

1467–77 Charles the Bold Duke of Burgundy. He allies with England and Aragon against Louis XI of France, his bitter enemy; and with Sigmund of Austria against the Swiss

1474 Siege of Neuss

1476 Battle of Murten

1476 Battle of Granson

1477 Battle of Nancy. Charles the Bold killed. His daughter has married Maximilian I of Austria who wins

1479 Battle of Guinegate. Treaty of Senlis divides the legacy

1477–99 Swabian War. Swiss establish

independence and separation from the Empire

1513 Swiss Confederation of 13 cantons

1477–99 Swiss Swabian War

1477 Habsburgs inherit Burgundy

1471–80 Turkish attacks on Styria

1477 Hungarian attacks on Austria

1485 Seizure of Vienna, occupation of Lower Austria, Carinthia and Styria by Matthias I Corvinus, King of Hungary, who dies 1490; Habsburgs recover territories including Vienna

Russia

1478 Ivan III annexes Novgorod

1480 Ivan III proclaims independence of Muscovy

Italy

1494–1559 Valois-Habsburg Wars for Italy (1499–1523 Italian wars involve Swiss mercenaries)

1494 Charles VIII of France begins wars for Naples, claiming Naples via the House of Anjou

1494 Charles conquers Naples

1495 Spanish and Habsburgs force him to retreat

1500 Louis XII of France takes Milan

1504 Treaty of Blois cedes Naples to Spain

By 1505 Habsburgs drive French from the south of Italy and take Naples

1511 Holy League to liberate Italy

1515 Battle of Marignano. Francis I of France defeats Swiss

1519–56 Habsburg Empire of Charles V

1519–56 Charles V (1516 inherits Spanish Empire; 1519 Austria and the Holy Roman Empire)

1521–6 War against Francis I of France

1525 Battle of Pavia. Habsburgs drive French from Milan

1525 Peasant revolt in Germany

1526–9 2nd war against Francis I.

Babur (Zahir ad-Din Muhammad) (1483–1530)
Founder of the Mogul Empire in India. A descendant of the great Mongol conquerors (including Genghis Khan and Timur), he succeeded to the throne of the insignificant kingdom of Fargana in 1494. His ambitions lay towards Samarkand (which had been Timur's capital), but here he found only frustration. His great enterprise to India met with spectacular success, striking against a Sultanate of Delhi riven and weakened by factionalism. His key victories at Panipat and Khanua in 1526 secured Delhi and Agra, and he subsequently extended his conquests to the frontier of Bengal. Cultured and convivial, he was a great poet, sportsman and conversationalist. His memoirs, *Babur-nameh*, are a classic.

Left: Babur, conqueror of northern India.

Naval warfare in the 16th century
Ocean-going ships were now increasingly assuming the form that would be familiar until the middle of the 19th century, larger and more robust than the tiny ships with which Columbus and the early explorers set out across the Atlantic and Indian Oceans. Increasing size afforded the strength and capacity for more armament, and, as on land, cannon were becoming more powerful, of longer range and more reliable. In the Mediterranean, however, the maneuverability of the galley – and the availability of slaves to use as rowers – maintained its supremacy as the mainstay of navies.
Above: *Galleys in combat at the Battle of Lepanto, the decisive victory of the Holy League over the Ottoman Turks in 1571.*

1527 Imperial army plunders Rome
1535 Habsburgs take Milan
1536–8 3rd war between Charles V and
    Francis I
1542–4 4th war between Charles V and
    Francis I
1546–7 Schmalkaldic War of south/central
    Germany
1547 Battle of Mühlberg. Habsburgs defeat
    German Protestants

1552–6 Charles V at war with France again.
    He abdicates 1556 splitting his empire
    into its Spanish and Austrian components
1559 Treaty of Câteau-Cambresis. French
    are excluded from Italy

Ottoman Empire in the Middle East
1516–17 Ottomans conquer Syria, Palestine
    and Mameluke Egypt
1520–66 Suleman I pushes the Ottoman
    Empire to its greatest extent
1529 Turks capture Algiers
1551 Turks take Tripoli
1565 Turks besiege Malta
1571 Turks take Cyprus
1574 Turks take Tunis

Mediterranean
1475–1546 Barbarossa raids Spanish and
    Italian coasts for Francis I of France
1529 Turks take Algiers
1535 Habsburg North African campaign
    against Barbarossa and seizure of Tunis
1541 Habsburg Algiers expedition fails
1551 Turks take Tripoli
1565 Turkish siege of Malta fails
1571 Battle of Lepanto. Don John of Austria
    leads Holy League fleet to victory over
    Turks
1571 Turks take Cyprus
1577 Ottoman-Habsburg truce. The Turkish
    threat wanes. Habsburgs are busy in the
    north; Ottomans in conflict with Persia

Ottomans in Europe
1526 Battle of Mohacs. Turks take most of
    Hungary
1529 First Turkish siege of Vienna
Turks take Hungary

India
1504–30 WARS OF BABUR
1526 Battle of Khanua: Babur defeats Rajput
    Confederation to conquer northern India
1526 Battle of Panipat: Babur defeats Sultan
    Ibrahim Lodi of Delhi and establishes the
    Moghul Empire, which becomes the

Above: A Warrior Monk, one of the formidable fighters who played a major part in 11th and 12th century warfare in Japan

Left: Toyotomi Hideyoshi (d.1598) leading the second Japanese invasion of Korea. **Above:** Japanese swordsmen in action.

*16th century
samurai, Japan's
warrior elite,
corresponding approx-
imately to the
knights of Western
Europe.
Samurai armor
was traditional and
complex, mainly
lamellar, made from
small scales
laced together.*

Above: *A Japanese warrior fires an early firearm.*

dominant power in India
1535–40 Campaigns of Humayan
1538 Bahmani State splits into 5 states
1539 Battle of Benares; defeated by usurper Sher–Shah
1540 Battle of Kanauj; again defeated by usurper Sher-Shah. Humayan, after exile, regains the throne in 1555 and extends the empire
1556–1605 Akbar, greatest of Mogul emperors
1556–1601 Campaigns of Akbar
1556 Second Battle of Panipat
1564 Five Deccan Kingdoms combine to destroy Vijayanagara
1610–29 Moghuls at war with Ahmadnagar
1623 Battle of Balochpur

Japan
1467–1615 'Period of the Warring States' as local warlords vie for supremacy
1467–77 Onin War
1561 Battle of Kawanakajima
1570–81 Siege of Ishiyama Honganji
1591 Siege of Kunoe
1592/3, 1597/8 Japanese invasions of Korea
1600 Battle of Sekigahara. Tokugawa decisively defeats his rivals, leading to the establishment of the Tokugawa shogunate
1637–8 Shimbara Revolt, the last uprising against the Togukawa shogunate. Peace in Japan. In 1639 Japan effectively cuts itself off from the outside world until the middle of the nineteenth century

Britain
1513–14 Anglo–Scottish War
1513 Battle of Flodden Field. Earl of Surrey defeats James IV of Scotland.
1545 Battle of Ancram Moor. Scots defeat English raiding party
1547 Battle of Pinkie. Somerset defeats Arran, regent of Scotland
1594–1603 Irish Nine Years War
1598–1603 Tyrone's Rebellion in Ireland

Above: *The Battle of Gravelines, culmination of the Spanish Armada expedition against England in 1588; painting by Philippe-Jacques de Loutherbourg.*

Maurice, Count of Nassau, Prince of Orange (1587–1625)

One of the major military innovators of his time, Maurice succeeded, in a series of victories, in securing the area that is today the Kingdom of the Netherlands, his campaigns of 1587 to 1609 being remembered in Dutch history as 'the closing of the garden'. In these years he took Sluys (1587), Breda (1590), Zutpen (1591), Nijmegen (1591) and inflicted defeats on the Spanish at Turnhout (1597) and Nieuport (1600). As Stadthouder and Captain-General of the United Provinces (from 1588) he reorganized and revitalized the Dutch army, introducing the battalion (550 men) to face the Spanish tercios, paying his troops properly and instilling improved discipline with regular drill. His scientific methods of siege warfare were based upon sound mathematical and engineering principles in a period when firearms and artillery were fast coming of age. The results of his campaigns were the recognition of the Netherlands as an independent state. When war began again in 1621 after the Twelve Years Truce he was less successful and died just weeks before the Spaniards retook Breda for Spain.

Maurice of Nassau.

1601 Spanish expeditionary force invades Ireland

1601 Battle of Kinsale. British defeat Tyrone

1531 Battle of Kappel. Swiss Catholics defeat Protestants of Zurich. Zwingli killed

Russia and Northern Europe

1552 Muscovy conquers Kazan Khanate

1569 Union of Lublin. Poland/Lithuania repulse. Muscovite expansion

1604–6 The 'False Demetrius' pretender invades Russia to depose Boris Godounov, the murderer of Dmitri, the last of the Rurik dynasty in 1598

1605 He enters Moscow

1610 Boyars retake Moscow and kill Demetrius

A second false Dmitri is a puppet of the Poles

1610–13 Time of Troubles – anarchy in Russia

1611 Poland takes Smolensk; Sweden invades Russia

1609–13 Russo-Polish War

1610 Battle of Klondnot

1611 Battle of Christianople

1612 Battle of Vringellen

1613 Battle of Wisby

1613 Michael Romanov elected Tsar and restores order

1617–18 Russian peace with Poland and Sweden

1615 Battle of Plescow

1621 Battle of Riga

1621–2 Battle of Kotzim

1634 Poland invades Russia

1637 Don Cossacks temporarily take Azov for Russia

1672–1725 Peter I the Great of Russia (sole ruler from 1689)

1695 Expedition against Azov fails

1696 Expedition succeeds in taking Azov

1698–9 Revolt of the Streltsi. Mass executions ensue

1703 Peter founds St Petersburg

Anglo-Spanish conflict

1587, 1596 English raid Cadiz

1588 Spanish Armada defeated in English Channel and off the Low Countries

China

1516 Portuguese base at Canton established

1563 Japanese pirates eliminated

1627 Abortive Ch'ing invasion of Korea

1628–44 Peasant rebellion in China

1636–7 Ch'ing conquest of Korea

1644–59 Ch'ing conquest of China

1644 Manchu take Peking

1644 Citzu-Ch'eng ends the Ming Dynasty and is immediately overthrown by the Ch'ing Dynasty to found the Manchu Dynasty

1594–7 Peasant Wars in Austria and Hungary

1605 Hungary invades Austria

Dutch War of Independence (Eighty Years War)

During the Dutch War and the Thirty Years War, North Italy is vital to Spain as the mustering–point for the 'Spanish Road' (Habsburg possessions) via the Valtellina, Alsace, Rhineland to the Low Countries, the English Channel being dominated by the Dutch and the English

1587–1625 CAMPAIGNS OF MAURICE OF NASSAU

1587–1609 Maurice secures the Netherlands ('The Closing of the Garden')

1600 Battle of Nieuport

1601–4 Siege and capture of Ostend by Maurice

1604 Maurice takes Sluys

1604 Spanish take Ostend

1607 Battle of Gibraltar. Dutch defeat Spanish at sea

April 1609 Twelve Years Truce

1621–48 Dutch War of Independence resumed and merges with Thirty Years War

1625 Capture of Breda

Gustavus Adolphus.

Gustavus II Adolphus (1594–1632)
One of the Great Captains of History and often considered the 'father of modern warfare', he created the first truly 'modern' army, which became the model for all the other powers of Europe. Succeeding to the Swedish throne in 1611, he reorganized the country's armed forces, adopting a regional regimental system (supported by mercenaries) and using the Dutch linear tactics to defeat mass tercios. His three-deep infantry formation gave increased flexibility of maneuver, combining shock effect with firepower. Shorter (eight-foot) pikes were easier to handle and deploy; lighter muskets with pre-packed cartridges increased the rate of fire. His artillery too became a vital tactical factor on the battlefield: 'leather' guns and light brigade artillery were more mobile and gave close support to the infantry. After early campaigns in the Baltic area, capturing Riga and taking possession of the Prussian ports, he became involved in the Thirty Years War. Breitenfeld (1631) signaled the emergence of Sweden as a major military power; but he met his death at Lützen the following year, at the head of his cavalry.

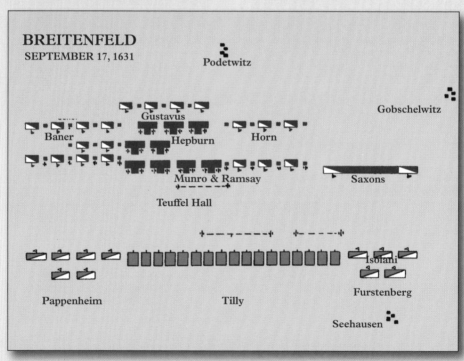

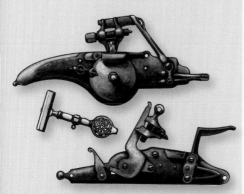

Top: *Dating from the early 1500s, the wheel-lock mechanism utilized the same principle as the mechanical cigarette lighter, in which the mineral for making the spark was held stationary and a wheel caused it to make a spark, which ignited the charge. The wheel was spun by clockwork and had to be wound by a key.* **Above:** *First recorded in 1683, the flintlock was a type of gunlock that ignited the charge by means of sparks produced by a spring-actuated cock striking a piece of flint against a vertically pivoted striking-plate.*

Battle of Breitenfeld

Context Thirty Years War, Swedish Phase

Date September 17, 1631

Location 5 miles north of Leipzig, Germany

Commanders/Forces Protestant army: King Gustavus Adolphus of Sweden and the Elector of Saxony commanding 36-40,000 Swedes and Saxons with 60-70 guns. Imperial/Catholic army: Count John de Tilly commanding 32,000 and 30 guns

Objectives Protestants aimed to capture Leipzig

Casualties Protestants 4,000 killed/wounded. Imperialists 7,000 killed/wounded and 6,000 taken prisoner

Victor Protestants

Consequences The Protestants captured Leipzig. Breitenfeld marked the emergence of Sweden as a major military power

1625–47 CAMPAIGNS OF FREDERICK HENRY OF ORANGE
1626 Battle of Lütter
1626 Battle of Dessau
1636 Frederick Henry captures Breda
1639 Battle of the Downs. Tromp defeats second Spanish Armada

France
1624–42 Richelieu First Minister of France
1626–30 Anglo-French War
1627–9 Huguenot Rebellion
1628 Siege and capture of La Rochelle
Buckingham attacks the Île de Rhé
1629–31 War of the Mantuan Succession. France versus Spain
1635–59 France and Spain at war, leaving Spain militarily exhausted.

THE FRONDE – FRENCH CIVIL WARS:
Jan–March 1649 First, *Fronde Parliamentaire* . Condé besieges Paris
1650–2 *Fronde* of the Princes
1652 Battle of Nemours
1652 Battle of Etampes
1658 Battle of the Dunes. Turenne captures Dunkirk (to England)
1659 Treaty of the Pyrenees

1618–48 Thirty Years War
Triggered by May 1618 Defenestration of Prague
1618–29 PHASE I. LOSS OF PALATINATE AND COLLAPSE OF GERMAN PROTESTANTISM
1620 Battle of White Mountain. Bohemian rebellion ended and conquest of Palatinate enabled
(1624–42 Richelieu first minister of France)
1626 Battle of Lütter compels withdrawal of Denmark. 1629 Peace of Lübeck
1630–5 PHASE II. RESTORATION OF PROTESTANTISM BY SWEDEN
1631 Battle of Breitenfeld restores Protestant fortunes and is the turning-point of the war
1631 Sack of Magdeburg
1632 Battle of Lützen. Victory, but death, of Gustavus Adolphus. Leads indirectly to

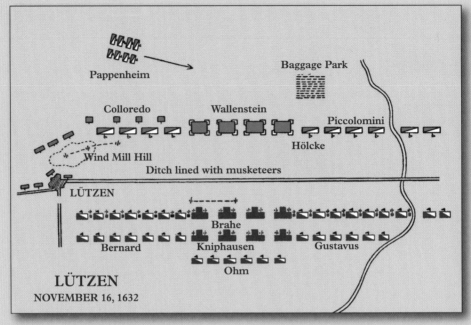

Henri de la Tour d'Auvergne, Vicomte Turenne (1611–1675)

France's most successful soldier of the seventeenth century, Turenne learnt the art of war from his uncle, Maurice of Nassau, and entered the French service in 1630. He rose to command France's armies during the Thirty Years War, reconquering Roussillon, winning battles at Freiburg (1644) and Zusmarshausen in 1648, and often sharing command with Condé. During the two French civil wars known as the *Fronde*, he found himself each time on the side opposite to Condé. He was defeated at Rethel in 1650, but was later reconciled with the court. During the second *Fronde* he had the better of Condé and subsequently defeated him at the Dunes in 1658 after having conquered much of the Spanish Netherlands. In 1677 he commanded in the wars against the Dutch, leading the triumphant campaign of 1675. His glorious career was cut short by a cannon ball that year. A master of strategy and tactics, he is acknowledged as one of the Great Captains of History, and his remains lie near to those of Napoleon in Les Invalides, Paris.

The Great Condé, Louis II de Bourbon,

Prince de Condé, Duc d'Enghien (1621–1686) Of French royal blood, Condé was, with Turenne, the greatest general of his time. His first victory came at Rocroi in 1643, when he was just 21 years of age. It was the greatest French victory for a century and marked the end

The Vicomte de Turenne.

Battle of Lützen

Context Thirty Years War, Swedish Phase

Date November 16, 1632

Location 15 miles south-west of Leipzig

Commanders/Forces Protestant army: Gustavus Adolphus commanding 16-19,000. Imperial army: Albrecht von Wallenstein commanding 15-20,000 infantry and 8-10,000 cavalry

Objectives Imperial army sought to cut the Swedish army's lines of communication from the Baltic and force the Elector of Saxony to leave the alliance with Sweden

Casualties Protestants c.5,000 killed/wounded; Gustavus Adolphus mortally wounded. Imperialists 6,000 killed/wounded

Victor Swedes

Consequences The Imperial army was frustrated in its aim; but the death of Gustavus Adolphus deprived the Protestants of the greatest general of his time

assassination of Wallenstein in Feb 1634

1634 Battle of Nördlingen undoes the work of Sweden. War becomes one of exhaustion between France/Sweden and Bavaria/Imperialists. Disease and starvation throughout Germany. End of religious phases of the war. 1635 Treaty of Prague. Negotiations ensue

1635–48 PHASE III. INTERVENTION OF FRANCE

1635 French ally with Dutch against Spain, begins the Dutch War of Independence with the Thirty Years War

(1642–1661 Mazarin first minister of France)

1643 Battle of Rocroi. Condé destroys the remnant of Spanish military prestige

1648 Battle of Zusmarshausen. Turenne and Wrangel defeat Imperialists and Bavarians

1648 Battle of Lens. Condé defeats the Spaniards

1648 Treaty of Westphalia ends Thirty Years War and Münster ends Spanish–Dutch War

of Spanish tercio supremacy and the rise of French military power. A series of victories followed with Turenne, including Freiburg, Philippsburg, Mainz and Nördlingen in 1645. His campaign in Flanders in 1646 was a brilliant success, as was his victory at Lens in 1648, following a brief campaign in Spain and defeat at Lérida the previous year. He was on Mazarin's side during the first *parliamentaire Fronde* of 1648–9 but turned against the Cardinal and was imprisoned in 1650, setting in motion the *Fronde* of the Princes – a major crisis for the regency of Anne of Austria and Mazarin. Released in 1651, he went into open rebellion until his position became untenable and he left France to fight for Spain. During this time he met defeat at the Battle of the Dunes in 1658. He was reconciled to Louis XIV the following year, thereafter invading Franche Comté in 1668 and invading the Netherlands with Turenne in 1672. At Seneffe two years later he halted the advance of the Prince of Orange. His personality was marked by princely arrogance coupled with an unrestrained temper, which must have been exacerbated in later life by crippling gout. He retired in 1675, the year in which his friend and colleague Turenne was killed.

The Great Condé.

Oliver Cromwell (1599–1658)

Arguably the greatest Englishman of the seventeenth century, Cromwell was essentially a politician and statesman, whose generalship was forced upon him by circumstance, revealing a soldier of genius. A Member of Parliament before and during the English Civil War, he raised his own regiment of 'Ironsides' and served as second-in-command of the Eastern Association army. Impatience with the lacklustre prosecution of the war by the Parliament's military leaders, he led the creation of the New Model Army, in which he soon became second-in-command. At Naseby the charge of his cavalry won the day. As an independent commander he proved his abilities at Preston, then at Dunbar (1650) and Worcester (1651). His campaign in Ireland (1649–50) earned him notoriety in Irish history for massacres following the capture of Drogheda and Wexford, but recent research has begun to absolve him. Essentially a moderate, he was driven to extreme measures by the duplicity and intransigence of the King, and took the lead in bringing Charles to trial and execution. Subsequent attempts to settle the government of the country proved tiresome and fruitless, and he soon became frustrated. His role as Lord Protector (1653 to his death) verged on monarchy. A central figure in British history, he was one of the great generals of the seventeenth century.

Sir Thomas Fairfax (1612–1671)

Captain-General of Parliament's New Model Army during the English Civil War, 'Black Tom' was a brave cavalryman and a skilled general. His apprenticeship to war was in 1629–31 in the Netherlands, and in 1640 he fought at Newburn in the Bishops' Wars. During the early years of the English Civil War he commanded the cavalry under his father in Yorkshire, taking Leeds and Wakefield in 1643, but being defeated at Adwalton Moor. He shared the victory at Winceby and in 1644 laid siege to York. At the Battle of Marston Moor he commanded the right wing of the Roundhead army. In 1645 Parliament appointed him Captain-General of the New Model Army, with which he won at Naseby and Langport; he cleared the Royalist West and in 1646 entered the Royalist capital of Oxford. In 1648 he crushed the Royalists at Maidstone and Colchester during the Second Civil War. Essentially a moderate man without the political motivation of many of his colleagues, he increasingly distanced himself from the victorious Parliament leadership and retired in 1651. Although he has often been eclipsed by Cromwell in accounts of the English Civil War, it was the military partnership of the two men that proved the war-winning factor in the Roundhead victory.

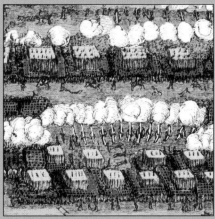

Above: A musketeer of the mid-seventeenth century (top) armed with a matchlock muzzle-loading gun, which he placed on an upright rest when shooting. These weapons were slow to fire, involving a laborious process of reloading, so musketeers were protected from cavalry by pikemen and deployed in dense squares, or tercios. The illustration below is a detail of a battle from this period showing artillery firing upon advancing tercios. On contact, infantry would contest 'push of pike' and hand-to-hand fighting. Cavalry, deployed on the flanks, would usually fight opposing cavalry, the victor turning in to attack the infantry in flank or from behind.

Poland

1609–13 Polish war against Russia

1611 Poles capture Smolensk

1617–29 Polish war against Sweden

Ongoing Polish war against Turkey

1625 Polish war against Sweden; 1629 Six Years Truce

1634 Poles invade Russia. Leads to Treaty of Viasma/Polyankova. Ladislas IV renounces claim to Russian throne

1648–68 Disastrous reign of John Casimir

Raids of Dnieper Cossacks; campaigns of Bogdan Chmielnuski

1648 Battle of Zolte Wody. Cossacks defeat Poles and take Lemberg

1651 Battle of Beresteszko. Poles defeated. Truce

c.1654 Bogdan and Russians invade Poland

1655–7 Sweden invades Poland. Civil War in Poland

1667 Cossack uprising in Poland

1672–6 Polish-Turkish War

1673 John Sobieski wins Battle of Khoczoim in Bessarabia

1674–96 John Sobieski King of Poland

Middle East

1623 Abbarttu the Great of Persia captures Baghdad

1638 Murad IV of Turkey recaptures Baghdad

India

1632 Hooghey taken from Portuguese

1649–53 Moghuls at war with Persia

1664–1710 Moghul persecution of non–Muslims

1675 Rajput revolt

English Civil Wars
1642–6 FIRST CIVIL WAR

Aug 22, 1642 King Charles I sets up standard at Nottingham: beginning of war

Sept 23, 1642 Battle of Powick Bridge. Rupert routs Parliamentarians

October 23, 1642 Battle of Edgehill. King defeats Earl of Essex

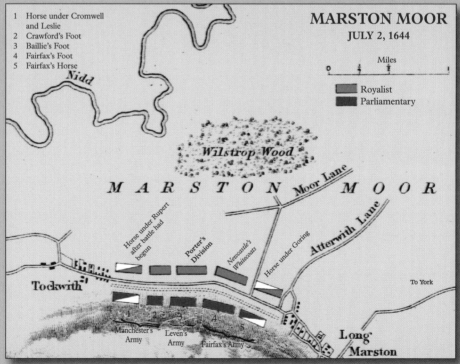

1 Horse under Cromwell
   and Leslie
2 Crawford's Foot
3 Baillie's Foot
4 Fairfax's Foot
5 Fairfax's Horse

MARSTON MOOR
JULY 2, 1644

Miles

Royalist
Parliamentary

Nidd

Wilstrop Wood

M A R S T O N   Moor Lane   M O O R

Horse under Rupert
after battle had
begun

Porter's
Division

Newcastle's
Whitecoats

Horse under Goring

Atterwith Lane

Tockwith

To York

Manchester's
Army

Leven's
Army

Fairfax's Army

Long
Marston

Oct 29, 1643 King makes Oxford his capital

November 13, 1643 Battle of Turnham Green. Royalists repulsed from London

Jan 19, 1643 Battle of Braddock Down. Hopton clears Cornwall of Parliamentarians

March 19, 1643 Battle of Hopton Heath. Royalist Northampton defeats Gell and Brereton

April 13, 1643 Battle of Ripple Field. Prince Maurice defeats Waller

April 23, 1643 Battle of Launceston. Hopton defeats Parliament army of Chudleigh

April 25, 1643 Battle of Sourton Down. Chudleigh defeats Hopton

May 13, 1643 Battle of Grantham. Cromwell defeats Cavendish

May 16, 1643 Battle of Stratton. Hopton defeats Stamford and secures south–west for the King

May 21, 1643 Sir Thomas Fairfax takes Wakefield

Battle of Marston Moor

Context English Civil War

Date July 2, 1644

Location 6 miles west of York, England

Commanders/Forces Royalists: Prince Rupert of the Rhine and the Marquis of Newcastle commanding c.11,000 foot and 6,000 cavalry. Parliament/Scots: Fairfax, Manchester and Leven commanding the forces of Yorkshire, the Eastern Association and Scotland, consisting of 12,200 infantry, 1,000 dragoons and 8,000 cavalry

Objectives Prince Rupert, having relieved the siege of York, sought a decisive battle

Casualties Unknown, but thought to be c.3,000 Royalists and c.2,000 Allied

Victor Parliament/Scots

Consequences The north was effectively lost to the King, and York surrendered July 16. Prince Rupert had squandered his brilliant success in relieving York by venturing upon an unnecessary battle, it being probable that the Allied army would have broken up in face of the prolongation of the siege

June 18, 1643 Battle of Chalgrove Field. Rupert defeats Parliamentarians

June 29, 1643 Battle of Adwalton Moor. Fairfaxes defeated by Newcastle's Royalists

July 5, 1643 Battle of Lansdown. Hopton defeats Waller

July 13, 1643 Battle of Roundway Down. Hopton and Prince Maurice destroy Waller's army

July 26, 1643 Bristol falls to Rupert

July 27, 1643 Battle of Gainsborough. Cromwell defeats Cavendish

Sept 20, 1643 Battle of Newbury I. King fails to prevent Essex's return to London

Sept 25, 1643 Solemn League and Covenant signed between Parliament and Scots

October 11, Battle of Winceby. Eastern Association defeats Royalists advancing south

Jan 25, 1644 Battle of Nantwich. Fairfax defeats Byron

March 21, 1644 Rupert relieves besieged Newark

March 29, 1644 Battle of Cheriton/ Alresford. Waller defeats Forth and Hopton

May 25 – June 11, 1644 Rupert takes Stockport, Bolton and Liverpool and marches to relieve besieged York

June 29, 1644 Battle of Cropredy Bridge. King defeats Waller

July 2, 1644 Battle of Marston Moor. Scots (Leven), Manchester and Fairfax defeat Rupert and Newcastle. Turning-point: the North is effectively lost to the King (July 16, York falls)

Aug 31, 1644 Battle of Castle Dore. King destroys Essex's army

Sept 1, 1644 Battle of Tippermuir. Montrose defeats Elgin's Covenanters

Sept 13, 1644 Battle of Aberdeen. Montrose defeats Elgin's Covenanters

Oct 27, 1644 Battle of Newbury II. King repulses Manchester and Waller

Feb 2, 1645 Battle of Inverlochy. Montrose defeats Campbells

April 1645 Formation of Parliament's New

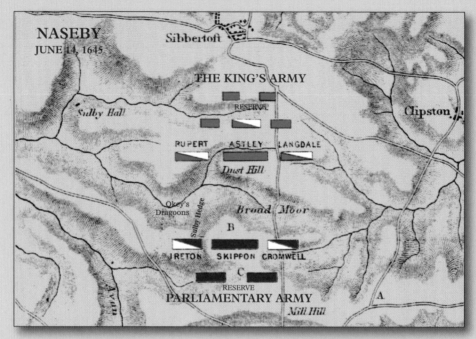

NASEBY
JUNE 14, 1645

Sibbertoft

THE KING'S ARMY

RESERVE

Sulby Hall

Clipston

RUPERT   ASTLEY   LANGDALE

Dust Hill

Okey's
Dragoons

Broad Moor

B

IRETON   SKIPPON   CROMWELL

C

RESERVE
PARLIAMENTARY ARMY

Mill Hill

A

Prince Rupert of the Rhine, Duke of Cumberland (1619–1682)

The quintessential dashing cavalier of romance, Prince Rupert was the third son of Frederick of the Palatinate. Joining his uncle at the outbreak of the English Civil War, he led the Royalist cavalry at Edgehill and First Newbury, captured Bristol in 1643 and carried out a spectacularly successful campaign in the North the following year. After relieving York, however, he demonstrated the impetuous side of his nature and ventured a battle against the odds at Marston Moor. This defeat lost the North for the King. As Commander-in-Chief of the Royalist army he found dissent among his fellow commanders preventing effective coordination. He took Leicester in 1645 but was defeated at Naseby and subsequently surrendered Bristol, to the anger of the King. From 1649 to 1652 he led a small squadron of Royalist buccaneers in a *guerre de course* against the new régime but was tirelessly pursued and worn down by Blake. After the Restoration he served as an admiral with Albemarle and the Duke of York in the Second and Third Anglo-Dutch wars, fighting at Southwold Bay (1665), the Four Days Fight (1667) and North Foreland (1667).

Above: *Prince Rupert was 24 years old at the beginning of the Civil War.*

Right: *Cromwell's victorious 'Ironsides' salute their general after the Battle of Naseby*

Battle of Naseby

Context English Civil War

Date June 14, 1645

Location 8 miles south-west of Market Harborough, Midlands of England

Commanders/Forces King Charles I commanding 4,000 infantry and 5,000 cavalry. Sir Thomas Fairfax commanding Parliament's New Model Army, consisting of 7,000 infantry and 6,000 cavalry

Objectives Parliament sought a decisive victory and the speedy end of the war

Casualties Royalists 6,000 killed/wounded/taken prisoner. Parliament less than 1,000 killed/wounded

Victor Parliament

Consequences The Royalist cause was lost in the Midlands with this defeat of the King's last major army. It was the decisive battle of the English Civil War

Model Army, commanded by Sir Thomas Fairfax with Cromwell in command of the cavalry

May 9, 1645 Battle of Auldearn. Montrose defeats Hurry's Covenanters

June 14, 1645 Battle of Naseby. Fairfax and Cromwell decisively defeat King, destroying his last significant field army

July 2, 1645 Battle of Alford. Montrose defeats Baillie's Covenanters

July 10, 1645 Battle of Langport. Fairfax defeats Goring

Aug 1, 1645 Battle of Colby Moor. Laugharne defeats Pembrokeshire Royalists

Sept 10, 1645 Rupert surrenders Bristol

Sept 13, 1645 Battle of Philiphaugh. Defeat of Montrose

Sept 24, 1645 Battle of Rowton Heath. Royalists defeated at Chester

March 12, 1646 Astley surrenders last Royalist army at Stow-in-the-Wold

Robert Blake (1599–1657)

One of England's greatest admirals, Blake fought for the Parliament in the defense of Bristol, Lyme Regis and Taunton during the English Civil war. In 1644 he became Parliament's General at Sea, in which role he hounded Prince Rupert's Royalist fleet to destruction (1650). The result was the recovery of the Scillies and Jersey. He fought during the First Anglo-Dutch War, defeating Tromp off Dover (1652) and Kentish Knock (1652), losing off Dungeness but winning again off Portland in 1653. In 1655 he campaigned against the Barbary pirates; in 1656–7 blockaded Spain over the winter; and in 1657 carried out a spectacular raid on Santa Cruz in the Canaries. He was instrumental in creating the new British navy and in the creation of *Fighting Instructions* in 1653, crucial to the development of the organization and tactical handling of fleets in battle. From this time onwards, Britain's navy was to become one of the great military forces on the world stage.

Michiel Adriaanzoon de Ruyter (1607–1676)

The Netherlands' greatest admiral, de Ruyter's naval victories against England did much to maintain Dutch power and prestige. After serving under Tromp in the First Anglo-Dutch War, he fought with the Danes in the First Northern War

Aug 8, 1647 Battle of Dunganhill.
Parliamentarian Jones defeats Irish

1648 SECOND CIVIL WAR

1648 Battle of Preston. Cromwell defeats
Royalists and Scots

Aug 28, 1648 Colchester surrenders to
Fairfax

Jan 30, 1649 King Charles I beheaded

1649 IRISH CAMPAIGN

Aug 2, 1649 Battle of Rathmines. Ormonde's
Royalists repulsed before Dublin

Sept–Dec 1649 Drogheda and Wexford
besieged and taken by Cromwell's army

1650–1 THIRD CIVIL WAR

April 27, 1650 Battle of Carbisdale.
Montrose's Royalists defeated

Sept 3, 1650 Battle of Dunbar. Cromwell

defeats Scots Covenanters

Sept 3, 1651 Battle of Worcester. Cromwell
defeats Charles II's Anglo–Scots army

Campaigns of the English Commonwealth

1650s England sends a fleet to the
Mediterranean against Barbary pirates

May 1655 England captures Jamaica

1662–83 England holds Tangier

Anglo-Dutch Wars (naval)

1652–4 1st ANGLO-DUTCH WAR

1652 Battle of Kentish Knock. Blake defeats
de With

1652 Battle of Dungeness. Tromp defeats
Blake

1653 Battle of Portland/Beachy Head.
Indecisive

1653 Battle of Gabbard/North
Foreland/Nieuport. Monck and Deane
defeat Tromp and de Ruyter

1653 Battle of Texel. Monck defeats Tromp,
who is killed

1665–7 2nd ANGLO-DUTCH WAR

1665 Battle of Solebay/Lowestoft. Duke of
York defeats Opdam

1666 Four Days Fight/Dover Strait. De
Ruyter and Tromp Jr defeat Albemarle
and Rupert

1666 Battle of North Foreland II. Albemarle
defeats de Ruyter

1672–4 3rd ANGLO-DUTCH WAR

1672 Battle of Southwold. De Ruyter
defeats York and d'Estrées

1673 Battle of Schooneveld Bank. De Ruyter
defeats Rupert and d'Estrées

1673 Battle of Texel II/Camperdown. De
Ruyter defeats Rupert and d'Estrées

China

1674–81 Rebellion of the Three Feudatores

1683 Chinese conquest of Formosa

1696 Chinese conquest of Mongolia

1705 Chinese invasion of Tibet

1720 Chinese conquest of Tibet

1740–3 Chinese–Indonesian War

1758–9 Chinese conquest of Kashgaria

and defeated the Swedes at Nyborg in 1659. He then campaigned off the Guinea coast and in the West Indies before leading major fleet actions in the Second Anglo-Dutch War, including the Four Days Fight in 1666. The following year his audacious invasion of the Medway, destroying much of the English fleet and capturing the English flagship, was spectacular. His greatest battles were fought during the Third Anglo-Dutch War (1672–4) and included victories at Sole Bay (1672), Ostend (1623) and Kijduin in 1673. Subsequently redeploying to the Mediterranean, he was mortally wounded off Sicily.

John Churchill, Duke of Marlborough (1650–1722)

One of Britain's greatest generals, Marlborough won a series of epic victories in the War of the Spanish Succession that turned the tide against the expansionism of Louis XIV's France. In 1685 he served at Sedgemoor during the Monmouth Rebellion but deserted James II in 1688 to welcome William of Orange as King of England. He served in Ireland and Flanders before becoming Captain General of the Allied armies in Flanders, at the head of the coalition created by William to counter the aggression of France in the Low Countries. In 10 successive campaigns he proved his skills as strategist, tactical and logistical organizer – and as soldier-diplomat. His greatest victories were Blenheim (1704), Ramillies (1706), Oudenarde (1708) and Malplaquet (1709). Well-loved by his troops, rewarded with a dukedom and the palace of Blenheim in Oxfordshire, he retired in 1711, the victim of shifting political sands.

Left: John Churchill, Duke of Marlborough and ancestor of Winston Churchill, who wrote his biography.

**Wars of Louis XIV (King of France
1643–1715; regency 1643–51)**
1659–1629 PHASE I
1668 Condé conquers Franche Comté
1672 France invades Holland, but Dutch
flood the countryside forcing withdrawal
next year
1674 Grand Alliance of the Hague against
Louis XIV
1674 Battle of Sinzheim and Ladenburg.
Turenne defeats Imperialists and
devastates the Palatinate
1675 Battles of Mülhausen, Colmar,
Türkheim. Again Turenne defeats the
Imperialists and forces the evacuation of
Alsace
1675 Battle of Sasbach. Turenne killed
1675 Battle of Fehrbellin. Brandenburg
defeats Sweden
1678 Treaty of Nijmegen
1667–8 War of Devolution against Spain
1679–97 PHASE II
French annexations (réunions) lead to 1681
Alliance of the Hague, of Dutch, Swedes,
Spanish and the Empire
1681 France invades Luxembourg
1684 French fleet bombards Genoa
1689–97 War of the League of Augsburg
(Nine Years War). Spain, Empire, Sweden
and Bavaria ally against France over the
Spanish succession
1688 Second French invasion of the
Palatinate
1688–9 Second devastation of the Palatinate
unites Europe against Louis XIV
1688 English 'Glorious Revolution':
Protestant William III replaces Catholic
James II
May 1689 Alliance of Vienna: Empire,
United Provinces, joined by England,
Spain and Savoy against France
Naval battles of Bantry Bay and Beachy
Head: French defeat England and Holland.
Louis XIV plans invasion of England with
camp at Cherbourg.
1692 Battle of La Hogue. Tourville defeated
by Russell

1689 France invades Low Countries
1692 Battle of Steinkirk. William III defeated
1693 Battle of Neerwinden (Landen)
William III defeated
French campaign in Italy: 1690 Battle of
Staffarde; 1693 Battle of Marsaglia
Jean Bart leads *guerre de course* in Channel
1696/7 Treaties of Turin and Ryswick
1697–1715 PHASE III
1700 Death of Charles II of Spain;
bequeaths Spanish Empire to Philip of
Anjou
(1700 Brandenburg becomes Kingdom of
Prussia)

1702–13 War of the Spanish Succession
French invade Netherlands
1701 Grand Alliance of the Hague against
the French
1702 Battle of Friedlingen
1703 Battle of Höchstadt
1704 Battle of Blenheim, Marlborough's
great victory. Allies conquer Bavaria
1704 Gibraltar taken by England
1706 Battle of Ramillies wins Belgium for
the Allies
1706 Battle of Turin
Philip V has to abandon Barcelona. France
loses Belgium, Milan and Spain in one
summer
1707 Battle of Almanza
1708 Battle of Oudenarde. Allies invade
France
1708–14 Sardinia is a British base
1708–83 Minorca is a British base
1709 Battle of Malplaquet, a Pyrrhic victory
for Marlborough, which prevents the
Allies invading France
1710 Battle of Lerida. Philip defeated
1710 Battles of Brihuega, Villviciosa. Allies
defeated, effectively restoring Spain to the
Bourbons
1711 French expedition takes Rio de Janeiro
1712 Battle of Denain. Villars wins France's
only major victory and the Allies lose
heart
1715 Treaty of Utrecht

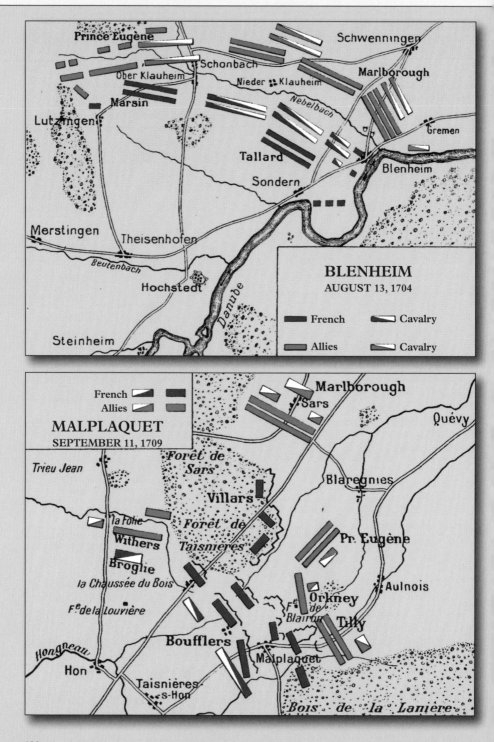

BLENHEIM
AUGUST 13, 1704

- French
- Allies
- Cavalry
- Cavalry

French
Allies

MALPLAQUET
SEPTEMBER 11, 1709

Battle of Blenheim

Context War of the Spanish Succession

Date August 13, 1704

Location Blindheim, 10 miles west of Donauworth, south Germany

Commanders/Forces Duke of Marlborough and Prince Eugene of Savoy commanding 52,000 men with 60 guns. Count Camille de Tallard commanding a French army of 56,000 men and 90 guns

Objectives The Allies aimed to break the deadlock in the Danube theater of operations and remove the French threat to Vienna

Casualties Allies 12,000 killed/wounded. French 20,000 killed/wounded and 14,000 taken prisoner

Victor Allies

Consequences Vienna was saved. The battle followed a brilliant march by the Allies which completely deceived the French. The Allies now had the initiative

Battle of Malplaquet

Context War of the Spanish Succession

Date September 11, 1709

Location 10 miles south of Mons

Commanders/Forces Duke of Marlborough and Prince Eugene of Savoy commanding Allied army of 110,000 men and 100 guns. Duke Claude de Villars and Louis de Boufflers commanding a French army of 80,000 men and 60 guns

Objectives The Allies aimed to take Mons, destroy the last French army and advance on Paris, thus ending the war

Casualties Allies 6,500 killed, 14,000 wounded. French 4,500 killed and 8,000 wounded

Victor Allies

Consequences The French were forced to quit the field, but the Allied victory was Pyrrhic. The bloodiest battle of the century, Malplaquet precluded any further Allied advance that year and turned British opinion against the war. It also speeded Marlborough's political downfall

Right: Marlborough gives orders during the Battle of Malplaquet, the fourth and last of his major battles. He aimed to destroy the last French army in the field, but Marshals Villars and Bouler occupied a formidable position, enhanced with earthworks. The battle was bloody, and though a technical victory for Marlborough, the French retired in good order. Losses (perhaps as many as 20,000 Allies to the French 12,000) affected opinion in England and fostered the growing demands for peace. This illustration is a detail from one of the great tapestries at Blenheim Palace.

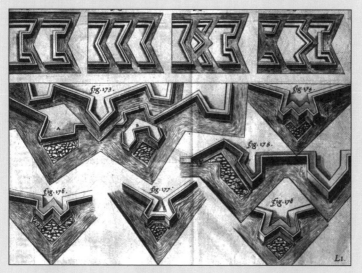

Left: Mid-seventeenth century designs for outworks, showing various forms of bastion. While the bulwark was intended as a strongpoint, permitting the application of fire to outflank attackers between bastions, it was itself vulnerable to being cut off and captured. These schemes show various ways of isolating an outwork so that, even if captured, the bulwark would reveal another layer of defenses behind it.

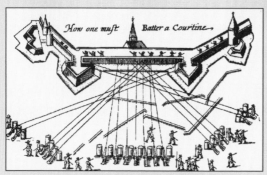

Left: Artillery in siege warfare as depicted in a manual of 1639 demonstrating the value of the bulwark. The curtain (between the bulwarks) is protected by cross-fire from the bulwarks; and (lower illustration) if the attackers do succeed in taking the bulwark, its narrow 'neck' is relatively easy to seal off with another layer of defense.

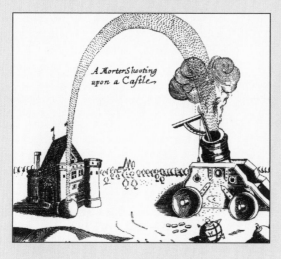

Left: A mortar, from a seventeenth century manual. Mortars were short, high-elevation guns which lobbed bombs at a high trajectory over the top of defenses. Less accurate than cannon, they were nevertheless destructive and could reach parts of the defenses that normal guns could not. Small infantry mortars, lightweight and man-portable, remain in use with the armies of today.

Americas

1711–12 Tuscarora War
1702–13 Queen Anne's War (War of The Spanish Succession in Europe)
1715–28 Yamassee War
1718–20 Franco-Spanish War (War of the Quadruple Alliance)
1721–5 Paraguayan Revolution
1740–8 King George's War (War of the Austrian Succession in Europe)

Turkey

After Suleiman the Magnificent the Ottoman Empire suffers a series of weak rulers
1606 End of frontier war with the Habsburgs
1621 Turkish-Polish conflict over the Dniester
1623 Abbas the Great of Persia captures Baghdad
1638 Murad IV (1623–40) recaptures Baghdad
1645–69 Turkish War for Crete (Candian War)
c.1648 Ottoman Empire invaded by Cossacks and Venetians
1663 Turks invade Hungary, Moravia, Silesia with a large army; a Holy League is formed to oppose them
1664 Battle of St Gothard on Raab. Imperial army defeats Turks
1664 Truce
1669 Turks take Candia (Crete). They invade Poland; 1672 Treaty of Buczacs. Polish Ukraine ceded to Turkey
1683–99 AUSTRO-TURKISH WAR
1683 Turks march on Vienna
1683 Battle of Petronell. Kara Mustafa defeats Charles of Lorraine. Sixty-day siege of Vienna
Battle of Vienna. John Sobieski defeats the Turks. Poland joins the Holy League, which already includes Austria, Venice, Malta and Russia
1686 They take Buda
1686 Venice takes the Morea, Athens and Dalmatia
1687 Battle of Mohacz. Turks defeated decisively and ejected from Hungary, which becomes a Habsburg kingdom
c.1689 Turks retake Nish and Belgrade
1691 Battle of Salankemen. Turks defeated
1697 Battle of Zenta. Turks defeated in war against Poles, the Austrian Empire, Venice and Hungary; and are expelled from Serbia and Bosnia
1699 Treaty of Karlowitz
1703 Janissary revolt
1714–18 Turkish War with Austria and Venice

Middle East

1717 Afghan revolt
1722–3 Russo-Persian War
1726–7, 1730–6 Persian-Turkish Wars
1737–8 Persian invasion of Afghanistan
1743–7 Turkish-Persian War
1768–74 1st Turkish War with Catherine of Russia
1769–73 Egyptian revolt
1774 Rohilla War
1775 Failed Spanish invasion of Algeria
1779–94 Persian Civil War
1795–7 Persian invasion of Georgia
1798 Persian invasion of Afghanistan

India

1738–9 Persian invasion of India
1744–8 1st Carnatic War
1746 Battle of Madras
1748 Battle of Pondicherry
1749–54 2nd Carnatic War
1751 Battle of Arcot

South-East Asia

1704–5 1st Javanese war of Succession
1714–16 Cambodian Civil War and Vietnamese invasion
1717 Siamese invasion of Cambodia
1719–23 2nd Javanese War of Succession
1739–49 Cambodian-Vietnamese war
1740–52 Mon revolt in Burma
1749–57 3rd Javanese war of Succession

Charles XII (1682–1728)
Like Napoleon, Charles XII found nemesis in Russia. A brilliant tactician, he led Sweden to victory in a series of encounters in the first decade of the 18th century. When the Great Northern War began in 1700, a coalition of Denmark, Saxony and Russia attacked Sweden's Baltic and north German possessions. At the age of 19 Charles established his reputation at Narva in 1700, driving the Russians back from Sweden's Baltic provinces. His generals had already forced Denmark out of the war; in a succession of campaigns following Narva, by 1706 Charles thrashed all his opponents. The Swedish–Russian enmity continued however and in 1707 he invaded Russia, winning a battle at Holowczyn, but gradually being drawn deeper into Russia. Eventually at Poltava in 1709 his army, worn down by the long campaign far from home, was confronted by Peter the Great's far superior numbers and destroyed. Charles spent an astonishing five years in Turkey before returning to Sweden incognito through hostile Germany. He at once set about defending the beleaguered Swedish empire, but it was too late. In 1718 he died of a head wound at the siege of Fredrikshald, Sweden's status as a great power dying with him. Brilliant as a tactician, he improved platoon firing and as at Narva made shock his chief weapon. But he was no logistician. He was also headstrong, restless, impulsive and lacking in strategic judgment.

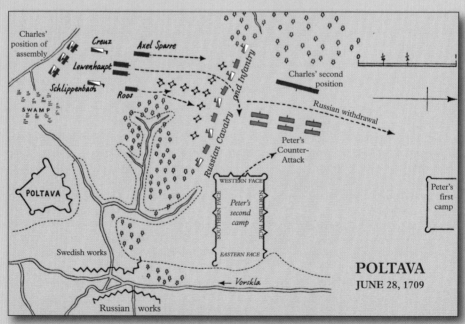

1755–60 Vietnam offensive in Cambodia
1760 Burmese invasion of Siam
1764–7 Burmese invasion of Siam
1765–9 Chinese-Burmese war
1769–73 Siamese-Vietnamese war
1773–1801 Vietnamese Civil War
1775–6 Burmese-Siamese war
1778 Siamese invasion of Laos
1780–2 Siamese invasion of Vietnam
1784–5 Burmese conquest of Arakan
1785–92 Burmese-Siamese war

1655–60 War of the North

1656 Secret Treaty of Marienburg. Brandenburg and Sweden agree partition of Poland
1655–7 Charles X of Sweden's invasion of Poland fails
1657–8 Swedish invasion of Denmark leads to treaty
1658–9 Second Swedish invasion of Denmark. Charles besieges Copenhagen but eventually surrenders to Dutch, Poles, Austrians and Danes. He dies 1660
1660 Treaties of Oliva and Copenhagen

Battle of Poltava

Context Great Northern War

Date June 28, 1709

Location Ukraine 85 miles south-west of Kharkov

Commanders/Forces Peter the Great of Russia commanding 42,000 regular troops and 35,000 irregulars. Charles XII of Sweden commanding 16,000 men

Objectives At the end of lines of communication that were tenuous at best, Charles was besieging Poltava but was forced to turn and fight Peter's approaching army

Casualties Russians 1,300 killed/wounded. Swedes 7,000 killed, 2,600 captured

Victor Russians

Consequences The remainder of the Swedish army surrendered several days later. The battle marked the end of Sweden as a great power and the appearance on the European stage of Russia as a military force

Sweden becomes involved in wars against Louis XIV; Russo-Polish conflict continues to 1667
1675 Battle of Fehrbellin. Elector of Brandenburg defeats Sweden, this marking the beginning of Sweden's military decline. Denmark, Brandenburg and Austria are at war with Sweden

The Wars of Charles XII
1700–21 THE GREAT NORTHERN WAR
1700 Charles forces peace on the Danes
1700 Battle of Narva. Charles defeats Russia, occupies Courland and Riga
1702 Charles invades Poland and enters Warsaw
1702 Battle of Klissow. Charles defeats Augustus of Poland. By 1705 the Swedes have conquered Poland. Meanwhile Peter the Great of Russia conquers Livonia and Estonia
1706 Battle of Fraustadt. Sweden defeats Poles, Russians and Germans
1706 Charles invades Saxony
1707 Sweden signs treaty with Augustus of Poland and the Habsburgs
(April 1707 Marlborough visits Charles at Altranstadt)
1707–9 Charles invades Russia
1708 Battle of Holowczyn
1709 Battle of Poltava. Peter the Great decisively defeats Charles who languishes for five years in Turkey
1710 Turkey joins the war against Russia
1711 Peace of the Pruth
1712 Danes invade Bremen
1712 Battle of Gadebusch. Swedes are victorious but subsequently forced to surrender at Tönning to superior forces. Russia invades Finland. Sweden ceases to be a power in Germany
1709–13 Charles remains at Bender
1713 Charles besieged at Kalibalik and made prisoner
1713 Treaty of Adrianople ends Russo-Turkish war
1714 Charles returns clandestinely to Sweden

Maurice, Comte de Saxe (1696–1750)
Significant for his writings as much as for his deeds, de Saxe fought for the French in the War of the Austrian Succession, taking Tournai in 1745 after defeating the allies (Dutch, British, Austrians) at Fontenoy. This led to the conquest of much of the Spanish Netherlands; in 1746 he took Brussels and two years later Maastricht. His *Mes Rêveries* (1732) was the most important and forward-thinking military treatise of the early 18th century. Maurice stressed the need for officer responsibility, uniform drill and training. Light infantry were to be used in large numbers; and de Saxe also proposed an all-arms formation that was the precursor of the Napoleonic corps d'armeé.

Left: *The Comte de Saxe.*

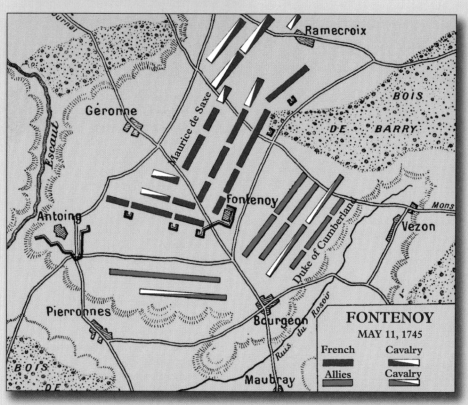

1715 Siege of Stralsund. Charles faces the armies of Russia, Prussia, Poland, Saxony, Hanover and Denmark

1719 Charles invades Norway and is killed at the siege of Frederickshald

1721 Treaty of Nystadt ends the Great Northern war

Britain
1679 SCOTTISH COVENANTER UPRISING
1679 Battle of Dumclog. Scottish Covenanters defeated

1679 Battle of Bothwell Bridge. Covenanter rising suppressed
1685 MONMOUTH REBELLION
1685 Battle of Sedgemoor. Pretender Monmouth defeated and captured
1688–91 WAR OF THE ENGLISH REVOLUTION
1689 Londonderry besieged but not taken by James II

1689 Battle of Killiecrankie. Highlanders ambush government force

1689 Battle of Dunkeld

1690 Battle of The Boyne. William III defeats James II decisively

1691 Battle of Aughrim. Irish rebels dispersed

1692 Battle of Glencoe. Treacherous government attack on the Macdonalds massacres 38

Battle of Fontenoy

Context War of the Austrian Succession

Date May 11, 1745

Location 5 miles east of Tournai, Belgium

Commanders/Forces Duke of Cumberland commanding British army of 53,000 men and 80 guns. Maurice de Saxe commanding a French army of 52,000 and 70 guns

Objectives Cumberland planned to break the French siege of Tournai, seen as the gateway to western Flanders

Casualties British 7,500. French 7,200

Victor French

Consequences The French took Tournai and most of the Austrian Netherlands

1715 JACOBITE REBELLION
1715 Battle of Sheriffmuir. Indecisive

1715 Battle of Preston. Rebels destroyed
1745–6 JACOBITE REBELLION
1745 Prestonpans. Charles Edward Stuart destroys government force then sorties into England

1746 Battle of Falkirk. Murray leads Jacobites to their last victory

1746 Battle of Culloden: Pretender 'Bonnie Prince Charlie' decisively defeated by Duke of Cumberland

Russia
1695–6 Russian conquest of Azov

1698–9 Revolt of the Streltsi in Russia

(See Great Northern War above)

1710–11 Russo-Turkish War

1703–11 Hungarian Revolt

1716–18 AUSTRO-TURKISH WAR
1717 Battle of Belgrade. Prince Eugene of Savoy's Austrian army defeats Turks

1727–9 Spanish War with Britain and France

1735–7 Spanish-Portuguese War

1736–9 Russo-Turkish War

1737–9 Austro-Turkish War

1739–43 Anglo-Spanish War of Captain Jenkins' Ear
1733–9 WAR OF THE POLISH SUCCESSION
This is fought in Poland, on the Rhine, in Northern Italy, Sicily and Naples. Rule of the Kingdom of Naples is transferred from the Habsburgs to the Burbons
1740–8 WAR OF THE AUSTRIAN SUCCESSION
1741 Battle of Mollwitz. Prussians defeat Austrians

1743 Battle of Dettingen. King George II of Britain defeats the French; the last battle to be commanded by a British monarch

1745 Battle of Hohenfriedburg. Frederick the Great of Prussia defeats Austro-Saxons

1745 Battle of Fontenoy. De Saxe's French army defeats Cumberland's Allied army

Frederick II the Great (1712–1786)

One of the Great Captains of History, Frederick was the man who turned Prussia into a major military power. Surviving a terrible early life with a violent, bullying father, Frederick inherited a highly organized military state – a machine he 'perfected' and took to war. In 1740 he seized Silesia and his battles to defend it proclaimed Prussia's new aggressive stance in Germany. During the Seven Years War his greatest battles were at Rossbach and Leuthen in 1757, but by 1759 he was beset by the converging forces of Austria, Russia and Sweden. The fact that Prussia survived is testimony to fast marching, hard fighting and Frederick's own indomitable genius. His influence on the conduct of war was of the greatest significance. His principles of war were fourfold – harsh discipline that reduced the individual soldier virtually to an automaton; great attention to prepared logistics; a stress on the offensive; and what he termed 'practicability' – which encompassed the use of the oblique order and aimed at local superiority on the battlefield. He was also an intellectual, the model of 'enlightened despotism' in the Age of Reason, a patron of Voltaire and an accomplished musician.

Above: *King Frederick the Great of Prussia.*

Right: *An incident at the Battle of Mollwitz in 1741, which secured the province of Silesia for Prussia. This was Frederick's first battle, and he made mistakes, as did his opponents. The battle was actually won by his general, Schwerin.*

1745 Battle of Sohr. Frederick the Great of Prussia defeats Austrians

1747 Battle of Laffeldt. Count Maurice de Saxe of France defeats Allies

1741–3 Russo-Swedish War

1756–63 Seven Years War

1756 Battle of Lobositz. Frederick the Great of Prussia defeats Austrians

1757 Battle of Prague. Frederick the Great of Prussia defeats Austrians

1757 Battle of Kolin. Marshal Leopold von Daun of Austria defeats Frederick the Great's Prussians

1757 Battle of Rossbach. Frederick the Great of Prussia defeats Franco-Austrians

1757 Battle of Leuthen. Frederick the Great of Prussia defeats Austrians

1758 Battle of Zorndorf. Frederick the Great of Prussia defeats Russians

1758 Battle of Hochkirch. Marshal Leopold von Daun of Austria defeats Frederick the Great

1759 Battle of Minden. Duke Ferdinand of Brunswick leads the Allies to defeat the French

1759 Battle of Kunersdorf. Lieutenant-General Gideon von Laudon of Austria

ROSSBACH

NOVEMBER 5, 1757

Franco-Austrians

Prussians

0   2   4ᴷ

Battle of Rossbach

Context Seven Years War

Date November 5, 1757

Location 26 miles south-west of Leipzig, Germany

Commanders/Forces Frederick the Great commanding 21–22,000 Prussians. Prince Charles de Soubise and Prince Joseph of Saxe-Hildburghausen commanding a Franco-Austrian army of 41,000

Objectives The Allied army was one of several major thrusts being propelled at beleaguered Prussia

Casualties Prussians 550 killed. Allies 3,000 killed, 5,000 taken prisoner

Victor Prussians

Consequences This brilliant victory enabled Frederick to meet the other armies invading Prussia. It also renewed the support of his ally, England

Robert, Lord Clive of Plassey (1725–1774)
The founder of the British Empire in India, Clive rose from humble beginnings as a clerk in the East India Company. In 1747 he became an ensign and began an unlikely military-political career. With audacity and much luck he was involved in numerous military expeditions against the Indians and French during the 2nd Carnatic War (1751–3). His defense of Arcot, which won Britain control of the Carnatic, made his reputation. His Bengal campaign of 1757 began as a response to the seizure of Calcutta by Nawab Siraj-ud-Daula and the story of the 'Black Hole' atrocity. Clive led the recapture of the city and defeated the Nawab at Plassey in a battle won by will-power and nerve against enormous odds. The result was British domination of Bengal. The establishment of the British Empire in India was to take many years, but his great victory had laid the foundation and Clive's subsequent role in extending and organising British India was profound.

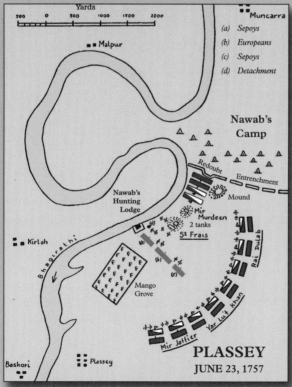

Above left: Statue to Clive in Westminster.

Below: Clive on the roof of the Nawab's hunting lodge, the only building on the battlefield, at Plassey surveying the enemy's position.

and Count Peter Soltikov of Russia defeat the Prussians

1760 Battle of Warburg. Anglo-Prussians under Duke Ferdinand of Brunswick defeat the French

1760 Battle of Liegnitz. Frederick the Great escapes Austro-Russian encirclement

1760 Battle of Torgau. Frederick the Great of Prussia defeats Austrians

SEVEN YEARS WAR IN INDIA

1756 Back Hole of Calcutta

1757 Clive captures Calcutta and wins Battle of Plassey, imposing British control over Bengal

Americas

1754–63 FRENCH AND INDIAN WAR IN NORTH AMERICA (corresponding to The Seven Years War in Europe)

Aug 9, 1757 Fort William Henry

June 3 – July 20, 1758 Louisburg

July 8, 1758 Fort Ticonderoga

Nov 24, 1758 Fort Duquesne

Sept 13, 1759 Wolfe captures Quebec

1763 Pontiac Rebellion

Battle of Plassey

Context Seven Years War

Date June 23, 1757

Location On the banks of the River Baggiruttee, central Bengal

Commanders/Forces Colonel Robert Clive leading about 3,000 British and Indian troops, with 8 cannon and 1 or 2 howitzers. The Nawab Suraj-ud-Daula leading 35–40,000 Bengali infantry, 18,000 mounted Pathans, plus 50 cannon and armored elephants.

Objectives Wanting to remove British influence in Bengal, the Nawab tried to overrun the Anglo-Indian entrenchments

Casualties Light. Anglo-Indian c.22 killed, 50 wounded. Bengalis c.500 killed

Victor British.

Consequences Clive's victory put Bengal firmly in British hands and helped establish the British Empire in India

1768–72 Polish Civil War leads to Russian invasion and the 1st partition of Poland

1768–74 Russo-Turkish War

1776–7 Spanish-Portuguese War

1777–9 War of the Bavarian Succession

1787–91 Austro-Turkish War

1788–90 Swedish War with Russia and Denmark

1792–5 Russo-Prussian invasion and 2nd partition of Poland

India

1766–9 1st Mysore War

1771 Mysore-Maratha War

1779–82 1st Maratha War

1780–3 2nd Mysore War

1789–92 3rd Mysore War

1790 Battle of Calicut

1791 Battle of Bangalore

1792 Battle of Seringapatam

1795–6 British expedition to Ceylon

1799 4th Mysore War

April 6 – May 3, 1799. British general Wellesley captures Seringapatam, ending third conflict with Tipu Sahib

1803–1805 Second Maratha War

Sept 23, 1803 Assaye. Wellesley defeats Marathas in a bloody fight against enormous odds

1817–18 British 3rd Maratha War

Americas

1769–99 Yankee-Pennamite War between settlers in the Wyoming Valley

1775–86 AMERICAN WAR OF INDEPENDENCE

1775 Battle of Lexington. British survive American militia attacks

1775 Battle of Bunker Hill. Gage/Howe of Britain defeat Americans

1775 Battle of Quebec. Carleton of Britain defeats Americans

1776 Battle of Long island. Howe defeats Americans

1776 Battle of White Plains. Howe defeats Americans

1776 Battle of Trenton. George Washington defeats British

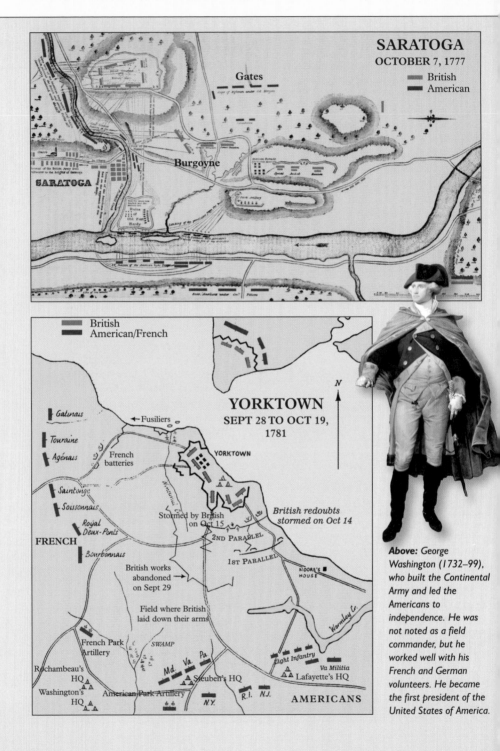

SARATOGA
OCTOBER 7, 1777

British
American

Gates

Burgoyne

SARATOGA

British
American/French

YORKTOWN
SEPT 28 TO OCT 19, 1781

N

Galinais

Touraine

Agénais

French batteries

YORKTOWN

Saintonge

Soissonnais

Royal Deux-Ponts

FRENCH

Stormed by British on Oct 15

British redoubts stormed on Oct 14

2ND PARALLEL

1ST PARALLEL

Bourbonnais

British works abandoned on Sept 29

MOORE'S HOUSE

Field where British laid down their arms

French Park Artillery

SWAMP

Rochambeau's HQ

Md Va Pa

Steuben's HQ

Light Infantry

Va Militia

Lafayette's HQ

Washington's HQ

American Park Artillery

N.Y.

R.I. N.J.

AMERICANS

Above: George Washington (1732–99), who built the Continental Army and led the Americans to independence. He was not noted as a field commander, but he worked well with his French and German volunteers. He became the first president of the United States of America.

Battle of Saratoga

Context American War of Independence

Date October 7, 1777

Location New York State

Commanders/Forces General Horatio Gates commanding 11,000 Americans. General John Burgoyne commanding 6,000 British troops

Objectives Burgoyne attempted to break free from the well-supplied American armies

Casualties British c.1,000 Americans c.150

Victor Americans

Consequences The turning-point of the war. British operations in the north were halted, and American independence began to be recognized internationally

Siege of Yorktown

Context American War of Independence

Date Sept 28 to Oct 19, 1781

Location East Virginia, 12 miles south-east of Williamsburg, overlooking the York River

Commanders/Forces General George Washington with 16,000 Americans, including militia and the French troops of General Jean-Baptiste, Comte de Rochambeau. General Charles, Earl Cornwallis, commanding 7,500 British, German and American Loyalist troops

Objectives Washington had marched through Virginia determined to find and exploit British weak points. Cornwallis intended to fortify a port position where he could be supplied by sea, but the Royal Navy temporarily lost control of the sea to the French

Casualties Light

Victor Americans

Consequences The loss of Yorktown was the *coup de grâce* to British rule in America. No further major military operations took place, and, with mounting costs, the British people lost the will to continue the war

1777 Battle of Princeton. Washington defeats British

1777 Battle of Brandywine. Howe defeats Americans

1777 Battle of Germantown. Howe defeats Americans

1777 Battle of Saratoga – Freeman's Farm and Bemis Heights. Gates of America defeats British; the turning-point of the war

1778 Battle of Monmouth. Clinton of Britain holds off Americans

1781 Battle of Guildford Court House. Cornwallis of Britain defeats Americans

1779–83 Siege of Gibraltar. Eliott of Britain defeats French/Spanish

1779 Battle of Savannah. Prevost of Britain defeats Americans

1780 Battle of Charleston. Clinton defeats Americans

1780 Rodney defeats Spanish at naval Battle of St Vincent

1780 Battle of Waxaws. Tarleton leading British and Loyalists defeats Americans

1780 Battle of Camden. Cornwallis defeats Americans

1789 Battle of King's Mountain. Colonels John Sevier, Isaac Shelby and Richard Campbell defeat British loyalists

1781 Battle of Cowpens. Morgan of America defeats British

1781 Battle of Yorktown. Washington and Jean-Baptiste de Rochambeau of France defeat British. The British surrender. Was the *coup de grâce* to British rule

1781 Battle of Eutaw Springs. Lieutenant-Colonel Alexander Stewart defeats Americans

1792–9 French Revolutionary and Napoleonic Wars
1792–1798 WAR OF THE FIRST COALITION
Sept 20, 1792 Valmy. Indecisive, but Prussians retreat and the French Republic survives

1792 Battle of Jemappes: the first French offensive victory of the war

George Brydges Rodney, 1st Baron Rodney (1719–1792)

One of the Royal Navy's greatest admirals of the 18th century. Rodney was present at Hawke's victory at Ushant in 1747 and fought with distinction during the Seven Years War. During the American Revolutionary War he won the battle of Cape St. Vincent, fought an indecisive battle off Martinique, and captured the island of St. Eustatius. Rodney's greatest victory at the Saintes in 1782 came at a crucial time in Britain's fortunes. It could not reverse the outcome of the American Revolutionary War, but it did avert the French threat to Britain's possessions in the West Indies and won back British control of the seas.

Left: Rodney.

Below: The 'Moonlight Battle' off Cape St Vincent, January 16, 1780, shows the Santo Domingo exploding, with Rodney's flagship Sandwich in the foreground.

Napoleon I (Napoleon Bonaparte)
(1769–1821)

The greatest general of modern times, who lent his name to an age. When the French Revolution broke out he was a lieutenant of artillery in the French Army. He made his mark in 1793 directing the artillery at the siege of Toulon. A general three years later, he began a series of spectacular campaigns: 1796–7 in Italy; 1798–9 in Egypt; 1800 in Italy again, after a daring trans-Alpine march; 1805 in Germany (the lightning Ulm–Austerlitz campaign); 1807 in Germany (the Jena campaign); and the 1807 Eylau–Friedland campaign against Russia. In 1799 a coup d'etat (18th *Brumaire*) brought him to power in France as First Consul; five years later he crowned himself Emperor of the French. 1807 was perhaps the zenith of his career. The Peninsular War, which began in 1808, became a steady drain on French resources and the crowned heads of Europe, always encouraged and often financed by his intransigent British enemies, were never reconciled to his domination of Europe. In 1809 war with Austria was dearly brought to a victorious conclusion at Wagram. In 1812 he began his war to enforce the Tsar's compliance with his anti-British Continental System. The result was an epic invasion of Russia and a catastrophic retreat. From this point Napoleon was essentially always on the defensive against an ever-growing ring of opponents. In 1813 the Battle of Leipzig lost him control of Germany. In 1814, despite a brilliant campaign against impossible odds, Napoleon was brought down and forced to abdicate. A year later he returned dramatically from exile on Elba only to meet his final defeat at Waterloo. Memoirs written during his years of exile on St. Helena helped establish his legend. Beyond that, however, he was a soldier and statesman of towering genius whose impact on the art of war reverberates to this day. Strategically, he emphasized the need to inflict a crushing blow upon an opponent's main army but, rather than being a great innovator, he showed *how* wars should be fought – with speed and decision – and the study of his campaigns and battles resonates with the the intensity of a great mind imposing its will on a volatile and dramatic train of events. Excessive ambition and an inability to recognize the limits of the possible were his undoing. He was murdered, in captivity on the South Atlantic island of St Helena, by the unforgiving Bourbons.

Horatio Nelson, Baron Nelson of the Nile
(1758–1805)

Arguably the greatest admiral in history, Nelson became a popular hero in his lifetime, and the circumstances of his death at the hour of victory at Trafalgar made him a legend. Entering the Royal Navy in 1770, he fought during the American Revolutionary War in the West Indies. In 1797 he played a crucial part at the Battle of Cape St. Vincent. His great victories began in 1798 at the Nile (Aboukir Bay) where he destroyed Bonaparte's Egyptian invasion fleet. At Copenhagen in 1801 he disobeyed his superior's order and won a victory that effectively ended the anti-British League of Armed Neutrality. At Trafalgar in 1805 he destroyed the combined fleets of France and Spain, the long-term results of which were to establish British naval supremacy for a century. During his career he was badly injured twice, in the right eye during operations on Corsica, and losing his right arm at Tenerife in 1797. Laying emphasis especially on individual initiative, his influence on the Royal Navy was profound.

Above: Nelson.

Above right: While ships of the line patrolled and fought the big battles at sea, many single-ship actions were fought across the world's oceans by frigates and smaller warships, protecting British merchantmen from French raiders.

Right: The Battle of Trafalgar.

Aug 27 – Dec 19, 1793 Toulon besieged by French, garrison having been taken over by Royalists with British naval support. Significant for Bonaparte's command of the French artillery

June 26, 1794 Fleurus. Jourdan's French defeat Austrians, leading to French capture of Netherlands

1796–7 Bonaparte's First Italian Campaign

May 10, 1796 Lodi. Bonaparte defeats and outmaneuvers Austrians, leading to capture of Mantua

Nov 15–17, 1796 Arcola. Bonaparte defeats the Austrians

Jan 14, 1797 Rivoli. Bonaparte defeats the Austrians' last attempt to relieve besieged Mantua

June 12, 1798 Battle of Vinegar Hill. Rebellion in Ireland ended

1798–1801 FRENCH EXPEDITION TO EGYPT

July 21, 1798 Pyramids. Bonaparte defeats Mameluke rulers of Egypt

July 25, 1799 The Nile/Aboukir Bay. Nelson destroys Bonaparte's fleet

March–May 1799 Unsuccessful siege of Acre by Bonaparte

March 21, 1801 Alexandria. French garrison of Egypt defeated by British expeditionary force under Abercromby

1798–1800 WAR OF THE SECOND COALITION

June 14, 1800 Marengo. Bonaparte's narrow victory over Austrians after epic trans-Alpine march into Italy

Dec 3, 1800 Hohenlinden. French victory over Austria in Germany

1805–6 WAR OF THE THIRD COALITION

1804 Napoleon crowns himself Emperor of the French

1805 Capitulation of Ulm. Mack, outmaneuvered and surrounded, surrenders an Austrian army to Napoleon

1805 Battle of Trafalgar. Nelson defeats the combined fleets of France and Spain. Britain attains mastery of the seas

The Wars of Napoleon were part continuation of the conflict that had started with the French Revolution, part the ambitions of the French emperor to build an empire and dominate Europe. A series of coalitions opposed him, inspired by the implacable hostility of Britain. At one time or another, almost all the nations of Europe were in arms against the French, and the warfare was continued across the oceans of the world. The peak of Napoleon's career, after a run of glittering triumphs on the battlefield, is generally thought to have come in 1807. Thereafter the long-running Peninsular War (the 'Spanish Ulcer') was a constant drain on French resources, while Britain dominated the seas after Trafalgar. The Moscow campaign of 1812 was the 'step too far' that led inexorably to Napoleon's downfall.

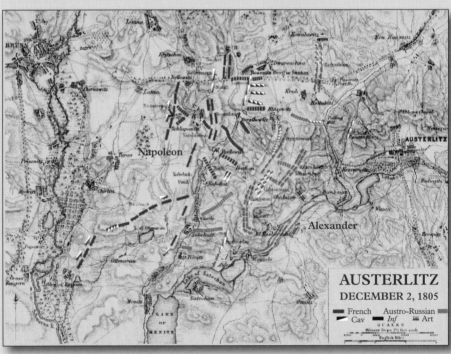

AUSTERLITZ
DECEMBER 2, 1805

French   Austro-Russian
Cav   Inf   Art

SCALES
Military Steps 2½ feet each
English Miles

Left: Panoramic view of the Battle of Austerlitz. Under the eye of the Emperor, the French troops emerge from the foggy valleys on to the Pratzen Heights, cutting the Allied army in two.

Above: Napoleon directing his victory at Wagram, 1809.

Battle of Austerlitz

Context War of the Third Coalition against Napoleon

Date December 2, 1805

Location South-east Czech Republic, 16 km east of Brno

Commanders/Forces Emperor Napoleon of the French commanding 50,000 infantry, 15,000 cavalry and 282 guns. Tsar Alexander of Russia commanding an Austro-Russian army of 70,000 infantry, 16,500 cavalry and 252 guns

Objectives Both sides sought a decisive battle

Casualties French c.10,000 killed/wounded. Allies 16,000 killed/wounded, 20,000 taken prisoner and 186 guns lost

Victor French

Consequences Seen by many as Napoleon's finest battle, Austerlitz eliminated Austria from the ranks of Napoleon's opponents, ended the Third Coalition and led to the establishment of the Confederation of the Rhine. (Battle also known as the Battle of the Three Emperors)

1805 Battle of Austerlitz. Napoleon defeats Austro-Russian army

1806–7 War of the Fourth Coalition

1806 Battles of Jena and Auerstadt. Napoleon defeats Prussia

1807 Battles of Eylau and Friedland. Napoleon defeats Russia

1807 Treaty of Tilsit confirms Napoleon's mastery of north-western Europe

1809 War of the Fifth Coalition

1809 Battles of Aspern–Essling and Wagram. Napoleon defeats Archduke Charles of Austria after initial repulse

1812–14 War of the Sixth Coalition

1812 Napoleon invades Russia to enforce Continental System measures against Britain. Battle of Borodino. Napoleon defeats Russians and occupies Moscow. Tsar will not make peace. Napoleon forced into disastrous retreat made worse by winter. Most of his army wiped out.

1813 Battle of Leipzig – 'Battle of the Nations'. Napoleon is defeated by armies of Austria, Russia, Prussia and Sweden

1814 Campaign of France. Napoleon's brilliant defensive campaign fails to prevent Allies converging on Paris. Napoleon abdicates and is banished to Elba.

1807–14 Peninsular War

July 19, 1808 Baylen. Shocking surrender of 28,000 French to Spanish, which destroys the 'myth' of French invincibility

Aug 21, 1808 Vimiero. British expeditionary force under Wellesley defeats Junot. Scandalous Convention of Cintra by Wellesley's superiors wastes the victory. Next year Napoleon personally leads French army into the peninsula

Jan 16, 1809 Corunna. Moore's reargard action enables evacuation of British expeditionary force by sea

July 27–28, 1809 Talavera. Wellesley defeats French army of Victor

Sept 27, 1809 Busaco. Wellesley (now Wellington) repulses Massena

Winter 1809/10 Wellington builds defensive Lines of Torres Vedras north of Lisbon

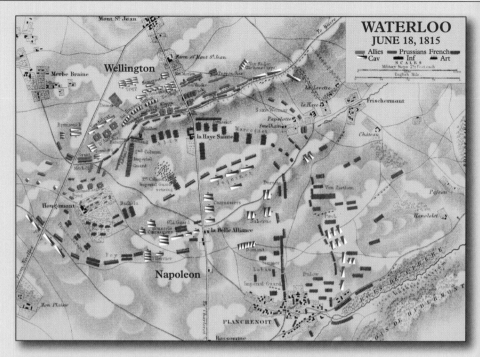

Arthur Wellesley, Duke of Wellington
(1769–1852)

Victor of the Peninsular War, Wellington – the 'Iron Duke' – was rather more than the 'Sepoy General' Napoleon considered him. He made his name in India with victories in the Maratha War at Assaye and Argaon. In 1807 he took part in the Copenhagen expedition, then defeated Junot at Vimiero in Portugal. Returning to Portugal in 1809, he fought a 5-year war to drive the French from the Peninsular. In 1809 he defeated Jourdan at Talavera. Outnumbered by Masséna's army in 1810, he defeated the French at Busaco before falling back behind his fortified Lines of Torres Vedras north of Lisbon. These foiled the French, who were eventually forced to retreat. In a series of victories – Fuentes de Oñoro (1811), Salamanca (1812) and Vitoria (1813), he drove the French over the Pyrenees, inflicting a final defeat at Toulon in 1814. Despite these huge achievements, he is best remembered for the victory at Waterloo (1815) which brought Napoleon's Hundred Days to an end. In the post-war era he was famous throughout Europe. Less successful was his Prime Ministership of Britain in 1828–30 and his lega-cy of opposition to the modernization of the army can be seen to have contributed to the deficiencies made apparent in the British army's performance during the Crimean War. During the Napoleonic Wars however, he proved himself Britain's greatest general since Marlborough. Patience, an eye for terrain and an ability to use British troops in line to destroy attacking French columns were the essentials of his generalship.

Right: Wellington.

Battle of Waterloo

Context Napoleon's 100 Days

Date June 18, 1815

Location 15 miles south of Brussels

Commanders/Forces Emperor Napoleon I commanding French Army of the North (c.72,000 men, 236 guns). Duke of Wellington commanding Allied (Anglo-Netherlands) Army (c.82,000 infantry, 14,500 cavalry, 204 guns), reinforced later in the battle by the Prussian Army (50,000) under Marshal Blücher

Objectives Napoleon aimed to defeat Wellington's army, open the road to Brussels and destroy the coalition that was ranged against him

Casualties French 42,000 killed, wounded, missing; Allied Army 15,000 killed, wounded, missing; Prussians 7,000

Victor Allies.

Consequences The final, decisive defeat of Napoleon I, who abdicated four days later

Above: *The British heavy cavalry charges the French Cuirassiers at Waterloo.*

May 3–5, 1811 Fuentes de Oñoro. Wellington repulses Masséna

May 16, 1811 Albuera

Jan 7–19, 1812 Cuidad Rodrigo besieged and captured by Wellington

March 16 – April 6, 1812 Badajoz besieged and captured by Wellington

July 22, 1812 Salamanca, Wellington defeats Marmont, opening the road to Madrid

June 21, 1813 Vitoria. Wellington defeats King Joseph (Bonaparte) and Marshal Jourdan, ending French control of Spain

April 10, 1814 Toulouse. After crossing the Pyrenees, Wellington defeats Soult, ending the Peninsular War. Napoleon abdicates the following day

1815 THE HUNDRED DAYS

1815 Napoleon returns to France. Battles of Quatre Bras and Ligny against Britain and Prussia are not decisive. Battle of Waterloo. Wellington and Blücher decisively defeat Napoleon, who abdicates again and is banished to St Helena

Anglo–American War, 1812–14 (War of 1812)

The young US navy's heavy figates win a series of single-ship actions including *Constitution* v. *Guerriere, United States* v. *Macedonian, Hornet* v. *Peacock* and *Constitution* v. *Java*, but HMS *Shannon* captures USS *Chesapeake*

Nov 11, 1813 Crysler's Farm. Second US invasion of Canada repulsed

July 5, 1814 Chippewa. US victory on Canadian border

July 25, 1814 Lundy's Lane. US invasion of Ontario repulsed

Aug 24, 1814 Bladensburg. US fail to halt British entering Washington

Jan 8, 1815 New Orleans. Jackson repulses Packenham's British after peace has been agreed between Britain and the USA

Europe

1808 Russo–Finnish War

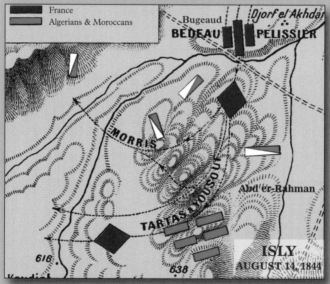

France

Algerians & Moroccans

Bugeaud

Djorf el Akhda

BEDEAU PELISSIER

MORRIS

TARTAS YOUSOU

Abd er-Rahman

610

638

ISLY
AUGUST 14, 1844

Top: *Napoleon III at the Battle of Solferino.*

Above: *Giuseppe Garibaldi (1807–82), guerrilla leader for Italian unification who became a popular hero.*

Battle of Isly River

Context French conquest of Algeria

Date August 14, 1844

Location Eastern Morocco

Commanders/Forces Marshal Bugeaud commanding 8,000 French infantry and cavalry. Algerian leader Abd el-Kader with up to 40,000 Algerians and Moroccans

Objectives French conquest of the interior of

Algeria. The Algerian leader was driven across the border into Morocco, where he was joined by Sultan Abd er-Rahman

Casualties French unknown. Algerians and Moroccans 1,500

Victor French

Consequences France gained complete control of Algeria, Abd el-Kader surrendering three years later

1804–13 Serbian insurrection
1815–17 Serbian insurrection
1806–12 Russo-Turkish War
1820 Neapolitan Revolution
1821 Sardinian Revolution
1821–3 Russo-Persian War
1821–8 Greek War of Independence
1821 Battle of Navarino
1823 French intervention in Spain
1825–8 Russo-Persian War
1828–9 Russo–Persian War
1830 French 'July' Revolution
1830–2 Polish insurrection
1831 Russo-Turkish War
1848 Revolutions and turmoil across Europe including French Revolution and revolts in Austria-Hungary
1848–9 Hungarian War of Independence

ITALIAN WARS OF INDEPENDENCE

June 4, 1859 Battle of Magenta. MacMahon's Franco-Piedmontese army defeats Austrians
June 24, 1859 Battle of Solferino. Napoleon III and Victor Emmanuel II (Franco-Piedmontese) defeat Austrians at a high cost – the carnage leads Napoleon to conclude peace and inspires the founding of the Red Cross

Middle East

1801–5 US-Tripolitanian War
1804–13 Russo-Persian War
1806–12 Russo-Turkish War
1807 Failed British invasion of Egypt
1807 Battle of Rosetta
1811–18 Egyptian war with Wahhabis
1815–16 US-Dutch war with Algiers
1816 Persian invasion of Afghanistan
1820–3 Russo-Persian War
1825–8 Russo-Persian War
1828–9 Russo-Turkish War

FRENCH CONQUEST OF ALGERIA

Aug 14, 1844 Battle of Isly. Using a 'Boar's Head' formation, Bugeaud's French decisively defeat Algerians
1831 Russo-Turkish War
1832–3 1st Turkish-Egyptian war

1836–8 Persian invasion of Afghanistan
1839–42 *FIRST BRITISH-AFGHAN WAR*
Nov 14, 1841 – April 16, 1842 Battle of Jellalabad
1839 Battle of Ghanzi
1839–47 Russian conquest of Khiva
1839–42 2nd Turkish-Egyptian War
1855 Persian invasion of Afghanistan
1856 British-Persian War
1859–60 Spanish-Moroccan War

South–East Asia

1810–11 British expedition to Indonesia
1812 Siamese invasion of Cambodia
1819 Burmese conquest of Assam
1823–6 1st British-Burmese war
1825–30 Great Java war
1826–7 Siamese-Laotian war
1831–4 Siamese invasion of Cambodia
1841–5 Siamese-Vietnamese war
1852–3 2nd British-Burmese war

India

1843 British conquest of Sind
Feb 17, 1843 Battle of Meeanee. Napier of Britain defeats the Amirs of Sind

1845–6 1ST ANGLO-SIKH WAR

Dec 18, 1845 Battle of Mudki. Gough of Britain defeats Sikhs
Dec 21–22, 1845 Battle of Ferozeshah. In the most bitterly contested battle the British fought in India, Gough defeats Sikhs
Jan 28, 1846 Battle of Aliwal. Smith destroys Sikh army
Feb 10, 1846 Battle of Sobraon. Gough defeats Sikhs

1848–9 2ND ANGLO-SIKH WAR

Jan 13, 1849 Battle of Chilianwallah. Sikhs hold off British
Feb 21, 1849 Battle of Gujerat. Gough defeats Skikhs/Afghans and Britain annexes the Punjab

Africa

1806 British take Cape Town
1806–7 Ashanti conquest of the Gold Coast

Simon Bolivar (1783–1830) 'The Liberator'
Revolutionary hero of the Latin-American Wars
of Independence. From a wealthy Creole family
in Venezuela, he was much influenced by the
Napoleonic idea of destiny and the ethos of the
French Revolution. In 1805 he vowed to liberate
his homeland. He participated in Miranda's ill-
fated first attempt, then became leader of the
movement. The early years were unsuccessful,
but in 1816 he began a two-year campaign that
established the independence of Venezuela. He
then entered Colombia and Ecuador to organize
the new nation of Gran Colombia. Two years
fighting in Peru and Bolivia followed, the
Spanish surrendering to his chief of staff, Sucre
in 1824. The work for which he is remembered
was now complete. There followed political and
constitutional wrangles, fueled by his own
authoritarian republicanism, which presaged the
civil wars that have bedevilled South America.

Top left: *The US-Mexican War – action during the
capture of Monterey by the American troops of
General Zachary Taylor in 1846, which facilitated
the further advance of the American forces south
into Mexico.*

Far left: *Churubusco, fought on the same day as
Contreras, August 20, 1847, was part of the
American battles to close up on Mexico City.*

Near left: *General Winfield Scott (1786–1866),
victor of Contreras/Churubusco, where his superior
use of artillery and flanking attacks kept US losses
to one tenth those of the Mexican defenders. An
American hero, despite disagreements and political
disputes, he remained loyal to the Federal cause
during the Civil War, despite being a Virginian, and
set out the 'Anaconda Plan' to divide and blockade
the South.*

1807 British occupy Alexandria
1807 British take St Louis (Senegal) from
  French
1818–19 Zulu Civil War
1820–39 Egypt conquers Sudan
1824–31 1st British-Ashanti war
1830–48 French conquest of Algeria
1832–3 Turkish-Egyptian war
1838 Boer-Zulu Battle of Blood River
1839–41 Turkish-Egyptian war
1856 Zulu Civil War
1858–68 Cape Wars
1859–60 Spanish-Moroccan war
1862–4 Transvaal-Orange Free State War

Americas
1806–7 British unofficial expeditions to
  Buenos Aires and Montevideo fail
1810–14 Chilean rebellion
1811 US Indian War
1811–25 Latin-American Wars of
  Independence
1818 US 1st Seminole War
1818 US invades Florida
1823 US Monroe doctrine forbids European
  involvement in American political affairs
1835–6 Texan War of Independence
1836 Siege of the Alamo and Battle of San
  Jacinto
1825–8 Brazil-Argentine War
Mackenzie's Rebellion in Canada
1827–9 Peruvian War
1829 Spanish involvement in Mexico
1832 US Black Hawk Indian War
1835–43 US 2nd Seminole Indian War
1836–9 Peruvian-Bolivian War
1838–9 French expedition to Mexico
1841 Peruvian invasion of Bolivia
1843–52 Argentine-Uruguayan War

1846–8 US-Mexican War
Sept 10–24, 1846 Battle of Monterey. Taylor
  defeats Mexicans and captures the city
Feb 22–23, 1847 Battle of Buena Vista.
  Taylor defeats Mexicans
Sept 8, 1847 Battle of Molino del Rey. Scott
  defeats Mexicans

Left: *The charge of the Heavy Brigade at the Battle of Balaclava, October 25, 1854. This was a most successful action, in marked contrast to the more famous charge of the Light Brigade: Scarlett's cavalry put some 2,000 Russians to flight at a cost of 78 British casualties.*

Left: *The second charge of the Guards at the Battle of Inkerman, when they retook the two-gun battery. The third significant battle of the Crimean War, Inkerman was fought in heavy fog, as the Allies drove off the Russians' determined effort to break the siege of Sevastopol.*

Sept 13, 1847 Battle of Chapultepec. Scott captures the fortress and advances to Mexico City defeating Santa Anna at Contreras/Churubusco
1849–51 Lopez's invasion of Cuba
1850–98 Series of US-Indian Wars
1856 US Kansas Civil War
1857–60 Mexican Civil War
1860–1 Colombian Civil War
1861–2 Spanish expedition to Mexico
1861–7 FRENCH EXPEDITION TO MEXICO
May 5, 1862 Battle of La Puebla: French are defeated, but subsequently capture Mexico City and install Maximilian I as Emperor
1867 Maximilian is defeated and executed by Juérez, who restores the Republic

China, Japan, Korea
1839–42 1st British-Chinese 'Opium War'
1850–64 China: Taiping rebellion; this civil war, one of the bloodiest conflicts in history, is thought to have resulted in the deaths of 20–30 million people
1856–60 2nd British–Chinese 'Opium War'
Aug 21, 1860 Battle of Taku Forts. Anglo-French forces, including Indians, under Grant and Cousin-Montauban storm forts and advance towards Beijing
1863–4 European bombardments of Kagoshima and Shimonoseki
1863–8 Civil War in Japan

1853–5 Crimean War
Sept 20, 1854 Battle of the Alma. British/French/Turkish Allies defeat Russians and advance to besiege Sevastopol
1854–5 Siege of Sevastopol
Oct 25, 1854 Battle of Balaclava. Raglan of Britain defeats Russians. Heroic failure of the Charge of the Light Brigade along the 'Valley of Death'
Nov 5, 1854 Battle of Inkerman. Raglan's British and French troops repulse Russians
Sept 28, 1854 – Sept 8, 1855 Fall of Sevastopol. Raglan of Britain and

The greatest of wars between the Napoleonic period and the First World War, the American Civil War caused some 600,000 deaths. The opposing sides were unevenly matched: the mainly urban, industrialized North (Union) with a population of 23 millions versus the largely agrarian, plantation-dominated South (Confederacy), with but 9 millions. The war was fought on two fronts. In the east, between the two capitals the Army of Northern Virginia, under the inspirational leadership of Robert E. Lee, proved more than a match for a series of Union generals. In the west, the capture of Vicksburg enabled the Union to split the South, leading to Sherman's 'March to the Sea' through the heart of the exhausted Confederacy.

Left: 'Stonewall' Jackson.

Below: Robert E. Lee.

Above: *The Battle of Cross Keys, June 8, 1862, as seen from the Union position. This was the penultimate action in Jackson's brilliant Shenandoah Valley Campaign.*

Thomas 'Stonewall' Jackson (1824–1863)

The ablest of Lee's generals, Jackson's sobriquet stems from his stolid defense at the first battle of the American Civil War, First Bull Run (1861). His partnership with Robert E. Lee in the Army of Northern Virginia was all but unbeatable, and he played vital roles at Second Bull Run (1862), Antietam (1862), Fredericksburg (1862) and Chancellorsville (1863). His masterpiece Shenandoah Valley campaign of summer 1862 remains a of model of the art of war. Jackson was killed accidentally by his own men during the Battle of Chancellorsville.

Robert E. Lee (1807–1870)

Legendary commander-in-chief of the Confederate Army during the American Civil War, Lee was possibly the greatest soldier since Napoleon. He served in the Mexican War and suppressed John Brown's insurrection at Harper's Ferry in 1859. Appointed C-in-C of Virginia's army on the outbreak of the Civil War, he attained field command in March 1862, organising the famed Army of Northern Virginia, which he led to a string of victories, including The Seven Days Battles (1862), Second Bull Run (1862), Fredericksburg (1862) and Chancellorsville (1863). His invasions of the North met with failure at Antietam (1862) and Gettysburg (1863), and his later campaigns defending Petersburg and Richmond were fought against impossible odds. He was much loved by his men and remains an enduring symbol of the South.

Below: The northern sector of the Antietam battlefield, looking toward Roulette Farm. Union troops are advancing from the right.

Canrobert of France eventually force Russians to abandon the fortress

Australasia

1804, 1806, 1808 Mutinies in Australia

1843–8 New Zealand: 1st Maori war

1860–79 New Zealand: 2nd Maori war

1861–5 American Civil War

April 12–14, 1861 Fort Sumter: bombardment and capture of the fort by Beauregard's Confederates makes war between North and South inevitable

July 21, 1861 First Battle of Bull Run. The first major battle of the war and the first use of rail transport for troops. Johnston's and Beauregard's Confederates fail to exploit victory. Confederate General Jackson's stubborn defense earns him the nickname 'Stonewall'

Feb 6–16, 1862 Battle of Fort Donelson. Grant wins first significant Federal victory

April 6–7, 1862 Battle of Shiloh (Pittsburg Landing). Grant eventually defeats Confederates and gives Federals strategic initiative in the west

May 31 – June 1, 1862 Battle of Seven Pines (Fair Oaks)

June 9, 1862 Battle of Port Republic. Jackson defeats Union and joins Lee's army

June 25 – July 1, 1862 Seven Days Battles. Lee forces Confederate retreat

Aug 9, 1862 Battle of Cedar Mountain. Inconclusive, but allows Confederates to advance north

Aug 28–30, 1862 Second Battle of Bull Run. Lee defeats Union army

Sept 13–15, 1862 Battle of Harper's Ferry. Jackson defeats Union garrison

Sept 17, 1862 Battle of Antietam (Sharpsburg). Politically and strategically crucial for the Union. Although Lee of the Confederacy wins a tactical victory, his losses force him to abandon his invasion of the north

Oct 3–4, 1862 Battle of Corinth. Rosecrans of the Union repulses Confederates

Left: Confederate infantry in action. Cobb's and Kershaw's troops behind the stone-wall at Fredericksburg, 1862.

Below left: Vicious hand-to-hand fighting characterized 'Bloody Angle' on the heavily wooded battlefield of Spotsylvania in 1864, the second encounter between Lee and Grant after the Wilderness battle.

Above right: April 16, 1863, Porter's flotilla arriving below Vicksburg, where they successfully passed by the Confederate batteries. The capture of Vicksburg by the North effectively split the Confederacy in two.

Right: Hooker's Federal troops attack up the rugged slopes of Lookout Mountain at the Battle of Chattanooga in 1863, Grant's last victory before being appointed General-in-Chief of the Union Army.

Above: Three of the commanders of the Union's Army of the Potomac, left to right: Ambrose Everett Burnside, defeated at Fredericksburg; Joseph Hooker defeated at Chancellorsville; and George Gordon Meade, victor at Gettysburg. *Right:* William Tecumseh Sherman, friend and lieutenant of Grant, whose 'March to the Sea' in November–December 1864 was the southern 'pincer' of the final Union strategy, complementing Grant's advance to the Confederate capital, Richmond.

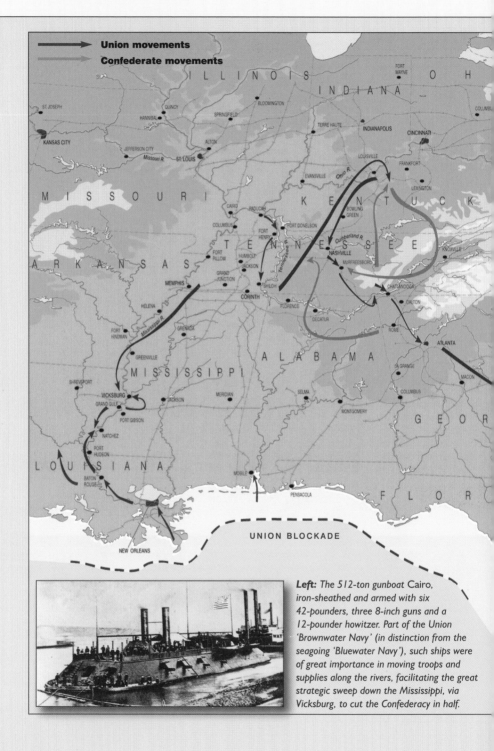

Left: The 512-ton gunboat Cairo, iron-sheathed and armed with six 42-pounders, three 8-inch guns and a 12-pounder howitzer. Part of the Union 'Brownwater Navy' (in distinction from the seagoing 'Bluewater Navy'), such ships were of great importance in moving troops and supplies along the rivers, facilitating the great strategic sweep down the Mississippi, via Vicksburg, to cut the Confederacy in half.

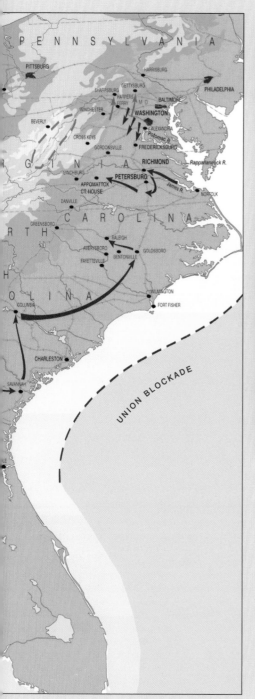

Ulysses S. Grant (1822–1885)

The North's greatest general during the American Civil War. Grant fought in the Mexican War, and served in the western theater of operations, capturing Fort Donelson 1862. He won at Shiloh (1862) and after a lengthy campaign captured Vicksburg in 1863. In March 1864 he was given command of all the Union armies and devised the North's winning strategy. The decisive thrusts were made in the west, while Grant pressed Lee back on Petersburg and Richmond, conditions of combat eventually becoming almost static, a foretaste of World War I. He receiving the Confederate general's surrender at Appomattox Court House on 9 April 1865. Grant went on to serve two terms as the 18th President of the USA from 1869 to 1877.

GETTYSBURG

JULY 1–3, 1863

Battle of Gettysburg

Context American Civil War

Date July 1–3, 1863

Location junction town in southern Pennsylvania

Commanders/Forces George Meade commanding the Union Army of the Potomac (*c*.95,000). Robert E. Lee commanding the Confederate Army of Northern Virginia (c.75,000)

Objectives Taking the war north, Lee aimed to inflict a decisive defeat on the Army of the Potomac, which was trying to intercept him

Casualties Union c. 3,000 killed, c.15,000 wounded, c.5,000 missing. Confederates c.4,000 killed, c.19,000 wounded, c.5,000 missing

Victor Union

Consequences Lee was halted with unsustainable casualties. The climax of the battle, Pickett's charge, has been called 'the high tide of the Confederacy'; from now on the South would be entirely on the defensive, making this, with the fall of Vicksburg the following day, the turning-point in the war

Above: A Union artillery battery at Gettysburg, the battle that ended Lee's second invasion of the North.

Left: The Battle of Gettysburg as depicted in a contemporary print.

Oct 8, 1862 Battle of Perryville.

Dec 13, 1862 Battle of Fredericksburg. Lee defeats Union

Dec 31 1862 – Jan 2, 1863 Battle of Stones River (Murfreesboro).

May 1–5, 1863 Battle of Chancellorsville. Lee defeats Union and prepares the second invasion of the North

May 19 – July 4, 1863 Battle of Vicksburg. Grant takes the fortress and splits the Confederacy in two in a crucial action

June 9, 1863 Battle of Brandy Station. Lee defeats Union but not decisively

July 1–3, 1863 Battle of Gettysburg. Meade of the Union defeats Lee's invasion force, inflicting unsustainable casualties

Sept 18–20, 1863 Battle of Chickamauga. Bragg wins tactical victory over Union

Nov 24–25, 1863 Battle of Chattanooga. Union breaks Confederate siege

May 5–6, 1864 Battle of the Wilderness. Grant of the Union holds off the Confederates and advances toward Richmond

May 8–18, 1864 Battle of Spotsylvania Court House. Grant defeats Confederates

May 31 – June 3, 1864 Battle of Cold Harbor. Lee repulses Federal attack

June 15–18, 1864 Battle of Petersburg. Confederates prevent capture of city

July 20 – Aug 31, 1864 Battle of Atlanta. Sherman captures the city

Dec 9–21, 1864 Battle of Savannah. Sherman of the Union takes the city

Dec 15–16, 1864 Battle of Nashville. Thomas conclusively defeats Confederates

April 1, 1865 Battle of Five Forks. Grant's Union cavalry under Sheridan defeat Confederates and force Lee to retreat

April 9, 1865 Battle of Appomattox Court House. Grant traps Confederates. Lee surrenders, effectively ending the war

American Indian Wars

Dec 21, 1866 Fetterman Massacre. Sioux led by Red Cloud and Crazy Horse kill

Above: *The charge of the Prussian 1st Guard Dragoon Regiment at Mars-la-Tour/Vionville, August 16, 1870.*
Below: *After the fall of Paris, on March 1, 1871, the German army marches in – a scene with an eery foretaste of 1940.*

Helmuth von Moltke (1800–1891)

Architect of Prussian victories against Denmark (1864), Austria (1866) and France (1870-1). After serving on the Prussian military mission to Turkey in 1832–9, he became Chief of the Prussian General Staff in 1858. He was the first soldier to recognize the importance of railways in the deployment of troops and munitions, and reorganized the Prussian army and its General Staff, making it a model for all other Western armies. His greatness lies not in being a field commander but rather the virtual creator of the military machine that united Germany and fought the First World War.

wagon train escort on the Powder River
June 25–26, 1876 Battle of Little Big Horn. Sitting Bull and Crazy Horse defeat US 7th Cavalry, killing Colonel Custer

Europe
1863–4 Polish insurrection
1864 Schleswig-Holstein War. The first phase of Bismarck's campaign to unify Germany, which results in 1870 in the formation of the German Empire
1866 AUSTRO-PRUSSIAN (SEVEN WEEKS) WAR
June 24, 1866 Second Battle of Custozza. Archduke Albert defeats Italians, allied with Prussia
July 3, 1866 Battle of Königgrätz (Sadowa): Prussia defeats Austrians and gives Prussia dominance in Central Europe
1866 Austro-Italian War

1870–1 Franco-Prussian War
Aug 6, 1870 Battle of Worth. Crown Prince Friedrich Wilhelm (Prussia) defeats French
Aug 16, 1870 Battle of Mars-la-Tour.
Aug 18, 1870 Battle of Gravelotte-St Privat. Von Moltke of Prussia eventually forces French to withdraw
Sept 1, 1870 Battle of Sedan: von Moltke of Prussia captures the town. Napoleon III of France goes into captivity and the Third Republic replaces the Second French Empire.
Sept 20, 1870 – Jan 28, 1871 Siege of Paris. Von Moltke starves the city into capitulation and ends the Franco–Prussian War

1873–6 Spanish Carlist War

Middle East
1878–80 2ND BRITISH-AFGHAN WAR
July 27, 1880 Battle of Maiwand. Ayub Khan destroys British brigade. Survivors retreat to Kandahar
Sept 1, 1880 Battle of Kandahar. Roberts relieves besieged British garrison and defeats Ayub Khan, replacing him on the throne with Abdur Rahman Khan

South-East Asia
1858–61 French conquest of Indo–China
1882–3 French-Vietnamese war
1873–7 Siamese-Laotian war
1873–95 continuing French expansion in Indo-China
1885 3rd British-Burmese war

India
1857–8 INDIAN MUTINY AGAINST BRITISH RULE
June 8 – Sept 20, 1857 Battle of Delhi. Wilson's British/Indian troops recapture the city
July 1 – Nov 19, 1857 Battle of Lucknow. British/Indians break rebel siege of garrison
Dec 6, 1857 Battle of Cawnpore. At a turning-point for the mutiny, Campbell routs the rebels
June 17–20, 1858 Battle of Gwalior. Rose defeats Indian rebels in last major battle of the mutiny
NORTH-WEST FRONTIER OF INDIA CAMPAIGNS
1897 Tirah
Oct 20, 1897 Battle of Dargai. Lockhart of Britain defeats Afridis and Orakzais
1888–98 Further British North-West India frontier campaigns and expeditions

China, Japan, Korea
1866 French expedition to Korea
1875–6 Japanese expedition to Korea
1877 Satsuma rebellion in Japan
1882–5 Chinese and Japanese expeditions to Korea
1883–1885 FRANCO–CHINESE WAR
Dec 14–16, 1883 Battle of Son-Tai. French capture Chinese–occupied fort
1894–5 Sino-Japanese War
1900 Boxer rebellion in China
June 20 – Aug 14, 1900 Battle for Beijing. International relief force breaks siege of Foreign Legations

Balkans
1877–8 RUSSO-TURKISH WAR
July 19 – Dec 10, 1877 Battle of Plevna.

Sir Garnet, later Lord, Wolseley (1833–1913)
The greatest of Britain's generals during the colonial wars of the nineteenth century. He fought in the Second Burma War, in the Crimea and the Indian Mutiny, where he lost the sight of an eye. In 1870 he led the Red River expedition in Canada; in 1873 the Ashanti campaign; in 1875 the campaign in Natal; and he took command in the later stages of the Anglo-Zulu War of 1879. In 1882 he led the conquest of Egypt, winning the Battle of Tel-el-Kebir, and two years later led the abortive Gordon rescue mission to Khartoum. His reforms of the British Army were significant in preparing it for the larger-scale operations of the Second Boer War and World War I.

Above: Sir Garnet Wolseley.

Above left: Led by the Highland Brigade, the British overrun Egyptian nationalists at Tel-el-Kebir in 1882, which gave Britain control of Egypt.

Left: British artillery charge over the parapet of the Egyptian lines at Tel-el-Kebir.

Shaka kaSenzagakhona (c.1787–1828)

Founder of the Zulu empire of the nineteenth century. In 1816 he usurped the chieftaincy of the Zulus and embarked upon wars of conquest with an army that he designed to be the most efficient fighting machine in Africa. Regiments were age-graded (*amabutho*) and made up of conscripts under forty years of age. Drill, discipline and mobility were the hallmarks of Shaka's military system, together with surprise tactics. A favorite stratagem involved encirclement by the *impondo zankomo* ('horns of the beast') attack formation. His conquests over a decade included most of Natal and modern Zululand. Among his principal battles were KwaGqoki (1816), where he survived attack by a superior force of Ndwande; Mhlatuze, when he inflicted the final defeat on the Ndwande, eliminating the last major rival to Zulu supremacy in southern Africa; and inDolowane, in 1826, when he brought an end to the Ndwande kingdom. He was assassinated by his half-brothers in 1828. His legacy was a powerful and proud military nation, which was to make its mark in history in the epic battles of 1879.

Krudener of Russia eventually defeats Turks

Nov 17–18, 1877 Battle of Kars. Melikoff takes the fortress for Russia in a surprise night attack

1885–6 Serbo-Bulgarian War

1896–7 Greco-Turkish War

Africa
1867–1868 ANGLO-ABYSSINIAN WAR

April 31, 1868 Battle of Aroghee. Napier's British/Indian troops, using breech-loading rifles for the first time, defeat Abyssinians

1868–72 Abyssinian Civil War

1873–4 2nd British-Ashanti war

1873–9 Egypt-Abyssinian war

1879 ANGLO-ZULU WAR

Jan 22, 1879 Battle of Isandhlwana. Ntshingwayo and Mavumengwana overrun British camp but suffer heavy casualties

Jan 22–23, 1879 Battle of Rorke's Drift. Lieutenant Chard leads a small band of British defenders in beating off repeated attacks and is relieved by Chelmsford the next day

March 29, 1879 Battle of Kambula. Wood (Britain) repulses Zulu attack

July 4, 1879 Battle of Ulundi. Chelmsford destroys a much larger Zulu army

1880–1 1ST ANGLO-BOER WAR

Jan 28, 1881 Battle of Laing's Nek. Joubert's Boers defeat British infantry

Feb 27, 1881 Battle of Majuba Hill. Joubert's Boer commandos defeat British, leading to armistice

1881 French occupy Tunis

1882 BRITISH-EGYPTIAN WAR

July 11, 1882 Bombardment of Alexandria

Sept 13, 1882 Battle of Tel-el-Kebir. Wolseley defeats Egyptians and imposes British control over Egypt

1883–4 Zulu Civil War

1883–9 Mahdist uprising and war with Abyssinia

1ST BRITISH SUDAN CAMPAIGN

Feb 29, 1884 Second Battle of El Teb. Graham defeats Mahdist army

Left: Dervish riflemen fire upon the British paddle-wheel gunboat Fateh, which was commanded by Lieitenant David Beatty, later to lead the British battlesruisers at the Battle of Jutland. Ten such gunboats were built for 'the river war' on the Nile, each armor-plated and armed with a mixture of quick-firing artillery including Maxim guns, Nordenfeldts, 6-pounders and 12-pounders.

Below: A panorama of the Battle of Omdurman as depicted in the pages of the Illustrated London News at the time. The gunboats supported the infantry ashore as they fought off the mass attack by the Madhist army.

Above: *General Sir Herbert Kitchener led the Anglo-Egyptian forces that re-possessed the Sudan in 1898, and was later C-in-C British forces in South Africa and India. At the conclusion of the Omdurman campaign he proceeded up the Nile to confront the French expedition of Marchand at Fashoda on the Nile. This tense meeting resulted in an Anglo-French agreement on spheres of influence in Africa.*

March 12, 1884 – Jan 26, 1885 Siege of Khartoum and death of General Gordon. Mahdi Mohammed Ahmed's rebels take the town, kill the garrison, and force most Anglo-Egyptian forces to withdraw from the Sudan

March 13, 1884 Battle of Tamai. Graham defeats Mahdists but fails to destroy their army

Jan 17, 1885 Battle of Abu Klea. British column marching to the relief of Khartoum beats off dervish attack

Jan 19, 1885 Battle of Abu Kru. British flying column defeats renewed dervish attacks

1888–90 German East Africa uprising

Dec 21, 1893 Battle of Agordat. Arimondi leads Italian defeat of Mahdists

1893 Spanish Riff war in Morocco

1893 Mashona-Matabele war

1893–4 3rd British-Ashanti war

1895–6 4th British-Ashanti war

1895–6 French conquer Madagascar

1895–6 Italian-Abyssinian war

1895–1896 ITALO-ABYSSINIAN WAR

March 1, 1896 Battle of Adowa. Emperor Menelek of Abyssinia wins independence by defeating Italian forces. At that time the biggest victory of irregulars over regular, well-equipped colonial troops

1896–8 ANGLO-EGYPTIAN RECONQUEST OF SUDAN

April 8, 1898 Battle of Atbara River. Kitchener leads Anglo-Egyptian destruction of Mahdist army, and continues to advance towards Mahdist capital, Omdurman

Sept 2, 1898 Battle of Omdurman. Kitchener's Anglo-Egyptian forces destroy Dervish army and end Mahdist rebellion

1897 British conquer Nigeria

1897–1901 Uganda uprising

Americas

1863 Colombia-Ecuador War

1864–6 Spanish war with Peru then Chile

1864–70 Lopez's war

1869–70 Canada: 1st Riel rebellion

Above: The US battleship Maine enters Havana Harbor in Cuba, where she blew up on the night of February 15, 1898. This was a precipitating cause of the war, but the precise cause of the explosion that caused the ship's demise remains a mystery.

Right: Colonel Theodore Roosevelt (later to become 26th President of the USA) and his Rough Riders atop the hill they captured at the Battle of San Juan.

Below: Oregon Volunteer Infantry firing by volley.

Below right: The Battle of Manila Bay.

1876–7 US Sioux and North Cheyenne War
1876 Battle of the Little Big Horn
1885 Canada: 2nd Riel rebellion
1890–1 US South Dakota war
1895–8 Cuban revolution

1898 SPANISH-AMERICAN WAR

Feb 15, 1898 Destruction of USS *Maine* in Havana (suspected to be by a mine) is catalyst to outbreak of war
May 1, 1898 Dewey leads US fleet into Manila Bay in the Philippines and destroys the Spanish fleet
June 1898 US troops invade Cuba
July 1, 1898 Battle of San Juan Hill. Americans under Shafter capture hill positions near Santiago de Cuba
July 3, 1898 Battle of Santiago de Cuba: Spanish Caribbean Squadron destroyed
Aug 13, 1898 US takes manila
Meanwhile US occupies Wake Island and Puerto Rico

1901 Colombian Civil War
1903 Panamanian revolution

1906–9 US intervention in Cuba
1907 Nicaraguan-Honduran war
1909–11 Honduran Civil War
1910–17 Mexican revolution
1912 Nicaraguan Civil War
1912 US intervention in Cuba

Pacific
1879–83 War of the Pacific
1899–1902 Philippine uprising

1899–1902 Second Anglo-Boer war
Oct 13, 1899 – May 17, 1900 Mafeking: Baden-Powell defies Boer siege
Oct 15, 1899 – 15 Feb 1900 Battle of Kimberley. British break Boer siege
Nov 2, 1899 – Feb 28, 1900 Siege of Ladysmith
Nov 28, 1899 Battle of Modder River. British forces encounter the Boers employing new, non-linear tactics
Dec 10, 1899 Battle of Stormberg. Olivier defeats British
Dec 10–11, 1899 Battle of Magersfontein. Cronje/De La Rey defeat British

The Boer offensives at the outset of the war resulted in the sieges of Ladysmith, Kimberley and Mafeking, and a number of subsequent battles were fought by the British to relieve these places.

Top left: British troops in action at the Battle of Farquhar's Farm, October 20, 1899, at which Joubert's Boer army repulsed Sir George White's British army, which fell back to become besieged in Ladysmith.

Below left: Boer troops, armed with the latest Mauser rifles, with which they consistently outshot the British.

Left: 'Charge!' A romantic illustration of British cavalry by Caton Woodville.

Top: Robert Baden-Powell (1857–1941), famed defender of Mafeking and later founder of the Boy Scout and Girl Guide movements.

Above right: Field Marshal Lord Roberts, VC, (1832–1914) was appointed to command British forces in South Africa, relieving Kimberley and advancing to Pretoria. 'Bobs' was a much-loved figure, having fought in the Indian Mutiny and distinguished himself in the 2nd Afghan war.

The Russo-Japanese War, the first great conflict of the twentieth century, demonstrated the new face of industrialized warfare and marked the emergence of Japan as a major world power – Yalu River was the first battle at which an Asiatic army defeated a European army using Western tactics and armament. The big battles, Yalu River, Liaoyang, Shaho River and Mukden were fought on long fronts (47 miles at Mukden) and became battles of attrition and exhaustion – a foretaste of World War I. At sea, the torpedo and mine made their first impact, and the Japanese succeeded in blockading the Russian ships in Port Arthur and Vladivostok, defeating their attempt to break out at the Battle of the Yellow Sea. The extraordinary voyage of the Russian Baltic Squadron ended at Tsushima, then the greatest sea battle since Trafalgar.

Above left: Russian artillery in action at the Battle of Liaoyang in 1904. This, the first major land battle of the war, was fought to a stalemate, although the Russians withdrew.

Left: The harbor at Port Arthur, besieged by the Japanese from May 1904 until its surrender on January 2, 1905, by which time Japanese artillery had sunk a number of the Russian warships at anchor.

Above: Admiral Haihachino Togo, victor of the Battles of the Yellow Sea and Tsushima, aboard his flagship, Mikasa.

Dec 15, 1899 Battle of Colenso. Botha defeats British

Jan 19–24, 1900 Battle of Spion Kop. Botha repulses British

Feb 18–27, 1900 Battle of Paardeberg. Roberts defeats Boers

1900 British reinforcements in great numbers give them unbeatable superiority; Boers resort to guerrilla warfare, eventually being worn down by starving the commandos into submission

1904 South-West African Hottentot uprising

1907 South Africa Zulu uprising

1904–5 Russo-Japanese War

Feb 8, 1904 Japanese torpedo-boat attack on Russian fleet at Port Arthur

Aug 10, 1904 Battle of the Yellow Sea: Japanese foil breakout of Russian fleet from Port Arthur

April 30 – May 1, 1904 Battle of the Yalu River. Oyama defeats the Russians and leads Japanese invasion of Manchuria

May 5, 1904 Japanese land and advance to the siege of Port Arthur

Aug 25 – Sept 3, 1904 Battle of Liaoyang. Both sides seek a major victory, but Oyama forces Russians to retreat

Oct 5–17, 1904 Battle of the Shaho River. An indecisive battle along a 40-mile front

Feb 21 – March 10, 1905 Battle of Mukden. Coming to the end of his manpower resources, Oyama attempts to crush the Russians but succeeds only in forcing a withdrawal.

May 27, 1905 Battle of Tsushima. The Russian Baltic Fleet, after an epic journey, is annihilated. Peace discussions ensue, Russia eventually evacuating Manchuria and Japan emerging as a major world power

1911 Chinese Civil War

Wars of Turkish Dissolution

1911–12 Italian war with Turkey. Italy annexes Libya, Tripolitania, Cyrenaica and occupies the Dodecanese

The first of the two cataclysmic conflicts of the twentieth century, World War I took the lives of nearly eight million combatants, plus those of unknown numbers of civilians. It was the first truly 'modern' war, fought with a terrible new arsenal of weapons that revolutionized warfare. Firearms, including machine-guns and artillery, dominated the land battlefield, above which air-craft were beginning to play a role that later in the century would become decisive. Poison gas added to the horror of stalemate battlefronts, where the living conditions of the troops became hellish. At sea the battleship was nearing the peak of development, but new threats from above and below the sea were already hastening its obsolescence – aircraft, submarines and mines.

Left: A typical British tank of World War I, a Mark IV machine-gun armed Female, seen in 1917 tackling a slope. The Male version was armed with a 6pdr gun in each of two sponsons. Even though slow and vulnerable, these tanks led the way in breaking the stalemate of trench warfare.

Right: A French soldier (poilu) of 1916.

Below: French Renault FT-17 two-man tank, the first operational tank to feature a rotating turret.

Left: Maxim Gun, c.1893. The first automatic machine-gun, Maxims slaughtered millions of men. Designed by an American and subsequently used throughout the world, the Maxim fired continuously as long the trigger was pressed and ammunition remained in the belt. The one shown here is German, World War I vintage.

Below: An Austrian howitzer.

1912–13 First and Second Balkan Wars: Balkan League (Serbia, Greece, Bulgaria, Montenegro) wrests most of European territory from the Ottomans; Albania is created an independent state and Serbia doubles in size.

1914–18 WORLD WAR I
WORLD WAR I: WESTERN FRONT

Aug 1914 Battle of the Frontiers. German armies sweep forward in a modification of the Schlieffen Plan

Sept 5–10, 1914 Battle of the Marne. Anglo-French armies repulse over-extended Germans

Sept 13–27, 1914 1st Battle of the Aisne

Sept–Oct 1914 'Race to the Sea'. Closure of the 'open flank' and establishment of stabilized Western Front (trench-lines from the English Channel to Switzerland)

Oct 18 – Nov 30, 1914 1st Battle of Ypres

April 22 – May 25, 1915 2nd Battle of Ypres

Feb 21 – Dec18, 1916 Battle of Verdun. Massive, repeated German assults fail to capture Verdun but cause huge casualties on each side

July 1 – Nov 18, 1916 Battle of the Somme. Major British/French offensive results in massive casualties

April 9–15, 1917 Battle of Arras

April 16 – May 9, 1917 2nd Battle of the Aisne

June 7–14, 1917 Battle of Messines

Aug–Nov 1917 3rd Battle of Ypres (Passchendaele)

Nov 20 – Dec 3, 1917 Battle of Cambrai. First mass use of tanks, by British, is successful but not follwed up

March 21 – April 5, 1918 German 'Kaiserschlacht' offensive on Western Front (Operation 'Michael') against British on the Somme fails (just) to break through and ends in German exhaustion

April 9–29, 1918 Lys German Offensive ('Georgette')

May 27 – June 4, 1918 Aisne German Offensive ('Blücher')

June 9–14, 1918 Matz/Montdidier German

WORLD WAR I GENERALS

Erich Ludendorff (1865–1937)

Strategist responsible for the conduct of German arms during the latter part of World War I. In the pre-war German Army he rose to command a section of the General Staff and participated in the (ultimately disastrous) revision of the Schlieffen Plan for the invasion of France under Moltke the Younger. Shortly before the outbreak of World War I his association with extreme nationalists threatened his career, but in 1914 he was appointed Chief of Staff to Hindenburg at Eighth Army on the Eastern front. Ludendorff's triumph at Tannenberg brought his senior great acclaim, and the two generals continued to fight the war on the Eastern Front until 1916. In August of that year the failure of the German assaults on Verdun prompted the Kaiser to bring the duo west, where Hindenburg assumed command of all German armed forces. As before, it was Ludendorff who in fact wielded the power and made the decisions. Eventually he staked all on a general offensive in the west, which opened in March 1918 – the Kaiserschlacht battles. It was a close-run thing, but by autumn the German momentum was spent and the Central Powers' last hope of victory had passed. After the war, Ludendorff did much to foster the 'stab in the back' explanation for the German defeat and served as a National Socialist member of parliament (1924–8). In 1918 his mental state had been strained by the stress of his position; in the inter-war years he became decidedly eccentric in his views, writing in 1935 (in a sinister reversal of Clausewitz) that peace was merely an interval in the natural state of war.

Douglas, 1st Earl Haig (1861–1928)

Principal British land forces commander during World War I. He fought in the Omdurman cam-paign of 1898 and in the Boer War of 1899–1902. On the outbreak of war he commanded I Corps, becoming C-in-C First Army in 1915 and then Commander-in-Chief of the British Expeditionary Force at the end of that year. He worked well with Foch during the last year of the war, but his reputation has always been controversial in the light of the devastating number of casualties suffered during the offensives on the Somme in particular. The Somme offensives were, in fact, to relieve pressure on the French at Verdun, but criticism has focused upon the prolonging of these offensives long after – in hindsight – they had proved to have failed. His order of the day to the troops facing the Kaiserschlacht offensive in 1918 is justly famous: 'With our backs to the wall, and believing in the justice of our cause, each one of us must fight on to the end…' In recent years historians have re-evaluated Haig's generalship, and have begun to portray him in a more favorable light. Increasingly he is credited with turning the British Army by 1918 into a superbly trained and equipped war-winning force.

Ferdinand Foch (1851–1929)

First World War Commander of Allied Forces from March 1918. An artilleryman, then profes-sor of tactics, he wrote a number of works on the theory and practise of war. In 1914 he commanded XX Corps in Nancy, his tenacity contributing to the victory of the Marne. After two years commanding Northern Army Group, he was made Chief of the General Staff to the French Minister of War, effectively 'adviser' to the Allied armies. He advocated a unified command but was not listened to until the German spring 1918 offensive struck. On 26 March he became generalissimo of the Allied armies to

Left: The old and the new – French cavalry contemplate a passing aircraft. While the role of the aircraft would grow as the war went on, the era of cavalry charges was past.

coordinate the Allied armies on the Western Front. In a titanic battle of wills with the executive commander of the German armies, Ludendorff, he reacted to each of the German offensives until, in Champagne, the German offensive ran out of steam. Now it was the Allies' turn to attack, this time advancing until the signing of the Armistice in November 1918. The man who brought the war to a victorious conclusion after four years of practical stalemate, Foch was the greatest French soldier of the twentieth century.

Below: Left to right – Kaiser Wilhelm II, the Emperor of Germany; Erich Ludendorff, mastermind behind the great German offensives of 1918; Sir Douglas Haig, commander of the British Expeditionary Force in France and Belgium; the French Marshal Foch, who became supreme general of Allied forces on the Western Front; Field Marshal Hindenburg, commander of the German forces on the Western Front at the end of the war; and General Pershing, commander of the United States' forces in Europe.

Offensive ('Gneisenau')
July 15–17, 1918 Marne-Rheims German Offensive ('Friedensturm')
These offensives yield large territorial gains for the Germans but exhaust the German army and fail to break the Allies. Ludendorff's last throw for victory fails
July 18 – November 11, 1918 Allied 'Hundred Days' offensives, leading to Armistice
July–Aug 1918 Reduction of the Marne Salient
Aug–Sept 1918 Reduction of the Amiens Salient
Aug–Sept 1918 Evacuation of Lys Salient
Sept 12–16, 1918 St Mihiel Offensive

WORLD WAR I: EASTERN (RUSSIAN) FRONT
Aug 26–30, 1914 Battle of Tannenberg. Hindenburg/Ludendorff victory prevents Russian capture of East Prussia
Aug 23 – Sept 26, 1914 Galician battles
Sept 9–14, 1914 Masurian Lakes I
Sept–Oct 1914 South-west Poland operations
Nov 11–25, 1914 Battle of Lodz
Feb 7–22, 1915 Battle of Masurian Lakes II
June 2 – May 27, 1915 Gorlice-Tarnow
July–Sept 1915 Russian withdrawal
March 1916 Lake Narotch Operations
June–Aug 1916 Brusilov Offensive
Aug–Sept 1916 Roumanian Offensive
Sept–Dec 1916 Roumania eliminated
March 1917 Russian Revolution
July 1917 Kerensky (2nd Brusilov) Offensive
Sept 1–5, 1917 Riga Operation
Dec 1917 Russian armistice

WORLD WAR I: ITALIAN FRONT
June–July 1915 1st Battle of the Isonzo
July–Sept 1915 2nd Battle of the Isonzo
Oct–Nov 1915 3rd Battle of the Isonzo
Nov 1915 4th Battle of the Isonzo
March 1916 5th Battle of the Isonzo
May 15 – June 17, 1916 Asiago Offensive
Aug 1916 6th Battle of the Isonzo
Sept 1916 7th Battle of the Isonzo
Oct 1916 8th Battle of the Isonzo
Nov 1916 9th Battle of the Isonzo

World War I was the heyday of the battleship – during the years leading to the outbreak of war, nations' strengths were judged by the numbers of battleships in their navies, and battleship-building programs became an intensely political issue.

The battleship had evolved from the old Nelsonian 'wooden walls' during the middle years of the nineteenth century, as steam power replaced sail, rifled artillery replaced muzzle-loaders, and ships became encased in armor. The American Civil War demonstrated these trends, most spectacularly in the Battle of Hampton Roads, the famous encounter between the iron-clads USS *Monitor* and the CSS *Virginia* (*ex-Merrimack*), when the two armor-clad ships bat-tered away at each other and almost overnight made wooden warships obsolete. By the end of the nineteenth century, the typical battleship was all-steel-built, with coal-fired engines, four 12-inch guns in revolving turrets plus a variety of secondary and smaller guns. The Battle of Tsushima in 1905 provided warship designers with much food for thought, especially the evidence that battles could now be fought at much longer ranges than previously believed – the Japanese had opened fire at 7,000 yards. The 'all-big-gun' *Dreadnought*, launched on February 10, 1906, caused a revolution in battleship design, outclassing by a large margin anything else afloat. She was larger, faster and far more powerful – the

Left: Dreadnought.

Right: The US battleship Michigan, launched in 1908, carried eight 12-inch guns, in centerline superfiring turrets. The lattice masts were peculiar to US ships.

Below: The German 1st and 2nd Battle Squadrons at Keil before the war, with Hegoland class battleships in the foreground.

main armament consisted of ten 12-inch guns (with a range of some 11 miles), and steam turbines raised her speed to 21 knots. During the years prior to the war, dreadnoughts became even bigger and faster, with artillery up to 15- and 16-inch caliber. Deployed in battle squadrons, these were the main combatants at the Battle of Jutland, in May 1916, the last of the great naval battles fought solely with surface ships. After World War I, submarines, mines, torpedoes and aircraft gradually reduced the dominance of battleships, although during World War II they remained potent commerce-raiders and provided valuable heavy artillery support for amphibious landings.

May–June 1917 10th Battle of the Isonzo
Aug–Sept 1917 11th Battle of the Isonzo
Oct 24 – Nov 7, 1917 Battle of Caporetto
June 15–22, 1918 Battle of the Piave
Oct 24 – Nov 4, 1918 Battle of Vittorio Veneto

WORLD WAR I: SERBIA/SALONIKA FRONTS
Aug 1914 1st Austrian invasion of Serbia
Sept 1914 2nd invasion of Serbia
Nov–Dec 1914 3rd invasion of Serbia
Oct–Nov 1915 4th invasion of Serbia
Oct 1915 Salonika Front established
Nov 1916 Fall of Monastir
Sept 1918 Final Allied Offensive

WORLD WAR I: GALLIPOLI FRONT
Nov 1914 Dardanelles bombarded
Feb–March 1915 Naval attempt to force passage of the Dardanelles fails
April–May 1915 Landings at Gallipoli
August Landings at Suvla Bay
Dec 1915–Jan 1916 Evacuation of Gallipoli expeditionary force

WORLD WAR I: MESOPOTAMIA FRONT
Nov–Dec 1914 Allied landing in Mesopotamia
Jan–July 1915 Allied advance in Mesopotamia
Sept 1915 1st Battle of Kut
Nov 22–25, 1915 Battle of Ctesiphon
Dec 8, 1915 – April 29, 1916 Siege and fall of Kut
Sept 1916 – Feb 1917 2nd British advance in Mesopotamia
Feb 1917 2nd Battle of Kut
March 1917 British capture Baghdad

WORLD WAR I: PALESTINE FRONT
Jan 1915 1st Turkish attack on Suez Canal
March 1917 1st Battle of Gaza
April 1917 2nd Battle of Gaza
Oct–Nov 1917 3rd Battle of Gaza
Nov–Dec Battles of Junction Station and Jerusalem
Sept 18 – Oct 31, 1918 Battle of Megiddo. Allenby's decisive victory leads to fall of Damascus and Aleppo

WORLD WAR I: NAVAL BATTLES
Nov 1, 1914 Battle of Coronel. British squadron defeated
Aug 28, 1914 1st Battle of Heligoland Bight

Dec 8, 1914 Battle of Falkland Islands. British battlecruisers avenge Coronel

Jan 24, 1915 Battle of Dogger Bank

May 31 – June 1, 1916 Battle of Jutland. Epic battle between British and German main fleets. Germans escape defeat

1917 2nd Battle of Heligoland Bight

WORLD WAR I: AFRICAN THEATER

June 1915 – Jan 1916 Allied operations against Germans in Cameroon

August 1915 Anglo-French capture German Togoland

Sept 1916 Allies take Dar-es-Salaam in German East Africa

Europe

1916 Easter Uprising in Ireland

1917–20 Russian Civil War

1919–22 Greco-Turkish War

1919–22 Russo-Polish War

Aug 16–25, 1920 Battle of Warsaw. Pilsudski advised by French General Weygand, smashes invading Russian Bolshevik army

Americas

1914 Veracruz US intervention

1915 US intervention in Haiti

1916 Villa raids US

1916 US intervention in Dominican Republic

1917 Cuban revolution

1918–19 Haitian revolt against USA

1921 Panama-Costa Rica conflict

1921–29 Chile-Peru Tacha-Arica dispute

1925 Nicaraguan Civil War. US intervention (to 1933)

1929 Bolivia-Paraguay border dispute

1932–35 Chaco War between Bolivia and Paraguay

1937 Haiti-Dominican Republic border dispute

Far East

1921 Chinese Civil War

1924 British troops intervene in Shanghai

1931–32 Sino-Japanese war over Manchuria; Japanese invade and establish there the puppet state of Manchukuo

1937–1945 SINO-JAPANESE WAR

April 1938 Battle of Taierchwang. General Li Tsung-jen defeats Japanese

Middle East

1919 3rd British-Afghan War

1920 USSR invades Persia

1928 Mutiny of Afghan Army

Above left: Heavy artillery was deployed in huge numbers by both sides in World War I, bringing down massive bombardments.

Below left: British officers in a fire-trench on the Salonika front early in the campaign.

Right: Manfred von Richthofen, the great German air ace, with his favorite aircraft, a Fokker Triplane. The 'Red Baron' downed 80 aircraft before being shot down on April 21, 1918.

The middle of the twentieth century saw the greatest war yet, with the added horrors of mass 'industrialized' murder of millions of Jews and other civilians. Bombing of cities brought civilians into the front-line. This was 'Total War'. Air power began to reign supreme, while German U-boats threatened to starve Britain into surrender, and armored vehicles dominated the battlefields, ushering in a new period of maneuver. The last act of the war introduced what seemed to be the ultimate weapon – the atomic bomb.

Left: German troops in action during the conquest of Poland, the opening campaign of World War II. The canisters at their waists are for gas masks, which were also carried by the Western Allies at the start of hostilities – both sides feared the other would use poison gas, as they had in World War I. In the event, this horror at least did not appear.

Below left: A German Panzer tank, this is a Mark IV, one of the mainstays of the German armored forces during the middle and later years of the war. It was the bold German use of tanks to spearhead their attacks in blitzkrieg ('lightning') offensives that confounded the Allies during the campaign in France and, later, in Russia.

Above left: Adolf Hitler (1889–1945), Chancellor of Germany and leader of the Nazi Party, who led Germany as 'Führer' ('leader') from 1933/4. Directly responsible for World War II, he oversaw the conquest of most of Western Europe and much of European Russia, bringing about the deaths of many millions of innocent people, and the murder by genocide of some seven million Jews and gypsies.

Above right: Benito Mussolini (1883–1945) was Fascist prime minister of Italy from 1922 and became a key member of Hitler's Axis alliance. His compatriots, however, were not entirely behind him in his pursuit of war, and he was ousted from power in 1943, leading, until his capture and death, a puppet regime at the behest of the Germans.

1934 Saudi attacks Yemen
1920–22 Irish War for Independence and 2nd Civil War

Europe
1936–39 Spanish Civil War
1939–40, 1941–5 Russo-Finnish War

1939–1945 WORLD WAR II
SEPT 1 – OCT 6, 1939 WORLD WAR II: POLISH CAMPAIGN. First German blitzkrieg overwhelms Poland and triggers war against Britain and France
NOV 13, 1939 – MARCH 12, 1940 WORLD WAR II: RUSSO-FINNISH WAR
Nov 30 1939 – Jan 8, 1940 Battle of Suomussalmi. Finns trap and destroy two Soviet divisions
Nov 30, 1939 – Feb 13, 1940 Mannerheim Line. Russia forces a way up the Karelian Isthmus
APRIL 9 – JUNE 8, 1940 WORLD WAR II: SCANDINAVIAN CAMPAIGN. German invasion of Denmark and Norway. British and French counter-invasion of Norway defeated (Narvik, Namsos, Aandalesnes)
WORLD WAR II: CAMPAIGN IN THE WEST, 1940
May 10 – June 22, 1940 France, Belgium and Holland. German blitzkrieg drives Britain out of the continent, overwhelms Holland, Belgium and France
May 21, 1940 Arras. British counterattack
May 26 – June 4, 1940 Dunkirk evacuation of British Expeditionary Force
Aug 19, 1942 Dieppe. Prototype amphibious landing by predominantly Canadian force
WORLD WAR II: AIR OPERATIONS, EUROPE
July 10 – Sept 15, 1940 Battle of Britain. German Luftwaffe fails to attain air superiority over British Isles preparatory to invasion
Sept 7, 1940 – May 10/11, 1941 The Blitz. Luftwaffe attempt to bomb Britain into submission fails
Nov c.7/8, 1941 onwards Strategic Bombing of Germany. RAF and (later) USAAF strategic strikes against enemy cities and

Erwin Johannes Eugen Rommel (1891–1944)
The 'Desert Fox', master of mobile warfare and charismatic leader of armored troops. Rommel won Prussia's highest decoration, the Pour le Mérite, during the First World War and published *Infantry Attacks* in 1937. He made his reputation as commander of 7th Panzer Division during the campaign in the west in 1940. The following year he was appointed to command the German expeditionary force to prop up the Italian régime in North Africa and launched an attack that all but ejected the British from Cyrenaica. His Afrika Korps successfully repulsed several British attacks until, reinforced, he attacked again in January 1942, capturing Tobruk after an epic battle at Gazala, and pursued the British into Egypt. He was defeated by Montgomery's superior forces at El Alamein in November. Retreating to Tunisia, to join German reinforcements, he took part in the losing battle for Tunisia. After com-manding German forces in northern Italy after the Italian surrender to the Allies, he was put in charge of the forces defending the coast of north-west France, where he warned the High Command of the need to push an Allied landing immediately back into the sea or risk complete failure. During the Battle for Normandy, he was severely wounded in an air attack (17 July). Implicated in the July bomb plot against Hitler, he was subsequently forced to commit suicide.

Sir Bernard Montgomery, 1st Viscount Montgomery (1887–1976)
Principal and most famous British general of the Second World War. In 1939 he commanded 3rd Division in the British Expeditionary Force, and after Dunkirk rose rapidly in rank. In August 1942 he was appointed to the command of Eighth Army, facing the triumphant Axis forces of Rommel on the frontier of Egypt. He defeated Rommel at El

Above: *Destination Tunisia. Allied troops make an unopposed landing to the west in North Africa in Operation 'Torch', while Montgomery's British Eighth Army sets off from the east in pursuit of Rommel, defeated at El Alamein.* **Right:** *Rommel and Montgomery.*

Alamein and led Eighth Army through the Tunisian and Sicilian campaigns and into Italy before being appointed land forces commander, under Eisenhower, for the 'Overlord' operation, in December 1943. During the Normandy campaign he was criticized for his difficulty in taking the key town of Caen; and in the subsequent operations in the Low Countries launched the Arnhem airborne operation that ended in failure. By now he had ruffled many feathers among his colleagues and, especially, his American allies, by his conceit and alarming outspokenness. He advocated a narrow-front strategy for the invasion of Germany, but this was rejected by Eisenhower. He took the surrender of enemy forces in northwest Germany. A great communicator with the ability to inspire his men with confidence, and a believer in averting casualties, Montgomery's egocentric character was an unfortunate limitation to his effectiveness as a coalition general.

installation; May 30/31, 1942 Cologne 1st 1000-bomber raid; March 5/6 – July 9/10, 1943 Battle of the Ruhr; May 16/17, 1943 Dambuster raid; July 24 – Aug 3, 1943 Hamburg; Aug 17, USAAF Schweinfurt/Regensburg; Nov 18/19, 1943 – March 24/25, 1944 Berlin; Feb 13/14, 1945 Dresden

WORLD WAR II: NORTH AFRICAN / MEDITERRANEAN / MIDDLE EASTERN CAMPAIGN

Dec 9 1940 – Feb 7, 1941 O'Connor's blitzkrieg destroys most of Italian forces in North Africa

June 1940 – May 1943 Siege of Malta. The island is attacked from the air and supplied perilously by sea

April 6–8, 1941 German/Italian invasion of Yugoslavia and Greece, completed by 20 April

May 20 – June 1, 1941 Crete. German airborne conquest

March 24 – April 25, 1941 Rommel's first offensive

Nov 18 – Dec 7, 1941 Operation 'Crusader'. British eject Rommel from Cyrenaica and relieve Tobruk

May 26 – June 21, 1942 Gazala. Rommel defeats British Eighth Army and captures Tobruk

July 1–27, 1942 First Battle of El Alamein. Rommel repulsed by Eighth Army

Aug 30 – Sept 2, 1942 Alam Halfa. Indecisive attack by Rommel

Oct 23 – Nov 4, 1942 Second Battle of El Alamein. Montgomery decisively defeats Rommel who retreats toward Tunisia

Nov 8, 1942 Operation 'Torch': Anglo-American amphibious landings in Morocco and Algeria. Germans reinforce Tunisia

Feb 14–22, 1943 Kasserine Pass. Rommel inflicts reverse on US II Corps in Tunisia

March 6, 1943 Medenine. Rommel repulsed

March 20–27, 1943 Mareth Line. Montgomery forces Rommel's retreat

WORLD WAR II: SICILY/ITALIAN CAMPAIGN

July 10, 1943 Allies invade Sicily. They enter

Top: Von Manstein.

Above: Zhukov.

Left: German troops of Sixth Army at Stalingrad. In the background is a Panzer IV tank.

Below left: A Russian T-34 tank, armed with an 85mm gun. Despite the technical superiority of some of the German tank designs, the fast, rugged T-34 has been judged the best all-round tank of the war and was built in sufficient numbers to overwhelm the panzers.

Erich von Manstein (1887–1973)

The son of a Prussian aristocrat, Manstein is considered as one of the ablest of the German generals during World War II. After he was wounded in World War I he served as a staff officer. He was von Rundstedt's Chief of Staff during the Polish Campaign in 1939. His inspired ideas for the campaign in the West were adopted by Hitler, even though opposed by Field Marshal von Brauchitsch, the Commander-in-Chief and Genral Halder, the Chief of Staff. The ensuing conquest of France was a military triumph during which Manstein commanded XXXVIII Corps. In Russia his Eleventh Army defeated the Soviets in the Crimea. During the Battle of Stalingrad he almost managed to relieve the Sixth Army trapped there. Then, commanding Army Group South in a counter-offensive, he won a major victory at Kharkov. After the German defeat at the Battle of Kursk in 1943 he led his forces through a series of defensive battles as the Germans were being pushed back by the Soviets. By March 1944 he had fallen out of favor with Hitler, and as a result he was dismissed and never held another command.

Georgi Zhukov (1896–1974)

Georgi Zhukov was the son of a peasant, serving in the Imperial Russian Army during World War I before joining the Red Army. When commanding the Soviet forces in Mongolia he defeated the Japanese Kwantung Army. In 1941 he became the Soviet Chief of the General Staff. In July 1941 he was posted to the armies east of Moscow. He was ordered to take command at Leningrad. He then returned to Moscow, counterattacking the Germans on December 6, 1941. Named Deputy Supreme Commander, he played a part in defeating the Germans at Stalingrad. The victory at Kursk merged into the Soviet Summer Offensive, when he co-ordinated the First and Second Ukrainian Fronts in the drive west. Zhukov personally took command of the First Ukrainian Front when its commander was wounded in February 1944. He helped to coordinate Operation 'Bagration', the summer offensive in 1944, in which the Soviets destroyed the Germans' Army Group Center. In November he was put in command of the First Belorussian Front, which had the most direct approach to Berlin. With the fall of Berlin he became the most celebrated of all the Soviet Marshals.

Messina on 17 Aug

Sept 3 and 9, 1943 Allies invade southern Italy

Sept 9–17, Battle of Salerno beachhead

Oct 12 – Nov 14, 1943 Volturno River. Major conflict for German defense line south of Rome

Jan 17 – May 22, 1944 Battle for Monte Cassino, major obstacle to Allied advance south of Rome

Jan 22 – May 23, 1944 Anzio landing to turn the Gustav Line. In desperate fighting, Allies almost defeated

June 4, 1944 Allies enter Rome

Aug 30 – Oct 28, 1944 Gothic Line. Allies struggle to breach last major German defense line in Italy

WORLD WAR II: EASTERN FRONT

June 22, 1941 Operation 'Barbarossa' launched. Germany invades USSR

July 17 – Aug 5, 1941 Smolensk. Major encirclement of Soviet forces

Sept 1, 1941 – Jan 27, 1944 Siege of Leningrad

Sept 9–26, 1941 Kiev. Major encirclement of Soviet forces

October 5–20, 1941 Vyazma-Bryansk. Major encirclement of Soviet forces

Oct 8, 1941 – April 30, 1942 Battle for Moscow. Hitler fails to capture Moscow. Central front stabilizes while German main thrust moves south

Oct 29, 1941 – July 3, 1942 Sevastopol. Manstein secures the Crimea for the Germans

June 28, 1942 German offensive toward Caucasus and lower Don River

Aug 10, 1942 German Sixth Army reaches Stalingrad

Aug 15, 1942 Gemans reach Caucasus mountains

Aug 19, 1942 – Feb 2, 1943 Stalingrad. German Sixth Army trapped and, after epic battle, forced to capitulate. The turning-point battle on the Eastern Front

Feb 16 – March 15, 1943 Kharkov. Manstein inflicts sharp reverse on Soviets

July 5–17, 1943 Kursk. Last major German

Left: *The American M-4 Sherman tank was the most widely produced and used tank of the American, British and Western Allied forces of World War II. Shown here is a Sherman armed with a 105mm howitzer.*

Dwight David Eisenhower (1890–1969)

At the age of 28 this popular, outgoing Texan was given the task of forming the US Army's first tank corps during World War I. From the Operations Branch in Washington he was sent to Great Britain in 1942 to lead the American staff there. He was a good choice in achieving the harmony needed within the Allied Forces' HQ. He commanded the invasion of French North Africa in November 1942. He was promoted to four-star general in February 1943. In December 1943 he was appointed as Supreme Commander in the Mediterranean theater of operations. Then, in January 1944, he was appointed as the Supreme Commander of the Allied Expeditionary Forces for the invasion of Europe. He was not a fighting general in the mold of Patton or Bradley but, as President Roosevelt believed, the best politician among any of the military commanders – which was exactly what the job called for. He did, however, insist on the 'broad front' strategy instead of the 'narrow front' as urged by Montgomery and Patton. The narrow front strategy might have ended the war earlier with powerful, deep thrusts

Above: *The Battle of the Atlantic was a hard-fought campaign between the German U-boats and Allied convoys taking supplies, equipment and troops across the Atlantic to Britain. Allied antisubmarine equipment and tactics triumphed in the end, with, crucially, the extension of air cover across the ocean.*

Below: *Germany's capital ships were blockaded in European ports for much of the war but made several sorties to attack Allied shipping. Bismarck's foray ended in her destruction without sinking a single merchantman, but not before she had sent HMS Hood, Britain's largest warship, to the bottom.*

Above: Eisenhower.
Right: Patton.

into German territory, making for Berlin, while the broader front was the slower but less risky option. He ended the war being looked upon as a hero, as much by the British as by the Americans. After the war he went on to be twice elected US President.

George Smith Patton Jr. (1885–1945)

America's favorite tank general, a charismatic, vigorous but controversial general dubbed by his men 'Old Blood and Guts'. He entered the US cavalry in 1909 and represented his country at the 1912 Olympics. A cavalryman through and through, he immediately saw the significance of the tank and became a vigorous proponent of armored warfare, of which he became one of the leading exponents. Following the 'Torch' landings, he commanded Western Task Force in North Africa then US II Corps. As commander of US Seventh Army, his exploits in Sicily – a dramatic and unplanned thrust to Palermo and Messina – earned him a reputation as a daring, aggressive leader. As commander of US Third Army, he led the right flank of the breakout from the Normandy beachhead and advanced across France with spectacular speed. His redeployment to strike at the southern flank of the German 'bulge' during the Ardennes offensive was brilliant, and his army crossed the Rhine at Mainz and Oppenheim in March 1945. Third Army thereafter sped across southern Germany, ending the war in Czechoslovakia. Volatile and pugnacious, he was often unadvisedly outspoken, but his battlefield accomplishments speak for themselves. He died as a result of a minor traffic accident in December 1945.

offensive on the Eastern Front and probably the largest tank battle ever fought

June 22 – Aug 27, 1944 Operation 'Bagration'. Soviet 'steamroller' liberates Byelorussia

Aug 1 – Oct 2, 1944 Warsaw. Failed Polish uprising significantly unsupported by Soviet offensive

April 16 – May 2, 1945 Berlin. Zhukov and Konev direct the Soviet conquest of Berlin. Hitler commits suicide amid the rubble

WORLD WAR II: NAVAL EVENTS (not covered in major theaters)

Dec 13, 1939 Battle of the River Plate. British cruiser squadron encounters German 'pocket battleship' *Graf Spee*, subsequently scuttled

April 9 and 13, 1940 Battle of Narvik. German destroyer force devastated by Royal Navy

BATTLE OF OF THE ATLANTIC.

German U–boat campaign against convoys to Britain, defeated by a combination of Allied air and naval technical advances and ULTRA codebreaking

Nov 11/12, 1940 Taranto raid by Royal Navy cripples part of Italian fleet

March 28, 1941 Battle of Cape Matapan. Cunningham's fleet defeats Italians

May 21–27, 1941 *Bismarck* action. German battleship sinks British battlecruiser *Hood* (24 May) before being sunk by Royal Navy forces

July 1–5, 1942 Destruction of Arctic Convoy PQ17

Dec 31, 1942 Battle of the Barents Sea: Germans repulsed in attack on an Arctic convoy

Dec 26, 1943 Battle of the North Cape: German battlecruiser *Scharnhorst* sunk

WORLD WAR II: CAMPAIGN IN THE WEST, 1944–5

June 6, 1944 D–Day. Montgomery directs successful Allied landing in Normandy

June 6 – July 25, 1944 Caen. Hard–fought battle to break out from the beachhead

Aug 13–21, 1944 Falaise Gap. Significant trapping of German forces in Normandy after 'Cobra' breakout on Allied right flank

Far left: *Admiral Yamamoto.*

Center left: *General MacArthur.*

Near left: *Admiral Chester Nimitz (1885–1966) took charge of the US Pacific Fleet after Pearl Harbor and directed Pacific Ocean Command thereafter directing the US amphibious thrusts across the Pacific toward Japan.*

Left: *'The Big Three' Allied leaders – British Prime Minister Winston Churchill, President Franklin Roosevelt and Soviet supremo Joseph Stalin, shown here at the Yalta Conference in February 1945.*

Below: *US Marines in action during the struggle for Okinawa, the last major battle of the Pacific campaign.*

Isoroku Yamamoto (1884–1943)
The man who planned and executed the raid on Pearl Harbor. Yamamoto served in the Russo-Japanese War and was wounded at the battle of Tsushima, losing two fingers from his left hand. Between the wars he studied English at Boston and gained a poor opinion of the US Navy but not of American power. Returning to Japan, he became one of the country's principal experts on military aviation, championing the aircraft carrier as the main naval weapon rather than the battleship, which, he said, was as useful in modern warfare as a samurai sword. He was, however, no warmonger and opposed Japan's bellicose stance. In that year he became commander of the Japanese Combined Fleet. If there had to be war, he saw Japan's only hope in a pre-emptive strike at the American fleet. This he planned and carried out with spectacular success. A string of victories followed until the disasters at Midway and Guadalcanal, the naval element of which he directed personally. He was killed on 18 April 1943, his aircraft intercepted by US fighters forewarned by codebreakers of his flight plan.

Douglas MacArthur (1880–1964)
One of the most controversial generals of the US Army. He graduated with the highest marks ever recorded at West Point and ended the First World War as a highly decorated brigadier. Between the wars he served as Army Chief of Staff (1930), and in 1935 was military advisor in the Philippines, after which he retired in 1937. In July 1941 he was recalled to become commander of US forces in the Far East, just in time to be defeated by the Japanese invasion of December that year. Retreating to Bataan and Corregidor, he was ordered to escape, uttering the famous promise, 'I shall return.' In April 1942 he commanded South West Pacific Area and began an island-hopping offensive that brought US forces back to the Philippines. He took the official surrender of the Japanese aboard USS *Missouri* in Tokyo Bay in September 1945, and thereafter became Supreme Commander Allied Forces, running Japan's transformation to democracy with astonishing success. In 1950 he became Commander-in-Chief of United Nations forces in Korea, stemming the North Korean advance and carrying out a spectacular landing at Inchon to outflank the enemy before driving deep into North Korea.

Aug 25, 1944 Allies enter Paris
Sept 17–25, 1944 Arnhem. Failed Allied airborne attempt to breach German riverine defense lines in Netherlands
Dec 16, 1944 – Jan 16, 1945 Battle of the Bulge (Ardennes). 'Last-throw' German counterattack fails
March 7–31, 1945 Rhine Crossings. Allies enter Germany
WORLD WAR II: PACIFIC THEATER
Dec 7, 1941 Pearl Harbor raid by Japanese devastates US fleet
Dec 22, 1941 – May 10, 1942 Japanese conquest of Philippines
Feb 27–8, 1942 Battle of the Java Sea. Japanese destroy Allied cruiser/destroyer squadron in Dutch East Indies
May 4–8, 1942 Battle of the Coral Sea. Tactical Japanese victory
June 4–7, 1942 Battle of Midway. Major turning-point defeat for Japanese, crippling their carrier fleet
Aug 7, 1942 – Feb 7, 1943 Guadalcanal. Air, land and sea battle is the second major turning-point in the Pacific theater
US amphibious landings and capture of stepping-stone islands across the Pacific:
Nov 20–23, 1943 Tarawa
Feb 1–4, 1944 Kwajalein
Feb 17–23, 1944 Eniwetok
June 15 – July 9, 1944 Saipan
July 21 – Aug 10, 1944 Guam
July 24–31, 1944 Tinian
Sept 15 – Nov 25, 1944 Peleliu
Feb 19 – March 16, 1945 Iwo Jima
April 1 – June 22, 1945 Okinawa
June 19–20, 1944 Battle of the Philippine Sea ('Great Marianas Turkey Shoot') breaks back of Japanese naval air power
Oct 20 – Dec 25, 1944 Leyte. Largest battle in naval history. US defeats last major offensive by Japanese fleet and secures landings in Philippines
Feb 3 – March 4, 1945 Battle for Manila
Aug 9–17, 1945 Soviet invasion and conquest of Manchuria from Japanese
Aug 6 and 9, 1945 Atomic bombing of

The Korean War was fought with essentially World War II equipment but with significant enhancements and technical developments. One of the most important was the mass deployment of jet aircraft, this war seeing the first jet-versus-jet combat.

Above: an M-40 155mm self-propelled gun, manned here by members of the Utah National Guard.

Below: US M-46 tanks in the harsh Korean winter.

Top right: US F-80 'Shooting Stars' returning from close air support operations to their forward airstrip.

Center right: Cacualty evacuation by helicopter, a significant advance in saving lives, to a MASH (Mobile Army Surgical Hospital).

Bottom right: GIs in foxholes exchange fire with communist forces along the Naktong River north of Taegu.

Hiroshima and Nagasaki

WORLD WAR II: SOUTH-EAST ASIA CAMPAIGN

Dec 8, 1941– Feb 15, 1941 Japanese conquest of Malaya

Dec 10, 1941 Japanese sink British Force Z (battleship *Prince of Wales* and battlecruiser *Repulse*)

Feb 8–15, 1942 Singapore surrenders, the worst British defeat since the 18th century

Feb and March – Aug 1944 Chindit raids behind Japanese lines

March 29 – June 22, 1944 Battle of Imphal/ Kohima. Slim's Fourteenth Army repulses attempted Japanese invasion of India

Nov 19, 1944 Slim begins Allied offensive into central Burma

Jan 27, 1945 British and Chinese advancing from north link up

March 20, 1945 Mandalay secured by Allies

May 3, 1945 Rangoon secured by Allies

Europe

1946 Greek Civil War

1954–9 Cyprus Emergency

1956 Hungarian Uprising

1968 Czechoslovakia Spring uprising and Warsaw Pact intervention

Far East

1945–9 Chinese Civil War and establishment of the Communist People's Republic of China

1950–3 Korean War

Korea has been split north–south since 1945 according to post-World War II occupation by the USSR and USA

June 25, 1950 North Korea invades South Korea, triggering a UN military response

Aug 1950 South Korean and UN forces are pinned to the 'Pusan perimeter' in the south of the peninsula

Sept 15, 1950 A UN offensive and amphibious landing at Inchon begins the counterattack; by the end of October the UN forces have overrun almost all North Korea

BALLISTIC MISSILES

Left: The US Jupiter intermediate-range ballistic missile, with a 1,500-mile range, was deployed from 1961 until 1963.

Below: Modern submarines, both conventional (diesel/electric) and nuclear powered, all have the distinctive teardrop-shaped hull. This is nuclear-powered attack submarine USS Asheville. The US Navy's submarine fleet is now completely nuclear powered.

Right: A US UGM-96A Trident T submarine-launched ballistic missile is launched from the nuclear-powered strategic missile submarine USS Nevada (SSBN-733). It can carry up to eight nuclear warheads with a range of over 4,500 miles.

24 November 1950 China joins the war without warning and drives the UN forces back south

April 22–30, 1951 Battle of Imjin River. British, Belgian and American troops force Chinese army to withdraw, inflicting 40 per cent casualties

By mid-1951 the lines are stabilized near where they started in 1950. UN forces commander General MacArthur recommends attacking China, but is dismissed by US President Truman

April 16–18, 1953 Battle of Pork Chop Hill. Trudeau (US/UN) drives off Chinese

Negotiations conclude on July 27, 1953 with a ceasefire; but North Korea and South Korea remain technically at war

1947/8 to 1989/90 The Cold War

At the close of World War II, Germany and Austria are occupied by the victors. Eastern Europe, 'liberated' from the Nazis, falls into Soviet sphere. Communist regimes are installed and in Churchill's words, an 'Iron Curtain' divides Europe. Tension grows between the USSR and the West. Berlin is divided and West Berlin forms an enclave of democracy within the Eastern bloc

1948–53 Height of the Cold War.

1949 Formation of North Atlantic Treaty Organization, between most of the European democracies and the North American powers

1949 USSR becomes an atomic power

1949 Berlin Airlift. USSR interdicts access to West Berlin, and the city is supplied by air from the West

1955 USSR forms Warsaw Pact

Intercontinental ballistic missiles increasingly form the principal deterrent between the superpowers, based on Mutual Assured Destruction, with fleets of bombers on constant stand-by and, later, nuclear-powered submarines deployed with targeted missiles aboard

1962 Cuban missile crisis. US spyplanes

After World War II, US global power projection has relied largely upon its huge nuclear-powered aircraft carriers.

Left: An F-4 Phantom of the US Navy on board USS Saratoga, 1964.

Below: The nuclear powered fleet carrier USS Nimitz. Approaching 100,000 tons displacement, these massive ships can each carry nearly 100 of the most capable combat aircraft in the world.

Right: The Royal Navy also used naval air power at long distance – in the South Atlantic Falklands War of 1982. The mainstay of the carrier-borne aircraft were the revolutionary Sea Harriers, able to take off and land vertically. They shot down 21 Argentine aircraft during the conflict.

discover Soviet missiles deployed in Cuba.
The world teeters on the brnk of nuclear
war, with Cuba blockaded by the US
Navy, before the USSR removes the
offending missiles

With the stalemate nuclear confrontation,
and armies stationed on either side of the
'Iron Curtain', the ideological and political
conflict between East and West is played
out by surrogate means in the Third
World

1980s Attempts by Mikhail Gorbachev to
democratize USSR. During the 1980s the
USSR finds it increasingly difficult to
maintain the 'arms race', the US constantly
outspending its rival and developing new
technologies such as Stealth aircraft and
the so-called 'Star Wars' anti-missile
system. Soviet involvement in Afghanistan
exacerbates the situation

1989/90 Collapse of Communist regimes in
Soviet-bloc Europe and reunification of
Germany

Americas

1945–65 Colombian Civil War
1947–49 Paraguayan Civil War and turmoil
1948 Nicaraguan invasion of Costa Rica
(Costa Rica Civil War)
1951–55 Ecuador-Peru border dispute
1952–59 Cuban revolution
1953 British intervention in Guiana
1955 Nicaraguan invasion of Costa Rica
1956–58 Haiti unrest
1959 Cuban-led invasion of Dominican
Republic repelled
1960–65 Brazil: Communist insurgency
1961 Cuba: US 'Bay of Pigs' invasion
repelled
1964 British Guiana state of emergency
1965 Dominican Republic Civil War and US
intervention
1979–91 El Salvador Civil War
FALKLANDS/MALVINAS WAR, 1982
May 27–28, 1982 Battle of Goose Green.
Jones/Keeble of Britain capture
Argentinian garrisons

Top: *Croatian troops firing a 12.7mm machine-gun mounted on a T-55 Main Battle Tank.*

Below left: *A US M2 Infantry Fighting Vehicle.*

Right: *The American-built M-60 tank formed the backbone of the US Army's tank forces in the 1960s and 1970s. The Israeli M-60 seen here has been up-armored with hi-tech reactive armor.*

Right: *The British six-wheeled Saladin armored car armed from the early 1960s with a 76mm main gun.*

Below: *Marine M1A1 Abrams tank during Operation 'Enduring Freedom'.*

June 11–14, 1982 Battle of Port Stanley. Moore's British forces defeat Argentinians and liberate the port

Oct 25–27, 1983 Grenada. Metcalf's US task force, with token Caribbean units, defeat Granadians/Cubans

1979–89 Nicaragua Civil War

1989 US invades Panama

1994 US intervention in Haiti

1995 Oklahoma City terrorist bombing

Middle East

1948–49 WAR OF ISRAELI INDEPENDENCE

1956 SUEZ CANAL CRISIS AND ARAB/ISRAELI WAR

Oct 29 – Nov 5, 1956 Battle of Sinai. Dayan fulfils all Israeli objectives, defeating Egyptian army and overrunning the Sinai

Nov 5–7, 1956 Battle of Suez Landings. UK/French Allies under Stockwell try to regain control of the nationalized Suez Canal, and advance along the canal until the UN demands a ceasefire

1958–67 Aden emergency

1967 ARAB/ISRAELI 'SIX DAY' WAR

June 5–8, 1967 Battle of Sinai. Israelis under Gavish destroy Egyptian army and set up defense line along Suez Canal

June 7, Israelis capture Jerusalem

June 9–10, 1967 Battle of Golan Heights. Elazar of Israel defeats Syrians and captures the plateau

1970 Jordanian conflict with Palestinians

1973 ARAB-ISRAELI OCTOBER (YOM KIPPUR / RAMADAN) WAR

Oct 6–8, 1973 Battle of Suez Canal Crossing. Under Ali and Shazli, Egypt crosses the canal to regain the Sinai and its honor. Israelis push back until US and USSR force a UN ceasefire resolution

Oct 6–10, 1973 Battle of Golan Heights. Hofi leads Israeli repulse of Syrians

South-East Asia

1948–60 Malayan emergency

1946–54 FRENCH INDOCHINA WAR

Nov 20, 1953 – May 7, 1954 Battle of Dien

Above: *In Vietnam, Bell UH-1 Iroquois 'Huey' helicopters were in such frequent use deploying US troops that they became emblematic of the war.*

Right: *A Marine moves a Viet Cong suspect to the rear during a search and clear operation fifteen miles west of Da Nang Air Base.*

Far right: *General Võ Nguyên Giáp, mastermind of the North Vietnamese strategy.*

Bien Phu. Giáp's Viet Minh capture
French base, forcing French to agree to
independence for Vietnam
1953 Vietnamese invasion of Laos
1955 Vietnamese Civil War
1959–76 Laos state of emergency
1961–75 VIETNAM WAR (US direct military
involvement 1961–73)
1964 Gulf of Tonkin incident
Oct 19 – Nov 26, 1965 Battle of Ia Drang
Valley. Kinnard's US 1st Cavalry inflicts
crippling losses on the North Vietnamese
and Viet Cong
Aug 18, 1966 Battle of Long Tan. Australians
under Jackson soundly defeated Viet
Cong
Feb 22 – May 14, 1967 Operation 'Junction
City'. Under Westmoreland, US/South
Vietnamese inflicted heavy defeat on
Communists, who retreated to
Cambodia, but claim to have devastated
American troops
Nov 19–23, 1967 Battle of Dak To (Hill 875).
North Vietnamese distracted American
attention from South Vietnam by laying an
ambush and fighting for the hill.
Jan 30 to Sept 23, 1968 Tet Offensive:
North Vietnamese forces launch massive
surprise attacks country-wide and enter
Saigon. It is a major defeat for the North,
but shocks the American public (who
follow its course on television) which
turns increasingly against continuation of
the war
Jan 21 – April 14, 1968 Siege of Khe Sanh. As
part of Tet Offensive, North Vietnamese
try to take American base. Lownds
succeeds in holding on until relieved
Jan 31 – Feb 25, 1968 Battle of Hue. Truong
(South Vietnamese)/LaHue (USA)
recapture city from North Vietnamese,
who had seized it in a surprise attack on
January 30/31
June 1969 Gradual withdrawal of US troops
begins
Jan 1973 US/North Vietnam agreement to
end the war

General Võ Nguyên Giáp (1912–)
Vietnamese general and statesman. Giáp joined
the Communist Party in 1931 to oppose French
rule in Indochina. During the 1930s he was a
schoolteacher and journalist, and a dedicated
reader of military history, particularly of
Napoleon and Sun Tzu. He fought against the
French in the First Indochina War (1946–54)
and the United States and her allies in the
Second Indochina War (1960–75). His greatest
victory was at the Battle of Dien Bien Phu in
1954, which led to the French withdrawal from
Vietnam. During the Second Indochina War, the
Tet Offensive of 1968 was a military failure for
Giáp but a moral defeat for the people of the
USA. The last US combat troops withdraw from
Vietnam in 1973.

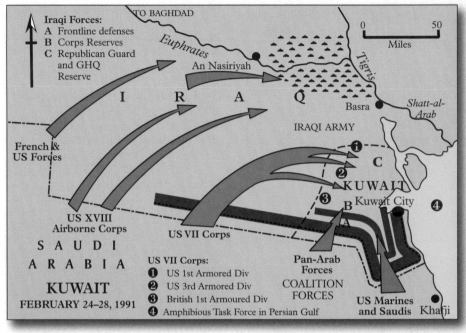

Iraqi Forces:
A Frontline defenses
B Corps Reserves
C Republican Guard and GHQ Reserve

TO BAGHDAD

Euphrates

An Nasiriyah

Tigris

0   50
Miles

I R A Q

Basra   Shatt-al-Arab

IRAQI ARMY

French & US Forces

❶
C
❷
KUWAIT
❸
B Kuwait City   ❹
A

US XVIII Airborne Corps

US VII Corps

SAUDI

ARABIA

KUWAIT

FEBRUARY 24–28, 1991

US VII Corps:
❶ US 1st Armored Div
❷ US 3rd Armored Div
❸ British 1st Armoured Div
❹ Amphibious Task Force in Persian Gulf

Pan-Arab Forces

COALITION FORCES

US Marines and Saudis   Khafji

Battle of Kuwait (Operation 'Desert Storm')

Context Gulf War

Date February 24–28, 1991

Location Kuwait and southern Iraq at the head of the Persian Gulf

Commanders/Forces General Norman Schwarzkopf commanding multi-national coalition forces comprising 665,000 troops. Possibly 500,000 Iraqi troops nominally commanded by President Saddam Hussein

Objectives Liberation of Kuwait from Iraqi occupation

Casualties Coalition *c*.500 killed or wounded. Iraq estimated 60,000 killed and 175,000 made prisoner

Victor Allies

Consequences Kuwait was freed and another Middle East crisis ended. But Saddam Hussein's despotic régime continued to make mischief in the region until terminated by another US-led invasion in 2003. This has, however, further destablized the Middle East.

Below: US M-1A1 Abrams Main Battle Tanks of the 3rd Armored Division advance during Operation 'Desert Storm'.

H. Norman Schwarzkopf (1934–)
The first great commander of the 'television age'. Schwarzkopf was highly decorated for his service in Vietnam (1965–6, 1969–70). Rising through the ranks, he commanded the ground forces involved in the invasion of Grenada in 1983. After the Iraqi invasion of Kuwait in 1990, he directed the massive multinational build-up of forces and led them to victory in Operation 'Desert Storm' in February 1991. A natural communicator whose character and charisma immediately won him worldwide fame, he brought to bear a deep understanding of military history and strategy to win a major coalition victory with minimal casualties.

March 29, 1973 Last US troops leave South Vietnam.
Jan 1974 North Vietnam resumes the war
April 30, 1975 North Vietnamese enter Saigon; South Vietnam surrenders

1964–66 Indonesian-Malaysian emergency
1970 Vietcong-Cambodian fighting
1973 Communist uprising in Cambodia
1975 Indonesia invades East Timor
1975 Khmer Rouge seizes control of Cambodia
1979 Sino-Vietnamese war
1979–89 Vietnamese intervention in Cambodia

Middle East
1975/6 Lebanese Civil War
1974 Turkish invasion of northern Cyprus
1978 Israeli invasion of southern Lebanon
1978 Iranian Revolution; fall of the Shah; establishment of Islamic Republic under Ayatollah Khomeini
1979 US embassy in Tehran occupied and staff held hostage
April 1980 Failure of US special operations raid to rescue Tehran hostages
April 30, 1980 Iranian Embassy siege in London ended by SAS attack on 5 May
1979–89 Russo-Afghan War
1980–9 Iran-Iraq War
1982 Israeli invasion of Lebanon (Operation 'Peace for Galilee')
1983–4 Israeli intervention in Lebanon
1986 Yemeni Civil War
1986 US bombs Libya (Operation 'Eldorado Canyon')
1987 Arab intifada against Israel begins
1990–1 GULF WAR
1990 Iraqi invasion of Kuwait
Feb 24–28, 1991 Operation 'Desert Storm'. Schwarzkopf's Coalition forces destroy the Iraqi army and liberate Kuwait
1992–94 Armenia-Azerbaijan war over Nagorno-Karabakh
1993 Tadjikistan State of Emergency
1994 Jordan-Israel formal peace (having

BATTLEFIELD MISSILES

A short-range ballistic missile (SRBM) is a ballistic missile with a range of about 1,000 km (600 miles) or less. They are usually capable of carrying nuclear weapons as well as conventional explosives and are of relatively low cost and ease of configuration.

Scud missiles were fired at a US Coast Guard station on the nearby Italian island of Lampedusa when Libya responded to US airstrikes in 1986. Missiles were used in several regional conflicts that included use by Soviet and Afghan Communist forces in Afghanistan and by Iranians and Iraqis against one another in the so-called 'War of the Cities' during the Iran-Iraq War (1980–88). Scuds were also used by Iraq during the Persian Gulf War against Israel and coalition targets in Saudi Arabia. More than a dozen Scuds were fired from Afghanistan at targets in Pakistan in 1988. A small number of Scud missiles were used in the 1994 civil war in Yemen and by Russian forces in Chechnya in 1996 and onwards.

Above right: The US Army Honest John battlefield missile was the first nuclear-capable surface-to-surface rocket in the US arsenal. It was first tested in 1951 and deployed in January 1953.

Left: The US Army Pershing missile was first test-launched in February 1960 and deployed in 1963 to West Germany. It had a maximum range of 460 miles. The warhead could be conventional explosive or nuclear.

Below right: The Soviet Scud missile and its derivatives constitute one of the few ballistic missiles to have been used in actual warfare. The Scud-A had a maximum range of 80 miles with the later Scud-D having a maximum range of 400 miles.

Above: The hatches of the 12 vertical-launch Tomahawk missile tubes stand open on the bow of the nuclear-powered attack submarine USS Oklahoma City (SSN-723).

Above: The launch of a BGM-109 Tomahawk cruise missile from its Armored Box Launcher (ABL) aboard a US destroyer. The missile has a speed of 550 mph (880 km/h) and a range of 2,500km. It can carry a conventional warhead of 1,000 lb (450 kg) or a BLU-97/B Combined Effects Bomb.

INFANTRY MISSILES

Left: The bazooka is a man-portable anti-tank rocket launcher, made famous during World War II where it was one of the primary infantry anti-tank weapons used by the US Armed Forces. It was one of the first weapons based on the High explosive anti-tank (HEAT) shell to enter service. It was nicknamed 'bazooka' from a vague resemblance to the musical instrument of the same name. The first bazookas had a calibre of 2.36 inches (right) and were superseded by the 3.5 inch 'Super Bazooka' (left).

Center left: Widely distributed worldwide is the RPG (Rocket Propelled Grenade). Today, modern armies such as that of the United States, have incorporated armor on their tanks that make them invulnerable to such grenades.

Below: A round fired from a SMAW (Shoulder Launched Multipurpose Assault Weapon). The SMAW is an 83mm man-portable weapon and has been in service with the US Army since the mid-1980s

Above: A Stinger missile is a short-range man-portable surface-to-air missile. The first entered service in 1981. To date it has been used by the military of the United States and 29 other countries and has been deployed successfully in numerous conflicts around the world.

Below: The AT4 Shoulder Mounted Anti-Armor Weapon is a one-shot weapon built in Sweden by Saab Bofors Dynamics. It gives infantry the ability to destroy or disable armored vehicles and fortifications, but it is not considered sufficient to defeat a modern main battle tank. The launcher and projectile are a single unit of ammunition, the launcher being discarded after use.

been technically at war since 1948)
1994–6 Russian intervention in Chechnya
1999–2000 Second Russian invasion of
    Chechnya; Battle for Grozny

India
1947–8 Indian War of Separation. Pakistan
    seizes a third of Kashmir
1961 Ceylon state of emergency
1965 Second Indo-Pakistan War
1969 Third Indo-Pakistan War
1984–89 Sri Lankan emergency
1984 Indian offensive in Punjab
1999 Kashmir: Indo-Pakistan border conflict

Africa
1952 Kenya: Mau-Mau emergency
1954–62 Algerian-French war of
    Independence
1959 Rhodesian emergency
1960 South Africa: Sharpeville massacre
1960–63 Congo
1961–75 Angolan War of Independence
1964 Rwanda: Tutsi massacres
1967–70 Nigerian Civil War
1971–9 Rhodesian Civil War; Rhodesia
    becomes Zimbabwe
1975–7 Chad Civil War
1975–91 Angolan Civil War
1976 Morocco invades West Sahara
July 1976 Entebbe raid by Israelis frees
    hostages
1977 Mogadisho incident
1977 Egyptian-Libyan conflict
1977 Ethiopia: Ogaden war
1977–8 Liberian Civil War
1979 Tanzania invades Uganda
1981 Zimbabwe uprising crushed
1983 Polisario attack Moroccans in West
    Sahara
1984–87 Chad war
1991 Ethiopian Civil War
1991 Somali Civil War / US intervention
1992–5 2nd Angolan Civil War
1993 Burundi Civil War
1994 Rwandan Civil War
1996–7 War of the African Great Lakes

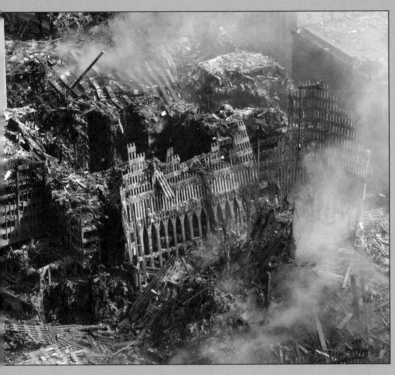

Right: Smoke bellows from the Pentagon after a hijacked commercial jetliner crashed into the building as part of the September 11, 2001 attack. The Pentagon crash followed an attack on the twin towers of the World Trade Center in New York City in one of the worst terrorist actions in history.

Left: Ground Zero, New York City. An aerial view shows only a small portion of the scene where the World Trade Center collapsed following the September 11 terrorist attack. Surrounding buildings were heavily damaged by the debris and massive force of the falling twin towers.

Below: US troops at Kandahar, Afghanistan, 2005.

The War on Terror was proclaimed by US President George W. Bush in 2001 in response to a dramatic attack by Islamic terrorists. On September 11 of that year, members of the Al Qaeda extreme Islamic fundamentalist group hijacked four civil airliners and succeeded in crashing two of them into the World Trade Center, New York, and another into the Pentagon, HQ of the US armed forces.

Two major military campaigns ensued, quite apart from the West's continuing intelligence and covert activities. In 2001 a US-led coalition invaded Afghanistan to oust the extreme Islamic Taleban regime there and to root out the Al Qaeda terrorists it was harboring. The Taleban were deposed but the terrorists not eliminated; subsequently the Taleban and local warlords reasserted themselves, necessitating the continued presence of Western troops in the country.

In 2003 the Americans (with participation by Britain and other Western allies) invaded Iraq, ostensibly to remove the dictator Saddam Hussein from power, eliminate alleged weapons of mass destruction in the country and sever supposed Iraqi links with terrorism. Saddam was removed, but weapons of mass destruction were not found, while a lack of American planning for the post-victory security of the country led to virtual civil war and internecine Islamic conflict, which Western forces struggled to contain.

Osama Bin Laden.   President George W. Bush.

Europe
1969–98 NORTHERN IRELAND TERROR CAMPAIGN
1969 Terrorist bombings by Protestant organizations and Irish Republican Army begin and continue over some three decades, interspersed with ceasefires and negotiations
1972 'Bloody Sunday': British paratroops open fire on civil rights protesters killing 13
1979 Lord Mountbatten murdered by IRA
1981 First IRA Bombings in London; subsequent targets include British Army bases in Germany and Gibraltar
1984 Brighton Bomb fails to kill British Prime Minister Margaret Thatcher
1991 IRA mortar attack on 10 Downing Street (home/office of the British Prime Minister)
1991–9 WAR OF YUGOSLAVIAN DISSOLUTION
1991–5 Serbia/Croatia/ Slovenia/Bosnia phase
1999 Serbia/Kosovo phase

War on Terrorism
Sept 11, 2001 Extremist Islamic group Al Qaeda make terrorist attack on USA: two hijacked civil airliners are crashed into the World Trade Center, New York, destroying it and killing more than 3,000 people; a third airliner hits the Pentagon.
Sept 18, 2001 USA declares War on Terrorism
While Islamic fundamentalist terror attacks target many countries, a substantial intelligence war is waged by Western security organizations to prevent or forestall them. Attacks include:
2002, 2005 Bali bombings
2003 Madrid train bombings
2005 London bombings

2001 US-led coalition invades Afghanistan and deposes extremist Taleban regime there; ongoing security operations continue thereafter

Above: *A US F-16 Fighting Falcon banks during a mission over Iraq armed with JDAM GPS satellite-guided bombs.* **Inset:** *The American GBU-31/32 Joint Direct Attack Munition (JDAM) is a tailkit that fits on general purpose unguided bombs and turns them into 'smart' – GPS-guided – bombs. Its range is up to 15 miles.*

Below: *The U.S. Navy's RQ-4A Global Hawk, an Unmanned Aerial Vehicle (UAV) – a pilotless aircraft, controlled from the ground. It has a cruising speed of* 404 mph and can stay in the air for 34 hours at a height of up to 65,000 feet (20,000 meters).

Right: *The Northrop Grumman B-2 Spirit stealth heavy bomber operated by the US Air Force. It is a second-generation stealth technology aircraft. It has seen combat during the Kosovo War in 1999, Afghanistan during Operation 'Enduring Freedom' and Iraq in Operation 'Iraqi Freedom'. Flying from mainland America, missions have lasted more than 30 hours and one mission in excess of 50 hours.*

IRAQ

Left: Iraqi men serving in the Indigenous Counter Insurgency Force pose for a photograph at their check point in Al Namer, Iraq, 2007.

Right An Afghan National Army soldier helps coalition forces search Ala Say Valley, Afghanistan, 2007, for suspected Taleban members.

Below: Assisting Iraqi police, US Marines patrol a street in Fallujah, Iraq, 2007.

The Iraq War

2003 US-led coalition invades Iraq and
deposes dictator Saddam Hussein;
ongoing security operations continue
thereafter in a practically civil-war
situation, with Shi'a and Sunni Muslims
using terror bombings against each other
and the West's security forces

Many other quasi-civil-war conflicts
continue, especially in the Middle East and
Africa, with various levels of involvement in
peace-making, peace-keeping and
humanitarian roles, by the United Nations,
NATO and the Western powers.

*Right: The Soviet
Kalashnikov assault
rifle, built for the Soviet
Army after World War
II, is the most
successful of all military
rifles – perhaps seventy
million have been made
to date, and production
continues in several
countries. Of 0.3in
caliber, with a thirty-
round box magazine, it
is comparatively
unsophisticated and
not the most accurate
of assault rifles. But it
is simple, sturdy,
efficient and rugged
enough to be used in
the most demanding of
conditions. It has
become an icon of
popular and terrorist
movements around the
world.*

THE GREAT BATTLES OF HISTORY: AN A–Z

BOLD TYPE INDICATES VICTOR; NO CLEAR VICTOR IS INDICATED BY AN ABSENCE OF BOLD

Abensberg	Apr 19–20, 1809	*Napoleon* [F] – Charles [A-H]
Aberdeen	Sept 13, 1644	*Montrose* [R] – Burleigh [Cov]
Aboukir	July 25, 1799	*Napoleon* [F] – Mustapha Pasha [T]
Abu Hamed	Aug 7, 1897	*Hunter* [Br] – Mohammed Zain [Mahd]
Abu Klea	Jan 17, 1885	*Stewart* [Br] – Mahdists
Abu Kru	Jan 19, 1885	*Stewart* [Br] – Mahdists
Accra	Aug 7, 1826	*British* – Ashantis
Acragas siege/battle	c.406BC	*Hamilcar/Himilco* [Carth] – Daphnaeus [Syrac]
Acre I	July 12, 1191	*Richard the Lionheart* [Crusaders] – Muslims
Acre II	Apr 6 – May 15, 1291	*Sultan Al-Ashraf* [Mus] – Amalric [Christ]
Acre III	Mar 18 – May 20, 1799	*Djezzar/Smith* [T] – Napoleon [F]
Acre IV	Nov 3, 1840	*Stopford* [Br/T] – Ibrahim Pasha [Eg]
Actium	Sept 2, 31BC	*Agrippa* [Octavian] – Antony/Cleopatra
Acultzingo	Apr 28, 1862	*Lorencez* [F] – Zaragoza [Mex]
Ad Decimum	Sept 14, 533	Gelimer [Van] – *Belisarius* [Rom]
Admagetobriga	61BC	*Ariovistus* [Sequani] – Eporedorix [Aedui]
Adowa	Mar 1, 1896	*Menelek* [Abyssinia] – Baratieri [It]
Adrianople I	July 3, 323	*Constantine* [Emp West] – Licinius [Emp East]
Adrianople II	Aug 9, 378	Valens [Emp East] – *Fritigern* [Goths]
Adrianople III	Apr 15, 1205	*Kaloyan* [Bul] – Baldwin [Crus]/Dandolo [Ven]
Adrianople IV	Mar 26, 1913	*Bulgarians/Greeks* – Shukri Pasha [T]
Aduatuca	53BC	*Ambiorix* [Eburones] – Titurius Sabinus [Rom]

Key to Nationalities

[A-H]	Austria-Hungary	[E Ang]	East Anglia	[Mahd]	Mahdists	[RoyHigh]	Royalist
[A-S]	Anglo-Saxons	[Eg]	Egypt	[Malt]	Malta		Highlanders
[A]	Austria	[Emp East]	Eastern Roman	[Mam]	Mamelukes	[Rep]	Republic
[Afg]	Afghanistan		Empire	[Man]	Mantua	[S Emp]	Southern Empire
[Alb]	Albania	[Emp West]	Western Roman	[Mar]	Marathas		(Japan)
[Alg]	Algeria		Empire	[Merc]	Mercia	[SA]	South Africa
[Amer]	USA/ America	[Eng]	England	[Mex]	Mexico	[Sab]	Sabines
[Arg]	Argentina	[F]	France	[Mex Lib]	Mexican Liberals	[Sam]	Samnites
[Ath]	Athens	[Fed]	Federals	[Mold]	Moldavia	[Sara]	Saracens
[Bat]	Batavian Republic	[Fin]	Finland	[Mog]	Moghuls	[Sard]	Sardinia
	(Dutch)	[Flem]	Flemish	[Mon]	Mongols	[Sax]	Saxony
[Bav]	Bavaria	[Flem Prot]	Flemish Protestants	[Mus]	Muslims	[Scots]	Scotland
[Bel]	Belgium	[Gari]	Garibaldians	[Mys]	Mysore	[Serb]	Serbia
[Boh]	Bohemia	[Gen]	Genoa	[N Emp]	Northern Empire	[Sic]	Sicily
[Bol]	Bolivia	[Ger]	Germany		(Japan)	[Sp]	Spain
[Bos]	Bosnia	[Ger Prot]	German Protestants	[Neap]	Naples	[Spar]	Sparta
[Br]	Britain	[Ghib]	Ghibellines	[New Eng]	New Englanders	[Sud]	Sudan
[Bran]	Brandenburg	[Govt]	Government	[Nor]	Normans	[Swed]	Sweden
[Braz]	Brazil	[Gr]	Greece	[Norw]	Norway	[Syr]	Syria
[Bul]	Bulgaria	[Han]	Hanover	[Northum]	Northumbria	[Syrac]	Syracuse
[Burg]	Burgundy	[Hess]	Hesse	[NZ]	New Zealand	[T]	Turks
[Burm]	Burma	[High]	Highlanders	[P]	Prussia	[Tar]	Tartars
[Byz]	Byzantium	[HRE]	Holy Roman Empire	[Palat]	Palatinate	[Teu]	Teutonic Knights
[Cæs]	Cæsarians	[Hug]	Huguenots	[Pann]	Pannonian Legions	[Tex]	Texas
[Can]	Canada	[Hung]	Hungary	[Pap]	Papal States	[Trans]	Transylvania
[Carl]	Carlists	[Huss]	Hussites	[Para]	Paraguay	[Tur]	Turkey
[Carth]	Carthage	[Imp]	Empire (Roman/	[Parl]	Parliament	[Ulst Prot]	Ulster
[Cast]	Castile		Byzantine/Japanese/	[Parth]	Parthians		Protestants
[Cat]	Catalan		Holy Roman)	[Pat]	Patriots	[UN]	United Nations
[Cath]	Catholics	[Imp/Pret]	Imperial Pretender	[Pelo]	Peloponnesians	[Uru]	Uruguay
[Cav]	Cavalry	[Ind]	Indians	[Per]	Persia	[US]	USA
[Chil]	Chile	[Ion]	Ionians	[Pied]	Piedmont	[Van]	Vandals
[Chin]	China	[Ir]	Ireland	[Pol]	Poland	[Ven]	Venice
[Christ]	Christians	[Isr]	Israel	[Pomp]	Pompeians	[Viet]	Vietnam
[Col]	Columbia	[It]	Italy	[Pon]	Pontics	[Virg]	Virginia
[Con]	Confederate States	[Jacob]	Jacobites	[Port]	Portugal	[Vis]	Visigoths
[Cong]	Congressists	[Jap]	Japan	[R]	Russia	[York]	Yorkists
[Cov]	Covenanters	[Kor]	Korea	[reb]	rebels	[W Sax]	West Saxons
[Cris]	Cristinos	[Lanc]	Lancastrians	[Rhod]	Rhodes	[Wa]	Walloons
[Crus]	Crusaders	[Lith]	Lithuania	[Rep]	Republic	[Wall]	Wallachians
[Dan]	Denmark	[Lyd]	Lydians	[Rom]	Rome	[Wes]	Wessex
[Dut]	Dutch	[Mac]	Macedonia	[Roy]	Royalists	[Würt]	Württemberg

Aegates Islands	241BC	*Catulus* [Rom] – Hanno [Carth]
Ægina	458BC	*Athenians* – Ægina
Aegospotami	405BC	*Lysander* [Pelo] – Conon [Ath]
Ægusa	Mar 10, 241BC	*Catulus* [Rom] – Hanno [Carth]
Agincourt	Oct 25, 1415	*Henry V* [Eng] – d'Albret [F]
Agnadello	May 14, 1509	*Louis XII* [F] – Trioulzio [Ven]
Agordat	Dec 21, 1893	*Arimondi* [It] – Ahmed Ali [Mahd]
Agra I	1708	*Bahadur* [Mog] – Muazim [reb]
Agra II	Oct 17, 1803	*Lake* [Br] – Sindhia [Mar]
Ahmed Khel	Apr 19, 1880	*Stewart* [Br] – Afghans
Ahmedabad	Feb 15, 1780	*Goddard* [Br] – Afghans /Mahrattas
Ahmednugger I	1599	*Akbar Khan* [Moghuls] – Chand Bibi [Deccan]
Ahmednuggur II	Aug 8–12, 1803	*Wellesley* [Br/Mys/Peshwa Mar] – Sindhia [Mar]/Deccan
Ain Jalut	1260	Kitboga [Mon] – *Qutuz* [Mam]
Aisne River I	Sept 14–18, 1914	*Joffre* [F] – Falkenhayn [Ger]
Aisne River II	Apr 16–20, 1917	Nivelle [F] – *Hindenburg/Ludendorff* [Ger]
Aisne River III	May 27 – June 17, 1918	*Ludendorff* [Ger] – Duchêne [F]
Aix Roads	Apr 10–11, 1809	*Gambier/Cochrane* [Br] – Williamez [F]
Aix-la-Chapelle	Mar 3, 1795	*Prince of Saxe-Coburg* [A] – Miranda [F]
Ajnadain	July 30, 634	*Khalid* [Mus] – Theodorus [Byz]
Akhalzic	Aug 27, 1828	*Paskievich* [R] – Turks
Aladja Dagh	Oct 15, 1877	*Grand Duke Michael* [R] – Mukhtar Pasha [T]
Alalia	535BC	*Etruscans/Phoenicians* – Phocaeans
Alam Halfa	Aug 30 – Sept 2, 1942	*Montgomery* [Br] – Rommel [Ger/It]
Alamo, siege of	Feb 23 – Mar 6, 1836	*Santa Anna* [Mex] – Travis/Bowie [Texans]
Aland	July 1714	*Apraxine* [R] – Erinschild [Swed]
Alarcos	July 18, 1195	*Yakub el Mansur* [Moors] – Alfonso VIII of Castile [Sp]
Albuera	May 16, 1811	*Beresford* [Br/Port/Sp] – Soult [F]
Alicudi	Jan 8, 1676	de Ruyter [Dut] – Duquesne [F]
Alcantara	1706	*Galway* [Br/Port] – Berwick [F]
Aleppo I	638	*Khalid ibn-al-Walid* [Mus] – Youkinna [Byz]
Aleppo II	Nov 11, 1400	*Timur* [Tartars] – Syrian Emirs [T]
Aleppo III	Aug 24, 1516	*Selim I* [T] – Kansu al-Gauri [Mam]
Alesia	52BC	*Cæsar* [Rom] – Vercingetorix [Gauls]
Alexandria I	Oct 48BC – Mar 47BC	*Caesar* [Rom] – Ptolemy XII [Eg]
Alexandria II	642	*Amr Ibn Al-As* [Mus] – city [Byz]
Alexandria III	Mar 21, 1801	*Abercrombie* [Br] – Menou [F]
Alexandria IV	July 11, 1882	*Seymour* [Br] – Arabi Pasha [Eg]
Alford	July 2, 1645	*Montrose* [Roy] – Baillie [Cov]
Algeciras Bay	July 6, 1801	Saumarez [Br] – *Linois* [F/Sp]
Alghero	1353	*Aragonese* – Genoese
Algiers I	July 8, 1775	de Castijon/O'Reilly [Sp] – city
Algiers II	Aug 26, 1816	*Exmouth/Van Capellan* [Br/Dut] – city
Alhama	Feb 28, 1482	*de Ortiga* [Sp] – town
Alhandega	939	Abd er-Rahman [Moors] – *Ramiro II* [Christians]
Alicante	June 29, 1706	*Byng* [Br] – town
Aligarh	Sept 4, 1803	*Lake/Morton* [Br] – Sindhia [Mar]
Aliwal	Jan 28, 1846	*Smith* [Br] – Runjoor Singh [Sikhs]
Aljubarrota	Aug 14, 1385	*John I* [Port] – John [Cast]
Alkmaar I	Aug 21 – Oct 8, 1573	*fortress* [Dut Pat] – de Toledo [Sp]
Alkmaar II	Oct 2, 1799	*Duke of York* [Br/R] – Brune [F]
Allia, The	July 16, 389BC	Quintus Sulpicius [Rom] – *Brennus* [Gauls]
Alma	Sept 20, 1854	*Raglan/St Arnaud* [Br/F] – Menshikov [R]
Almanza	Apr 25, 1707	*Berwick* [F/Sp] – Galway [Br/Port]
Almenara	July 10, 1710	*Stanhope* [Br] – Philip V [Sp]
Almorah	Apr 25, 1815	*Nicolls/Gardiner* [Br] – town
Alnwick I	Nov 13, 1093	Malcolm Canmore [Scots] – *English*
Alnwick II	June 13, 1174	William the Lion [Scots] – *English*
Alsen	June 29, 1864	*Prussians* – Danes
Altendorf	Aug 24, 1632	*Wallenstein* [Imp] – Gustavus Adolphus [Swed/Ger]
Alto Pascio	1325	*Castracane of Lucca* [Ghib] – Guelfs
Amakusa	1638	Masada Shiro [reb] – *Nobutsuna* [Shogun]
Amalinde	1818	Gaikas – *Ndlambi*

Ambate	1532	*Atahualpa* [Incas] – Huascar [Incas]
Amberg	Aug 24, 1796	*Charles* [A] – Jourdan [F]
Ambracian Gulf	435BC	Corinthians – *Corcyreans*
Ambur	1749	*Muzaffar Jung/Chunda Sahib/de Bussy* [reb/F] –
Anwar-ud-din [Carnatics]		
Amida	359	Fortress [Rom] – *Sapor II* [Per]
Amiens	Aug 8–11, 1918	Ludendorff [Ger] – Foch [F]
Amoaful	Jan 31, 1874	*Wolseley* [Br] – Coffee [Ashantis]
Amorium	838	*Motassem* [Mus] – Theophilus [Gr]
Amphipolis	Mar 422BC	Cleon [Ath] – *Brasidas* [Spar]
Amstetten	Nov 5, 1805	*Murat/Lannes* [F] – Russians
Añaquito	Jan 18, 1546	*Pizarro* [Sp Conquistadors] – Nuñez [Sp Conquistadors]
Ancona	Sept 1860	*Persano/Cialdini* [Pied] – La Moricière [Pap]
Ancrum Moor	Feb 17, 1545	*Earl of Angus* [Scots] – Evans [Eng]
Ancyræ	242BC	Seleucus Callinicus [Syr] – *Hierax* [rebels]
Angora	July 30, 1402	*Timur* [Tartars] – Bayazid I [T]
Antietam	Sept 17, 1862	Lee [Con] – McClellan [Fed]
Antioch I	244BC	Seleucus Callinicus [Syr] – *Ptolemy Energetes* [Eg]
Antioch II	218	*Varius Avitus* [rebel] – Macrinus [Rom]
Antioch III	613	*Chosroes II* [Per] – Byzantines
Antioch IV	June 5–28, 1098	*Bohemund/Raymond* [Crus] – Kerboga of Mosul [T]
Antioch V	Oct 21, 1097 – June 3, 1098	*Bohemund/Raymond* [Crus] – Yagi Siyan [T]
Antium	May 30, 1387	*Pisani* [Ven] – Fieschi [Gen]
Antwerp I	Oct 3, 1576	*Spanish mutineers* – city [Wa]
Antwerp II	Aug 17, 1585	*Farnese* [Sp] – city
Antwerp III	Nov – Dec 1832	*French* – Chassé [Bel]
Antwerp IV	Oct 1–9, 1914	*Falkenhayn* [Ger] – King Albert I [Bel]
Anzio	Jan 22 – May 23, 1944	*Lucas/Truscott* [US] – Mackensen [Ger]
Aong	July 15, 1857	*Havelock* [Br] – [mutineers]
Aquae Sextiae	102BC	Teutobod [Teu] – *Marius* [Rom]
Aquileia	Sept 5–6, 394	*Theodosius* [East] – Eugenius [West]
Arausio	105BC	*Boiorix* [Gauls] – Cæpio/Mallius Maximus [Rom]
Araxes, The	589	*Maurice* [Rom] – Bahram [Per]
Arbedo	June 30, 1422	Swiss – *Carmagnola* [Duchy of Milan]
Arbela: see *Gaugamela*		
Arcis-sur-Aube	Mar 20–1, 1814	Schwarzenberg [Allies] – Napoleon [F]
Arcola	Nov 15–17, 1796	*Napoleon* [F] – Alvintzi [A]
Arcot	Sept – Oct 1751	*Clive* [Br/Sepoys] – Chunda Sahib [Carnatics/F]
Ardennes	Dec 16, 1944 – Jan 28, 1945	*Bradley* [US] – Rundstedt [Ger]
Argaum	Nov 29, 1803	*Wellesley* [Br/Mys/Peshwa Mar] – Sindhia/Berar [Mar]
Argentaria	May 378	*Gratianus* [Rom] – Priarius [Alemanni]
Argentoratum	Aug 357	*Julian* [Rom] – Chnodomar [Alemanni]
Arginusæ	406BC	*Thrasyllus* [Ath] – Callicratidas [Pelop]
Argonne Forest	Sept 26 – Nov 11, 1918	*Pershing/Foch* [US/F/Br] – Ludendorff/Groener [Ger]
Argos	195BC	Nabis [Spar] – *Flaminius* [Rom/Mac]
Arius, The	214BC	Antiochus [Syr] – Arsaces III/Euthydemus [Parth]
Arkenholm	May 12, 1455	*James II* [Scots] – Douglas brothers [rebels]
Arklow	June 9, 1798	*Needham* [Br] – Murphy [Irish rebels]
Armada, The	July 31 – Aug 8, 1588	*Lord Howard of Effingham* [Eng] – Duke of Medina Sidonia [Sp]
Arnhem	Sept 17–26, 1944	*Rundstedt* [Ger] – Montgomery [Allies]
Arques	Sept 21, 1589	*Henri IV* [Hug] – Duc de Mayenne [Leaguers]
Arrah (Mutiny)	July 25 – Aug 3, 1857	*Boyle* [Br/Sikhs] – Kur Singh [Sepoys]
Arras	Apr 9 – May 15, 1917	*Haig* [Br] – Hindenburg [Ger]
Arretium	283BC	L. Cæcilius Metellus – *Etruscans*
Arroyo dos Molinos	Oct 28, 1811	*Hill* [Br/Port] – Girard [F]
Arroyo Grande	Dec 6, 1842	*Oribe* [Arg] – Rivera [Uru]
Arsouf	Sept 7, 1191	*King Richard* [Eng/Crusaders] – Saladin [Turks]
Artois I	Sept 27 – Oct 12, 1914	*Germans* – French/British
Artois II	May 9 – June 18, 1915	Falkenhayn [Ger] – Joffre [F]
Artois-Loos	Sept 25 – Oct 8, 1915	Falkenhayn [Ger] – Haig [Br]/d'Urbal [F]
Ascalon	Aug 12, 1099	*Godefroi* [Crus] – al-Afdal [Eg]
Asculum I	279BC	Sulpicius Saverrio/P. Decius Mus [Rom] – *Pyrrhus* [Epirots]
Asculum II	89BC	*Strabo* [Rom] – Judacilius [It]

Ashdown	Jan 8, 871	*Alfred* [W Sax] – Bagsac/Halfdene [Danes]
Asiago	May 15 – June 17, 1916	Cadorna [It] – Hotzendorff [A]
Askultsik	1828	Turks – *Paskievich* [R]
Aspendus	191BC	Hannibal [Syr] – *Eudamus* [Rhod]
Aspern-Essling	May 21–2, 1809	*Archduke Charles* [A] – Napoleon [F]
Aspromonte	Aug 29, 1862	*Pallavicini* [Roy] – Garibaldi ['Red Shirts']
Assandun (Ashingdon)	Oct 18, 1016	*Canute* [Danes] – Edmund Ironside [A-S]
Assaye	Sept 23, 1803	*Wellesley* [Br/Mys/Peshwa Mar] – Sindhia [Mar]
Astrakhan I	1554–6	*Ivan IV* [R] – Mongols
Astrakhan II	1569	Selim II [T] – *town* [R]
Atbara	Apr 8, 1898	*Kitchener* [Br/Eg] – Mahmoud [Mahd]
Atlanta I	July 22, 1864	Hood [Con] – *McPherson* [Fed]
Atlanta II	Aug 27–31, 1864	*Sherman* [Fed] – Hood [Con]
Auerstadt	Oct 14, 1806	*Davoût* [F] – Brunswick [P]
Aughrim	July 12, 1691	*Ginkel* [Br] – St-Ruth/Lucan[F/Ir reb]
Augsburg	910	*Magyars* – Germans
Augusta	Aug 22, 1676	Duquesne [F] – de la Cerda [Sp/Dut Allies]
Auldearn	May 9, 1645	*Montrose* [Roy High] – Hurry [Cov]
Auray	Sept 29, 1364	*Chandos* [Eng] – du Guesclin/de Blois [F]
Aussig	1426	*Prokop* [Hussite] – Ger Catholics
Austerlitz	Dec 2, 1805	*Napoleon* [F] – Kutuzov [A-R]
Avaricum	53BC	Vercingetorix [Gauls] – *Cæsar* [Rom]
Avus	198BC	Philip [Mac] – *T. Quinctius Flaminius* [Rom]
Axarquia	Mar 20, 1483	Marquis of Cadiz [Sp] – Abul Hasan [Moors]
Ayacucho	Dec 9, 1824	*Sucre* [Patriots] – de la Serna [Sp]
Aylesford	456	*Hengist/Horsa* [Jutes] – Vortigern [Britons]
Azimghur	Apr 15, 1858	Layard [Br] – Kur Singh [mutineers]
Azores	1591	Howard [Br] – *Bassano* [Sp]
Badajoz	Apr 6, 1812	*Wellington* [Br/Port] – Phillipon [F/Sp/Hess]
Baghdad I	Feb 15, 1258	*Hulagu* [Mon] – Mustasim [Abbasid]
Baghdad II	July 23, 1401	*Timur* [Tar] – city
Baghdad III	1534	*Suleiman I* [T] – Shah Thamosp [Per]
Baghdad IV	March 4–11, 1917	*Maude* [Br] – Pasha [T]
Bagradas	49BC	Curio [Cæs] – *Juba/Saburra* [Numidians]
Bahur	Aug 1752	*Lawrence* [Br/levies] – Kirkjean[F]
Bai ju	506BC	*Sun Tzu* [Wu] – Ch'u
Balaclava	Oct 25, 1854	*Raglan* [Br] – Menshikov
Ball's Bluff	Oct 21, 1861	*Evans* [Con] – Stone/Baker [Fed]
Ballinamuck	Sept 8, 1798	*Cornwallis* [Br] – Humbert [F]
Ballymore	June 3, 1798	Walpole [Roy] – *Murphy* [rebels]
Balochpur	1623	*Jahangir* [Mog] – Khurram [rebels]
Baltimore	Sept 12, 1814	*Stricker* [Amer] – Ross/Brooke [Br]
Bamian	1221	*Genghis Khan* [Mon] – city
Banda	Apr 19, 1858	*Whitlock* [Br] – Nawab of Banda [mutineers]
Banda Islands	Mar 8, 1796	*Rainier* [Br] – islands
Bands, The	961	*Indulph* [Scots] – Danes
Bangalore	Mar 7–21, 1791	*Cornwallis* [Br/Mar] – Tipu Sultan [Mysore]
Banitsa	Nov 1912	*Turks* – Greeks
Bannockburn	June 24, 1314	*Bruce* [Scots] – Edward II [Eng]
Bapaume	Jan 2–3, 1871	Faidherbe [F] – von Göben [Ger]
Barbosthenian Mtns	192BC	Narbis [Spar] – *Philopœmen* [Achæan League]
Barcelona	Sept 14, 1705	*Earl of Peterborough* [Br/Dut] – city
Barnet	Apr 14, 1471	*Edward IV* [York] – Earl of Warwick [Lanc]
Barquisimeto	1813	*Bolivar* [Col] – Spanish Royalists
Barrosa	Mar 4, 1811	*Graham* [Br] – Victor [F]
Bar-sur-Aube	Feb 27, 1814	*Wittgenstein/Wrede* [Allies] – Oudinot [F]
Basing	871	*Danes* – W Saxons
Bassano	Sept 8, 1796	*Napoleon* [F] – Wurmser [A]
Bassein	Nov 13, 1780	*Goddard* [Br] – garrison [Mahr]
Bassorah	665	*Caliph Ali* [Mus] – Telha/Zobin [rebels]
Bastogne	Dec 19–26, 1944	*McAuliffe* [US] – Manteuffel [Ger]
Bataan-Corregidor	Apr – May 6, 1942	*Homma* [Jap] – King/Wainwright [US]
Batavia	Aug 8, 1811	*Auchmuty* [Br] – town [Dut]

Batoche	May 9–12, 1885	*Middleton* [Can] – Riel [Ind]
Batowitz	1653	*Bogdan* [Wall] – John II [Pol]
Baugé	Mar 22, 1421	*Armagnacs* – Duke of Clarence [Br]
Bautzen	May 20–1, 1813	*Napoleon* [F] – Blücher/Wittgenstein [P/R]
Baylen	July 19, 1808	*Castaños* [Sp] – Dupont [F]
Bayonne	Apr 14, 1814	*Hope* [Br/Port] – Thouvenot [F]
Baza	June–Dec 1489	*Ferdinand* [Sp] – Sidi Yahye [Moor]
Beachy Head	July 10, 1690	*de Tourville* [F] – Torrington [Br/Dut]
Beaumont	Aug 30, 1870	*Prince of Saxony* [Ger] – de Failly [F]
Beaune-la-Rolande	Nov 28, 1870	*Duke of Mecklenburg* [Ger] – Crouzat [F]
Beauséjour	June 19, 1755	*Monckton* [Br] – de Vergor [F]
Beda Fomm	Feb 6–7, 1941	*O'Connor* [Br] – Graziani [It]
Bedr	623	*Mohammed* – Koreish
Bedriacum I	Apr 14, 69	Otho [Imp] – *Valens* [Vitellians]
Bedriacum II	Dec 69	Vitellians – *Antonius Primus* [Flavians]
Beecher's Island	Sept 17–27, 1868	Forsyth [US] – Roman Nose [Cheyenne]
Bega	1696	*Mustapha II* [T] – Imperialists
Belfort I	Nov 3, 1870 – Feb 15, 1871	Denfert-Rochereau – *Germans*
Belfort II	Jan 15–17, 1871	*Werder* [Ger] – Bourbaki/Garibaldi [F]
Belgrade I	Sept 1456	Mohammed II [T] – Hunyadi [city]
Belgrade II	1521	*Suleiman I* [T] – city
Belgrade III	Aug 16, 1717	*Prince Eugene* [A] – Ibrahim Pasha [T]
Belgrade IV	Oct 8, 1789	*Laudon* [A] – Turks
Belle Isle I	June 8, 1761	*Hodgson* [Br] – island
Belle Isle II	June 17, 1795	*Cornwallis* [Br] – Villaret-Joyeuse [F]
Belleau Wood	June 6 – July 1, 1918	Ludendorff [Ger] – *Pershing* [US]
Belmont	Nov 23, 1899	*Methuen* [Br] – Boers
Benburb	June 5, 1646	*O'Neill* [Ir rebels] – Monro [Parl]
Bender	Aug 1768	*Panin* [R] – Turks
Benevente	Dec 29, 1808	*Otway* [Br] – Lefebvre-Desnonëttes [F]
Benevento	Feb 26, 1266	Manfred [Neap] – *Charles of Anjou* [F]
Beneventum I	275BC	Pyrrhus [Epirots/It] – *M. Curius Dentatus* [Rom]
Beneventum II	214BC	Hanno [Carth] – *Tiberius Gracchus* [Rom]
Beneventum III	212BC	*Cn. Fluvius* [Rom] – Hanno [Carth]
Bennington	Aug 16, 1777	*Stark* [Amer] – Baum [Br/Hess]
Berezina	Nov 26–8, 1812	*Napoleon* [F] – Kutuzov [R]
Bergen	Apr 13, 1759	*de Broglie* [F] – Ferdinand of Brunswick [P]
Bergen-op-Zoom I	July 15 – Sept 18, 1747	*Lowendahl* [F] – Cronstrun [Dut/Br]
Bergen-op-Zoom II	Mar 8, 1775	*Bizouet* [F] – Cooke [Br]
Bergen-op-Zoom III	Sept 19, 1799	*Vandamme* [F] – York [Br/R]
Bergen-op-Zoom IV	Oct 2, 1799	*York* [Br/R] – Vandamme [F]
Bergfried	Feb 3, 1807	*Leval* [F] – Russians
Berlin	Apr 20 – May 2, 1945	*Konev* [R] – Weidling [Ger]
Béthune	July 14, 1707	du Puy Vauban [F] – *Schulemburg* [Imp]
Betioca	1813	*Bolivar* [Col] – Spanish Royalists
Betwa, The	Apr 1, 1858	*Rose* [Br] – Tantia Topi [mutineers]
Beylan	1831	*Ibrahim Pasha* [Syr/Eg] – Turks
Bhurtpore I	Jan 7 – Feb 21, 1805	*Lake* [Br] – fortress
Bhurtpore II	Dec 1825 – Jan 18, 1826	*Combermere* [Br] – Fortress
Biak Island	May 27 – June 28, 1944	*Doe* [US] – Kimura [Jap]
Biberac	Oct 1796	*Moreau* [F] – Latour [A]
Bibracte	July 58BC	*Cæsar* [Rom] – Helvetii
Bilbao I	Nov 9, 1836	Carlists – *Christinos*
Bilbao II	Mar 31 – June 19, 1937	*Mola/Dávila* [Sp Nationalists] – Encomienda/Ulibarri [Sp Republicans]
Biruan	1221	*Jellaluddin* [Mus] – Katuku [Tar]
Bismarck Operation	May 18–27, 1941	*Tovey* [Br] – Lütjens [Ger]
Bismarck Sea	Mar 2–5, 1943	*Kenney* [US/Australians] – Kimura [Jap]
Bithur	Aug 16, 1857	*Havelock* [Br] – mutineers
Bitonto	May 25, 1734	Imperialists – *Mortemar* [Sp]
Blackheath	June 22, 1497	*Henry VII* [Roy] – Flammock/Audley [rebels]
Blackwater	1598	*O'Neill* [Ir] – Bagnall [Eng]
Bladensburg	Aug 24, 1814	*Ross* [Br] – Winder [Amer]

Battle	Date	Combatants
Blanquefort	Nov 1, 1450	*Amanien* [F] – English
Blenheim	Aug 13, 1704	*Marlborough/Prince Eugene* [Br/Imp] – Tallard [F/Bav]
Bloemfontein	Mar 31, 1900	*Roberts* [Br] – Boers
Blood River	Dec 16, 1838	*Pretorius* [Boers] – Dingaan [Zulus]
Bloore Heath	Sept 23, 1459	*Earl of Salisbury* [York] – Henry VI [Lanc]
Blueberg	Jan 8, 1806	*Baird* [Br] – Janssens [F/Dut]
Bois-le-Duc	Nov 12, 1794	*Duke of York* [F/A] – Moreau [F]
Bokhara	Mar 1220	*Genghis Khan* [Mon] – Khwarazmians/Bokhariots
Bonsaso	Jan 21, 1824	*Ashantis* – McCarthy [Br]
Boomplaats	Aug 29, 1848	*Smith* [Br] – Pretorius [Boers]
Borghetto	May 30, 1796	*Napoleon* [F] – Beaulieu [A]
Bornhöved	1227	*Henry of Schwerin* [Ger] – Waldemar II [Dan]
Borny	Aug 15, 1870	Steinmetz [P] – Bazaine [F]
Borodino	Sept 7, 1812	*Napoleon* [F] – Kutuzov [R]
Boroughbridge	Mar 16, 1322	*Edward II* [Roy] – Hereford/Lancaster [rebels]
Borysthenes, The	1512	*Sigismund I* [Pol] – Muscovites
Bosra	632	*Serjabil/Khaled* [Mus] – fortress
Bosworth Field	Aug 22, 1485	*Henry VII* [Lanc] – Richard III [York]
Bothwell Bridge	July 2, 1679	*Duke of Monmouth* [Roy] – Hamilton [Cov]
Boudicca, defeat of	61	Boudicca [Britons] – *Suetonius* [Rom]
Boulogne	Sept 14, 1544	*Henry VIII* [Eng] – town
Bourbon	July 8, 1810	*Keatinge* [Br] – island
Bouvines	July 27, 1214	*Philip Augustus* [F] – Otto IV [Ger/Flem/Eng]
Boyaca	Aug 7, 1819	*Bolivar* [Col] – Barreiro [Sp Roy]
Boyne, The	July 1, 1690	*William III* [Br] – James II [Ir]
Braddock Down	Jan 19, 1643	*Hopton* [Roy] – Ruthven [Parl]
Bramham Moor	Feb 20, 1408	*Rokeby* – Earl of Northumberland [rebels]
Brandy Station	June 9, 1863	Hooker/Pleasanton [Fed] – Stuart [Con]
Brandywine	Sept 11, 1777	*Howe* [Br] – Washington [Amer]
Bregenz	Jan 1408	Leaguers – *Burghers of Constance*
Breitenfeld I	Sept 17, 1631	*Gustavus Adolphus* [Swed] – Tilly/Pappenheim [League]
Breitenfeld II	Nov 2, 1642	*Torstensson* [Swed] – Archduke Leopold/Piccolomini [Imp]
Brémule	Aug 20, 1119	*Henry I* [Eng] – Louis VI [F]
Brentford	Nov 12, 1642	*Prince Rupert* [Roy] – Holles [Parl]
Brescia	Mar 31, 1849	*Von Haynau* [A] – city
Breslau	Nov 22, 1757	*Prince Charles of Lorraine* [A] – Duke of Brunswick-Bevern [P]
Brest	Aug 10, 1512	*Lord Edward Howard* [Eng] – de Thenouënel [F]
Bridge of Dee	June 18, 1639	*Montrose* [Cov] – Lord Aboyne [Roy]
Briell	Apr 1, 1572	*de la Marck/Treslong* [Beggars of the Sea] – Spanish
Brienne	Jan 29, 1814	*Napoleon* [F/Sp] – Blücher [R/P]
Brihuega	Dec 10, 1710	*Vendôme* [F] – Stanhope [Br]
Britain, Battle of / Blitz	July 10, 1940 – May 11, 1941	*Dowding* [Br] – Göring [Ger]
Brunanburgh	937	*Athelstan* [Wes] – Anlaf/Owen of Cumberland/Constantine [Dan/Scots/Picts]
Bucharest	1771	Mousson Oglou [T] – *Romanzoff* [R]
Buena Vista	Feb 22–3, 1847	*Taylor* [Amer] – Santa Anna [Mex]
Buenos Aires I	June 27, 1806	city – *Beresford* [Br]
Buenos Aires II	Aug 12, 1806	*de Liniers* [Arg/Sp] – Beresford [Br]
Buenos Aires III	July 5, 1807	de Liniers [Arg/Sp] – Whitelocke [Br]
Buenos Aires IV	Nov 6, 1872	*Sarmiento* [Arg] – Mitre/Aredondo [rebels]
Bull Run I	July 21, 1861	*Beauregard* [Con] – McDowell [Fed]
Bull Run II	Aug 29–30, 1862	*Jackson* [Con] – Pope [Fed]
Bunker Hill	June 17, 1775	*Gage* [Br] – Ward [Amer]
Burlington Heights	May 5, 1813	*Procter* [Br] – Harrison [Amer]
Burma	Apr 3 – May 10, 1942	*Terauchi* [Jap] – British/Chinese
Busaco	Sept 27, 1810	*Wellington* [Br] – Masséna [F]
Buxar	Oct 23, 1764	*Munro* [Br/Sepoys] – Shujah-ud-Daula [Bengalis]
Byzantium I	318BC	*Antigonus* [Mac] – Clytus [Asiatic rebels]
Byzantium II	323	*Constantine the Great* [Emp West] – city
Cabala	379BC	*Dionysius* [Syrac] – Mago [Carth]
Cadesia	636	*Said* [Mus] – Rustam [Per]
Cadiz I	Apr 19, 1587	*Drake* [Eng] – Spanish
Cadiz II	June–July 1596	*Howard/Essex* [Eng/Dut] – Spanish

Castalla	Apr 13, 1813	*Murray* [Allies] – Suchet [F]
Castelfidardo	Sept 18, 1860	*Cialdini* [Sard] – La Moricière [Pap]
Castelnaudary	Sept 1, 1632	*Louis XIII* – Duc de Montmorenci [rebels]
Castiglione I	Sept 8, 1706	*de Medavi* [F] – Prince of Hesse [Imp]
Castiglione II	Aug 5, 1796	*Napoleon* [F] – Wurmser [A]
Castillejos	Jan 1, 1860	*Prim* [Sp] – Moors
Castillon	July 17, 1453	*Bureau* [F] – Earl of Shrewsbury [Br]
Castlebar	Aug 27, 1798	*Humbert* [F] – Lake [Br]
Castricum	Oct 6, 1799	*Brune* [F] – York [Br/R]
Catalaunian Plains: see Châlons III		
Catana	387BC	Leptines [Syrac] – *Carthaginians*
Caudine Forks	322BC	*Pontius* [Sab] – T. Veturius Calvinus/Spurius Postumus [Rom]
Cecryphalea	458BC	Peloponnesians – *Athenians*
Cedar Creek	Oct 19, 1864	*Wright* [Fed] – Early [Con]
Cedar Mountain	Aug 9, 1862	*Jackson* [Con] – Banks [Fed]
Cepeda	Oct 23, 1859	*Urquiza* [Arg Confederation] – Mitre [Buenos Aires]
Cephisus	1307	*Catalans* – de Brienne
Cerignola	Apr 26, 1503	*de Córdoba* [Sp] – Duc de Nemours [F]
Cerisolles	Apr 14, 1544	*de Bourbon* [F] – del Vasto [Imp]
Ceva	Apr 16–17, 1796	*Colli* [A] – Augereau [F]
Chacabuco	Feb 12, 1817	*San Martin* [Chil] – Marcoto [Sp Roy]
Chæronea I	Sept 1, 338BC	*Philip* [Mac] – Chares/Theagenes [Ath/Theb]
Chæronea II	86BC	*Sulla* [Rom] – Archelaus [Pontus]
Chalcis	429BC	*Phormio* [Ath] – [Pelo]
Chalgrove Field	June 18, 1643	*Prince Rupert* [Roy] – Hampden [Parl]
Châlons I	271	*Aurelian* [Rom] – Tetricus [rebels]
Châlons II	July 366	*Valentinian* [Rom] – Vadomair [Alemanni]
Châlons III	June 451	*Aetius/Theodoric* [Rom/Vis] – Atilla [Huns]
Châlons IV	1274	*English knights* – French knights
Champagne I	Dec 20, 1914 – Mar 17, 1915	Falkenhayn [Ger] – Joffre [F]
Champagne II	Sept 25 – Nov 6, 1915	Falkenhayn [Ger] – Joffre [F]
Champagne-Marne River	July 15–19, 1918	Ludendorff [Ger] – Foch [F]
Champaubert	Feb 10, 1814	*Napoleon* [F] – Blucher [R/P]
Chancellorsville	May 1–6, 1863	*Lee* [Con] – Hooker [Fed]
Chanda	May 9, 1818	*Adams* [Br] – Rajah of Nagpore [fortress]
Chandernagore	Mar 23, 1757	*Clive/Watson* [Br] – French
Changama	Sept 3, 1767	*Smith* [Br] – Hyder Ali/Nizam Ali
Charasia	Oct 6, 1879	*Roberts* [Br] – Yakub Khan [Afghans]
Charenton, fortress	Feb 8, 1649	*Condé* [Roy] – Clauleu [Parl]
Château-Thierry	Feb 12, 1814	*Napoleon* [F] – York [Allies]
Châteaugay	Oct 26, 1813	*De Salaberry* [Br/Can] – Hampton [US]
Châteauneuf-Raudon	1380	*du Guesclin* [F] – de Ros [Br]
Chattanooga	Nov 24–5, 1863	*Grant* [Fed] – Bragg [Con]
Che-mul-pho	Feb 8, 1904	*Uriu* [Jap] – Russians
Cherbourg	June 22–7, 1944	*Collins* [Alllies] – Schlieben [Ger]
Chernaya	Aug 16, 1855	*Marmora* [F/Sard] – Gorchakov [R]
Chesapeake Bay	Sept 5, 1781	*de Grasse* [F] – Graves [Br]
Chesme	July 6–7, 1770	*Orlov* [R] – Turks
Chetaté	Jan 6–9, 1854	Fischbuch [R] – *Ahmed Pasha* [T]
Chiari	Sept 1, 1701	*Prince Eugene* [Imp] – Duke of Savoy [F/Sp]
Chickamauga	Sept 19–20, 1863	Bragg [Con] – Rosecrans [Fed]
Chillianwalla	Jan 13, 1849	Gough [Br] – Shere Singh [Sikhs]
Chiloe	Jan 19, 1826	Quintanella [Sp] – *Chileans*
Chinese Farm	Oct 16–18, 1973	*Adan* [Isr] – Ismail [Eg]
Chios I	357BC	*town* – Chabrias/Chares [Ath]
Chios II	201BC	Philip [Mac] – *Theophiliscus/Attalus* [Rhodes/Pergamum]
Chios III	Feb 9, 1695	Venice – Turks
Chios IV	July 5, 1769	*Spiritoff* [R] – Capitan Pasha [T]
Chios V	July 5, 1770	*Orlov* [R] – Turks
Chiozza	June 24, 1380	Doria [Gen] – *Pisani* [Ven]
Chippewa River	July 5, 1814	*Brown* [Amer] – Riall [Br]
Chitor I	1300	*Ala-ud-Din* [Pathans] – Lakhsman [Rajputs]
Chitor II	1535	*Bahadur Shah* [Gujeratis] – Bikrmajit

Chitor III	1568	**Akbar** [Delhi Mog] – Jagmal [Rajputs]
Chocim	Nov 11, 1673	**Sobieski** [Pol/Lith] – Hussein Pasha [Ottomans]
Choczim	1769	Galitzin [R] – **Mohammed Emin Pasha** [T]
Chong-ju	Apr 1904	**Japanese** – Mischtchenko [Cossacks]
Chotusitz	May 17, 1742	**Frederick the Great** [P] – Prince Charles of Lorraine [A]
Christianople	1611	**Gustavus Adolphus** [Swed] – fortress
Chrysler's Farm	Nov 11, 1813	**Morrison** [Br] – Wilkinson [US]
Chrysopolis	323	Licinius [Emp East] – **Constantine** [Emp West]
Chunar	1538	Shir Khan Sur [Bengal] – **Humayun** [Mog]
Cibalis	Oct 8, 315	**Constantine the Great** [Emp West] – Licinius [Emp East]
Cinco de Mayo: see Puebla		
Ciudad Rodrigo	Jan 19, 1812	**Wellington** [Br] – Barrié [F]
Ciuna	315BC	Caius Mænius [Rom] – Pontius [Sam]
Civitella	1033	**Guiscard** [Nor] – Pope Leo IX [Ger/It]
Clissau	July 13, 1702	**Charles XII** [Swed] – Frederick Augustus [Pol/Sax]
Clontarf	Apr 24, 1014	Danes – **Boru** [Ir]
Clusium	225BC	**Gauls** – Romans
Cnidus	394BC	Pisander [Spar] – **Pharnabazus/Conon** [Per/Ath]
Cocherel	May 16, 1364	De Grailli [Navarrese] – **du Guesclin** [F]
Cold Harbor	June 3–12, 1864	**Lee** [Con] – Grant [Fed]
Colenso	Dec 15, 1899	**Botha** [Boers] – Buller [Br]
Colline Gate	82BC	**Sulla** [Rom Aristocrats] – Pontius [Rom/Samnites]
Colombey	Aug 11, 1870	Bazaine [F] – von Steinmetz [Ger]
Colombo	Feb 15, 1796	town [Dut] – **Rainier/Stuart** [Br]
Compedion	281BC	Lysimachus [Mac] – **Seleucus** [Syr]
Constantine	Oct 1837	**Damrémont/Valée** [F] – city
Constantinople I	716	**City/Bulgarians** – Mosleneh [Mus]
Constantinople II	July 25, 1261	**Stragopulos** [Byz] – Baldwin II
Constantinople III	May 25, 1453	**Mohammed II** [T] – Constantine XI [Gr]
Constitution/Guerrière	Aug 19, 1812	**Hull** [US] – Dacres [Br]
Constitution/Java	Dec 29, 1812	**Bainbridge** [US] – Lambert [Br]
Convoy PQ17	July 2–13, 1942	**Germans** – Pound [Br]
Copenhagen I	Apr 2, 1801	**Parker/Nelson** [Br] – Fischer [Dan]
Copenhagen II	Sept 2–5, 1807	**Cathcart/Gambier** [Br] – Peimann [Dan]
Copratus, The	316BC	Antigonus [Mac] – **Eumenes** [Asiatics]
Coral Sea	May 7–8, 1942	Fletcher [US] – Inouye [Jap]
Cordova	Aug 1010	**Sulaiman/Sancho** [Berbers/Sp] – Almudy [Moors]
Corfu	July 8, 1716	Andrea Corner [Venice] – Turks
Corinth I	429BC	Cnemus [Pelo] – **Phormio** [Ath]
Corinth II	394–390BC	Spartans – Athenians/Corinthians/ Thebans/Argives
Corinth (USA)	Oct 3–4, 1862	**Rosecrans** [Fed] – Van Dorn [Con]
Coronea	Aug 394BC	Athenians/Argives/Thebans/ Corinthians – **Agesilaus** [Spar]
Coroneia	447BC	Tolmides [Ath] – **Bœotians**
Coronel	Nov 1, 1914	**Spee** [Ger] – Cradock [Br]
Corrichie	1562	**Mary Queen of Scots** – Huntly [rebels]
Cortenuova	1237	**Frederick II** [Imp] – Guelfs
Corumba	1877	**Paraguayans** – Brazilians
Corunna	Jan 16, 1809	**Moore** [Br] – Soult [F]
Corygaum	Jan 1, 1818	**Staunton** [Br] – Peshwa Baji Rao II [Mar]
Cos	258	**Macedon** – Egyptians
Coulmiers	Nov 9, 1870	**d'Aurelle de Paladines** [F] – von der Tann [Ger]
Courcelles	1198	**Richard I** [Eng] – Philip Augustus [F]
Courtrai	July 11, 1302	D'Artois [F] – **de Dampierre** [Flem]
Coutras	Oct 20, 1587	**Henry of Navarre** [Hug] – Duc de Joyeuse [Cath]
Covelong	1752	fortress [F] – **Clive** [Br]
Coverypank	Feb 1752	**Clive** [Br] – Rajah Sahib
Craonne	Mar 7, 1814	**Napoleon** [F] – Blücher [Allies]
Cravant	Aug 1, 1423	**Earl of Salisbury** [Burg/Eng] – Buchan/Stewart [F]
Crayford	456	**Hengist** [Jutes] – Vortigern [Britons]
Crécy	Aug 26, 1346	**Edward III** [Eng] – Philip VI [F]
Crefeld	June 23, 1758	**Prince Ferdinand of Brunswick** [P] – de Clermont [F]
Cremona	Feb 1, 1702	**Prince Eugene** [Imp] – de Villeroi [city]
Crete	May 1941	**Student** [Ger] – Freyberg [Allies]

Crimisus	June 340BC	*Timoleon* [Sic] – Hamilcar/Hasdrubal [Carth]
Cronion	379BC	Dioysius [Syrac] – *Cathaginians*
Cross Keys	June 8, 1862	*Ewell* [Con] – Frémont [Fed]
Crotona	983	Otho II [Ger] – *Greeks/Saracens*
Ctesiphon	Nov 22–26, 1915	*Nur-ud-din* [T] – Townsend [Br]
Cuaspad	Dec 6, 1862	Flores [Ecu] – *Mosquera* [Col]
Cuddalore I	July 6, 1782	Hughes [Br] – Suffren [F]
Cuddalore II	June 20, 1783	Hughes [Br] – Suffren [F]
Culloden	Apr 16, 1746	*Duke of Cumberland* [Roy] – Young Pretender [Jacob]
Cumae	474BC	*Hiero* [Syrac] – Etruscans
Cunaxa	401BC	Artaxerxes [Per] – Cyrus/Clearchus [Per/Gr]
Curupayty	Sept 22, 1866	*Diaz* [Para] – Flores [Braz/Arg/Uru]
Custozza	June 24, 1866	*Archduke Albert* [A] – La Marmora [It]
Cutwa	July 19, 1763	*Adams* [Br/Sepoys] – Mir Cossim [Bengal]
Cuzco	1533	*Pizarro* [Sp] – Incas
Cynoscephalæ I	July 364BC	*Pelopidas* [Thebans/Thessalians] – Alexander of Pheræ
Cynoscephalæ II	197BC	*Flamininus* [Rom] – Philip [Mac]
Cynossema	411BC	Mindarus [Pelo] – *Thrasybulus/Thrasyllus* [Ath]
Cyssus	191BC	*Caius Livius* [Rom] – Polyxenides [Antiochus]
Cyzicus I	410BC	*Alcibiades* [Ath] – Mindarus [Pelo]
Cyzicus II	88BC	Mithridates [Pontics] – *Lucullus* [Rom]
Cyzicus III	193	*Septimius Severus* [Pann] – C. P. Niger Justus [Syr]
Czarnovo	Dec 24, 1806	*Napoleon* [F] – Tolstoy [R]
Czaslau	1742	*Frederick the Great* [P] – Charles of Lorraine [A]
Daegastan	603	*Æthelfrith* [Northumbrians] – Aidan [Picts/Scots]
Dakar	Sept 22–25, 1940	*de Gaulle* [Free F/Br] – French
Dalmanutha	Aug 21–28, 1900	*Roberts/Buller* [Br] – Botha [Boers]
Damascus I	633	*Khaled* [Mus] – city [Gr/Rom]
Damascus II	Jan 25, 1401	*Timur* [Tar] – city
Damascus III	1917–18	*Allenby* [Br] – Turks
Damme	Apr 1213	*Earl of Salisbury* [Br] – French
Dan-no-ura	1185	*Noriyori/Yoshitsune* [Minamoto clan] – Munemori [Taira clan]
Danzig I	Mar 10 – May 24, 1807	*Lefebvre* [F] – Kalkreuth [P/R]
Danzig II	Jan 16 – Nov 29, 1813	*Duke of Württemberg* [Allies] – Rapp [F]
Dara	530	*Belisarius* [Rom] – Persians/Arabs
Dardanelles I	June 26, 1656	*Lorenzo Marcello* [Venice] – Turks
Dardanelles II	July 17, 1657	*Turks* – Lazaro Mocenigo [Venice]
Dardanelles III	Sept 20, 1698	Venice – Turks
Dardanelles IV	Feb 19 – Mar 18, 1915	*von Sanders* [T] – Sackville Carden [Br]/de Robeck [F]
Dargai	Oct 18–20, 1897	*Yeatman-Biggs* [Br] – Afridis
Dego	Apr 14–15, 1796	*Napoleon/Massena* [F] – Beaulieu [A]
Deig	Dec 11–24, 1804	*Lake* [Br] – Holkar [Mar]
Delhi I	1297	Kuttugh Khan [Mon] – Aladain Khalji [Ind]
Delhi II	1398	*Timur* [Tar] – Mahmud Tughlak [Ind]
Delhi III	Sept 10, 1803	*Lake* [Br] – Bourquain [Mar]
Delhi IV	June–Sept 1857	*Wilson* [Br] – mutineers
Delium	424BC	Hippocrates [Ath] – *Pagondas* [Bœotians]
Delphi	355BC	*Philomelus* [Phocians] – Locrians
Denain	1712	Earl of Albemarle [Allies] – *Villiers* [F]
Dennewitz	Sept 6, 1813	*Bernadotte* [Allies] – Ney [F]
Deorham	577	*Ceawlin* [Wessex] – British
Desert Storm: *see* Kuwait		
Dessau	Apr 25, 1626	*Wallenstein* [Imp] – Von Mansfeldt [Ger Prot]
Dettingen	June 27, 1743	*George II* [Allies] – Duc de Noailles [F]
Deutschbrod	Jan 10, 1422	*Zisca* [Huss] – Sigismund [Ger]
Devicotta	1740	fortress [Tanjores] – *Lawrence* [Br]
Diamond Hill	June 11–12, 1900	Botha [Boers] – *Roberts* [Br]
Dienbiènphu	Mar 13–May 7, 1954	*Giap* [Viet] – de Castries [F]
Dieppe Raid	Aug 19, 1942	*Germans* – Roberts [Br/Can]
Dipæ	471BC	*Spartans* – Arcadians
Diu I	Feb 2, 1509	*Almeida* [Port] – Indian Muslims
Diu II	Sept 1537	*de Silveira* [Port] – Suleiman/ Bahadur Shah/Khojah Zofar [T]
Diu III	1545	*Juan de Castro* [Port] – Khojah Zofar/Rami Khan [Gujeratis]

Djerbeh	1560	*Piycála Pasha* [T] – Christians
Dnieper	June 28–29, 1788	Nassau-Siegen [R] – el Ghazi [T]
Dniester	Sept 9, 1769	*Prince Gallitzin* [R] – Ali Moldovani Pasha [T]
Dodowah	Aug 7, 1826	*Hope Smith* [Br] – Ashantis
Döffingen	1388	*German League* – Charles IV [HRE]
Dogger Bank I	Aug 5, 1781	Parker [Br] – Zoutman [Dut]
Dogger Bank II	Jan 24, 1915	Hipper [Ger] – *Beatty* [Br]
Dollar	875	*Thorstem* [Danes] – Constantine [Alban]
Dolni-Dubnik	Nov 1, 1876	*Gourko* [R] – Turks
Domokos	May 17, 1879	Edhem Pasha [T] – Crown Prince of Greece [Gr]
Donauwörth	July 2, 1704	*Duke of Marlborough* [Br/Imp] – Tallard [F/Bav]
Dorylaeum	July 1, 1097	*Bohemund/Godfrey/Raymond* [Crus] – Kilij Arslan [Seljuk]
Douai	Apr 25, 1710	*Marlborough/Prince Eugene* [Allies] – d'Albergotti [F]
Dover	May 29, 1652	Blake [Eng] – Tromp [Dut]
Downs, The	Oct 21, 1639	*Tromp* [Dut] – de Oquendo [Sp]
Drepanum	249BC	Publius Claudius [Rom] – *Adherbal* [Carth]
Dresden	Aug 26–7, 1813	*Napoleon* [F] – Schwarzenberg [Allies]
Dreux	Dec 19, 1562	*Guise* [Catholics] – Condé/Coligny [Hug]
Driefontein	Mar 10, 1900	*Roberts* [Br] – De Wet [Boers]
Dristen	973	Swatoslaus [R] – *Zimisces* [Gr]
Drogheda I	Dec 1641	*Tichborne* [Br] – O'Neil [Ir reb]
Drogheda II	Sept 12, 1649	*Cromwell* [Parl] – Aston [Ir Roy]
Drumclog	June 11, 1679	*Hamilton* [Cov] – Claverhouse [Roy]
Dubba	Mar 24, 1843	*Napier* [Br] – Amir Shere Mahomed [Baluchis]
Dunamunde	July 9, 1701	*Charles XII* [Swed] – Von Stenau [R/Sax]
Dunbar I	Apr 27, 1296	*Edward I* [Br] – Earl of Athol [Scots]
Dunbar II	1339	Earl of Salisbury [Br] – *Agnes Countess of March* [Scots]
Dunbar III	Sept 3, 1650	*Cromwell/Monck* [Parl] – Leslie [Scots Roy]
Dundalk	Oct 5, 1318	Edward Bruce [Scots] – *de Bermingham* [Eng/Ir]
Dunes	June 14, 1658	*Turenne* [F/Eng] – Don John of Austria/Creat Condé [Sp]
Dunganhill	Aug 8, 1647	*Jones* [Br] – Irish rebels
Dungeness	Dec 10, 1652	*Tromp* [Dut] – Robert Blake [Eng]
Dunkeld	Aug 21, 1689	Cleland [Camerons] – Cannon [Highlanders]
Dunsinnan	1054	Macbeth [Scots] – *Earl of Northumberland* [A-S]
Düppel	Mar 30 – Apr 17, 1864	*Prince Frederick Charles* [P] – fortress [Dan]
Dupplin Muir	12, Aug 1332	*Baliol* [barons] – David King of Scotland
Durazzo	July 17, 1081 – Feb 8, 1082	Palæologus/Comnenus [Gr/Mac] – *Guiscard* [Nor]
Durben	1260	Teutonic Knights – *Lithuanians*
Dürrenstein	Nov 11, 1805	*Mortier* [F] – Miloradovith [R]
Durrës	1081	*Italo-Normans* – Byzantines
Dussindale	1549	*Earl of Warwick* [Roy] – Kett [rebels]
Dwina, The	1701	*Charles XII* [Swed] – von Stenau [Sax]
Dyle	896	Normans – *Arnulph* [Ger]
Dyrrhachium	48BC	Julius Cæsar – *Pompey*
East Pakistan	Dec 3–16, 1971	*India* – Pakistan
Eastern Solomons	Aug 23–25, 1942	Nagumo [Jap] – *Fletcher* [US}
Ebelsberg	May 3, 1809	*Masséna* [F] – Archduke Charles [A]
Eckmühl	Apr 22, 1809	*Davoût/Lannes* [F] – Archduke Charles [A]
Edessa I	259	Valerian [Rom] – *Sapor I* [Per]
Edessa II	Nov–Dec 1144	*Zangi* [Syrian Muslims] – Joscelin II [Crus]
Edgecote	July 26, 1469	*Warwick* [Lanc] – Pembroke [York]
Edgehill	Oct 23, 1642	*Charles I* [Roy] – Essex [Parl]
Edirne (Adrianopolis)	811	*Krum* [Bulgars] – Nicephorus [Byz]
El Alamein I	July 1–27, 1942	*Auchinleck* [Br] – Rommel [Ger/It]
El Alamein II	Oct 23 – Nov 4, 1942	*Montgomery* [Br] – Rommel [Ger/It]
El Arish	Feb 19, 1799	*Napoleon* [F] – Ibrahim [T]
El Boden	Sept 25, 1811	*Picton* [Br/Port] – Montbrun [F]
El Caney: see San Juan Hill		
El Teb I	Feb 4, 1883	*Osman Digna* [Dervishes] – Baker Pasha [Br]
El Teb II	Feb 29, 1884	*Graham* [Br] – Osman Digna [Dervishes]
Elandslaagte	Oct 21, 1899	*Hamilton* [Br] – Kock [Boers]
Elasson	Oct 23, 1912	*Crown Prince Constantine* [Gr] – Turks
Elchingen	Oct 14, 1805	*Ney* [F] – Riesch [A]

Elena	1877	**Melikoff** [R] – Muhktar Pasha [T]
Elephants	275BC	**Antiochus** [Seleucids] – Galatians
Elinga	206BC	Hanno [Carth] – **Scipio Africanus** [Rom]
Ellendune	825	Beornwulf [Mercians] – **Egbert** [W Sax]
Elleporus	389BC	**Dionysius** [Syrac] – Heloris [Italiots]
Elteka	c.700BC	Assyrians – **Judaeans/Egyptians**
Embata	356BC	Chares [Ath] – **Chians**
Emesa	272	**Aurelian** [Rom] – Zenobia [Palmyrenians]
Englefield	Dec 870	**Aethelred/Alfred** [W Sax] – Danes
Entholm	June 11, 1676	**van Tromp** [Dut/Dan] – Swedes
Ephesus	499BC	Aristagorus [Ath/Ion] – **Artaphernes** [Per]
Erzurum-Erzincan	Jan 17 – Aug 24, 1916	**Yuderich** [R] – Pasha [T]
Eshowe	Jan 28 – Apr 4, 1879	**Pearson** [Br] – Zulus
Espinosa	Nov 10, 1808	**Victor** [F] – Blake [Sp]
Etampes	604	**Brunehilde** [Burg] – Clothaire II [Neustrians]
Ethandun	878	**Alfred** [W Sax] – Guthrum [Danes]
Eurymedon	467/6BC	Persians – **Cimon** [Ath/Delians]
Eutaw Springs	Sept 8, 1781	**Stuart** [Br] – Greene [Amer]
Evesham	Aug 4, 1265	**Prince Edward** [Roy] – de Montfort [barons]
Eylau	Feb 8, 1807	**Napoleon** [F] – Bennigsen [R/P]
Faenza	541	Romans – **Totila** [Goths]
Fair Oaks	May 31 – June 1, 1862	McClellan [Fed] – Johnston [Con]
Falkirk I	July 22, 1298	**Edward I** [Eng] – Wallace [Scots]
Falkirk II	Jan 17, 1746	**Young Pretender/Murray** [Jacob] – Hawley [Roy]
Falkland Islands I	Dec 8, 1914	**Sturdee** [Br] – Spee [Ger]
Falkland Islands II	1982	**Woodward** [Br] – Argentinians
Famagusta	Oct 1570	**Mustapha Pasha** [T] – Bragadino [Ven/Cyp]
Fariskur	Apr 6, 1250	**Muslims** – King Louis IX [Crusaders]
Farrington Bridge	July 27, 1549	**Russell** [Roy] – Cornish rebels
Faughart	Oct 5, 1318	**De Bermingham** [Eng/Ir] – Edward Bruce [Scots]
Faventia	82BC	Norbanus – **Metellus** [Sullans]
Fehrbellin	June 28, 1675	**Frederick William** [Bran] – Charles XI [Swed]
Ferozeshah	Dec 21, 1845	**Gough** [Br] – Lal Singh [Sikhs]
Fethanleag	584	**Ceawlin** [W Sax] – Cutha [Britons]
Fetterman Massacre	Dec 21, 1866	Fetterman [US] – **Red Cloud/Crazy Horse** [Sioux]
Firket	June 7, 1896	**Kitchener** [Br/Eg] – Hamada [Mahd]
Fisher's Hill	Sept 22, 1864	**Sheridan** [Fed] – Early [Con]
Fismes	Mar 17, 1814	**Blücher** [Allies] – Marmont [F]
Flanders	May 1940	**Rundstedt** [Ger] – British/French/Belgians
Fleurus I	Aug 29, 1622	**Spinola** [Sp] – von Mansfeld/Christian of Brunswick [Ger]
Fleurus II	July 1, 1690	**Luxembourg** [F] – Prince of Waldeck [Br/Dut/Ger/Sp]
Fleurus III	June 26, 1794	**Jourdan** [F] – Saxe-Coburg [Allies]
Flodden	Sept 9, 1513	**Earl of Surrey** [Br] – James IV [Scots]
Florence	406	Radagasius [Ger] – **city/Stilicho** [Rom]
Flushing	July 30 – Aug 16, 1809	**Chatham** [Br] – town
Focchies	May 12, 1649	**Giacomo Riva** [Venice] – Turks
Fockani	July 21, 1789	**Suvorov/Saxe-Coburg** [R/A] – Yusuf Pasha [T]
Fontenoy	May 11, 1745	**Saxe** [F] – Duke of Cumberland [Br/Dut/A]
Formigny	Apr 15, 1450	**Comte de Clermont** [F] – Kyriel [Br]
Fornham St Genevieve	1173	de Beaumont [rebels] – **de Lucy** [Roy]
Fornovo	July 6, 1495	**Charles VIII** [F/Swiss] – Gonzaga [Ven/Man/Milan]
Fort Donelson	Apr 14–16, 1862	**Grant** [Fed] – Buckner [Con]
Fort Frontenac	Aug 26, 1758	**Bradstreet** [Br/Colonials] – Noyan [F]
Fort McHenry	Sept 12–13, 1812	Cockburn [Br] – fortress [US]
Fort St David I	Apr 29, 1758	Pococke [Br] – Comte d'Ache [F]
Fort St David II	June 2, 1758	**Lally** [F] – fortress [Br]
Fort Sumter	Apr 12–14, 1860	**Beauregard** [Con] – Anderson [Fed]
Fort Ticonderoga	July 8, 1758	**Abercromby** [Br] – Montcalm [F]
Fort William Henry	Aug 6–9, 1757	**Montcalm** [F/Can] – Monro [Br/Colonials]
Forum Terebronii	251	Decius [Rom] – **Cuiva** [Goths]
Four Days Fight/	June 11–14, 1666	**de Ruyter** [Dut] – Albemarle/Prince Rupert [Eng]
Dover Strait/The Goodwins		
Fraga	1134	**Almoravids** – Aragonese

France (Battle for)	May – June 25, 1940	*von Rundstedt* – Gamelin [F]
Frankenhausen	May 15, 1525	*Saxony/Hesse/Brunswick* – Münzer [peasants]
Frankfurt-on-Oder	Apr 2, 1631	*Gustavus Adolphus* [Swed] – town
Franklin	Nov 30, 1864	*Schofield* [Fed] – Hood [Con]
Frastenz	Apr 20, 1499	*Wolleb* [Swiss] – Maximilian [A]
Fraubrunnen	Jan 1376	*Bernese* – von Coucy ['Guglers']
Frauenstadt	Feb 12, 1706	*Reinschild* [Swed] – Schulemburg [R/Sax]
Fredericksburg	Dec 13, 1862	*Lee* [Con] – Burnside [Fed]
Fredericshall	Dec 1718	*Fortress* – Charles XII [Swed]
Freibourg	Aug 3, 5, 9, 1644	*Great Condé/Turenne* [F] – von Mercy [Bav]
Freteval	1194	*Richard Cœur de Lion* [Eng] – Philip Augustus [F]
Friedberg	Aug 24, 1796	*Moreau* [F] – Latour [A]
Friedland	June 14, 1807	*Napoleon* [F] – Bennigsen [R]
Frontiers of France	1914	*Germans* – Belgians/French
Fröschwiller	Dec 22, 1793	*Hoche* [F] – Brunswick [P]
Fuengirola	Oct 13, 1810	*Sébastiani* [F] – Blagney [Br]
Fuentes de Oñoro	May 5, 1811	*Wellington* [Br] – Masséna [F]
Fulford	Sept 20, 1066	*Hardrada* [Norse] – Edwin/Morcar [A-S]
Furruckabad	Nov 17, 1804	*Lake* [Br] – Holkar [Mar]
Fushimi	1868	*Satsuma/Choshu* – Yoshinobu [Aizu/Kuwana]
Futehpur	July 12, 1857	*Havelock* [Br] – [mutineers]
Gabbard Bank / North Foreland / Nieuport	June 12–13, 1653	*Monck/Deane* [Eng] – Martin Van Tromp/Witte de With [Dut]
Gadebusch	Dec 20, 1712	*Stenbock* [Swed] – Danes/Saxons
Galicia	Aug 23 – Sept 26, 1914	Conrad [A] – Ivanov [R]
Gallipoli	Apr 25, 1915 – Jan 9, 1916	*von Sanders* [T] – Hamilton/Monro [Br]
Gandamak	Jan 13, 1842	*Akbar* [Afghans] – Elphinstone [Br]
Gangut	1714	*Peter the Great* [R] – Ehrenskiöld [Swed]
Garcia Hernandez	July 23, 1812	*Bock* [Br] – Foy [F]
Garigliano I	Dec 29, 1503	*De Córdoba* [Sp] – Marquis of Saluzzo [F/It]
Garigliano II	Oct 1850	*Cialdini* [It] – Francis II [Neap]
Gate Pah	Apr 29, 1864	Cameron [Br] – Maoris
Gaugamela	Oct 1, 331BC	*Alexander* [Mac] – Darius [Per]
Gaza I	312BC	*Seleucus/Ptolemy* [Syr/Eg] – Demetrius Poliorcetes [Mac]
Gaza II	Mar 26 and Apr 17, 1917	*Murray/Dobell* [Br] – Kressenstein [T]
Gaza III	Oct 31 – Dec 9, 1917	*Allenby* [Br] – Turks
Gazala	May 27 – June 18, 1942	*Rommel* [Ger/It] – Ritchie [Br]
Gebora	Feb 19, 1811	*Soult* [F] – Mendizabal [Sp]
Geisberg	Dec 26, 1793	*Hoche* [F] – Wurmser [A]
Gelt, The	Feb 1570	*Hunsdon* [Roy] – Dacre [Borderers]
Gemblours	Jan 31, 1578	*Don John of Austria* [Sp] – Goignies [Dut]
Genoa I	Dec 6–10, 1746	*Genoese* – Botta [A]
Genoa II	Mar 14, 1795	*Hotham* [Br] – Martin [F]
Geok Tepe I	Sept 9, 1878	*fortress* [Turkomans] – Lomakine [R]
Geok Tepe II	Jan 8–17, 1880	fortress – *Skobeloff* [R]
Geok Tepe III	Jan 8–17, 1881	*Skobeloff* [R] – fortress [Turkomans]
Gerberoi	1080	*William the Conqueror* [Nor] – Robert [Nor]
Gergovia	Apr–May 52BC	Julius Cæsar [Rom] – *Vercingetorix* [Gauls]
Germaghah	1193	*Genghis Khan* [Mon] – Sankun
Germantown	Oct 4, 1777	*Howe* [Br] – Washington [Amer]
Gerona	June 4 – Dec 10, 1809	*Verdier* [F] – Alvarez [Sp]
Gettysburg	July 1–3, 1863	*Meade* [Fed] – Lee [Con]
Ghanzi	July 23, 1839	*Keane* [Br/Bombay Army] – Afghans
Gheria	Aug 2, 1763	Mir Cossim [Bengalis] – *Adams* [Br]
Gibbel Rutts	May 26, 1798	*Duff* [regulars] – Irish rebels
Gibraltar I	July 23–4, 1704	*Byng* [Br/Dut] – de Salinas [Sp]
Gibraltar II	1779–83	*Elliot* [Br] – Alvarez/de Crillon/ Moreno [F/Sp]
Gihon, The	1362	*Khan* [Getes] – Timur [Tar]
Gingi	1689–92	Rajah Ram [town] – *Zulfikar Khan/Kambaksh/Aurungzebe*
Gislikon	Nov 23, 1847	*Dufour* [Fed] – Salis-Soglio [Sonderbund]
Glen Fruin	1604	Duke of Argyll [Roy] – *Highlanders*
Glen Malone	1580	*Irish* – De Wilton [Br]
Glenlivet	Oct 4, 1594	*Earl of Errol/Earl of Huntly* [rebels] – Earl of Argyll [Roy]

Glenmarreston	638	*Donald Bree* [Scots] – Angles
Glorious 1st June (Ushant II)	June 1, 1794	Howe [Br] – Villaret-Joyeuse [F]
Goa I	1510	*Albuquerque* [Port] – Kumal Khan [Bijapore]
Goa II	1570	*De Ataida* [Port] – Ali Adil Shah [Bijapore]
Goits	May 30, 1848	*Charles Albert of Savoy* [Pied] – Radetsky [A]
Golan Heights I	June 5–10, 1967	*Elazar* [Isr] – Souedan [Syr]
Golan Heights II	Oct 6–22, 1973	*Israelis* – Syrians/Iraqis/Jordanians
Golden Rock	Aug 7, 1753	*Lawrence/Monakji* [Br/Tanjore] – French/Mysoris
Golymin	Dec 26, 1806	*Augereau* [F] – Gallitzin [R]
Goraria	Nov 23–4, 1857	*Stuart* [Br] – mutineers
Gorlice-Tarnow	May 2 – Sept 1915	Hindenburg [Ger] – Russians
Gorni-Dubnik	Oct 24, 1877	*Gourko* [R] – Achmet Hefzi Pasha [T]
Gorodeczno	Aug 12, 1812	*Reynier/Schwarzenberg* [F/A] – Tormazov [R]
Granada I	1319	Pedro/John of Castile [Sp] – *Moors*
Granada II	Apr 26 – Jan 2, 1492	*Ferdinand* [Sp] – Abu Abdullah [Moor]
Grandella	1266	Manfred [Two Sicilies] – *Charles of Anjou* [F]
Grangam	1721	Swedes – *Golitshin* [R]
Granicus, The	334BC	*Alexander the Great* [Mac] – Memnon of Rhodes [Per/Gr]
Granson	Mar 2, 1476	*Swiss* – Charles the Bold [Burg]
Grant's Hill	Sept 14, 1758	*Indians/de Ligneris* – Grant [Highlanders/Provincials]
Gravelines	July 13, 1558	*d'Egmont* [Sp/Ger/Flem] – des Thermes [F/Ger]
Gravelotte-St Privat	Aug 18, 1870	*von Moltke* [Ger] – Bazaine [F]
Great Meadows	July 3, 1752	*de Villiers* [F] – Washington [Virg]
Greece, battle for	Apr 6–20, 1941	*List* [Ger] – Papagos [Gr]/Wilson [Br]
Grenada	July 6, 1779	Byron [Br] – d'Estaing [F]
Grochow	Feb 25, 1831	*Prince Michael Radziwill* [Pol] – Diebitsch [R]
Grossbeeren	Aug 23, 1813	*Bernadotte* [Allies] – Oudinot [F]
Gross-Jägersdorf	Aug 30, 1757	*Apraxine* [R] – Lehwaldt [P]
Grozka	1739	Neipperg [A] – *Grand Vizier* [T]
Grunnervaldt	1404	*Vladislas IV* [Pol] – Teutonic knights
Guadalcanal (land)	Aug 7, 1942 – Feb 9, 1943	*Ghormley* [US] – Hayakutake [Jap]
Guadalcanal (naval)	Nov 13–15, 1942	*Various admirals* [US] – Various admirals [Jap]
Guadeloupe I	Dec 10, 1794	*French* – island
Guadeloupe II	July 3, 1794	*Jervis* [Br] – island
Guad-el-Ras	Mar 23, 1859	*O'Donnell* [Sp] – Moors
Guam	July 21 – Aug 10, 1944	*Geiger* [US] – Japanese
Guastalla	Sept 19, 1734	Prince of Württemberg [Imp] – *de Coligny* [F]
Guildford Courthouse	Mar 15, 1781	*Cornwallis* [Br] – Greene [Amer]
Guinegate	Aug 16, 1513	*Henry VIII/Maximilian I* [Eng/Imp] – French
Gujerat	Feb 21, 1849	*Gough* [Br] – Shere Singh/Chuttur Singh [Sikhs]
Gumbinnen	Aug 20, 1914	Molke [Ger] – Grand Duke Nicholas [R]
Gunzburg	Oct 9, 1805	*Ney* [F] – d'Aspre [A]
Gwalior I	Aug 3, 1780	*Popham* [Br/Sepoys] – Fortress [Mahr]
Gwalior II	June 20, 1858	*Rose* [Br] – Rani of Jhansi /Tantia Topi [mutineers]
Haarlem	Dec 11, 1572 – July 12, 1573	*De Toledo* [Sp] – Ripperda [city]
Hadranum	344BC	*Timoleon* – Hiketas
Haelen	Aug 12, 1914	*de Witte* [Bel] – Marwitz [Ger]
Hahozkai	1274	*Japanese* – Lin Fok Heng [Tar]
Haliartus	395BC	Lysander [Spar] – *town* [Thebans]
Halidon Hill	July 19, 1333	*Edward III* [Eng] – Archibald Douglas [Scots]
Halieis	459BC	*Athenians* – Corinth/Epidamnus
Hampton Roads	Mar 8–9, 1862	Buchanan [Con] – Marston [Fed]
Hanau	Oct 30–31, 1813	*Napoleon* [F] – Wrede [A/Bav]
Hardenberg	June 1–15, 1580	*Schenck* [Roy] – Hohenlo [Dut Pat]
Harlaw	July 24, 1411	*Earl of Mar* [Lowlanders] – Donald [Highlanders]
Harpers Ferry I	Oct 16–18, 1859	*Lee* – John Brown [Abolitionists]
Harpers Ferry II	Sept 14–15, 1862	*Jackson* [Con] – Miles [Fed]
Hashin	Mar 20, 1885	*Graham* [Br] – Osman Digna [Sud]
Haslach	Oct 11, 1805	*Dupont* [F] – Schwarzenberg [A]
Hastenbeck	July 26, 1757	*d'Estrées* [F] – Duke of Cumberland [Han/Br]
Hastings	Oct 14, 1066	*William the Conqueror* [Nor] – Harold [A-S]
Hattin	July 4, 1187	*Saladin* [Sara] – Guy [Crus]

Battle	Date	Combatants
Hatvan	Apr 2, 1849	Schlick [A] – *Hungarians*
Havana I	Oct 12, 1748	Reggio [Sp] – *Knowles* [Br]
Havana II	June–Aug 1762	*Albemarle/Pococke* [Br] – city [Sp]
Heathfield	633	*Penda* [Merc] – Edwin [Northum]
Heavenfield	634	*Oswald* [Northum] – Cadwallon [Britons]
Hedgeley Moor	Apr 25, 1464	Margaret of Anjou/Percy [Lanc] – *Montague* [York]
Heiliger-Zee	May 23, 1568	*Louis of Nassau* ['Beggars of the Sea'] – Aremberg [Sp]
Heilsberg	June 10, 1807	*Soult* [F] – Bennigsen [R]
Hekitai-Kan	1595	*Kobayagawa Takakage* [Jap] – Li Chin [Chin]
Heligoland	Aug 31, 1807	*Russell* [Br] – island [Danes]
Heligoland Bight I	Aug 28, 1914	*Beatty* [Br] – Germans
Heligoland Bight II	Nov 17, 1917	Germans – British
Heliopolis	Mar 20, 1800	*Kléber* [F] – Ibrahim Bey [T]
Hellespont	323	*Crispus* [Emp West] – Amandus [Emp East]
Helorus	492BC	*Hippocrates* – Syracusans
Helsingborg	Feb 1710	*Steinbock* [Swed] – Danes
Hemushagu	1595	Konishi Yukinaga [Jap] – *Li Chin* [Chin]
Hengestesdun	835	*Egbert* [Wes] – Danes/Cornish
Hennersdorf	Nov 24, 1745	*Frederick the Great* [P] – Charles of Lorraine [A/Sax]
Heraclea	280BC	*Pyrrhus* [Epirots] – P. Laverius Lævinus [Rom]
Heraclea	313	*Licinius* [Illyrians] – Maximinus
Herat I	1220–1	city – *Sudah Bahadur* [Tar]
Herat II	Nov 22, 1837 – Sept 9, 1838	Muhammed [Per] – *Yar Muhammed* [Afg]
Herdonea	210BC	*Hannibal* [Carth] – Cnæus Fulvius [Rom]
Héricourt	Nov 13, 1474	*Swiss* – Charles the Bold [Burg]
Hermannstadt	1442	*Hunyadi* [Hung] – Mejid Bey [T]
Hernani I	Aug 29, 1836	Evans [Br] – *Carlists*
Hernani II	Mar 15–16, 1837	Evans [Br] – Don Sebastian [Carl]
Herrera	Aug 23, 1837	*Don Carlos/Moreno* [Carl] – Buerens [Cris]
Herrings, The	Feb 12, 1429	*Fastolfe* [Eng] – Clermont/Stewart [F]
Hexham	May 15, 1464	*Montague* [York] – Somerset [Lanc]
Himera I	480BC	*Gelon* [Syrac/Agrigentines] – Hamilcar [Carth]
Himera II	409BC	town – *Hannibal* [Carth]
Hlobane	Mar 28, 1879	*Wood/Buller* [Br] – Zulus
Hochkirch	Oct 14, 1758	Frederick the Great [P] – Daun [A]
Höchst	June 10, 1622	*Tilly* [Imp] – Christian of Brunswick [Palat]
Hochstadt	June 19, 1800	*Moreau* [F] – Kray [A]
Hoglund	July 17, 1788	Greig [R] – Sudermanland [Swed]
Hohenfriedberg	June 4, 1745	*Frederick the Great* [P] – Charles of Lorraine [A/Sax]
Hohenlinden	Dec 3, 1800	*Moreau* [F] – Archduke John [A]
Hollabrünn	Nov 16, 1805	*Lannes* [F] – Bagration [R]
Homildon Hill	Sept 14, 1402	*Percy* [Eng] – Earl of Douglas [Scots]
Honain	629	*Mohammed* [Mus] – Pagan Arabs
Hondschoote	Sept 6–8, 1793	*Houchard* [F] – York [Br/Han]
Hong Kong	Dec 18–25, 1941	*Japanese* – Maltby [Br]
Hooghly, The	Nov 24–5, 1759	*Wilson* [Br] – Dutch
Huesca I	1105	Ali [Moors] – *Alfonso VI of Castile* [Sp]
Huesca II	Mar 24, 1837	*Don Carlos/Don Sebastian* [Carl] – Irribarreu [Cris/Br]
Humblebeck	1700	*Charles XII* [Swed] – Danes
Hydaspes, The	326BC	*Alexander the Great* [Mac/Asiatics] – Porus [Ind]
Hyderabad: *see* Dubba		
Hyrcanian Rock	588	*Bahram* [Per] – Turks
Hysiæ	c.669/668BC	Spartans – *Argos*
Ichinotani	1189	*Norigoris/Yoshitsune* [Shogun] – Tairas
Idistaviso	16	*Germanicus* [Rom] – Arminius [Ger]
Ilerda	July–Aug 49	*Julius Cæsar* [Cæs] –Afranius/Petrius [Pomp]
Ilipa	206BC	*Scipio Africanus* [Rom] – Mago/Hasdrubal [Carth]
Immac	June 7, 218	*Elagabalus* [Syr] – Macrinus [Imp/Pret]
Imola	Feb 3, 1797	*Victor* [F/It] – Colli [Pap]
Imphal/Kohima	Mar 7 – July 18, 1944	*Slim* [Br] – Mutaguchi [Jap]
Inchon	Sept 15–25, 1950	*Almond* [UN] – North Koreans
Indus, The	1221	*Genghis Khan* [Tar] – Jellalladin [Khwarazm]
Ingavi	Nov 20, 1841	*Ballivián* [Bol] – Gamarra [Peru]

232

Inkerman	Nov 5, 1854	*Raglan* [Br/F] – Prince Menschikov [R]
Inveraray	1510	*Bruce* [Scots] – Mowbray [Eng]
Inverkeithing	1317	English – *Earl of Fife* [Scots]
Inverlochy	Feb 2, 1645	*Montrose* [Roy High] – Argyll [Lowland Cov]
Ioannina	Mar 3, 1913	*Crown Prince Constantine* [Gr] – Turks
Ipsus	301BC	*Seleucus/Lysimachus* [Syr] – Antigonus/Demetrius [Mac]
Iraq	Mar 20 – Apr 15, 2003	*Franks* [US/Coalition] – Saddam Hussein [Iraq]
Irun	May 18, 1837	*Evans* [Cris/Br] – fortress [Carl]
Isandlwana	Jan 22, 1879	*Ntshingwayo* [Zulus] – Durnford [Br]
Isaszcq	Apr 6, 1849	*Görgey* [Hung] – Jellachich [Cro]
Isly	Aug 14, 1844	*Bugeaud* [F] – Abd-el-Kader [Alg]
Ismail	Dec 22, 1790	*Suvorov* [R] – Fortress
Isonzo River (I – XI)	June 23, 1915 – Sept 15, 1917	Cadorna [It] – Hotzendorff [A-H]
Issus I	333BC	*Alexander the Great* [Mac] – Darius [Per]
Issus II	194	*Septimius Severus* [Pann] – C. P. Niger Justus [Syr]
Issus III	1488	Bajazet II [T] – *Sultan of Egypt*
Itabitsu	Oct 740	Hirotsuke [rebels] – *Ono-no-Atsuma* [Jap Imp]
Ivry	Mar 14, 1590	*Henri IV* [Hug] – Duc de Mayenne [Cath]
Iwo Jima	Feb 19 – Mar 26, 1945	*Schmidt* [US] – Tadamichi [Jap]
Jadar River	Aug 12–21, 1914	Potiorek [A] – Putnik [Serb]
Jaffa	Mar 7 1799	*Napoleon* [F] – Abon-Saad [T]
Jalalabad	Nov 1841 – Apr 1842	Sale [Br] – Afghans
Jalula	Dec 637	*Said* [Mus] – Yezdegerd [Per]
Jamaica	May 1655	Island [Sp] – *Penn/Venables* [Br]
Japanese Sea	Aug 14, 1904	*Kamimura* [Jap] – Yessen [R]
Jarnac	Mar 13, 1569	*de Tavannes/Duc d'Anjou* [Cath] – Prince de Condé/Coligny [Hug]
Jassy	Sept 20, 1620	*Zolkiewski* [Pol] – Osman II [T]
Java Sea	Feb 27–28, 1942	*Takagi* [Jap] – Doorman [Dut/Allies]
Jemappes	Nov 6, 1792	*Dumouriez* [F] – Archduke Albert [A]
Jena	Oct 14, 1806	*Napoleon* [F] – Hohenlohe [P]
Jenin-Nablus	June 5–7, 1967	*Elazar* [Isr] – Jordan
Jerba	1560	*Piali Pasha* [T] – Doria [Sp/Genoa]
Jersey	1550	*Winter* [Eng] – French
Jerusalem I	70	city [Jews] – *Titus* [Rom]
Jerusalem II	637	Sophronius [city] – *Abu Obeidah/Khalif Omar* [Mus]
Jerusalem III	June 9 – July 18, 1099	*Godefroi* [Crus] – Iftikhar/city [Mus]
Jerusalem IV	Sept 20 – Oct 2, 1187	*Saladin* [Mus] – Crusaders/city
Jerusalem V	1244	*Khwarazmians* – Crusaders/city
Jerusalem VI	June 5–7, 1967	*Gur* [Isr] – Ala Ali [Jordan]
Jhansi (Relief of)	Apr 3, 1858	*Rose* [Br] – Tantia Topi [mutineers]
Jidballi	Jan 10, 1904	*Egerton* [Br] – 'Mad Mullah' [Somalis]
Jiron	Feb 28, 1829	Lamar [Peru] – Sucre [Col]
Johannesburg	1900	*Roberts* [Br] – Boers
Julian, defeat of	June 8, 363	Julian [Rom] – *Sapor II* [Per]
Junin	Aug 6, 1824	*Bolivar/Sucre* [Col] – Cauterac [Sp Roy]
Jutland	May 31 – June 1, 1916	Scheer [Ger] – Jellicoe [Br]
Kabul I	Jan 1842	Elphinstone [Br] – *Akbar Khan* [Afg]
Kabul II	Sept 15, 1879	*Pollock* [Br] – Afghans
Kagoshima	Aug 18, 1876	Saigo Takamori [rebels] – *Taruhito* [Jap Imp]
Kagul	Aug 3, 1770	*Rumiantsev* [R] – Halil Pasha [T]
Kaiping	Jan 10, 1895	Chinese – *Nogi* [Jap]
Kaiserslautern	Nov 28–30, 1793	*Brunswick* [P] – Hoche [F]
Kalat	Nov 13, 1839	*Willshire* [Br] – Mehrab Khan [Baluchis]
Kalisch	1706	Meyerfeld [Swed] – *Mentschikoff* [R/Pol]
Kalpi	May 22, 1858	*Rose* [Br] – Tantia Topi/Rani of Jhansi [mutineers]
Kalunga	Oct–Nov 1814	*Gillespie* [Br] – Amarsing Thapa [Gurkhas]
Kamarut	July 8, 1824	*Campbell* [Br] – Tuamba Wangyee [Burm]
Kandahar I	1221	Tuli Khan [Tar] – *Jellalladin* [Khwarazm]
Kandahar II	Mar 1545	*Humayun* [Mog] – Mirza Askari [Afg]
Kandahar III	1638	*Shah Jahan* [Mog] – city [Per]
Kandahar IV	1648	city [Mog] – *Abbas II* [Per]
Kandahar V	Sept 1, 1880	*Roberts* [Br] – Ayub Khan [Afghans]
Kápolna	Feb 26–7, 1849	*Windischgrätz* [A] – Dembinski [Hung]

Kappel	Oct 10, 1531	*Swiss Catholic cantons* – Göldli/Lavater [Zurichers]
Kara Burur	Aug 11, 1791	*Ouschakoff* [R] – Turks
Karaku	1218	Genghis Khan [Tar] – Sultan Mehemet [Khwarazmians]
Karamuran	1225	*Genghis Khan* [Tar] – Shidasker of Rangat [T/Chin]
Kargaula	1774	Pugatcheff [Cossacks] – *Prince Gallitzin* [R]
Kars I	Nov 26, 1848	*Russians* – Williams [T]
Kars II	Nov 18, 1877	*Melikov* [R] – Hussein Pasha [T]
Kashgil	Nov 3–5, 1882	*Mahdists* – Hicks Pasha [Eg]
Kashmir I	Sept 1–25, 1965	India – Pakistan
Kashmir II	Dec 3–16, 1971	India – Pakistan
Kassassin	Aug 28, 1882	*Graham* [Br] – Arabi Pasha [Eg]
Kasserine Pass	Feb 14–22, 1943	*Rommel* [Ger] – Fredendall [US]
Kastoria	Nov 1912	*Turks* – Greeks
Katzbach	Aug 26, 1813	*Blücher* [P] – Macdonald [F]
Kazan	1774	Pugatcheff [Cossacks] – *Michelson* [R]
Kemmendine	June 10, 1824	*Campbell* [Br] – Burmans
Kentish Knock	Oct 8, 1652	*Blake* [Eng] – Witte de With [Dut]
Keresztes	Oct 24–6, 1596	*Mohammed III* [T] – Archduke Maximilian/ Prince Sigismund of Transylvania [Imp/Trans]
Khajwa	Jan 8, 1659	*Aurangzeb* [reb] – Shah Jahan [Mog]
Kharisme	1220	*Tartars* – Himartekin [city]
Khartoum	Mar 12, 1884 – Jan 26, 1885	*Mohammed Ahmed* [Dervishes] – Gordon [Br]
Khe Sanh	Jan 21 – Apr 8, 1968	*Lowndes* [US] – North Vietnamese
Khotin: see Stavuchani		
Kiev	Sept 19, 1941	*Rundstedt* [Ger] – Russians
Killala	Sept 23, 1798	*Trench* [Br] – Irish rebels
Killiecrankie	July 27, 1689	*Graham* [Highland Jacobites] – Mackay [Roy]
Kilsyth	Aug 15, 1645	*Montrose* [Roy] – Baillie [Cov]
Kinloss	1009	*Sweyn* [Danes] – Malcolm II [Scots]
Kinnesaw Mountain	June 27, 1864	Sherman [Fed] – *Johnston* [Con]
Kinsale	Dec 23, 1601	D'Aguila [Sp]/Tyrone [Ir reb] – *Mountjoy/Earl of Thomond* [Roy]
Kiöge	July 1677	*Juel* [Danes] – Horn [Swed]
Kirch-Denkern	July 16, 1761	*Prince Ferdinand* [P] – Soubise/Duc de Broglie [F]
Kirkeban	Feb 10, 1885	*Earle* [Br] – Dervishes
Kirkee	Nov 5, 1817	*Burr* [Br] – Peshwa Baji Rao II [Mar]
Kirk-Kilissa	Oct 22–5, 1912	*Bulgaria* – Abdalla Pasha [T]
Kiso	Sept 1180	*Yoshinaka* [Minamotos] – Taira-no-Kiyomori
Kiu-lien-cheng	May 1, 1904	*Kuroki* [Jap] – Sassulitch [R]
Kizil-Tepe	June 25, 1877	Melikov [R] – *Mahktar Pasha* [T]
Kjöge Bay I	July 11, 1677	*Juel* [Dan/Dut Allies] – Horn [Swed]
Kjöge Bay II	Oct 4, 1710	Gyldenlove [Dan] – Wachmeister [Swed]
Klausenburg	May 1660	*Mohammed Koprulu* [T] – George Rakoczy II [Trans]
Klushino	Sept 1610	*Zolkiewski* [Pol] – Shuisky [R]
Koenigswartha	May 19, 1813	Peyri [It] – *de Tolly* [R]
Kojende	1219	*Tuchi Khan* [Tar] – Timar Malek [Khwarazmians]
Kokein	Dec 15, 1824	*Campbell* [Br] – Maka Bandula [Burm]
Kolin	June 18, 1757	*Daun* [A] – Frederick the Great [P]
Komandorski Is.	March 26, 1943	McMorris [US] – Hosagaya [Jap]
Komatsu	Sept 5, 1062	Sadatoki [Jap rebels] – *Yoriyoshi* [Imp]
Komorn	Apr 26, 1849	*Klapka/Damjanics* [Hung] – Austrians
Koniah	Dec 21, 1832	*Ibrahim Pasha* [Eg/Syr] – Reschid Pasha [T]
Königgrätz	July 3, 1866	*von Moltke* [P] – von Benedek [A]
Kossova	June 15, 1389	*Murad I* [T] – Lazar [Serb/Bos/Alb]
Kotzim	Sept 1621	*Chodkiewicz/Lubomirski* [Pol] – Osman II [T]
Kovel-Stanislav	June 4 – Sept 20, 1916	Czar Nicholas [R] – Austro-Germans
Krak des Chevaliers	1271	*Baybars I* [Mam] – Hospitallers
Krakovicz	Jan 17, 1475	*Stephen of Moldavia* [Moldavia/ Hung] – Suleiman Pasha [T]
Krasnoi	Nov 14–18, 1812	Napoleon [F] – *Miloradovitch* [R]
Kressenbrunn	1261	*Ottocar II* [Teu] – Bela IV [Hung]
Kringellen	Aug 29, 1612	*Norwegians* – Sinclair [Scots]
Kronia	1738	*Wallis/Neipperg* [Imp] – Turks

Kronstadt	June 3–4, 1790	*Kruse* [R] – Swedish
Kroszka	July 23, 1739	*El Hadj Mohammed Pasha* [T] – Wallis [A]
Kulevcha	June 11, 1829	*Diebitsch* [R] – Reschid Pasha [T]
Kulm-Priestea	Aug 30, 1813	*Ostermann-Tolstoy/Kleist* [A/R/P] – Vandamme [F]
Kumai	Feb 1355	*Yoshinori* [Imp] – Moronoshi/Tokliushi [Jap rebels]
Kumanovo	Oct 24, 1912	*Serbia* – Turks
Kunersdorf	Aug 12, 1759	*Landon/Soltikoff* [A/R] – Frederick the Great [P]
Kunobitza	1443	Amurath II [T] – *Hunyadi* [Hung]
Kursk	Feb 8, 1943	*Russians* – Germans
Kustinitza	1443	*Hunyadi/Ladislas* [Hung] – Murad [T]
Kut-al-Imara I	Sept 28, 1915	*Townsend* [Br] – Nur-ud-din [T]
Kut-al-Imara II	Dec 8, 1915 – Apr 29, 1916	*Nur-ud-din* [T] – Townsend [Br]
Kuwait ('Desert Storm')	Feb 23–8, 1991	*Schwarzkopf* [Coalition] – Saddam Hussein [Iraq]
Kwajalein-Eniwetok	Jan 31 – Feb 4, 1944	*Spruance* [US] – Akiyama [Jap]
Kyrene	570BC	Apries [Eg] – Greeks
L'Ecluse	1340	*English* – French
La Favorita	Jan 16, 1797	*Napoleon* [F] – Provera [A]
La Fère Champenoise	Mar 25, 1814	*Schwarzenberg* [Allies] – Marmont/Mortier [F]
La Hogue	May 19–20, 1692	*Russell/Allemande* [Eng/Dut] – de Tourville [F]
La Jauda	711	*Tarik* [Mus] – Roderick [Visigoths]
La Paz	Jan 1865	Belza [Bol] – *Melgarejo* [Bol]
La Placilla	Aug 28, 1891	*Del Canto* [Cong] – Barbosa [Balmacediste]
La Puebla	Mar 4 – May 17, 1863	*Forey* [F] – Ortega [Mex]
La Rochelle I	June 22, 1372	*Don Ambrosio Bercenegra* [Sp/F] – Earl of Pembroke [Eng]
La Rochelle II	Oct 29, 1628	*Richelieu* [Roy] – Guiton [Hug]
La Rothière	Jan 30, 1814	*Napoleon* [F] – Blücher [R/P/Würt]
Lade I	494BC	*Darius* [Per] – Dionysius [Ionian fleet]
Lade II	201BC	Theophiliscus [Rhod] – Heraclides [Mac]
Lagos Bay I	June 27–8, 1693	*De Tourville* [F] – Rooke [Br/Dut]
Lagos Bay II	Aug 18–19, 1759	*Boscawen* [Br] – de la Clue [F]
Lahore	1296	Amir Daood [Mon] – *Alaf Khan* [Delhi]
Laing's Nek	Jan 28, 1881	*Joubert* [Boers] – Colley [Br]
Lake Champlain	Sept 11, 1814	*Macdonough* [Amer] – Downie [Br]
Lake Erie	Sept 10, 1813	*Perry* [Amer] – Barclay [Br]
Lake George	Sept 8, 1755	*Johnson* [Amer] – Dieskau [F/Ind]
Lake Kerguel	July 1391	Tokatmich [R] – *Timur* [Tar]
Lake Peipus	Apr 5, 1242	*Nevski* [Novgorod] – Teutonic Knights
Lake Regillus	496BC	Rome – Latin League
Lake Trasimene	Apr 217BC	Flaminius [Rom] – *Hannibal* [Carth]
Lake Vadimo	283BC	*P. Cornelius Dolabella* [Rom] – Gauls/Etruscans
Landau	Sept 12, 1702	*Prince Louis of Baden* [Imp] – De Melac [fortress]
Landeshut	Apr 21, 1809	*Napoleon* [F] – Hiller [A]
Landskrone	July 14, 1676	*Charles XI* [Swed] – Christian V [Danes]
Langensalza	June 27–9, 1866	*von Falkenstein* [P] – von Arenschildt [Han]
Langport	July 10, 1645	*Fairfax/Cromwell* [Parl] – Goring [Roy]
Langside	May 13, 1568	*Murray* [Regent] – Argyll [Scots Cath]
Lannoy	Jan 1567	*Noircarmes* [Sp] – Cornaille [Flem Prot]
Lansdowne Hill	July 5, 1643	*Hopton* [Roy] – Waller [Parl]
Laon	Mar 9–10, 1814	*Blücher* [Allies] – Ney/Marmont [F]
Larcay	Dec 1829	Zastera [Govt] – *Prieto* [Unit]
Largs	Oct 2, 1263	Haco [Norse] – *Scots*
Larissa	171BC	P. Licinius Crassus [Rom] – *Perseus* [Mac]
Larissus, The	209BC	*Philipœmen* [Achæans] – Ætolians/Eleans
Las Navas de Tolosa	June 10, 1212	*Alfonso VIII of Castile* [Christ] – Mohammed I of Granada [Almohads]
Las Salinas	Apr 20, 1538	Pizarro [Sp Conquistadors] – Almagro [Sp Conquistadors]
Laswaree	Nov 1, 1803	*Lake* [Br] – Sindhia [Mar]
Lauffeld	July 2, 1747	*Saxe* [F] – Prince of Orange/Cumberland [A/Br]
Laupen	June 21, 1339	*Von Erlach* [Swiss] – Kiburg/Nidau [Burg]
Lautulæ	316BC	*Pontius* [Samnites] – Q. Fabius Maximus [Rom]
Le Cateau	Aug 26, 1914	*Kluck* [Ger] – Smith Dorrien [Br]
Le Mans	Jan 10–12, 1870	*Prince Frederick Charles* [Ger] – Chanzy [F]
Lech, The	Apr 15–16, 1632	*Gustavus Adolphus* [Swed/Ger Prot] – Tilly [Imp]

Battle	Date	Combatants
Lechfeld	955	*Otto I* [Germans] – Magyars
Legnano	May 29, 1176	*Lombard League* – Frederick Barbarossa [Imp]
Leignitz	Apr 9, 1241	*Kaidu* [Mongols] – Henry/Wenceslaus [Christians]
Leipzig I	Sept 7, 1631	*Tilly* [Imp] – Gustavus Adolphus/George [Swed/Sax]
Leipzig II	Oct 16–19, 1813	*Schwarzenberg/Blucher/Bernadotte* [A/R/P] – Napoleon [F]
Leitskau	Aug 27, 1813	Girard [F] – *Hirschberg/Czernitcheff* [P/Cossacks]
Lemberg I	Sept 3, 1914–15	Austro/Germans – Russians
Lemberg II	July 1 – Aug 1, 1917	*Hindenburg* [Ger] – Brusilov [R]
Lemnos I	July 12 and 16, 1717	Venice – Turks
Lemnos II	June 30, 1807	*Seniavin* [R] – Turks
Lens	Aug 2, 1648	*The Great Condé* [F] – Archduke Leopold William [Imp/Sp]
Leontini	211BC	City [Syrac/rebels] – *M. Marcellus* [Rom]
Lepanto	Oct 7, 1571	*Don John of Austria* [Sp/Ven] – Ali Pasha [T]
Lerida	May 12 – June 17, 1647	*Don Jorge Britt* [Sp] – The Great Condé [F]
Lérida	Sept 1642	*De la Motte-Houdancourt* [F] – Leganez [Sp]
Lesno	1709	*Peter the Great* [R] – Levenhaupt [Swed]
Leucopetra	146BC	*Lucius Mummius* [Rom] – Diacus [Achæan League]
Leuctra	July 371BC	Cleombrotus [Spar] – *Epaminondas* [Thebes]
Leuthen	Dec 5, 1757	*Frederick the Great* [P] – Prince Charles of Lorraine/Daun [A]
Lewes	May 14, 1264	*de Montfort* [barons] – Henry III/Prince Edward [Roy]
Lexington and Concord	Apr 19, 1775	*Smith* [Br] – Parker/Barrett [Amer Minutemen]
Lexington	Oct 19, 1864	*Price* [Con] – Blunt [Fed]
Leyden	May 26 – Oct 3, 1574	*city* – Valdez [Wa/Ger]
Leyte Gulf	Oct 23–26, 1944	*Nimitz* [US] – Toyoda [Jap]
Liége	Aug 14, 1914	*von Emmich* [Ger] – King Albert I [Bel]
Liegnitz	Aug 15, 1760	*Frederick the Great* [P] – Landon [A]
Ligny	June 16, 1815	*Napoleon* [F] – Blücher [P]
Lille	Aug 12 – Oct 25, 1708	*Prince Eugene* [Imp] – de Boufflers [F]
Lilybæum	250–241BC	*C. Attilius/L. Manlius* [Rom] – Hamilcar [Carth]
Lincoln	Feb 2, 1141	King Stephen – *Earl of Gloucester*
Lindley	May 27, 1900	*De Wet* [Boers] – Spragge [Br]
Linköping	1598	*Charles the Regent* [Swed Prot reb] – Sigismund III [Pol/Swed Cath Roy]
Liparian Islands	257BC	*C. Attilius* [Rom] – Carthaginians
Lissa I	Mar 13, 1811	*Hoste* [Br] – Dubourdieu [F/Ven]
Lissa II	July 20, 1866	*Tegetthoff* [A] – Persano [It]
Little Big Horn	June 23, 1876	*Crazy Horse* [Sioux Ind] – Custer [US Cav]
Loano	Nov 24, 1795	*Schérer* [F] – Vins [A]
Lodi	May 10, 1796	*Napoleon* [F] – Beaulieu [A/Sard]
Lodz	Nov 11–25, 1914	Mackensen [Ger] – Rennenkampf [R]
Loftcha	Sept 3, 1877	*Prince Imeretinsky* [R] – Adil Pasha [T]
Loigny-Pouprey	Dec 1, 1867	*Grand Duke of Mecklenburg* [Ger] – d'Aurelle de Paladines [F]
Loja	July 4, 1482	*Ali Atar* [Moors] – Ferdinand the Catholic [Sp]
Lonato	Aug 3, 1796	*Napoleon* [F] – Quasdanovich [A]
Londonderry	Apr 19 – July 30, 1689	*Baker/Kirke* [Ulst Prot] – James II [Roy]
Long Island	Aug 27, 1776	*Howe* [Br] – Putnam [Amer]
Lorraine	Aug 14–22, 1914	*Germans* – French
Loudon Hill	May 1307	*Bruce* [Scots] – Pembroke [Eng]
Louisbourg	June 16, 1745	*Pepperell/Warren* [New Eng/Br] – fortress
Louvain	891	*Arnulph* [Ger] – Vikings
Löwenberg	Aug 21, 1813	*Napoleon* [F] – Blücher [P]
Lowestoft/Solebay	June 13, 1665	*Duke of York/Prince Rupert* [Eng] – van Obdam [Dut]
Lowositz	Oct 1, 1756	*Frederick the Great* [P] – von Browne [A]
Lübeck	Nov 6, 1806	*Soult/Bernadotte* [F] – Blücher [P]
Lugdunum (Lyons)	197	Clodius Albinus [Imp Britain] – *Septimius Severus* [Rom]
Lüleburgaz	Oct 28–3, 1912	*Bulgaria* – Abdalla Pasha [T]
Luncarty	980	*Kenneth III* [Scots] – Danes
Lunceña	Apr 1483	*Comte de Cabra* [Sp] – Abdullah/Ali Atar [Moors]
Lunden	1676	Charles XI [Swed] – Christian V [Danes]
Lundy's Lane	July 25, 1814	*Riall* [Br] – Brown [Amer]
Lutetia	52BC	*Labienus* [Rom] – Gauls
Lutter am Barenberge	Aug 24–7, 1626	*Tilly* [Imp] – Christian IV [Dan/Ger]
Lützen I	Nov 16, 1632	*Gustavus Adolphus* [Swed] – Wallenstein [Imp]

Lützen II	May 2, 1813	*Napoleon* [F] – Wittgenstein/Blücher [R/P]
Luzzara	Aug 15, 1702	*Prince Eugene* [Imp] – Duc d'Anjou [F]
Lynn Haven Bay	Sept 5, 1781	Graves [Br] – French
Lys River (Ypres IV)	Apr 2–29, 1918	Ludendorff [Ger] – Foch/Haig[F/Br]
Maastricht	Mar 12 – Apr 8, 1579	Melchior [city] – *Prince Alexander Farnese of Parma* [Sp]
Macalo	Oct 11, 1427	*Carmagnola* [Ven] – Malatesta [Milan]
Madeira	Dec 26, 1807	*Cochrane/Bowyer* [Br] – island
Madonna del' Olmo	Sept 30, 1744	*Prince Louis de Conti/Don Philip* [F/Sp] – Charles Emmanuel [A/Sardinia]
Madras I	Sept 14–25, 1746	*Dupleix/La Bourdonnais* [F] – city [Br]
Madras II (St Thomé)	Nov 4, 1746	*Paradis* [F/Sepoys] – Maphuze Khan [Carnatic]
Madras III	Dec 16, 1758 – Feb 1759	Lawrence [Br] – Lally-Tollendal [F]
Mafeking	Oct 14, 1899 – May 17, 1900	*Baden-Powell* [Br] – Cronje/Snyman [Boers], relieved Mahon/Plumer [Br]
Magdeburg, siege	Nov 1630 – May 20, 1631	*Pappenheim/Tilly* [Imp] – Falkenberg [Swed]
Magenta	June 4, 1859	*MacMahon* [F] – Gyulay [A]
Magersfontein	Dec 11, 1899	*Cronje/De La Rey* [Boers] – Methuen [Br]
Magnano	Apr 5, 1799	*Kray* [A] – Schérer [F]
Magnesia	190BC	Antiochus the Great [Syr] – *Cnæus Domitius/Eumenes* [Rom/Pergamum]
Maharajpore	Dec 29, 1843	*Gough* [Br] – Marathas
Mahidpore	Dec 23, 1817	*Hislop* [Br] – Indore Marathas
Maida	July 6, 1806	*Stuart* [Br] – Reynier [F]
Mainz	Oct 29, 1795	*Clerfayt* [A] – Pichegru [F]
Maiwand	July 26, 1880	*Ayub Khan* [Afg] – Burrows [Br/Bengalis]
Majorca	1706	*Leake* [Br] – Spanish
Majuba Hill	Feb 27, 1881	*Joubert* [Boers] – Colley [Br]
Malacca	1513	Sultan Mohammed [Malays] – *Albuquerque* [Port]
Malaga I	Apr 17 – Aug 18, 1487	Hamet Zeli [Moors] – *Ferdinand the Catholic* [Sp]
Malaga II	Aug 13, 1704	*Rooke* [Br/Dut] – Comte de Toulouse [F]
Malaga III	Aug 24, 1704	Shovell [Br] – Saint-Aubin [F]
Malakov	Sept 8, 1855	*Pélissier* [F] – fort [R]
Malaya	Dec 8, 1941 – Jan 31, 1942	*Yamashita* [Jap] – Percival [Br]
Malborghetto	March 23, 1797	*Masséna* [F] – Archduke Charles [A]
Maldon	991	Brihtnoth [A-S] – *Olaf Triggvason* [Danes]
Malegnano	June 8, 1859	*Baraguay d'Hilliers* [F] – Austrians
Maloyaroslavets	Oct 24, 1812	Eugène [F] – *Kutuzov* [R]
Malplaquet	Sept 11, 1709	*Marlborough/Prince Eugene* [Br/Imp] – Villars/Boufflers [F]
Malta I	May 19 – Sept 11, 1565	*Lavalette* [Knights of Malta] – Mustapha Pasha/Piale [T]
Malta II	Sept 5, 1800	*Martin/Pigott* [Br] – French
Mandonia	338BC	Archidamus [Gr] – *Lucanians*
Mangalore	June 20, 1783 – Jan 26, 1784	*Campbell* [Br] – Tipu Sultan
Manila	May 1, 1898	*Dewey* [US] – Montojo [Sp]
Mannerheim Line	Feb 1–13, 1940	*Timoshenko* [R] – von Mannerheim [Finns]
Mansura	Feb 8, 1250	*Fakr-Ed-Din* [Mus] – King Louis IX [F/Crusaders]
Mantinea I	418BC	*Agis* [Spar/Tegeans] – Laches/Nicostratus [Ath]
Mantinea II	362BC	*Epaminondas* [Bœotians] – Athen/Sparta/Mantinea
Mantinea III	207BC	*Philopœmen* [Achæans] – Machanidas [Spar]
Mantua	June 4, 1796 – Feb 2, 1797	*Napoleon* [F] – Canto d'Yrles/Wurmser [A]
Manzikert	1071	*Alp Arslan* [T] – Romanus [Byz]
Maogamaicha	363	fortress [Per] – *Julian* [Rom]
Marathon	Sept 490BC	*Miltiades* [Ath/Platæans] – Datis [Per]
Marcianopolis	376	Lupicinus [Rom] – *Fritigern* [Goths]
Mardis	315	*Constantine* [Emp West] – Licinius [Emp East]
Marengo	June 14, 1800	*Napoleon* [F] – Melas [A]
Margus	May 285	Carinus – *Diocletian*
Marignano	Sept 13–14, 1515	*Francis I* [F/Ven] – von Winkelried [Swiss]
Marne River I	Sept 8, 1914	*Joffre* [F] – von Moltke [Ger]
Marne River II	July 15 – Aug 4, 1918	Ludendorff [Ger] – Foch [F]
Marosch, The	101	Decebalus [Dacians] – *Trajan* [Rom]
Marsaglia	Oct 4, 1693	*de Catinat* [F] – Duke of Savoy [A/Sp/Eng]
Mars-la-Tour	Aug 16, 1870	*Prince Friedrich Karl* [Ger] – Bazaine [F]
Marston Moor	July 2, 1644	*Manchester/Leven/Fairfax* [Parl] – Prince Rupert [Roy]

Martinesti	Sept 23, 1789	*Prince of Coburg/Suvorov* [A/R] – Osman Pasha [T]
Martinique I	Apr 17, 1780	Rodney [Br] – de Guichon [F]
Martinique II	1793	*Jervis/Grey* [Br] – French
Martinique III	Feb 24, 1809	*Cochrane/Beckwith* [Br] – de Joyeuse [F]
Martyropolis	588	*Bahram* [Per] – Romans
Maserfield	642	Oswald [Northumbrians] – *Penda* [Mercians]
Masulipatam	Mar 1759	*Forde* [Br] – Lally [F]
Masurian Lakes I	Sept 9–14, 1914	*von Moltke* [Ger] – Zhilinsky [R]
Masurian Lakes II	Feb 7–22, 1915	Hindenburg [Ger] – Russians
Matapan I	July 19, 1717	*Diedo* [Venice and allies] – Kapudan Pasha Ibrahim Pasha [Tur]
Matapan II	March 26–29, 1941	*Cunningham* [Br] – Iachino [It]
Matchevitz	Oct 10, 1794	*De Fersen* [R] – Kosciusko [Pol]
Matchin	July 10, 1794	*Prince Repnin* [R] – Yussuf Pasha [T]
Mauritius	Dec 3, 1810	*Abercromby* [Br] – Decaen [F]
Maxen	Nov 21, 1759	*Daun* [A] – Finck [P]
Maya	July 25, 1813	*Pringle* [Br/Port] – d'Erlon [F]
Maypo	Apr 5, 1818	*San Martin* [Chil Pat] – Osorio [Sp Roy]
Medellin	Mar 29, 1809	*Victor* [F] – Cuesta [Sp]
Medenine	Mar 6, 1943	*Montgomery* [Br] – Rommel [Ger]
Medina	625	*Mohammed* [Mus] – Abu Sophian [Koreish]
Medina del Rioseco	July 14, 1808	*Bessières* [F] – Cuesta/Blake [Sp]
Meerut	1398	Fortress – *Timur* [Tar]
Meerut (Mutiny)	May 10, 1857	*Sepoys* – Garrison [Br]
Megaletaphrus	740BC	Aristomenes [Messenians] – *Spartans*
Megalopolis I	331BC	Agis [Spar] – *Antipater* [Mac]
Megalopolis II	226BC	*Cleomenes* [Spar] – Aratus [Achæans]
Megiddo I	1469BC	*Thutmosis III* [Eg] – rebels
Megiddo II	610BC	*Necho* [Eg] – Josiah [Judah]
Megiddo III	Sept 19–21, 1918	*Allenby* [Br] – von Sanders [T]
Meiktila	Feb 28 – Mar 3, 1945	*Slim* [Br] – Katamura [Jap]
Meldorp	1500	John of Denmark [Danes] – *Dithmarsh*
Melitene	578	Tiberius [Imp] – Chosroes [Per]
Memphis	638	*Amron* [Mus] – city
Memphis (town)	June 6, 1862	*Davis* [Fed] – Montgomery [Con]
Menin	Sept 13, 1793	*Houchard* [F] – Prince of Orange [Dut]
Mensourah	1249	Louis IX [F] – *Moslems*
Mentana	Nov 3, 1866	de Failly [F/Pap] – Garibaldi [It]
Mergentheim	May 2, 1645	Turenne [F] – *Mercy* [Imp]
Merida	712	city [Sp] – *Musa* [Moors]
Mersa Matruh	June 27–28, 1942	*Germans* – British
Merseburg	934	*Henry the Fowler* [Ger] – Hungarians
Merta	1561	Rajput Rajah of Malwar – *Sharf-ud-din Hussein*
Merton	871	Alfred [W Sax] – *Danes*
Merv	651	*Othman* [Islam] – Firuz II [Sassanids]
Messina	Oct 2, 1284	*de Lauria* [Sic/Cat] – Charles of Anjou [F]
Messines	Apr 10–11, 1917	Haig [Br] – Prince Rupprecht of Bavaria [Ger]
Metaurus	207BC	*Claudius Nero/Marcus Livius* [Rom] – Hasdrubal [Carth]
Methven	June 19, 1306	Bruce [Scots] – *Earl of Pembroke* [Eng]
Metz	Oct 27, 1870	*Prince Frederick Charles* [Ger] – Bazaine [F]
Mexico City: *see* Tenochtitlan		
Miani (Meeanee)	Feb 17, 1843	*Napier* [Br] – Amirs of Sind [Baluchis]
Middelburg	Winter 1593 – Feb 18, 1594	Mondragon [Sp] – Patriots
Midway	June 4–7, 1942	*Nimitz* [US] – Yamamoto [Jap]
Milazzo	July 20, 1860	*Garibaldi* [It Volunteers] – Bosco [Neap]
Miletopolis	86BC	*Flavius Fimbria* [Rom] – Mithridates [Pontics]
Mill Springs	Jan 19–20, 1862	*Thomas* [Fed] – Crittenden [Con]
Millesimo	Apr 14, 1796	*Napoleon* [F] – Provera [A]
Minden	Aug 1, 1759	*Ferdinand of Brunswick* [Han/Br/P] – Louis de Contades [F]
Ming Chiao	c1523BC	Shao Dynasty – *Shang Dynasty*
Mingolsheim	Apr 27, 1622	*von Mansfeldt* [Ger Prot] – Tilly [Bav]
Minorca I	May 20, 1756	de la Galissonière [F] – Blakeney/Byng [Br]
Minorca II	July 22, 1781 – Feb 5, 1782	de Crillon [F/Sp] – Murray [Br]
Miohosaki	Sept 764	Oshikatsa [Jap rebels] – *Saiki-no-Sanya* [Imp]

Battle	Date	Combatants
Miraflores	Jan 15, 1881	*Baquedano* [Chil] – Peruvians
Missolonghi	Apr 27, 1825 – Apr 23, 1826	*Reshid Pasha* [T] – Greeks
Mita Caban	1362	*Timur* [Tar] – Khan Elias [Getes]
Miyako I	June 1353	*Moronoshi* [rebels] – Yoshinori [Emp of the South]
Miyako II	Dec 30, 1391	Mitsuyaki [Idzumo/Idzumi] – *Gokameyama* [Emp of the South]
Mobile Bay	Aug 5, 1864	*Farragut* [Fed] – Buchanon [Con]
Modder River	Nov 28, 1899	*Methuen* [Br] – Cronje/De La Rey [Boers]
Mohacz I	Aug 29, 1526	*Suleiman the Magnificent* [T] – Louis II/Tomore [Hung]
Mohacz II	Aug 12, 1687	*Charles of Lorraine/Emanuel of Bavaria* [A/Hung/Pol] – Mohammed IV [T]
Mohilev	July 23, 1812	*Davout* [F] – Raievsky [R]
Mohrungen	Jan 25, 1807	Bernadotte [F] – *Markov* [R]
Molins del Rey	Dec 21, 1808	*St Cyr* [F] – del Caldagues [Sp]
Mollwitz	Apr 10, 1741	*Von Schwerin* [P] – Neipperg [A]
Monarda	Mar 18, 1501	Di Cifuentes/de Aguilar [Sp] – *Moors*
Monastir	Nov 5, 1912	*Serbia/Greece* – Turks
Mondovi	Apr 21, 1796	*Napoleon* [F] – Colli [A/Pied]
Monogahela, The	July 9, 1755	*Contrecœur* [F/Ind] – Braddock [Br/Virg]
Mons	Aug 23, 1914	*Kluck* [Ger] – French [Br]
Mons Graupius	84	*Agricola* [Rom] – Galgacus [Caledonians]
Mons Lactarius	Mar 553	*Narses* [Rom] – Teias [Goths]
Mons-en-Puelle	1304	*Philip IV* [F] – Flemings
Montcontour	Oct 3, 1569	*Duc d'Anjou/de Tavannes* [Cath] – Le Béarnais [Hug]
Monte Aperto	Sept 4, 1260	Guelfs – *Manfred of Sicily* [Ghib]
Monte Caseros	Feb 3, 1852	*Urquiza* [reb] – Rosas [Arg]
Monte Cassino: see Cassino		
Montebello I	June 9, 1800	*Napoleon* [F] – Ott [A]
Montebello II	May 20, 1859	Stadion [A] – *Forey* [F]
Montenotte	Apr 12, 1796	*Napoleon* [F] – Beaulieu [A]
Montereau	Feb 18, 1814	*Napoleon* [F] – Schwarzenberg [Allies]
Monterrey	Sept 20–4, 1846	*Taylor* [Amer] – de Ampudia [Mex]
Montevideo I	Feb 3, 1807	*Auchmuty* [Br] – city
Montevideo II	Oct 8, 1851	*Urquiza* [Uru/Braz/Para] – Oribe [Arg]
Montevideo III	Aug 1863	Flores [Uru Colorados] – *Medina* [Uru Blancos]
Montfaucon	Sept 886	*Eudes* [F] – Normans
Montiel	1369	*du Guesclin* [F reb] – Pedro II of Castile [Sp]
Montlhéry	July 13, 1465	Louis XI [Roy] – *Charles The Bold* [League of Public Weal]
Montmartre: see Paris I		
Montmirail	Feb 11, 1814	*Napoleon* [F] – Yorck [Allies]
Montmorenci	July 31, 1759	*Montcalm* [F] – Wolfe [Br]
Montreal	Sept 8, 1760	*Amherst* [Br] – Lévis [F]
Moodkee	Dec 18, 1845	*Gough* [Br] – Tej Singh [Sikhs]
Mookesheyde	Apr 14, 1574	*Don Sancho d'Avila* [Sp] – Count Louis of Nassau [Dut]
Morat	June 22, 1476	*Waldmann* [Swiss] – Charles the Bold [Burg]
Morawa	Nov 3, 1443	*Hunyadi* [Hung] – Murad II [T]
Morazzone	1848	Garibaldi [It] – *d'Aspre* [A]
Morella	May 23–30, 1840	Cabrera [Carlists] – *Espartero* [Crist]
Morgarten	Nov 15, 1315	*Swiss Cantons* – Archduke Leopold [A]
Morshedabad	July 24, 1763	*Adams* [Br] – Mir Cossim [Bengalis]
Mortara	Mar 21, 1849	Duke of Savoy/Darando [Pied] – *Radetsky* [A]
Mortimer's Cross	Feb 2, 1461	*Edward* [York] – Earl of Pembroke/Earl of Wiltshire [Lanc]
Mortlack	1010	Sweyn [Danes] – *Malcolm II* [Scots]
Moscow	Dec 1941 – Jan 1942	*Zhukov* [R] – Bock [Ger]
Möskirch	May 5, 1800	*Moreau* [F] – Kray [A]
Motya	398BC	*Dionysius* [Syrac] – city [Carth]
Mount Gaurus	342BC	*Valerius Corvus* [Rom] – Samnites
Mount Panium	198BC	*Antiochus the Great* [Syr] – Scopas [Gr/Eg]
Mount Seleucus	Aug 10, 353	Megnentius [rebels] – *Constantius* [Rom]
Mount Tabor	Apr 17, 1799	*Napoleon* [F] – Achmed [T]
Mount Taurus	804	*Harroun-al-Raschid* [Mus] – Nicephorus I [Gr]
Mount Tifata	83BC	*Sulla* [Rom] – Norbanus [Rom]
Mühlberg	Apr 24, 1547	*Duke of Alva* – Frederick of Saxony/Landgrave of Hesse [Ger Prot]

Mühldorf	1322	*Louis the Bavarian* [Imp] – Frederick Duke of Austria [rebels]
Mühlhausen	58BC	*Julius Cæsar* [Rom] – Ariovistus [Sequani]
Mukden	Feb 21 – Mar 10, 1905	*Oyama* [Jap] – Kuropatkin [R]
Mulhouse	Aug 7–10, 1914	*Heeringen* [Ger] – Bonneau [F]
Multan	Sept 1848 – Jan 22, 1849	*Whish* [Br] – Mulraj [Sikhs]
Munda	Mar 17, 45BC	Sextus/Labienus [Pomp] – *Julius Cæsar* [Cæsarians]
Muret	Sept 12, 1213	*de Montfort* [F Cath] – Count of Toulouse/ Pedro II of Aragon [Albigensians]
Murfreesboro	Dec 31, 1862 – Jan 2, 1863	Bragg [Con] – Rosecrans [Fed]
Mursa	Sept 28, 351	Magnentius – *Constantius*
Muta	629	Zaid/Khaled [Mus] – *Heraclius* [Imp]
Mutina	Apr 16–27, 43BC	Mark Antony – Hirtius/Octavius/Vibius Pansa
Mycale	Aug 479BC	*Leotychidas* [Gr] – Persians
Mylæ I	260BC	*Caius Duilius* [Rom] – Hannibal [Carth]
Mylae II: see Naulochus		
Myonnesus	190BC	*Caius Livius* [Rom] – Polyxenides [Syr]
Mytilene I	428–427BC	City/Alcidas [Pelo] – *Paches* [Ath]
Mytilene II	406BC	*Callicratidas* [Pelo] – Conon [Ath]
Näfels	Apr 9, 1388	Tockenburg [A] – *Glarus* [Swiss]
Nagy-Sarló	Apr 19, 1849	*Görgey* [Hung] – Austrians
Nahavend	637	*Said* [Mus] – Persians
Naissus	269	*Claudius Gothicus* [Imp] – Goths
Namur	Aug 20–25, 1914	*von Bülow* [Ger] – Belgians
Nangis	Feb 17, 1814	Count de Pahlen [R] – *Victor* [F]
Nanshan	May 26, 1904	*Oku* [Jap] – Stoessel [R]
Naroch Lake	Mar 18 – Apr 14, 1916	Czar Nicholas [R] – Hindenburg [Ger]
Narva	Nov 20, 1700	*Charles XII* [Swed] – Dolgorouky [R]
Narvik I	Apr 10, 1940	*Norwegians/British* – Germans
Narvik II	Apr 24 – May 26, 1940	*Norwegians/British/French* – Germans
Naseby	June 14, 1645	*Fairfax/Cromwell* [Parl] – Prince Rupert/Charles I [Roy]
Nashville	Dec 15–16, 1863	*Thomas* [Fed] – Hood [Con]
Naulochus	Sept 3, 36BC	Sextus Pompey [Pompeians] – *Agrippa* [Triumvirs]
Naupactus	429BC	*Phormio* [Ath] – Cnemas [Pelo]
Navarino	Oct 20, 1827	*Codrington/de Rigny/Heiden* [Br/Fr/R] – Ibrahim Pasha [T/Eg]
Navarrete	Apr 3, 1367	*Black Prince* [Eng] – du Guesclin/de Trastamare [F/Cast]
Naxos	Sept 376BC	*Chabrias* [Ath] – Pollio [Spar]
Nechtan's Mere	May 20, 685	*Brude* [Picts] – Ecgfrith [Northumbrians]
Nedao	455	Huns – Huns
Neerwinden I	July 29, 1693	*Luxembourg* [F] – William III [Br/Dut]
Neerwinden II	Mar 18, 1793	*Saxe-Coburg* [A] – Dumouriez [F]
Negapatam I	July 25, 1746	Peyton [Br] – La Bourdonnais [F]
Negapatam II	Oct 21, 1781	*Braithwaite* [Br] – garrison [Dut/Mys]
Negapatam III	1782	Hughes [Br] – Suffren [F]
Neon	354BC	Philomelus [Phocians] – *Thebans/Locrians*
Neuve-Chapelle	Mar 10–13, 1915	Falkenhayn [Ger] – French [Br]
Neuwied	Apr 18, 1797	*Hoche* [F] – Werneck [A]
Neville's Cross	Oct 17, 1346	*Percy/Neville* [Eng] – David II [Scots]
New Market	May 15, 1864	*Breckenridge* [Con] – Sigel [Fed]
New Orleans	Jan 8, 1815	*Jackson* [Amer] – Pakenham [Br]
New Ross	June 5, 1799	*Johnstone* [regulars] – Roche/Harvey [rebels]
Newbury	Sept 20, 1643	Charles I [Roy] – Essex [Parl]
Newtown Butler	Aug 2, 1689	*Wolseley* [Prot] – MacCarthy [Cath]
Niagara	June 1759	*Prideaux/Johnson* [Br/Ind] – Pouchot [F]
Nicaea I	193	*Septimus Severus* [Pann] – C. P. Niger Justus [Syr]
Nicaea II	May 14 – June 19, 1097	*Crusaders/Alexius* [Byz] – Saracens
Nicholson's Nek	Oct 30, 1899	*Joubert* [Boers] – Carleton [Br]
Nicopolis I	66BC	*Pompey* [Rom] – Mithridates [Pon]
Nicopolis II	47BC	Domitius Calvinus [Rom] – Pharnaces [Bosporans]
Nieuport I	July 2, 1600	*Maurice of Orange* [Dut] – Archduke Albert [Sp]
Nieuport II: see Dunes		
Nikko	1868	*Saigo Takamori* [Imp] – Otori Keisuke [Shogun]
Nikopol	1396	*Bajazet I* [T] – John The Fearless [F/Hung]

Nile (Aboukir Bay)	Aug 1, 1798	*Nelson* [Br] – Brueys [F]
Nile Delta	Feb 47BC	*Julius Cæsar/Mithridates* [Cæs] – Ptolemy [Pomp]
Nineveh	Dec 1, 627	*Heraclius* [Imp] – Rhazates [Per]
Niquitas	1813	*Bolivar* [Col] – Spanish Royalists
Nisib	June 23, 1839	*Ibrahim* [Syr/Eg] – Hafiz Pasha [T]
Nisibis I	338	*fortress* – Sapor II [Per]
Nisibis II	346	*fortress* – Sapor II [Per]
Nisibis III	350	*Lucilianus* [fortress] – Sapor II [Per]
Nissa	1064	Sweyn II [Danes] – *Harald Hardrada* [Norse]
Nive	Dec 9–12, 1813	*Wellington* [Br/Port] – Soult [F]
Nivelle	Nov 10, 1813	*Wellington* [Br] – Soult [F]
Noisseville	Aug 31, 1870	Bazaine [F] – *Prince Frederick Charles* [Ger]
Nördlingen I	Sept 6, 1634	*Ferdinand of Hungary* [Imp] – Duke of Saxe-Weimar/Count Horn [Ger/Swed]
Nördlingen II	Aug 3, 1645	*The Great Condé* [F] – Mercy [Imp]
Normandy	June 6 – July 27, 1944	*Montgomery* [Allies] – Rommel [Ger]
North Cape	Dec 26, 1943	*Fraser* [Br] – Bey [Ger]
North Foreland I	June 2–6, 1653	Monck [Eng] – Tromp [Dut]
North Foreland II	July 25, 1666	*Albemarle/Prince Rupert* [Eng] – van Tromp/de Ruyter [Dut]
Northampton	July 10, 1460	Henry VI [Lanc] – *Earl of Warwick* [York]
Noryang	Nov 1598	*Yi Sun-sin* [Kor] – Japanese
Notion	407BC	*Lysander* [Pelo] – Athenians
Nova Carthago	209BC	Mago [Carth] – *Scipio* [Rom]
Novara	June 6, 1515	*Swiss* – La Tremouille [F]
Novara	Mar 23, 1849	*Radetsky* [A] – Chrzanowski [Pied]
Novi Ligure	Aug 15, 1799	*Suvorov* [R/A] – Joubert [F]
Noyon-Montdidier	1918	Ludendorff [Ger] – Foch [F]
Nuadydroog	Oct 19, 1791	*Cornwallis* [Br/Mar] – Mysore
Oberstein	1533	*Tarnowski* [Pol] – Bogdan [Wallachians]
Obligado	Nov 20, 1845	*French/British* – Mansilla [Arg]
Ocaña	Nov 19, 1809	*Soult* [F] – Areizaga [Sp]
Ocean Pond: see Olustee		
Ochakov I	1737	*Count Münnich* [R] – fortress [T/Bos]
Ochakov II	1788	*Potemkin* [R] – fortress
Ockley	851	Danes – *Ethelwulf* [W Sax]
Oeland: see Entholm		
Oeland I	June 11, 1676	*Tromp* [Dan/Dut Allies] – Creutz [Swed]
Oeland II	July 26, 1789	Duke Carl [Swed] – Chichagov [Ru]
Œnophyta	457BC	*Myronides* [Ath] – Thebans/Bœotians
Ofen	May 4–21, 1849	Hentzi [A] – *Görgey* [Hung]
Ohud	623	Mohammed [Mus] – *Abu Sophian* [Koreish]
Okinawa	Apr 1 – July 2, 1945	*Buckner* [US] – Ushijima [Jap]
Okpo	May 1592	*Yi Sun-sin* [Kor] – Japanese
Olmedo	1467	Archbishop of Toledo [rebels] – *Henry of Castile* [Sp Roy]
Olmütz	May 1758	*Town* [A] – Frederick the Great [P]
Olpæ	426BC	*Demosthenes* [Ath] – Eurylochus [Ambraciots]
Oltenitza	Nov 4, 1853	*Omar Pasha* [T] – Russians
Olustee	Feb 20, 1864	*Finegan* [Con] – Seymour [Fed]
Omdurman	Sept 2, 1898	*Kitchener* [Br/Eg/Sud] – The Khalifa Abdullahi [Dervishes]
Oondwa Nullah	Sept 1763	*Adams* [Br] – Mir Cossim
Ooscata	Aug 23, 1768	*Morari Rao* [Mahr] – Hyder Ali [Mys]
Opequan Creek	Sept 19, 1864	*Sheridan* [Fed] – Early [Con]
Oporto	May 12, 1809	*Wellesley* [Br] – Soult [F]
Oran	May 17, 1509	*Jiménez/Navarro* [Sp] – Moors
Orchomenus	85BC	Archelaus [Pontic] – *Sulla* [Rom]
Ordovici, The	50	*Ostorius Scapula* [Rom] – Caractacus [Britons]
Orléans I	Oct 12, 1428–1429	*Dunois/Joan of Arc* [F] – Duke of Bedford/Suffolk [Eng]
Orléans II	Dec 2–4, 1870	*Friedrich Karl* [G] – d'Aurelle de Paladines [F]
Orthez	Feb 27, 1814	*Wellington* [Br/Port] – Soult [F]
Oruro	1862	*Acha* [Bol Govt] – Perez [rebels]
Oslo	Apr 9–10, 1940	*Germans* – Norwegians
Ostend	July 5, 1601 – Sept 14, 1604	*Archduke Albert* [Sp] – Town
Ostia	1500	Guerri [F] – *de Cordova* [Sp]

Ostrach	Mar 21, 1799	*Charles* [A] – Jourdan [F]
Ostrolenka	1853	*Omar Pasha* [T] – Russians
Ostrovno	July 25–6, 1812	*Murat* [F] – Ostermann-Tolstoi [R]
Oswego	Aug 11, 1756	*Montcalm* [F] – Mercer [Provincials/Br]
Otrar	1219	Gazer Khan [city] – *Oktai/Zagatai* [Mon]
Otterburn	Aug 19, 1388	*Douglas* [Scots] – Henry Percy [Eng]
Otumba	July 8, 1520	*Cortés* [Sp] – Aztecs
Oudenarde	July 11, 1708	*Marlborough/Prince Eugene* [Br/Imp] – Duke of Burgundy/Vendôme [F]
Paardeberg	Feb 18–27, 1900	*French/Kitchener* [Br] – Cronje [Boers]
Pabon	Sept 17, 1861	*Mitre* [Buenos Aires] – Urquiza [Arg Confed]
Pagahar	1825	*Campbell* [Br] – Zay-ya-Thayan [Burm]
Pagasæan Gulf	352BC	OnoMarus [Phocians] – *Philip* [Mac]
Palais Gallien	Sept 5, 1649	de la Meilleraic [Royal] – Duc de Bouillon/ Duc de la Rochefoucauld [Bordelais]
Palermo I	June 2, 1676	*Comte de Vivonne* [F] – Spanish/Dutch
Palermo II	May 26–27, 1848	*Garibaldi* [It] – Lanza [Neap]
Palestrina	May 9, 1849	*Garibaldi* [It] – Ferdinand [Neap]
Palestro	May 30, 1859	*Napoleon* [F/Pied] – Gyusas [A]
Palmyra	272	*Aurelian* [Rom] – city
Palo Alto	May 8, 1846	*Taylor* [US] – Arista [Mex]
Panama	Apr 25, 1680	*Coxon* [Buccaneers] – Spanish
Panama City	Jan 2, 1671	*Henry Morgan* [Buccaneers] – Guzman [Sp garrison]
Pandosia	331BC	Alexander of Epirus [Gr] – *Lucanians*
Panipat I	Apr 20, 1526	*Babur* [Mog] – Ibrahim [Delhi]
Panipat II	Nov 5, 1556	*Akbar* [Mog] – Hemu [Hindu Rajahs]
Panipat III	Jan 14, 1761	Marathas – *Ahmed Shah Abdali* [Afg]
Panormus	250BC	*L. Cæcilius Metellus* [Rom] – Hasdrubal [Carth]
Parætakene Mtns	316BC	*Antigonus* [Mac] – Eumenes [Asiatics]
Parambakum	Sept 10, 1780	*Hyder Ali* [Mys] – Munro/Baillie [Br]
Paraná	1866	Lopez [Para] – *Porto Alegre* [Braz/Arg/Uru]
Paris I	Mar 30, 1814	*Schwarzenberg* [Allies] – Marmont [F]
Paris II	Sept 19, 1870 – Jan 28, 1871	*von Moltke* [Ger] – Trochu [city]
Parkany	Aug–Sept 1663	*Ahmed Kopralu Pasha* [T] – Count Forgach [Hung]
Parma	June 29, 1734	*De Coigny* [F] – de Mercy [Imp]
Paros Island	July 1651	Mocenigo [Venice] – Turks
Paso de la Patria	May 24, 1866	Lopez [Para] – *Porto Alegre* [Braz/Arg/Uru]
Passchendaele	Oct 12 – Nov 10, 1917	Haig [Br] – von Armin [Ger]
Patay	June 18, 1429	*Joan of Arc/Duc d'Alençon* [F] – Talbot/Fastolfe [Eng]
Patila	1394	*Timur* [Tar] – Shah Mansur [Per]
Pavia I	271	*Aurelian* [Rom] – Alemanni
Pavia II	568–571	*Alboin* [Lombards] – city
Pavia III	May 22, 1431	*Milanese* – Trevisani [Ven]
Pavia IV	Feb 25, 1525	*Lannoy* [Imp] – Francis I [F]
Pea Ridge	Mar 7–8, 1862	Van Dorn [Con] – Curtis [Fed]
Peach Tree Creek	July 20, 1864	*Thomas* [Fed] – Hood [Con]
Pearl Harbor	Dec 7, 1941	*Nagumo* [Jap] – USA
Peking	1215	*Genghis Khan* [Mon] – city
Peking	June 20 – Aug 14, 1900	*Macdonald/Seymour* [Allies] – Chinese [Pro-Boxer]
Pelekanon	1329	*Orkhan* [T] – Andronicus the Younger [Imp]
Pelischat	Aug 30, 1877	Turks – *Zotoff* [R]
Pelusium I	525BC	*Cambyses* [Per] – Psamtek [Eg]
Pelusium II	321BC	Perdiccas [Mac] – *Ptolemy Lagus* [Eg]
Pen Selwood	1016	*Edmund Ironside* [A-S] – Canute [Danes]
Peña Cerrada	June 21, 1838	Gergue [Carlists] – *Espartero* [Cris]
Penobscot Bay	July 25 – Aug 14, 1779	*Collier* [Br] – Americans
Pered	June 21, 1849	Görgey [Hung] – *Prince Windischgrätz* [A/R]
Perisabor	May 363	fortress [Sassanids] – *Julian* [Rom]
Perpignan	1474–5	*Du Lude* [F] – fortress [Sp]
Perryville	Oct 8, 1862	Buell [Fed] – Bragg [Con]
Persepolis	316BC	*Antigonus* [Mac] – Eumenes [Asiatics]
Peshawar	1001	*Mahmud of Ghuzni* [Afg] – Jaipal of Lahore [Punjabis]
Petersburg	June 15–18, 1864	*Beauregard* [Con] – Butler/Smith [Fed]

Petersburg, siege	June 30, 1864 – Apr 3, 1865	Lee [Con] – *Grant* [Fed]
Peterwardein	Aug 5, 1716	*Prince Eugene* [Imp] – Darnad Ali Pasha [T]
Pharsalus I	Aug 9, 48BC	Pompey [Pompeians] – *Cæsar* [Cæsarians]
Pharsalus II	May 6, 1897	*Edhem Pasha* [T] – Greeks
Philiphaugh	Sept 13, 1645	*Leslie* [Cov] – Montrose [Roy]
Philippi (twin battle)	42BC	Brutus/Cassius [Republicans] – *Octavius/Antony* [Triumvirs]
Philippine Sea	June 19–20, 1944	*Mitscher* [US]/Allies – Toyoda [Jap]
Philippopolis I	251	City – *Cniva* [Goths]
Philippopolis II	Feb 17, 1878	*Gourko* [R] – Fuad Pasha/Shakir Pasha [T]
Philippsburg	1734	*Duke of Berwick* [F] – Fortress [Imp]
Phyllacia	233BC	*Demetrius* [Macedon] – Achaean League
Piave River	June 15–22, 1918	Straussenburg [A] – Diaz [It]
Pieters Hill	Feb 19–27, 1900	*Buller* [Br] – Boers
Pinkie Cleugh	Sept 10, 1547	*Somerset* [Eng] – Earl of Huntly [Scots]
Pirna	Aug 26, 1813	*Vandamme* [F] – Eugène of Württemberg [Allies]
Pirot	Nov 26–7, 1885	*Prince Alexander* [Bul] – Milan [Serbians]
Placentia	271	Aurelian [Rom] – Alemanni
Plains of Abraham	Sept 13, 1759	*Wolfe* [Br] – Montcalm [F]
Plassey	June 23, 1757	*Clive* [Br] – Suraj-ud-Daula [Bengal]
Platæa I	479BC	*Pausanias* [Gr] – Mardonius [Per]
Platæa II	429–427BC	City [Platæans/Ath] – *Archidamus* [Spar]
Plattsburg	Sept 11, 1814	*Macomb* [Amer] – Prevost [Br]
Plescow	Aug 20, 1615	Gustavus Adolphus [Swed] – fortress [R]
Plevna	July 20 – Dec 10, 1877	*Krudener/Grand Duke Michael* [R] – Osman Pasha [T]
Podhaic	1667	*Sobieski* [Pol] – Cossacks/Tartars
Podol	June 26, 1866	*Prince Frederick Charles* [P] – Clam-Gallas [A]
Poitiers I	507	*Clovis* [Franks] – Alaric II [Visigoths]
Poitiers II	Sept 19, 1356	*Edward the Black Prince* [Eng] – John [F]
Pola	1380	*Doria* [Gen] – Pisani [Ven]
Pollentia	Apr 6, 402	Alaric [Goths] – *Stilicho* [Rom]
Pollilur	Aug 27, 1781	*Coote* [Br] – Haidar Ali [Mys]
Polonka	1667	Russians – *Czarnieçki* [Pol]
Polotsk I	Aug 16–18, 1812	*Oudinot/Saint Cyr* [F/Bav] – Wittgenstein [R]
Polotsk II	Oct 18–20, 1812	*Oudinot* [F] – Wittgenstein [R]
Poltava	June 8, 1709	*Peter the Great* [R] – Charles XII [Swed]
Pondicherry I	Aug–Oct 1748	Boscawen [Br] – *Dupleix* [F]
Pondicherry II	Aug 1760 – Jan 15, 1761	*Coote/Monson* [Br] – Lally-Tollendal [F]
Pondicherry III	June 20, 1783	Hughes [Br] – de Suffren [F]
Pondicherry IV	Aug 10, 1778	*Vernon* [Br] – Tronjolly [F]
Pont Valain	1370	*du Guesclin* [F] – Granson [Eng]
Poona	Oct 25, 1802	*Holkar of Indore* [reb] – Peshwa/Sindhia [Mar]
Populonia	282BC	*Rome* – Etruscans
Port Arthur I	Feb 8, 1904	*Togo* [Jap] – Stark [R]
Port Arthur II	Apr 13, 1904	*Japanese* – Makarov [R]
Port Republic	June 9, 1862	*Jackson* [Con] – Shields [Fed]
Porte St Antoine	July 2, 1652	*Turenne* [Roy] – Condé [insurgents]
Portland	Feb 28 – March 2, 1653	Blake [Eng] – Tromp [Dut]
Porto Bello I	July 1668	fortress – *Henry Morgan* [Buccaneers]
Porto Bello II	Nov 21, 1740	*Vernon* [Br] – fortress [Sp]
Porto Novo	July 1, 1780	*Coote* [Br/Sepoys] – Hyder Ali [Mys]
Porto Praya Bay	Apr 16, 1781	*de Suffren* [F] – Johnstone [Br]
Poserna	May 1, 1813	*Ney* [F] – Winzingerode [Allies]
Potidæa	432–429BC	*Athenians* – Aristæus [Corinth]
Potosi	Apr 1825	*Bolivar* [Bol] – Olaneta [Sp Roy]
Prague	May 6, 1757	*Frederick the Great* [P] – Charles of Lorraine [A]
Prairie Grove	Dec 7, 1862	*Blunt/Herron* [Fed] – Hindman [Con]
Preston I	Aug 17–19, 1648	*Cromwell* [Parl] – Langdale [Roy]
Preston II	Nov 12, 1715	Wills [Roy] – Forster [Jacob]
Prestonpans	Sept 21, 1745	*Young Pretender* [Jacob] – Cope [Roy]
Princeton	Jan 3, 1777	*Washington* [Amer] – Mawhood [Br]
Pruth, The	July 13, 1711	*Bultaghi* [T] – Peter the Great [R]
Pteria	c.547BC	Cyrus [Per] – Croesus [Lyd]
Puebla	May 5, 1862	Lorencez [F] – *Zaragoza* [Mex]

Puente	Feb 16, 1816	Lorrices [Col Pat] – *Morillo* [Sp Roy]
Puente de la Reyna	Oct 6, 1871	*Ollo* [Carlists] – Moriones [Rep]
Pultusk	Apr 12, 1703	*Charles XII* [Swed] – von Stenau [Sax]
Pultusk	Dec 26, 1806	Bennigsen [R] – Lannes [F]
Puna	Apr 27 – May 3, 1687	*Davis* [Buccaneers] – Spanish
Punniar	Dec 29, 1843	*Grey* [Br] – Marathas
Punta Delgada	1582	*Santa Cruz* [Sp] – Philip Strozzi [F]
Pusan I	Aug 1592	*Yi Sun-sin* [Kor] – Japanese
Pusan II	Aug 5 – Sept 15, 1950	*Walker* [UN] – Choe Yong Gun [North Koreans]
Pydna	June 22, 168BC	*Æmilius Paulus* [Rom] – Perseus [Mac]
Pylos	425BC	*Demosthenes* [Ath] – Thrasymelidas [Spar]
Pyongyang	Sept 15, 1894	*Nodzu* [Jap] – Chinese
Pyramids	July 21, 1798	*Napoleon* [F] – Murad Bey [Mam]
Qadisiya, The	June 637	*Said* [Mus] – Rustam [Per]
Quadesh	1275BC	Ramses II [Eg] – Muwatalli [Hittites]
Quang Tri	Apr 26 – May 1, 1972	North Vietnamese – South Vietnamese
Quatre Bras	June 16, 1815	*Wellington* [Br/Allies] – Ney [F]
Quebec: see Plains of Abraham		
Quebec I	Apr 27, 1760	de Lévis [F] – Murray [Br]
Quebec II	Apr 27 – May 15, 1760	*Murray* [Br] – de Lévis [F]
Queenston Heights	Oct 13, 1812	*Brock* [Br] – van Rensselaer [Amer]
Quiberon	July 16–20, 1795	*Hoche* [F] – French royalists/Br
Quiberon Bay I	56BC	*Brutus* [Rom] – Veneti
Quiberon Bay II	Nov 20, 1759	*Hawke* [Br] – de Conflans [F]
Quipuaypan	1532	*Atahualpa* [Incas] – Huascar [Incas]
Quistello	July, 1734	*Prince Eugene* [Imp] – Duc de Broglie [F]
Raab	June 14, 1809	*Eugène* [F] – Archduke John [A]
Radcot Bridge	1387	De Vere [Roy] – *Earl of Derby* [Lords Appellant]
Ragatz	Mar, 1446	*Swiss Confederation* – Austrians
Raisin River	Jan 22, 1813	*Proctor* [Br] – Harrison [US]
Rajahmundry	Dec 9, 1758	*Forde* [Br] – Conflans [F]
Rakersberg	1416	Ahmed Bey [T] – *Ernest of Styria* [A]
Ramadi	Sept 28–9, 1917	*Maude* [Br] – Turks
Ramillies	May 23, 1706	*Marlborough* [Br/Imp] – de Villeroi [F]
Ramleh I	1101	*Baldwin* [Crus] – Saad el-Dawleh [Eg]
Ramleh II	1177	Saladin [Sara] – *de Châtillon* [Christians]
Rangoon	May 10 – Dec 15, 1824	*Campbell* [Br] – Burmese
Raphia	223BC	*Ptolemy Philopator* [Eg] – Antiochus the Great [Syr]
Rastatt	July 5, 1796	*Moreau* [F] – Archduke Charles [A]
Raszyn	Apr 19, 1809	*Archduke Ferdinand* [A] – Poniatowski [F/Pol]
Rathenow	June 25, 1675	*Frederick William* [Bran] – Charles XI [Swed]
Rathmines	Aug 2, 1649	*Jones* [Parl] – Ormonde [Roy]
Ratisbon	Apr 23, 1809	*Napoleon* [F] – Charles [A]
Rava Russkaya	Sept 3–11, 1914	*Russians* – Austrians
Ravenna	729	Leo the Iconoclast [Gr] – *Pope Gregory II* [It]
Ravenna	Apr 11, 1512	de Foix [F] – Holy League
Ré, Isle de	July 17 – Oct 29, 1627	*island/Schomberg* [F] – Duke of Buckingham [Eng]
Reading	Jan 871	*Danes* – Aethelred/Alfred [W Sax]
Rebec	1524	*De Bourbon* [Imp] – Bonnivet [F]
Reddersberg	Apr 3–4, 1900	*De Wet* [Boers] – British
Réunion	July 8–10, 1810	*Keatinge* [Br/NZ] – St Susanne [F]
Revel	1790	*Port* [R] – Duke of Sudermanland [Swed]
Revolax	Apr 27, 1808	*Klingspor* [Swed] – Bonlatoff [R]
Rheims	Mar 13, 1814	*Napoleon* [F] – St-Priest [P/R]
Rheinfelden	Feb 28 – Mar 1, 1638	*Bernard of Saxe-Weimar* [Ger Prot] – de Wert [Imp]
Rhodes	1306–10	*Hospitallers* – Byzantines
Rhodes I	Aug 15, 1309	*Fulk de Villaret* [F/Hospitallers] – Rhodians
Rhodes II	May 23 – Aug 20, 1480	*d'Aubusson* [Knights] – Mehmet II [T]
Rhodes III	July 28 – Dec 21, 1522	*Suleiman the Magnificent* [T] – de l'Isle Adam [Knights]
Riachuelo	June 11, 1865	Paraguayans – *Brazilians*
Richmond (Kentucky)	Aug 30, 1862	*Kirby Smith* [Con] – Manson/Nelson [Fed]
Richmond (Virginia)	Mar 8, 1865	Lee [Virg] – *Grant* [Fed]
Ridanieh	Jan 22, 1517	*Selim I* [T] – Tooman Bey [Eg]

Rietfontein	Oct 24, 1899	*Free Staters* [Boers] – White [Br]
Rieti	Mar 21, 1821	*Austrians* – Pepe [Neap]
Riga I	Aug – Sept 15, 1621	*Gustavus Adolphus* [Swed] – city [Pol]
Riga II	Sept 1–5, 1917	*Hutier* [Ger] – Klembovsky [R]
Rimnik	Sept 22, 1789	*Saxe-Coburg/Suvorov* [A/R] – Grand Vizier [T]
Rinya	July 21, 1556	*Nadasdy* [A/Hung] – Ali Pasha [T]
River Plate	Dec 13, 1939	*Harwood* [Br] – Langsdorff [Ger]
Rivoli	Jan 14, 1797	*Napoleon* [F] – Alvintzi [A]
Roanoke Island	Feb 7–8, 1862	*Burnside* [Fed] – Wise [Con]
Rocoux	Oct 11, 1746	*de Saxe* [F] – Charles of Lorraine [Imp]
Rocroi	May 19, 1643	*Great Condé* [F] – de Melo [Sp]
Roliça	Aug 17, 1808	*Wellesley* [Br/Port] – Delaborda [F]
Rome I	410	*Alaric* [Visigoths] – city
Rome II	537	*Belisarius* [Emp East/city] – Vitiges [Goths]
Rome III	May 546	*Totila* [Goths] – Bassas [city]
Rome IV	549	*Totila* [Goths] – Demetrius [city]
Rome V	May 9, 1527	*de Bourbon* [Imp] – City
Rome VI	Apr 29 – June 29, 1849	*Oudinot* [F] – Garibaldi [It]
Romerswael	Jan 29, 1574	Boisot ['Beggars of the Sea'] – Romero [Sp]
Roncesvalles	778	*Loup II* [Basques/Gascons] – Charlemagne [Franks]
Roncesvalles	July 25, 1813	*Wellington* [Br/Port] – Soult [F]
Roosebeke (Rosbecque)	Nov 27, 1382	van Arteveldt [Flem] – *Charles VI* [F]
Rorke's Drift	Jan 22, 1879	*Bromhead/Chard* [Br] – Dabulamanzi [Zulus]
Roseburgh	Aug 3, 1460	*James II* [Scots] – town [Eng]
Rosetta	Apr 20, 1807	*Turks* – Fraser [Br]
Roskilde	Aug 29, 1807	Wellesley [Br] – Castenskiold [Dan]
Rossbach	Nov 5, 1757	*Frederick the Great* [P] – Soubise [F/A]
Rostock	June 1677	*Juel* [Dan] – Horn [Swed]
Rottofreddo	July 1746	Prince Lichtenstein [A] – Maillebois [F]
Rouen	1418	de Boutillier/city – *Henry V* [Br]
Roundway Down	July 13, 1643	*Prince Maurice* [Roy] – Waller/Hazlerigg [Parl]
Rouvray: see The Herrings		
Roveredo	Sept 4, 1796	*Masséna* [F] – Davidovich [A]
Rudnik Ridges	Sept 7 – Dec 15, 1914	Potiorek [A] – Putnik [Serb]
Rügen	Aug 8, 1715	Raben [Dan] – Sparre [Swed]
Rullion Green	Nov 1666	*Dalziel* [Roy] – Wallace [Cov]
Rumania	Aug 28, 1916 – Jan 1917	*Austro-Germans* – Rumanians
Rumersheim	Aug 26, 1709	*de Villiers* [F] – Mercy [Imp]
Ruspina	Jan 3, 46BC	Julius Cæsar [Cæs] – Labienus [Pomp]
Rynemants	Aug 1, 1578	Bossu/de la Noue [Dut Pat] – Don John of Austria [Sp]
Saalfeld	Oct 10, 1806	*Lannes* [F] – Prince Louis [P]
Sabugal	Apr 3, 1811	*Wellington* [Br/Port] – Reynier [F]
Sacile	Apr 16, 1809	*Archduke John* [A] – Eugène [F/It]
Sackets Harbor	May 28–9, 1813	*Brown* [US] – Prevost [Br]
Sacripontus	82BC	*Sulla* – Marius
Sadowa: see Königgrätz		
Sagunto	Sept 23 – Oct 26, 1811	fortress/Blake [Sp] – *Soult* [F]
Saguntom	219BC	*Hannibal* [Carth] – city
Sahagun	Dec 21, 1808	*Paget* [Br] – Debelle [F]
Saigon	1860–61	*French* – Vietnamese
Saintes	July 21, 1242	*Louis IX* [F] – Henry III [Eng]
Saintes, The	Apr 12, 1782	*Rodney* [Br] – de Grasse [F]
Saint-Mihiel	Sept 12–16, 1918	*Pershing* [US] – Germans
Saipan	June 15 – July 7, 1944	*Holland Smith* [US] – Yoshitsugu [Jap]
Salado	1344	*Alfonso IV/Alfonso XI* [Port/Cast] – Abu Hamed [Moors]
Salamanca	July 22, 1812	*Wellington* [Br/Port] – Marmont [F]
Salamanca (Mexico)	Mar 10, 1858	*Osollo* [Mex Govt] – Parrodi [Mex Lib]
Salamis (Greece)	480BC	*Themistocles/Eurybiades* [Gr] – Persians
Salamis I (Cyprus)	450BC	*Cimon* [Ath fleet] – Persians
Salamis II (Cyprus)	306BC	*Demetrius Poliorcetes* [Mac] – Ptolemy [Eg]
Salano	1340	*Alfonso XI* [Sp] – Abu 'l Hasan [Moors]
Saldanha Bay	17, Aug 1796	*Elphinstone* [Br] – garrison
Salerno	Sept 9–16, 1943	*Clark* [US] – Vietinghoff [Ger]

Salonika	Sept 1915 – Sept 29, 1918	Austro-Germans/Bulgarians – Allies
Samaghar	June 1658	Dara [Great Mogul] – *Aurungzebe/Marad*
Samarkand	June 1220	Alub Khan [T/Khwarazmians] – *Genghis Khan* [Mon]
Sampford Courtney	Aug 17, 1549	*Russell* [Roy] – Arundel [rebels]
San Isidoro	Apr 1870	Paraguayans – *Camera* [Arg/Braz/Uru]
San Jacinto I	Apr 21, 1836	*Houston* [Tex] – Santa Anna [Mex]
San Jacinto II	Feb 1, 1867	*Escobedo* [Mex Lib] – Miramon [Mex Conservatives]
San Juan Hill / El Caney	July 1, 1898	*Shafter* [US] – Linares [Sp]
San Lazaro	June 1746	*Prince Lichtenstein* [A] – Maillebois [F/Sp]
San Sebastian I	Aug 31, 1813	*Wellington* [Br/Port] – Rey [F]
San Sebastian II	Feb 1836	*Wylde/Evans* [Cristinos/Br/Sp] – Sagastibelza [Carlists]
Sandwich	1350	*Edward III* [Eng] – Spanish
Sanna's Post	Mar 31, 1900	Broadwood [Br] – *De Wet* [Boers]
Santa Cruz I	Apr 20, 1657	*Blake* [Br] – Spanish
Santa Cruz II Islands	Oct 25–6, 1942	*Kondo* [Jap] – Kincaid [US]
Santa Lucia	1842	*Caxias* [Braz Govt] – Feliciano [rebels]
Santa Vittoria	July 26, 1702	*Duc de Vendôme* [F/Sp] – Visconti [Imp]
Santarém	May 16, 1834	*Saldanha* [Port Govt] – Dom Miguel [reb]
Sante	1236	*Lithuanians/Semigalians* – Teutonic Knights
Santiago	July 3, 1898	*Schley/Sampson* [US] – Cervera [Sp]
Santo Domingo	Feb 6, 1806	*Duckworth* [Br] – Laissague [F]
Sapienza	1490	*Kemal Reis* [T] – Venetians
Saragossa I	Aug 20, 1700	*Archduke Charles* [A/Br/Dut/Port] – Spanish
Saragossa II	June 15 – Aug 17, 1808	*Palafox* [Sp] – Verdiet [F]
Saragossa III	Dec 20, 1808 – Feb 20, 1809	*Lannes* [F] – Palafox [Sp]
Saratoga I	Sept 19, 1777	*Gates* [Amer] – Burgoyne [Br]
Saratoga II	Oct 7, 1777	*Gates* [Amer] – Burgoyne [Br]
Sardis	280BC	*Eumenes* [Pergamum] – Antigonus Soter [Syr]
Sarikamis	Dec 29, 1914 – Jan 3, 1915	*Myshlayevski* [R] – Pasa [T]
Sárkány	Dec 30, 1848	*Windischgrätz* [A] – Perczel [Hung]
Sasbach	July 27, 1675	Turenne [F] – Montecuccoli [A]
Sauchieburn	June 18, 1488	*Angus* [rebels] – James III [Scots]
Saucourt	861	*Louis III* [Neustrians] – Norsemen
Saugor (Relief)	Feb 3, 1858	*Rose* [Br/Bombay Army] – Rebels
Savandroog	Dec 21, 1791	*Cornwallis* [Br/Mar] – Mysore
Savo Island	Aug 9, 1942	*Mikawa* [Jap] – Turner [US]
Saxa Rubra	Oct 28, 312	*Constantine* [Imp] – Maxentius [It]
Scarpheia	146BC	*Matellus* [Rom] – Critolaus [Achæans]
Scheveningen/Texel I	Aug 8–10, 1653	*Monck* [Eng] – Tromp [Dut]
Schipka Pass I	Jan 8, 1877	*Gourko* R] – Vessil Pasha [T]
Schipka Pass II	Aug 21, 1877	Darozhinsky [R] – Suleiman Pasha [T]
Schipka Pass III	Sept 16, 1877	*Russians* – Suleiman Pasha [T]
Schleiz	Oct 9, 1806	*Bernadotte* [F] – Tauenzein [Sax]
Schooneveldt I	June 7, 1673	de Ruyter [Dut] – Prince Rupert/d'Estrées [Eng/F]
Schooneveldt II	June 14, 1673	*de Ruyter* [Dut] – Prince Rupert/d'Estrées [Eng/F]
Schwechat	Oct 30, 1848	*Windischgrätz* [A] – Moga [Hung]
Scutari I	May 1474	*Loredano* [Ven] – Suleiman Pasha [T]
Scutari II	June – Sept 8, 1478	*Antonio di Lezze* [Ven] – Mohammed II [T]
Secchia, The	Sept 14, 1734	*Köningsegg* [Imp] – Duc de Broglie [F]
Sedan	Sept 1, 1870	Ducrot [F] – *von Moltke* [Ger]
Sedgemoor	July 6, 1685	*Feversham* [Roy] – Monmouth [rebels]
Seetabuldee	Nov 26 – Dec 24, 1817	*Scott* [Br] – Peshwa Baji Rao II [Mar]
Segeswár	July 31, 1849	*Bem* [Hung] – Haynau/Paskiewich [A/R]
Segoyvela	713	*Musa* [Mus] – Roderick [Visigoths]
Seine Mouth	Aug 15, 1416	*Bedford* [Br] – French
Sekhukhune	Nov 28 – Dec 2, 1879	*Wolseley* [Br/Swazis] – Pedi
Sekigahara	Oct 21, 1600	*Ieyasu* [Shogun] – Mitsunari [rebels]
Selby	Apr 11, 1644	*Fairfax* [Parl] – Bellasis [Roy]
Selinus	409BC	*Hannibal* [Carth] – city
Sellasia	222BC	*Philip V* [Macedon] – Aetolians
Seminara	Oct 1495	de Cordova/Ferdinand of Naples [Sp/Neap] – *d'Aubigny* [F]
Sempach	July 9, 1386	*Swiss Confederates* – Leopold III [A]
Seneff	Aug 11, 1674	The Great Condé [F] – Prince of Orange [Flem/Sp]

Sentinum	295BC	*Q. Fabius Maximus/Publius Decius* [Rom] – Gellius Equatius [Sam/Gauls]
Sepeia	494BC	*Cleomenes* [Spar] – Argives
Serbia	Oct 6–23, 1915	*Mackenson* [A] – Putnik [Serb]
Seringapatam I	Feb 6/7 – Mar 19, 1792	*Cornwallis* [Br/Mar] – Tipu Sultan [Mys]
Seringapatam II	May 4, 1799	*Harris/Baird* [Br] – Tipu Sultan [Mys]
Seringham	1753	Laurence [Br] – Astruc [F/Mahr/Mys]
Seskar	1790	*Kruze* [R] – Duke of Sudermanland [Swed]
Seta	1183	*Noriyori/Yoshitsune* [Yoritomo] – Yoshinaka [rebels]
Sevastopol I	Sept 28, 1854 – Sept 8, 1855	*St Arnaud/Canrobert/Raglan* [F/Br] – Menshikov/Gorchakov [R]
Sevastopol II	Dec 17, 1941–4	*Russians* – Germans/Rumanians
Seven Oaks	July 1, 1450	*Cade* [rebels] – Stafford [Roy]
Seven Pines: see Fair Oaks		
Shahjehan	1221	Tuli Khan [Tar] – Bugha [T]
Shaldiran	Aug 24, 1514	*Selim I* [T] – Dhah Ismael [Per]
Shannon/Chesapeake	June 1, 1813	*Broke* [Br] – Lawrence [Amer]
Sharqat	Oct 29–30, 1918	*Cobbe* [Br] – Hakki [T]
Sheerness	June 7, 1667	de Ruyter [Dut] – English
Sheriffmuir	Nov 13, 1715	Earl of Mar [Jacob] – Duke of Argyll [Roy]
Sherpur	Dec 23, 1879	*Roberts* [Br] – Mohammed Jan [Afg]
Sherstone	1016	Edmund Ironside [A-S] – Canute [Danes]
Shijo Nawate	1339	*Takaugi/Tadayoshi* [N Emp] – Masatsura [S Emp]
Shiloh	Apr 6–7, 1862	*Grant* [Fed] – Johnston /Beauregard [Con]
Shinowara	Apr 1183	*Yoshinaka* [rebels] – Taira-no-Kore [Imp]
Shirogawa	Sept 24, 1876	*Taruhito* [Imp] – Saigo Rebels
Sholinghur	Sept 27, 1781	*Coote* [Br/Sepoys] – Hyder Ali [Mys]
Shrewsbury	July 21, 1403	*Henry IV* [Roy] – 'Hotspur' Percy [rebels]
Sidassir	Mar 6, 1799	*Montresor* [Br] – Tipu Sahib [Mys]
Sidi Barrani	Dec 9–11, 1940	*Wavell* [Br] – Graziani [It]
Sievershausen	July 9, 1553	*Maurice of Saxony* [Ger] – Margrave Albert [Bran]
Siffin	656	Caliph Ali [Mus] – Moawiyeh [reb]
Sikajoki	Apr 18, 1808	*Klingspor* [Swed] – Buxhöwden [R]
Silistria	Mar–June 1854	*fortress* [T] – Paskevich [R]
Simancas	934	*Ramiro II* [Sp Christ] – Abd er-Rahman [Umayyads]
Simnitza	June 26, 1877	*Grand Duke Nicholas* [R] – Sistova [T]
Sinai I	Oct 29 – Nov 6, 1956	*Dayan* [Isr] – Amer [Eg]
Sinai II	June 5–9, 1967	*Israelis* – Egypt
Singapore	Jan 31 – Feb 15, 1942	*Yamashita* [Jap] – Percival [Br]
Singara I	348	Constantius [Emp East] – *Sapor II* [Per]
Singara II	360	garrison [Rom] – *Sapor II* [Per]
Sinope	Nov 30, 1853	Nakhimov [R] – Hussein [T]
Sinsheim	Oct 4, 1674	*Turenne* [F] – Caprara/Duke of Lorraine [Imp]
Skalitz	June 28, 1866	*Steinmetz* [P] – Ramming [A]
Slivnitza	Nov 17–19, 1885	*Alexander* [Bul] – Milan [Serbs]
Sluys	June 24, 1340	*Morley/Fitzalan* [Eng] – Quiéret [F]
Smolensk I	Sept 22, 1708	*Charles XII* [Swed] – Cossacks/Tartars
Smolensk II	Aug 17–18, 1812	*Napoleon* [F] – Barclay de Tolly [R]
Smolensk III	Aug 5, 1941	*von Kluge* [Ger] – Russians
Sobraon	Feb 10, 1846	*Gough/Smith* [Br] – Runjoor Singh [Sikhs]
Soczawa	1676	*Sobieski* [Pol] – Mohammed IV [T]
Sohr	Sept 30, 1745	*Frederick the Great* [P] – Prince Charles of Lorraine [A]
Soissons	486	*Clovis* [Salian Franks] – Syagrius [Rom]
Sole Bay: see Southwold		
Solferino	June 24, 1859	*Napoleon III/Victor Emmanuel* [F/Pied] – Emperor Franz Josef [A]
Solway Moss	Dec 14, 1542	*Dacre/Musgrave* [Eng] – Sinclair [Scots]
Somme River I	July 1 – Nov 18, 1916	Falkenhayn/Hindenburg [Ger] – Haig [Br]
Somme River II	Mar 21 – Apr 5, 1918	Haig [Br] – Ludendorff [Ger]
Somnauth	1024	city – *Mahmud of Ghuzni* [Afg]
Somosierra	Nov 30, 1808	*Napoleon* [F] – San Juan [Sp]
Sorata	1780	city – *Christobal* [Inca rebels]
Sorauren	July 28–30, 1813	*Wellington* [Br/Port] – Soult [F]
South China Sea	Dec 10, 1941	*Japanese* – Phillips [Br]

South Mountain	Sept 14, 1862	McClellan [Fed] – Lee [Con]
Southwark	July 5, 1450	*Gough* [Londoners] – Cade [rebels]
Southwold (Sole Bay)	June 7, 1672	de Ruyter [Dut] – Comte d'Estrées/Duke of York [F/Eng]
Spanish Armada	July 31 – Aug 8, 1588	*Howard of Effingham* [Eng] – Medina Sidonia [Sp]
Spion Kop	Jan 24–5, 1900	*Botha* [Boers] – Buller/Warren [Br]
Spira	Nov 15, 1703	*Tallard* [F] – Prince of Hesse [Imp]
Splitter	Jan 1679	Horn [Swed] – *Frederick William* [Bran]
Spotsylvania	May 8–18, 1864	Lee [Con] – Grant [Fed]
St Albans I	May 22, 1455	*Duke of York* [York] – Henry VI [Lanc]
St Albans II	Feb 17, 1461	*Somerset/Exeter* [Lanc] – Warwick [York]
St Aubin du Cormier	1487	*La Tremouille* [Roy] – de Rieux [rebels]
St Denis	Nov 10, 1567	*Montmorency* [Cath] – Prince de Condé/de Coligny [Hug]
St Denis (Canada)	Nov 23, 1837	*Nelson* [reb] – Gore [Br/Can]
St Eustache	Dec 14, 1837	*Colborne* [Govt] – Rebels [Girod]
St George	Oct–Dec 1500	*de Córdoba/Pesaro* [Sp/Ven] – Garrison [T]
St Gotthard	Aug 1, 1664	*Montecuccoli* [F/Ger] – Ahmed Koprulu Pasha [T]
St Jakob an der Mirs	Sept 1444	*Dauphin* [Armagnacs] – Confederate Swiss
St Jean de Luz	Nov 9, 1813	*Hope* [Br/Port] – Soult [F]
St Kitts I	May 10, 1667	*Harman* [Br] – Kruysen/de la Barre
St Kitts II	Jan 25–26, 1782	Hood [Br] – de Grasse [F]
St Louis (Senegal)	July 13, 1809	garrison [F] – *Columbine* [Br]
St Lucia	Apr 4, 1794	*Jervis* [Br] – island [F]
St Mary's Clyst	Aug 4, 1549	*Russell* [Roy] – Arundel [rebels]
St Pierre	Dec 13, 1813	*Hill* [Br/Port] – Soult [F]
St Quentin	Aug 10, 1557	Montmorency [F/Ger] – *Egmont* [Sp/Flem]
St Quentin	Jan 19, 1871	*von Göben* [Ger] – Faidherbe [F]
St Thomas	Dec 21, 1807	Island [Dan] – *Cochrane/Bowyer* [Br]
St Thomé: see Madras II		
St Vincent	Feb 14, 1792	*Jervis* [Br] – Cordova [Sp]
Stadtlohn	Aug 9, 1623	*Tilly* [Imp] – Christian of Brunswick [Prot]
Staffarda	Aug 18, 1690	*Catinat* [F] – Victor Amadeus [Imp]
Stalingrad	Aug 19, 1942 – Feb 2, 1943	*Yeremenko* [R] – Paulus [Ger]
Stallupénen	Aug 17, 1914	Germans – Russians
Stamford Bridge I	Sept 25, 1066	*Harold* [A-S] – Harold Hardrada/Tostig [Norse]
Stamford Bridge II	Aug 1453	Neville – Egremont
Standard, The	Aug 22, 1138	*Thurstan/Raoul* [Eng] – David [Scots]
Stavuchani	Aug 28, 1739	*Münnich* [R] – Veli Pasha [T]
Ste Croix	Dec 25, 1807	island [Dan] – *Cochrane/Bowyer* [Br]
Steinkirk	Aug 8, 1692	William III [Br/Dut] – *Luxembourg* [F]
Stiklestad	June 30, 1030	Olaf II [Norw] – *Canute* [Danes/peasants]
Stirling	Sept 11, 1297	*Wallace* [Scots] – Earl of Surrey [Eng]
Stockach I	Mar 25, 1799	*Archduke Charles* [A] – Jourdan [F]
Stockach II	May 3, 1800	*Moreau* [F] – Kray [A]
Stoke Field	June 16, 1487	*Henry VII* [Roy] – Simnel [rebels]
Stollhofen	May 22, 1707	*Villars* [F] – Margrave of Baden-Baden [A]
Stones River: see Murfreesboro		
Stoney Creek	June 6, 1813	*Vincent* [Br] – Winder/Chandler [US]
Stony Point	July 15–16, 1779	*Wayne* [Amer] – Johnson [Br]
Stormberg	Dec 10, 1899	Gatacre [Br] – *Olivier* [Boers]
Stralsund, siege	July 5 – Sept 1628	*town* – Wallenstein [Imp]
Stralsund	Oct 19, 1715	*Frederick William III/Frederick IV* [P/Danes] – Charles XII [Swed]
Stratton	May 16, 1643	*Hopton* [Roy] – Waller [Parl]
Suez-Adabiya	Oct 23–4, 1973	*Adan* [Isr] – Ismail [Eg]
Sugar-loaf Rock	Sept 20, 1753	*Laurence* [Br] – Astruc [F]
Suomussalmi	Nov 30, 1939 – Jan 8, 1940	*van Mannerheim* [Finns] – Timoshenko [R]
Surinam	May 5, 1804	garrison [Dut] – *Hood/Green* [Br]
Sursuti, The I	1191	Mohammed Ghori [Afg] – *King of Delhi* [Hindus]
Sursuti, The II	1192	*Mohammed Ghori* [Afg] – Rajah of Ajmir [Rajputs]
Sveaborg	Feb – May 3, 1808	*Suchtelen* [R] – Kronstedt [Swed/Fin]
Svensksund I	Aug 24, 1789	*Nassau-Siegen* [R] – Ehrensvärd [Swed]
Svensksund I	July 9–10, 1790	*Swedes* – Russians
Sybota	433BC	Corinthians – Corcyreans/Athenians

Syracuse I	415–413BC	*City/Gylippus/Hermocrates* [Syrac/Spar] – Lamachus/Nicias/Demosthenes [Ath]
Syracuse II	387BC	*Dionysius* [city] – Himilco [Carth]
Syrte I	Dec 17, 1941	Iachino [It] – Vian [Br]
Syrte II	March 22, 1942	*Vian* [Br] – Iachino [It]
Szalánkemen	Aug 19, 1691	*Margrave Louis* [Imp] – Mustafa Koprulu Pasha [T]
Szigeth	Aug 5 – Sept 8, 1566	*Suleiman The Magnificent* [T] – Zrinyi [Hung]
Tacna	May 26, 1880	*Baquedano* [Chil] – Campero [Bol/Peru]
Tacubaya	Apr 11, 1859	*Marquez* [Mex Conservatives] – Degollado [Liberals]
Taginae	July 552	Totila [Goths] – *Narses* [Rom]
Tagliacozzo	Aug 25, 1268	*Charles of Anjou* [Guelfs] – Conradin/ Duke of Austria [Ghib]
Taiken Gate	1157	Shitoku [Jap rebels] – *Bifukumonia/Tadamichi* [Imp]
Taillebourg	1242	*Louis IX* [F] – Henry III [Eng]
Takashima	1281	Chang Pak [Chin] – *Shoni Kagesuke* [Kiushiu]
Taku Forts I	June 25, 1859	Vansittart [Br] – Chinese
Taku Forts II	Aug 21, 1860	*Hope Grant/Montauban* [Br/F] – *Hang Foo* [Chin]
Taku Forts III	June 17, 1900	*Allies* – Chinese [Pro-Boxer]
Talana Hill	Oct 20, 1899	*Symons/Möller* [Br] – Joubert [Boers]
Talavera	July 27–28, 1809	*Wellesley/Cuesta* [Br/Sp] – Jourdan/Victor [F]
Talkhan	1221	fortress – *Genghis Khan* [Mon]
Tamai	Mar 13, 1884	*Graham* [Br] – Osman Digna [Dervishes]
Tanagra	457BC	*Spartans/Peloponnesians* – Athenians
Tanhangpo	June 1592	*Yi Sun-sin* [Kor] – Japanese
Tanjore I	Aug 1758	Monacji [garrison] – Lally-Tollendal [F]
Tanjore II	Aug 20, 1773	*Smith* [Br] – Laljaji/Monacji [fortress]
Tannenberg I	July 15, 1410	*Jagiello/Witawt* [Pol/Lith] – Teutonic Knights
Tannenberg II	Aug 26–30, 1914	*Hindenburg/Ludendorff* [Ger] – Zhilinsky [R]
Tansara Saka	1876	*Taruhito* [Imp] – Japanese rebels
Tapae	101BC	*Trajan* [Rome] – Deceballus [Dacians]
Taranto I	Mar 1, 1502	*de Córdoba* [Sp] – Conde di Potenza [Neap]
Taranto II	Nov 12, 1940	*Cunningham* [Br] – [It]
Tarawa-Makin	Nov 13–23, 1943	*Smith* [US] – Shibasaki [Jap]
Tashkessen	Dec 28, 1877	Baker Pasha [T] – Kourloff [R]
Tassafaronga	Nov 30, 1942	*Tanaka* [Jap] – Wright [US]
Taus	Aug 14, 1431	*Ziska* [Huss] – Sigismund [Imp]
Tayeizan	1868	*Imperialists* – Shogun
Tchesme	July 7, 1770	*Orloff* [R] – Turks
Tearless Battle	368BC	Arcadians – *Archidamus* [Spar]
Tecoac	Nov 16, 1876	*Díaz* [reb] – de Tejada [Mex]
Tegea	473BC	*Spartans* – Arcadians/Argives
Telamon	225BC	Gauls – *Aemilius Papus/Atilius Regulus* [Rom]
Tel-el-Kebir	Sept 13, 1882	*Wolseley* [Br] – Arabi [Eg]
Telissu	June 14–15, 1904	*Oku* [Jap] – De Stakelberg [R]
Tellicherry	June 1780	*Garrison/Abington* [Br] – Sirdar Ali Khan [Mys]
Temesvar	Aug 9, 1849	*Haynau* [A] – Dembinski [Hung]
Tenchebrai	Sept 28, 1106	*Henry I* [Eng] – Robert of Normandy [Normans]
Tendra	Sept 8–9, 1790	*Ushakov* [R] – Said Bey [T]
Tengen	Apr 19, 1809	*Davout* [F] – Hohenzollern [A]
Tenochtitlan I	June 30, 1520	*Aztecs* – Cortés [Sp Conquistadors]
Tertry	687	*Pepin II* [Austrasians] – Thierry III [Neustrians]
Tet Offensive	Jan 30 – Feb 29, 1968	*US/South Vietnamese* – Viet Cong/North Vietnamese
Tettenhall	Aug 5, 910	Danes – *Edward the Elder* [W Sax]
Tetuan	Feb 4, 1860	*O'Donnell* [Sp] – Moors
Teutoburger Wald	9	Quintilius Varus [Rom] – *Arminius (Hermann)* [Ger]
Tewkesbury	4 May, 1471	*Edward IV* [York] – Somerset [Lanc]
Texel	June 2–3, 1653	*Monck/Blake* [Br] – van Tromp [Dut]
Texel II /Camperdown	Aug 21, 1673	*de Ruyter* [Dut] – Prince Rupert/d'Estrées [Eng/F]
Thala	22	*Fortress* [Rom] – Tacfarinas [nomads]
Thames (Canada)	Oct 5, 1813	*Harrison* [US] – Proctor [Br/Shawnee]
Thapsus	Apr 6, 46BC	Julius Cæsar [Cæs] – Metellus Scipio/Juba/Labienus/ Sextus [Pomp]
Thebes	Sept 335BC	*Perdiccas* [Mac] – Thebans

Battle	Date	Combatants
Thermopylæ I	480BC	Leonidas [Spar/Thebans/Greeks] – **Xerxes** [Per]
Thermopylæ II	191BC	**Glabrio/Cato** [Rom] – Antiochus the Great [Syr]
The Saints	Apr 12, 1782	**Rodney** [Br] – de Grasse [F]
The Sound	Nov 8, 1658	**van Obdam** [Dut] – Wrangel [Swed]
Thetford	870	**Danes** – Edward [E Ang]
Thorn	Sept – Oct 22, 1702	**Charles XII** [Swed] – Robel [Pol]
Thurii	282BC	**Caius Fabricius** [Rom] – Lucanians/Bruttians
Thymbra	546BC	Croesus [Lyd/Eg] – **Cyrus** [Per]
Tiberias	June 1187	**Saladin** [Sara] – Guy de Lusignan [Crus]
Ticinus	218BC	**Hannibal** [Carth] – P. Cornelius Scipio [Rom]
Ticonderoga I	July 8, 1758	**Montcalm** [F/Can] – Abercrombie [Br]
Ticonderoga II	July 22–6, 1759	**Amherst** [Br] – Bourlamaque/Hébécourt [F/Can]
Ticonderoga III	June 6–7, 1777	**Burgoyne** [Br] – St Clair [Amer]
Tidone River	June 17, 1799	**Suvorov** [R] – Macdonald [F]
Tientsin	June 17–23, 1900	**Seymour** [Br]/**Lisum** [US] Allies – Chinese [Pro-Boxer]
Tiflis	1386	**Timur** [Tar] – Queen of Georgia [Caucasians]
Tigranocerta	69BC	**Lucullus** [Rom] – Tigranes [Pontics/Armenians]
Tigris	363	**Julian** [Rom] – Persians
Tinian	July 24 – Aug 1, 1944	**Schmidt** [US] – Japanese
Tippermuir	Sept 1, 1644	**Montrose** [Scots Roy] – Elcho [Cov]
Toba	1868	**Satsuma/Choshu** – Yoshinobu [Aiza/Kuwana]
Tobruk I	Jan 22, 1941	**Wavell** [Br] – Italians
Tobruk II	June 20–1, 1942	**Rommel** [Ger]/It – Klopper [SA]/Br
Tofrek	Mar 22, 1885	**McNeill** [Br] – Mahdists
Tolbiac	496	**Clovis** [Franks] – Alemanni
Tolentino	May 3, 1815	**Bianchi** [A] – Murat [It]
Torgau	Nov 3, 1760	**Frederick the Great** [P] – Daun [A]
Tornhout	Jan 24, 1597	**Maurice of Nassau** [Dut] – Jean De Rie [Sp]
Toro	Mar 1, 1476	**Ferdinand the Catholic** – Alfonso of Portugal [Port/Sp]
Toulon I	July – Aug 1707	fortress – Shovell [Dut/Br]
Toulon II	Feb 11, 1744	de Court/Navarro [F/Sp] – Matthews [Br]
Toulon III	Aug 29 – Dec 18, 1793	**Dugommier** [F] – Mulgrave [Br]
Toulouse	Apr 10, 1814	**Wellington** [Br/Port] – Soult [F]
Tourcoing	May 18, 1794	**Souham** [F] – Saxe-Coburg [Allies]
Tournai I	Oct – Nov 30, 1581	**Alexander of Parma** [Roy] – garrison
Tournai II	June 27 – Sept 3, 1709	**Marlborough** [Br/Dut/Ger] – de Villiers [F]
Tours	Oct 732	**Charles Martel** [Franks] – Abderrahman Ibu Abdillah [Sara]
Towton	Mar 29, 1461	**Edward IV** [York] – Henry VI [Lanc]
Trafalgar	Oct 21, 1805	**Nelson** [Br] – Villeneuve [F/Sp]
Trautenau	June 27, 1866	**Gablenz** [A] – Von Bonin [P]
Trebbia I	Dec 218BC	**Hannibal** [Carth] – Sempronius [Rom]
Trebbia II	June 17–20, 1799	**Suvorov** [R/A] – Macdonald [F]
Trebizond	1461	city – **Mohammed II** [T]
Trenton	Dec 26, 1776	**Washington** [Amer] – Rall [Br/Hess]
Tricameron	Nov 533	**Belisarius** [Rom] – Gelimer/Zano [Van]
Trincomalee I	Aug 10, 1759	Pococke [Br] – Comte d'Aché [F]
Trincomalee II	Sept 26–7, 1767	**Smith** [Br] – Hyder Ali/Nizam Ali
Trincomalee III	Apr 12, 1782	Hughes [Br] – Suffren [F]
Trincomalee IV	Sept 3, 1782	Hughes [Br] – Suffren [F]
Trinidad	Feb 17, 1797	**Harvey/Abercrombie** [Br] – island [F]
Tripoli	1289	**Sultan Khalil** – Knights
Tripoli (Africa)	647	**Abdulla Ibn Zubayr** [Mus] – Greg [Imp]
Trivadi	1760	**Hyder Ali** [Mys] – Moore [Br]
Trout Brook	July 6, 1758	Abercrombie [Br] – French
Truceia	593	**Fredegond** [Neustrians] – Childebert II [Austrasians]
Tsingtao	18 Sept – Nov 8, 1914	**Japanese** – Germans
Tsushima I	1419	Chinese/Koreans – **Barons of Kiushiu** [Jap]
Tsushima II	May 27–8, 1905	**Togo** [Jap] – Rozhdestvenski [R]
Tudela	Nov 23, 1808	**Lannes** [F] – Castaños/Palafox [Sp]
Tunis I	255BC	Regulus [Rom] – **Xanthippus** [Carth]
Tunis II	1270	Louis IX [F Crus] – city
Turbigo	June 3, 1859	**MacMahon** [F] – Clam-Gallas [A]
Turckheim	Jan 5, 1675	**Turenne** [F] – Montecuccoli [A]

Turcoing	1794	*Souham* [F] – Duke of York [Br]
Turin I	312	*Constantine [Rom]* – Maxentius
Turin II	Sept 7, 1706	*Eugène* [Imp] – Duc d'Orléans [F]
Turnhout	Aug 22, 1597	*Maurice of Nassau* [Dut] – Archduke Albert [Sp]
Tyre	332BC	*Alexander the Great* [Mac] – city
Ucles	1108	Don Sancho of Castile [Sp] – *Ali* [Moors]
Uji	1180	*Shigehera* [Tairans] – Prince Yukiiye/Yorimasa [Jap]
Ulm I	1377	*German League* – Charles IV [HRE]
Ulm II	May 16, 1799	*Moreau* [F] – Kray [A]
Ulm III	Oct 15, 1805	*Napoleon* [F] – Mack [A]
Ulundi	July 4, 1879	*Chelmsford* [Br] – Cetshwayo [Zulus]
Uppsala I	1520	*Otho of Krumpen* [Danes] – Christina Gyllenstierna [Swed]
Uppsala II	1521	*Gustavus Vasa* [Swed] – Bishop of Uppsala [Danes]
Urbicas, The	456	*Theodoric II* [Vis] – Rechiari [Suevi]
Urica	Dec 5, 1814	*Boves* [Sp] – Ribas [Patriots]
Urosan	1595	*Kiyomasa/Hideaki/Hidemoto* [Jap] – Tik Ho [Chin/Kor]
Usagre	May 25, 1811	*Lumley* [Br] – Latour-Maubourg [F]
Ushant I	July 27, 1778	Keppel [Br] – d'Estaing [F]
Ushant II: *see* Glorious 1st June		
Utica	694	*Hassan* [Mus] – Imperialists
Utsonomiya	1868	*Saigo Takamori* [Imp] – Otori Keisuke [Shogun]
Vaal Krantz	Feb 5–7, 1900	Buller [Br] – Boers
Valencia	Jan 9, 1812	*Suchet* [F] – Blake [Sp]
Valenciennes I	Dec 1566 – Mar 23, 1567	*Noircarmes* [Sp/Ger] – city
Valenciennes II	July 16, 1656	*de Manesses/Condé* [Sp] – Turenne/La Ferté [F]
Valenciennes III	May 21–3, 1793	*Saxe-Coburg* [A] – Custine [F]
Val-ès-Dunes	1047	*William of Normandy* [Nor] – rebels
Valjouan	Feb 17, 1814	*Grouchy/Gérard* [F] – Wrede [Allies]
Valletta	Sept 1798 – Sept 5, 1800	*Ball* [Br/Malta] – Vaubois [F]
Valmy	Sept 20, 1792	*Kellermann/Dumouriez* [F] – Duke of Brunswick [P]
Valparaiso	Mar 31, 1866	city – *Mendez Nuñez* [Sp]
Valutino	Aug 19, 1812	*Ney* [F] – Barclay de Tolly [R]
Varaville	1058	*William of Normandy* [Normans] – Henri I [F/Angevins]
Varese	May 25, 1859	*Garibaldi* [It] – Urban [A]
Varmas	1813	*Bolivar* [Col Pat] – Spanish Royalists
Varna	Nov 10, 1444	*Murad II* [T] – Hunyadi/Ladislaus [Christ]
Vasaq	1442	*Hunyadi* [Hung] – Shiabeddin Pasha [T]
Vauchamps	Feb 14, 1814	*Napoleon* [F] – Blücher [Allies]
Veleneze	Sept 29, 1848	Móga [Hung] – Jellachich [Croats]
Velestinos	May 5, 1897	*Hakki Pasha* [T] – Smolenski [Gr]
Velletri	May 19, 1849	*Roselli* [Garibaldians] – Ferdinand of Naples [Neap]
Vellore (Mutiny)	July 10, 1806	*Gillespie* [Br] – Sepoys
Venije	Nov 5, 1912	*Crown Prince Constantine* [Gr] – Turks
Vera	Oct 7, 1813	*Wellington* [Br/Port/Sp] – Taupin [F]
Vercellæ	July 30, 101BC	*Marius* [Rom] – Boiorix [Cimbri]
Verdun	Feb 21 – Dec 18, 1916	Falkenhayn [Ger] – Petain [F]
Verneuil	Aug 17, 1424	*Duke of Bedford* [Eng] – Buchan/Douglas/Alençon [Scots/F]
Vernon	1198	*Richard I* [Eng] – Philip Augustus [F]
Verona	312	*Constantine* [Rom] – Pompeianus [rebels]
Veseris	339BC	*Manlius Torquatus/Decius Mus* [Rom] – Latins
Viazma	Nov 3, 1812	Eugène/Davoût [F] – *Kutuzov* [R]
Viborg	1157	Sweyn III of Denmark – *Waldemar*
Vicksburg	May 19 – July 4, 1863	*Grant* [Fed] – Pemberton [Con]
Vienna I	Sept 27 – Oct 14, 1529	*Count of Salm/von Roggendorf* [city] – Suleiman the Magnificent [T]
Vienna II	Sept 12, 1683	*city/Sobieski* [Pol/Imp] – Kara Mustafa Pasha [T]
Vigo Bay	Oct 12, 1702	*Rooke/Ormonde* [Br/Dut] – French/Spanish
Villach	1492	Ali Pasha [T] – *de Khevenhuller* [Christ]
Villaviciosa	Dec 10, 1710	*Philip of Anjou/Vendôme* [F] – Starhemberg [Imp]
Villers-en-Cauchies	Apr 24, 1794	*Ott* [Br/A] – French
Villeta	Dec 11, 1867	Lopez [Para] – *Brazilians/Uruguayans/Argentinians*
Villiers	Nov 30 – Dec 3, 1870	Ducrot [F] – *Württembergers*
Vimeiro	Aug 21, 1808	*Wellesley* [Br/Port] – Junot [F]

Vimy Ridge	Apr 9–14, 1917	Horne/Allenby [Br] – Falkenhausen [Ger]
Vincy	717	**Charles Martel** [Austrasians] – Childeric [Neustrians]
Vinegar Hill	June 12, 1798	**Lake** [Br reg] – Murphy [Ir rebels]
Vinkovo	Oct 18, 1812	**Bagration** [R] – Murat [F]
Vistula River-Warsaw	Oct 15–21, 1914	Hindenburg [Ger] – Ivanov [R]
Vitebsk	July 28, 1812	**Napoleon** [F] – De Jolly [R]
Vittoria	June 21, 1813	**Wellington** [Br/Port] – Joseph/Jourdan [F]
Vittorio Veneto	Oct 24 – Nov 4, 1918	Straussenburg [A] – Diaz [It]
Vögelinseck	May 15, 1402	**Swiss Imperialists** – rebels
Volcaean Marsh	7	**Tiberius** [Rome] – Pannonians
Volturno	Oct 26, 1860	**Garibaldi** [It] – Afan de Riva [Neap]
Vouillé	507	**Clovis** [Franks] – Alaric II [Vis]
Vyazma	Oct 4–13, 1941	von Bock [Ger] – Timoshenko/Konev [R]
Wagram	July 6, 1809	**Napoleon** [F] – Archduke Charles [A]
Waizan	Apr 10, 1840	**Damjanics** [Hung] – Götz/Jablonowski [A]
Wakamatsu	Sept 22, 1868	**Imperialists** – Shogun
Wake Island	Dec 22–3, 1941	**Japanese** – USA
Wakefield	Dec 30, 1460	**Somerset/Percy** [Lanc] – Richard Duke of York [York]
Waltersdorf	Feb 5, 1807	**Ney** [F] – Lestocq [P]
Wandewash I	Jan 22, 1760	**Coote** [Br] – Lally-Tollendal [F]
Wandewash II	Dec 1780	**Flint** [fort] – Hyder Ali [Mys]
Warburg	July 31, 1759	**Prince Ferdinand** [P/Br] – De May [F]
Warsaw I	Sept 6–8, 1831	**Paskievich** [R] – Dembinski [Pol]
Warsaw II	May 4–5, 1915	Germans – Russians
Warsaw III	Aug 1 – Oct 2, 1944	**Bach-Zelewski** [Ger] – Bor-Komorowski [Pol]
Waterloo	June 18, 1815	**Wellington/Blücher** [Br/Dut/Bel/Nassau/P] – Napoleon [F]
Watrelots	Jan 1567	**de Rassinghem** [Sp] – Teriel [Flem Prot]
Wattignies	Oct 15–16, 1793	**Jourdan** [F] – Saxe-Coburg [A]
Wavre	June 18/19, 1815	**Grouchy** [F] – Thielmann [P]
Wednesfield	911	Danes – **Edward the Elder** [W Sax]
Wei-hai-Wei	Feb 4–9, 1895	Ting [Chin] – **Oyamo/Ito** [Jap]
Weissenburg	Aug 4, 1870	**Crown Prince of Prussia** [Ger] – MacMahon/Douay [F]
Werben	July 22, 1631	**Gustavus Adolphus** [Swed] – Tilly [Imp]
Wertingen	Oct 8, 1805	**Murat** [F] – Auffenberg [A]
Wetzlar	June 16, 1796	**Charles** [A] – Jourdan [F]
White Mountain (Weisser Berg)	Nov 8, 1620	**Maximillian/Tilly** [Imp] – Frederick [Boh]
Wiasma	Nov 3, 1812	**Davout** [F] – Miloradovich [R]
Wilderness, The	May 5–6, 1864	**Grant** [Fed] – Lee [Con]
Williamsburg	May 5, 1862	Longstreet [Con] – McClellan [Fed]
Wilson's Creek	Aug 10, 1861	Lyon [Fed] – **McCulloch** [Con]
Wimpfen	Apr 26, 1622	**Tilly/de Córdoba** [Imp] – Margrave of Baden [Palat]
Winchester I (USA)	May 25, 1862	**Jackson** [Con] – Banks [Fed]
Winchester II (USA)	June 13–14, 1862	**Ewell** [Con] – Milroy [Fed]
Winchester III (USA)	Sept 19, 1864	**Sheridan** [Fed] – Early [Con]
Windhoek	1915	**Botha** [SA] – Heydebrek [Ger]
Wisby	1613	Gustavus Adolphus [Swed] – Christian IV [Danes]
Wisloch	Apr 16, 1622	**von Mansfeldt** [Palat] – Tilly [Imp]
Worcester	Sept 3, 1651	**Cromwell** [Parl] – Charles II [Roy]
Wörth	Aug 6, 1870	**Crown Prince of Prussia** [Ger] – MacMahon [F]
Wrotham Heath	Jan 1554	Isley [Kentish rebels] – **Abergavenny** [Roy]
Würzburg	Sept 3, 1796	**Archduke Charles** [A] – Jourdan [F]
Wynandael	Sept 28, 1808	**Webb** [Br] – de la Motte [F]
Xeres	July 19–26, 711	**Tarik** [Mus] – Roderic [Sp]
Yalu River	Sept 17, 1894	Ting [Chin] – **Ito** [Jap]
Yamazaki	1582	**Ota** – Mitsuhide
Yarmuk	Aug 636	**Khalid** [Mus] – Theodore [Byz]
Yashima	1184	Taira – **Yoshitsune Minamoto** [Rebels]
Yawata	Jan 1353	N Emperor of Japan – **Moroushi** [S Emp]
Yellow Sea	Aug 10, 1904	**Togo** [Jap] – Russians
Yellow Tavern	May 11, 1864	**Sheridan** [Fed] – Stuart [Con]
Yenikale, Gulf of	July 1790	Turks – Onschakoff [R]
Yorktown I	Sept 28 – Oct 19, 1781	**Washington** [Amer/F] – Cornwallis [Br]

Yorktown II	Apr 4 – May 4, 1862	*McClellan* [Fed] – Magruder [Con]
Ypres I	Oct 19 – Nov 22, 1914	Falkenhayn [Ger] – Joffre/Foch [F]
Ypres II	Apr 22 – May 25, 1915	Falkenhayn [Ger] – French [Br]
Ypres III	31 July – Nov 10, 1917	Haig [Br] – von Armin [Ger]
Ypres IV: *see* Lys River		
Yugoslavia	Apr 6–17, 1941	*Germans/Italians/Hungarians* – Yugoslavians
Zab I, The	591	Bahram [Per] – *Narses* [Rom]
Zab II, The	Jan 750	*Khataba* [Abbasids] – Marwan [Umayyads]
Zallaka	Oct 23, 1088	*Tashfin* [Moors] – Alfonso VI of Castile [Sp Christ]
Zama	202BC	Hannibal [Carth] – *Scipio Africanus* [Rom]
Zamora I	901	*Alfonso the Great* [Sp Christ] – Abdallah [Moors]
Zamora II	939	*Ramiro II* [Sp Christ] – Abd er-Rahman [Moors]
Zeim	Apr 20, 1877	Melikoff [R] – *Mukhtar Pasha* [T]
Zela I	67BC	Triarius [Rom] – *Mithridates* [Pon]
Zela II	Aug 2, 47BC	*Julius Cæsar* [Rom] – Pharnaces [Bosporans]
Zell	Nov 8, 1805	*Davoût/Marmont* [F] – Merveldt [A]
Zendecan	1039	*Moghrul Beg* [Seljuks] – Musrud [Afg]
Zenta	Sept 11, 1697	*Prince Eugene* [A] – Elwas Mohammed [T]
Zeugminum	1168	*Manuel I* [Gr] – Hungarians
Ziezicksee	1302	*Grimaldi/di Rieti* [Gen] – Flemish
Zlotsow	1676	*Sobieski* [Pol] – Mohammed IV [T/Tar]
Zorawno	Sept–Oct, 1676	Sobieski [Pol] – Ibrahim Pasha [T/Tar]
Zorndorf	Aug 25, 1758	*Frederick the Great* [P] – Fermor [R]
Zurich I	June 4–7, 1799	*Archduke Charles* [A] – Masséna [F]
Zurich II	Aug 14, 1799	*Archduke Charles* [A] – Masséna [F]
Zurich III	Sept 2, 1799	*Masséna* [F] – Korsakov [R/Allies]
Zusmarshausen	May 17, 1648	*Turenne/Wrangel* [F/Swed] – Melander /Montecuccoli [Imp]
Zutphen	Sept 22, 1586	*Farnese, Duke of Parma* [Sp] – Earl of Leicester [Br/Dut]
Zuyder Zee	Oct 11, 1573	Bossu [Sp] – *Dirkzoon* [Dut]

FURTHER READING

Military history is well served with whole libraries of excellent books covering every conceivable aspect of military conflict. The titles listed below offer a brief selection of useful works, with emphasis on general books about wars, campaigns and military eras, plus atlases of military history and a number dealing with individual battles.

Archibald, E. H. H., *The Fighting Ship in the Royal Navy 897–1984*, 1984

Armitage, Sir Michael, *The Royal Air Force*, 1993, 1999

Arnold, James R., *Ardennes 1944*, 1990

– *Tet Offensive 1968*, 1990

– *Chickamauga 1863*, 1992

– *Shiloh 1862*, 1998

Austin, Paul Britten, *1812: The March on Moscow*, 1993

– *1812: Napoleon in Moscow*, 1995

– *1812: The Great Retreat*, 1996

Badsey, Stephen, *Normandy 1944*, 1990

– *Arnhem 1944*, 1993

Banks, Arthur, *A Military History and Atlas of the First World War*, 1975

Barnett, Corelli, *Marlborough*, 1974

– *The Swordbearers: Studies in Supreme Command in the First World War*, 1981

Barthop, M., *The Zulu War*, 1980

Beevor, Anthony, *Stalingrad*, 1998

– *Berlin: The Downfall, 1945*, 2003

Bennett, Geoffrey, *The Battle of Jutland*, 1964

– *Naval Battles of the First World War*, 1974

Black, Jeremy, *European Warfare 1660–1815*, 1994

– *The Cambridge Illustrated Atlas of Warfare: Renaissance to Revolution, 1492–1792*, 1996

Bond, Brian, *Victorian Military Campaigns*, 1967

Bruce, J., *British Aeroplanes 1914–1918*, 1969

Burne, A. H., *The Art of War on Land*, 1944

– *Battlefields of England*, 1950

– *More Battlefields of England*, 1952

– and Young, P., *The Great Civil War: a Military History of the First Civil War*, 1959

Caesar, Julius, *The Conquest of Gaul*, 1956 52/1 BC, various modern translations

Calvocoressi, P., *Top Secret Ultra*, 1980

– and Wint, Guy, *Total War: Causes and Courses of the Second World War*, 1972

Castle, Ian, *Aspern and Wagram 1809*, 1994

– *Colenso 1899*, 1995

– *Majuba 1881*, 1996

– *Eggmühl 1809*, 1998

– and Knight, Ian, *Fearful Hard Times: The Siege and Relief of Eshowe, 1879*, 1994

Chandler, David G., *A Traveller's Guide to the Battlefields of Europe*, 2 vols, 1965

– *The Campaigns of Napoleon*, 1967

– *Marlborough as Military Commander*, 1973

– *Napoleon*, 1974

– *The Art of War in the Age of Marlborough*, 1976

– *Dictionary of the Napoleonic Wars*, 1979

– *Austerlitz 1805*, 1990

– (ed.), *Great Battles of the British Army*, 1991

– *Jena 1806*, 1993

Christiansen, E., *The Northern Crusades: The Baltic and Catholic Frontier 1100–1525*, 1980

Churchill, Winston S., *The Story of the Malakand Field Force*, 1898

– *The River War*, 1899

– *Marlborough, His Life and Times*, 2 vols, 1933–38

– *The World Crisis, 1911–1918*, 1923–31

– *The Second World War*, 6 vols, 1948–53,

Clarendon, Earl of, *The History of the Rebellion and Civil War in England*, 1702

Clark, Allan, *Barbarossa: The Russian-German Conflict 1941–1945*, 1995

Clausewitz, Carl von, *On War*, 1832

Cloughley Brian, *A History of the Pakistan Army*, 1999

Clowes, William Laird, *The Royal Navy – A History from the earliest times to 1900*, 1997

Coates, John, *An Atlas of Australia's Wars*, vol VII in *The Australian Centenary History of Defence*, 2001

Connell, J. Mark, *Ardennes: The Battle of the Bulge, 1944–45*, 2003

Contamine, P., *War in the Middle Ages*, 1984

Corbett, J. S., *England in the Seven Years' War*, 2 vols, 1907

Costello, John, and Hughes, Terry, *The Battle of the Atlantic*, 1977

– *The Pacific War, 1941–45*, 1981

Crawford, Mark, *Encyclopedia of the Mexican-American War*, 1999

Creasey, E. S., *The Fifteen Decisive Battles of the Western World*, 1851

Creveld, Martin van, *Supplying War*, 1977

Cross, Robin (ed.), *The Guinness Encyclopedia of Warfare*, 1991

Davis Hanson, Victor, *Wars of the Ancient Greeks*, 1999

Dear, I. C. B. (ed.), *The Oxford Companion to the Second World War*, 1995

Delbrück, H., *History of the Art of War*, 4 vols, 1900–20, English translation 1975–85

Douhet, G., *The Command of the Air*, 1943

Duffy, Christopher, J., *Borodino and the War of 1812*, 1972

– *The Army of Frederick the Great*, 1974

– *Austerlitz, 1805*, 1976

– *The Army of Maria Theresa*, 1977

– *Fire and Stone: The Science of Fortress Warfare 1660–1860*, 1996

Dupuy, R. E. and T. N., *The HarperCollins Encyclopedia of Military History*, 1991

Dupuy, T. N., Johnson, Curt, and Bongard, David L., *The Harper Encylopedia of Military Biography*, 1992

Eggenberger, D., *A Dictionary of Battles*, 1967

Erickson, John, *Stalin's War with Germany*, 2 vols, 1975, 1983

Eshel, D., *Chariots of the Desert*, 1989

Esposito, V. J., *The West Point Atlas of American Wars*, 2 vols, 1959

– and Elting J. R., (eds), *A Military History and Atlas of the Napoleonic Wars*, 1964

Evans, Anthony A., *Gulf War: Desert Shield and Desert Storm, 1990–1991*, 2003

– *World War II, An Illustrated Miscellany*, 2005

Falls, Captain Cyril, *The Art of War from the Age of Napoleon to the Present Day*, 1961

– *The First World War*, 1960

Farrar-Hockley, A. H., *The Somme*, 1964

– *The British Part in the Korean War*, 1990

Farwell, Byron, *Queen Victoria's Little Wars*, 1973

Ferril, A., *The Fall of the Roman Empire: The Military Explanation*, 1986

Firth, C. H., *Cromwell's Army*, 1902

Fletcher, Ian, *Salamanca 1812*, 1997

Foch, Marshal F, *The Memoirs of Marshal Foch*, 1931

Foote, Shelby, *The Civil War*, 1963

Fortescue, Sir John, *History of the British Army, 1899–1920*

Forty, George, *Land Warfare: The Encyclopedia of 20th Century Conflict*, 1997

Francis, D., *The First Peninsular War, 1702–13*, 1975

Frankland, N., *The Bombing Offensive against Germany*, 1965

Frere-Cook, Gervis, and Macksey, Kenneth, *The Guinness History of Sea Warfare*, 1975

Fuller, J. F. C., *The Foundations of the Science of War*, 1926

– *The Decisive Battles of the Western World and their Influence on History*, 3 vols, 1954–56

– *The Conduct of War 1789–1961*, 1961

– *A Military History of the Western World*, 1967

Gardiner, Samuel R, *History of the Great Civil War, 1642–1649*, 1893

Geraghty, Tony, *Who Dares Wins – The Special Air Service, 1950 to the Falklands*, 1980, 1992

Gilbert, Martin, *The First World War*, 1944

Glover, M., *The Peninsular War, 1807–14: A Concise Military History*, 1974

Gorlitz, W., *History of the German General Staff, 1675–1945*, 1953

Gravett, C., *German Medieval Armies 1300–1500*, 1985

Gray, Randal, and Argyle, Christopher, *Chronicle of the First World War*, 2 vols 1990, 1991

Greenhalgh, Peter, *Pompey: The Roman Alexander*, 1980

Gunston, Bill (ed.), *The Encyclopedia of World Air Power*, 1980

Hackett, General Sir John (ed.), *The Third World War: August 1985*, 1978

– *The Third World War: The Untold Story*, 1982

– *Warfare in the Ancient World*, 1989

Harbottle, T. B., *Dictionary of Battles*, 1901

Hastings, M., *Montrose: The King's Champion*, 1977

– *Overlord – D-Day and the Battle for Normandy*, 1984

– *The Korean War*, 1987

– *Armageddon: The Battle for Germany, 1944–45*, 2004

– *Nemesis: The Battle for Japan, 1944–45*, 2007

– and Jenkins, S., *The Battle for the Falklands*, 1983

Haythornthwaite, Philip J., *The Napoleonic Source Book*, 1990

– *The World War One Source Book*, 1992

– *The Armies of Wellington*, 1994

– *The Colonial Wars Source Book*, 1995

– *Who Was Who in the Napoleonic Wars*, 1998

Herzog, Chaim, *The Arab–Israeli Wars*, 1982

– and Grichon, M., *Battles of the Bible*, 1997

Hoffmann, Karl, *Erwin Rommel, 1891–1944*, 2004

Hofschroer, Peter, *The Waterloo Campaign: Wellington, His German Allies and the Battles of Ligny and Quatre Bras*, 1998

Hogg, Ian V., *A History of Artillery*, 1974

– and Weeks, John, *Military Smallarms of the Twentieth Century*, 1973 and subsequent editions

Holmes, Richard (ed.), *The World Atlas of Warfare*, 1988

Hood, Jean (ed.), *Submarine*, 2007

Horne, Alistair, *To Lose a Battle – France 1940*, 1979

Howard, Michael E., *The Franco–Prussian War*, 1961

– *War in European History*, 1976

Hughes, Major General B. P., *Firepower – Weapon Effectiveness on the Battlefield*, 1974

Hughes, Q., *Military Architecture*, 1974

Ito, Masanori, *The End of the Imperial Japanese Navy*, 1986

Jackson, W. G. F., *The Battle for Italy*, 1975

– *The North African Campaign 1940–43*, 1975

James, W., *The Naval History of Great Britain from the Declaration of War by the French Republic in 1793 to the Accession of George IV*, 1837

Jomini, A.-H., *Summary of the Art of War*, 1838

Jones, A., *The Art of War in the Western World*, 1987

Jones, H. A., *The War in the Air*, vol, II, 1928; vol, III, 1931; vol, IV, 1934

Jones, R. V., *Most Secret War*, 1979

Judd, D., *The Crimean War*, 1975

Katcher, Philip, *The American Civil War Source Book*, 1992

Keegan, John (ed.), *The Times Atlas of the Second World War*, 1989

– *A History of Warfare*, 1993

Kennedy, Frances H. (ed.), *The Civil War Battlefield Guide*, 1990

Kennedy, Paul, *The Rise and Fall of the Great Powers*, 1988

Kilduff, P., *Germany's First Air Force, 1914–1918*, 1991

– *Richthofen: Beyond the Legend of the Red Baron*, 1993

Kinglake, A. W., *The Invasion of the Crimea*, 9 vols, 1868

Knight, Ian, *The Zulus*, 1989

– *Brave Men's Blood: The Epic of the Zulu War*, 1990

– *Nothing Remains But To Fight: The Defence of Rorke's Drift, 1818–1879*, 1995

– *Great Zulu Battles 1838–1906*, 1998

Kohn, G., *Dictionary of Wars*, 1986

Kostyal, K. M., *Stonewall Jackson: A Life Portrait*, 1999

Laband, John, *Rope of Sand: The Rise and Fall of the Zulu Kingdom in the Nineteenth Century*, 1995; also published 1997 under the title *The Fall of the Zulu Nation*

Lachouque, H., *Waterloo*, 1975

– *The Anatomy of Glory*, 1978

Laffin, J. *Brassey's Battles*, 1986

Lambert, Nicholas, *Sir John Fisher's Naval Revolution*, 1999

Lamberton, W., *Fighter Aircraft of the 1914–1918 War*, 1960

Lavery, Brian, *Churchill goes to War: Winston's Wartime Journeys*, 2007

– *Nelson's Navy – The Ships, Men and Organisation 1793–1815*, 1989

Lewin, R., *Ultra Goes To War*, 1978

Lewis, Michael, *The Spanish Armada*, 1960

FURTHER READING

Liddell-Hart, B. H., *The Ghost of Napoleon*, 1933
– *The Other Side of the Hill*, 1948
– *The Real War, 1914–1918*, 1964
– *History of the First World War*, 1970
– *History of the Second World War*, 1970
Livesey, A., *The Viking Atlas of World War I*, 1994
Longford, E., *Wellington, the Years of the Sword*, 1968
Longstreet, S., *War Cries on Horseback – The History of the Indian Wars*, 1970
Lucas, James, *War in the Desert: The Eighth Army at El Alamein*, 1982
Lyon, David, *Sea Battles in Close-Up: The Age of Nelson*, 1996
Macksey, Kenneth, *The Guinness History of Land Warfare*, 1973
– *Military Errors of World War Two*, 1987
Mahan, A., *The Influence of Sea Power upon History 1660–1783*, 1890
Marley, David F., *Wars of the Americas*, 1998
Mattingly, Garrett, *The Defeat of the Spanish Armada*, 1965
McCarthy, Chris, *The Somme – The Day by Day Account*, 1993
Messenger, Charles, *World War Two Chronological Atlas*, 1989
– *The Second World War in the West*, 1999
Middlebrook, Martin, *The Kaiser's Battle: 21 March 1918*, 1978
Montgomery of Alamein, Field Marshal Viscount, *A History of Warfare*, 1968
Morris, D., *The Washing of the Spears*, 1966
Morrissey, Brendan, *Boston 1775*, 1995
– *Yorktown 1781*, 1997
Mueller, Joseph N., *Guadalcanal 1942*, 1992
Napier, W. F. P., *History of the War in the Peninsula, 1832–40*
Nash, D. B., *Imperial German Army Handbook, 1914–1918*, 1980
Nebenzahl, K., (ed), *Atlas of the American Revolution*, 1974
Nicolle, David, *The Normans*, 1987
– *The Crusades*, 1988
– *Attila and the Nomad Hordes: Warfare on the Eurasian Steppes, 4th to 12th Centuries*, 1990
– *Hattin 1187*, 1993
– *Medieval Warfare Source Book*, 1995
– *Arms & Armour of the Crusading Era 1050–1350: Western Europe and the Crusader States*, 1999
Nofi, Albert A., *The Gettysburg Campaign*, 1996
Norman, A. V. B., and Pottinger, Don, *English Weapons and Warfare, 449–1660*, 1966
Oman, Sir Charles, *History of the War in the Peninsula*, 1902–30
– *A History of the Art of War in the Middle Ages*, 1924
Overy, R., *The Air War 1939–1945*, 1980
Padfield, Peter, *The Battleship Era*, 1972
Pakenham, T., *The Boer War*, 1979
Parkes, Dr. Oscar, *British Battleships*, 1957
Pemsel, Helmut, *Atlas of Naval Warfare*, 1977
Perrett, Bryan, *A History of Blitzkrieg*, 1983
– *Desert Warfare*, 1988
– *The Battle Book*, 1992
Pitt, Barrie, *1918 – The Last Act*, 1962

– and Pitt, Frances, *The Chronological Atlas of World War II*, 1989
Pope, Stephen, and Robbins, Keith, *The Cassell Dictionary of the Napoleonic Wars*, 1999
Price, A., *The Hardest Day*, 1979
Price, Anthony, *The Eyes of the Fleet – A Popular History of Frigates and Frigate Captains, 1793–1815*, 1990
Rickenbacker, E., *Fighting the Flying Circus*, 1967
Riley-Smith, Jonathan, *The Atlas of the Crusades*, 1991
Robertson, B., *Air Aces of the 1914–1918 War*, 1959
Rothenburg, G. E., *The Art of War in the Age of Napoleon*, 1965
Runciman, S., *A History of the Crusades*, 1994
Ryan, Cornelius, *The Longest Day*, 1960
Shepperd, Alan, *France 1940*, 1990
Sixsmith, E. K. G., *Douglas Haig*, 1976
Smith, Digby, *The Greenhill Napoleonic Wars Data Book*, 1998
Smurthwaite, David, *The Ordnance Survey Complete Guide to the Battlefields of Britain*, 1989
Sokolovsky, V., *Soviet Military Strategy*, 1975
Stevens, Norman S., *Antietam 1862*, 1994
Stone, David, *'First Reich': Inside the German Army during the War with France, 1870–71*, 2002
– *Wars of the Cold War*, 2004
– *Fighting for the Fatherland*, 2006
Strachan, Hew, *The First World War*, vol 1: *To Arms*, 2001
Strawson, J., *The Italian Campaign*, 1987
Sun Tzu, trans, R. D., Sawyer, *Art of War*, 1994,
Suskind, Richard, *The Crusades*, 1962
Sweetman, John, *Balaclava 1854*, 1990
Tan Qixiang (ed.), *The Historical Atlas of China* (8 vols), 1981 onwards,
Terraine, John, *The Great War, 1914–1918*, 1977
Thomas, H., *The Spanish Civil War*, 1961
Thompson, L., *The US Army in Vietnam*, 1990
Tsouras, P., *Changing Orders: Evolution of the World's Armies, 1945 to the Present*, 1994
Tucker, John, and Winstock, Lewis S., (eds), *The English Civil War: A Military Handbook*, 1972
Tunstall, Brian, *Naval Warfare in the Age of Sail*, 1990
Turnbull, Stephen, *The Samurai: A Military History*, 1977
– *The Book of the Samurai*, 1982
– *The Book of the Medieval Knight*, 1985
– *The Samurai Source Book*, 1998
Urban, M., *War in Afghanistan*, 1990
Walter, John, *The Kaiser's Pirates: German Surface Raiders in World War One*, 1994
Warner, Oliver, *Great Sea Battles*, 1963
Warner, Philip, *World War One: A Chronological Narrative*, 1981
Watts, Anthony J., *The Royal Navy: An Illustrated History*, 1994
Webster, Graham, *The Roman Imperial Army*, 1969
Wedgwood, C. V., *The Thirty Years War*, 1938
Weller, J., *Wellington in the Peninsula, 1808–1814*, 1962
– *Wellington at Waterloo*, 1967
– *Wellington in India*, 1972
Wise, Terence, *The Wars of the Crusades 1096–1291*, 1978
Young, P., *Napoleon's Marshals*, 1973
– and Holmes, R., *The English Civil War*, 1974
Zaloga, Steven, *Bagration 1944*, 1996